A
MARITIME
HISTORY
OF
SOMERSET

VOLUME TWO

Somerset Archaeological
& Natural History Society

A
MARITIME
HISTORY
OF SOMERSET

VOLUME TWO

Adrian J. Webb

SOMERSET ARCHAEOLOGICAL AND NATURAL HISTORY SOCIETY

COVER ILLUSTRATIONS

Front: Ferry crossing the Avon at Rownham, reproduced with
permission of Bristol Museums, Galleries & Archives,
reference BMG K6260.
Back: The Minehead swimming pool from the editor's collection.
The slipway at Pill is reproduced from a painting in a private
collection.

The views expressed in this volume are those of the authors and not
those of the Somerset Archaeological and Natural History Society.

Typeset in Garamond.
Typeset and designed by David Worthy and Adrian Webb.
Printed by 4Word, Bristol.

ISBN 978 0 902152 26 7

Contents

Abbreviations

BAR   British Archaeological Reports
BRO   Bristol Record Office
BRS   Bristol Record Society
CEFAS   Centre for Environment, Fisheries & Aquaculture Science
CSPD   Calendar of State Papers Domestic
CSPD   Calendar of State Papers Domestic
DEFRA   Department for Environment, Food and Rural Affairs
ICES   International Council for the Exploration of the Sea
LIDAR   Light Detection and Ranging
LPFD   Letters and Papers Foreign and Domestic
MHS   Maritime History of Somerset
MSY   Maximum Sustainable Yield
SANHS   Somerset Archaeological and Natural History Society
SHC   Somerset Heritage Centre
SRS   Somerset Record Society
TAC   total allowable catches
TNA   The National Archive [of England and Wales]

Acknowledgements

COMPILING THIS VOLUME of new studies into aspects of Somerset's extensive and diverse maritime history has been a pleasure, although a protracted process. I am grateful to my fellow authors for their contributions and patience. My biggest debts are to David Worthy for once again pulling together the text, images, tables and figures into publishable order and making this an attractive volume for the reader. Philip Ashford kindly gave lots of advice, encouragement and an enormous amount of time towards this publication. In order to overcome the final hurdles of production, I am in debt to Commodore Bill Kelly R.N. for his kind assistance. Finally, I would like to thank my family for their support whilst working on this volume and not undertaking my full share of our collective domestic duties.

The reproduction permissions have been agreed between the copyright holders and the individual authors. Illustrations (as marked in the text) are reproduced with the permission of the following individuals and organisations, which we gratefully acknowledge their assistance: Philip Ashford, Hilary Binding, Bristol Museums Galleries & Archives, David Bromwich, Ian Coleby, Phil Hockin, Gary Holden, Captain Paul Hughes, Andy King, The Society of Antiquaries (London), Somerset Archaeological and Natural History Society, Somerset Heritage Centre, Chris Webster of the Somerset Historic Environmental Record, United Kingdom Hydrographic Office, Margaret Webb and David Worthy. Special thanks go to Ian Coleby for his cartographic skills used to produce the maps in this volume.

A final note of thanks must go to the Publications Committee and the members of SANHS Board, without whom this function of the Society would not run. The Committee have all helped in one way or another to make the Society's publications a success and not a burden on its finances. This particular series has also been supported by The South West Maritime History Society, to whom I am extremely grateful.

Foreword

SOMERSET'S spectacular and interesting coast, with its variety, beauty and special atmosphere, has inspired writers and artists for generations. This volume of Maritime History is full of information, clearly expressed, about some of the practical effects of the sea on the way of life and opportunities of Somerset people, from far in the past up to the present day. It comes from the expert knowledge and extensive research of the authors, and is given added interest by including descriptions of many of those who were involved at the time. The many illustrations are an attractive and useful feature, with drawings, photographs, maps and diagrams, and help to set the scene.

It is a pleasure to welcome the writing of such an informative and readable addition to our knowledge of the sea and its influence on Somerset.

Elizabeth Gass

Lady Elizabeth Gass, D.C.V.O.
Patron of the Somerset Archaeological and Natural History Society

Introduction

VOLUME TWO IN THIS SERIES contains as much content as volume one, but more variety in fewer chapters. One theme which is common to the first three chapters, but not covered exclusively, is that of travel. From this it can be seen how Somerset was witness to the movement of thousands of people by water during the Age of Sail, as well as afterwards on the ferries crossing the Avon and Bristol Channel. Philip Ashford shows how travel was undertaken for a variety of reasons, not just in pursuit of commerce (a theme which can be found in volume one), but to avoid religious persecution, for family or personal reasons, and, more so as time progressed, for the pleasure of travel itself. Ashford also identifies how the western ports and harbours were used for embarking and receiving hundreds of troops on Government service. How those maritime communities were affected by such movements has yet to be fully examined.

Communities thrived and declined, in part at least, due to different maritime factors. Places such as Pill, Rownham, Minehead, Burnham-on-Sea and Weston-super-Mare changed from a reliance on their age-old staple sources of income, *i.e.* ferry passengers and the money they spent with local businesses, trade and fishing, into new communities reliant on new sources of revenue. For Minehead, Burnham and Weston their metamorphosis was dramatic and irreversible, but for Pill, on a much smaller scale, the loss of income was notable. Fortunately for Pill, both before and after the construction of the Avonmouth Bridge, employment came in the form of jobs created by Avonmouth Docks, where maritime trade occurs on a scale not witnessed by any other port or harbour in Somerset. Today the economies of those seaside conurbations hang upon tourism, and their development can be seen in Sue Berry's chapter on this subject. Recent unseasonable weather has caused those economies to lose out on the seasonal trade, that, ironically, was boosted in 2011 and 2012 by above average temperatures in April and September. How the weather affected tourism in Somerset in the Victorian period, especially when there was no weather forecasting available on the radio to keep visitors away, has yet to be investigated.

Such extremes of bad weather often had disastrous effects on vessels sailing off the Somerset coast. The experiences of some of those who survived those extremes can be found in Ashford's chapter. This does not include a detailed study of 'wreck and rescue', as this has, to a certain extent, been researched by many people, including by Farr,[1] Smith,[2] Tovey[3] and the Larns[4] but there is much that is of interest on this subject. Ashford has also unearthed evidence to show some of the other causes, or potential causes, of disaster off the Somerset coast. For example, a drunken captain who was so incapable that he could not give any orders to the pilots, which could have been catastrophic but fortunately was not, although later in the voyage they all ended up on a sandbank.[5] Similarly knowing where you were once at sea was not always straight forward. One seaman when asked what the ship's position was replied, "If ye'd only but show me the ould Head of Kinsale I'd tell ye where ye are in a twinkling; but devil a bit of me knows one o' these waves from t'other".[6] Although only a handful of examples are given, there must have been many, many more cases of negligent practices that caused many lives to be lost off the Somerset coast.

One aspect of the many accounts of travel was the need for easy access to a safe harbour, not only for the protection of shipping and life at sea, but also for the improved management of cargo handling. Both of these would have led to an increase in trade, something that the Luttrells of Dunster were concerned with when they employed Joseph Surbey, in 1701, to survey their principal harbour at Minehead. Surbey's design was similar in style to those at other harbours in the Bristol Channel, especially in Devon,[7] and it helped ensure that Minehead remained a viable port during the eighteenth century. Captain Paul Hughes shows in great detail the lengths to which Surbey went to in order for the project to be a success. This research complements Ashford's and Hussey's chapters in volume one in this series, where aspects of the trade of West Somerset and the development of near-by Porlock are documented.[8]

Less well documented than the ships that traded to and from Somerset's coast, is the amount of vessels involved in sea fishing from Somerset's ports and harbours. On the south and east coasts of Britain fishing was undertaken by fleets of vessels. For example, at Brixham 76 trawlers were in operation in 1785 and in the 1820s the number had risen to 89, which by 1890 were 300 in number. In the Bristol Channel the situation was very different. Bill Kelly shows how a fleet operated from Minehead, part of which may have been drawn by a land surveyor in the 1680s (reproduced as image 5.16),[9] but how big this fleet was is far from clear, as is the size of the catches they brought back to port. Through a careful study of many different factors, Kelly has also predicted the future course of sea fishing off the Somerset coast. It will be interesting to see if his prediction for the Bristol Channel's unique marine food web connections is better understood, or not, in years to come. Perhaps these findings can be examined in a future volume in this series, if books are still being published in 50 years time. He has also shown how the protection of Lundy has seen a resurgence in different types of fish. But an exceptionally wet winter, in 2012/2013, has meant an unusually large amount of fresh water has drained into the Bristol Channel, causing sea anglers difficulty in catching as much fish as in previous much drier years.

The seas and rivers, or in the case of this volume, the Bristol Channel, which connects the studies published here, is shown to have been both a giver and taker of livelihoods. Its destructive power brought a civil engineer to the West Country from London, to design a new pier at Minehead to offer ships protection from it. It also transported thousands of ships over a period of hundreds of years safely from one destination to another, mainly Ireland or South Wales, but occasionally much further afield. At the same time some Somerset people were making their living through fishing, working the ferries at Pill or Rownham, or servicing the ever-growing tourist industry. Today there are no commercial trawlers working from Somerset, only vessels being hired by charter parties so their owners can still make a living off the coast and river ferries are a distant memory of a bygone age.

Adrian Webb
Taunton

Note: A third volume of studies into aspect of Somerset's rich and varied maritime history is in progress. If you wish to be involved with this volume please contact the SANHS office.

References
1. G.E. Farr, *Wreck and rescue in the Bristol Channel: story of the English lifeboats* (1966).
2. G. Smith, *Shipwrecks of the Bristol Channel* (1991).
3. R. Tovey, *A chronology of Bristol Channel shipwrecks* (n.d.).
4. R. and B. Larn, *Shipwreck index of the British Isles volume 5 – West Coast and Wales* (2000).
5. T. C. Crocker (ed.), *The tour of the French traveller, M. De La Boullaye Le Gouz in Ireland in 1644* (1837), 1-5.
6. *The London University Magazine* vol. 1 (1829), 185-7.
7. M. Stammers, *The industrial archaeology of docks and harbours* (2007), 26.
8. See chapters three and four.
9. Somerset Heritage Centre, DD/L1/10/35A a survey of the Luttrell estate in West Somerset, 1687.

List of Illustrations

List of Tables

List of Figures

Four Hundred Years of Maritime Travel via the Somerset Coast, 1435-1835

Philip Ashford

THE MOTIVATION for, timing, and outcome of passages to and from the Somerset coast are examined in this chapter, which is based upon over two hundred accounts from a wide range of sources. However, a main purpose of this discourse is to give an authentic voice to the experience of maritime travel in the Bristol Channel prior to the Age of Steam, through the use of (predominantly) contemporary accounts, thus bringing a very personal perspective to Somerset's maritime history. Aspects of Tudor, Stuart and Georgian trade from the Somerset ports are explored by various authors elsewhere in *A maritime history of Somerset volume one: trade and commerce*, which identified

a wide distribution of destinations for vessels whose journeys originated on the Somerset coast. The resulting trade routes meant possibilities for personal travel opened up for many people from all walks of life and it is clear they did not only travel in designated passenger vessels, such as the Irish packets, but at times used cargo vessels, fishing vessels and even warships to complete their passages. Many accounts of journeys to the predominant international destination, Ireland, survive but

---

Illustration 1.1: Map of the Bristol and St George's Channels depicting the most significant passenger routes from the Somerset coast described in this chapter. (Author)

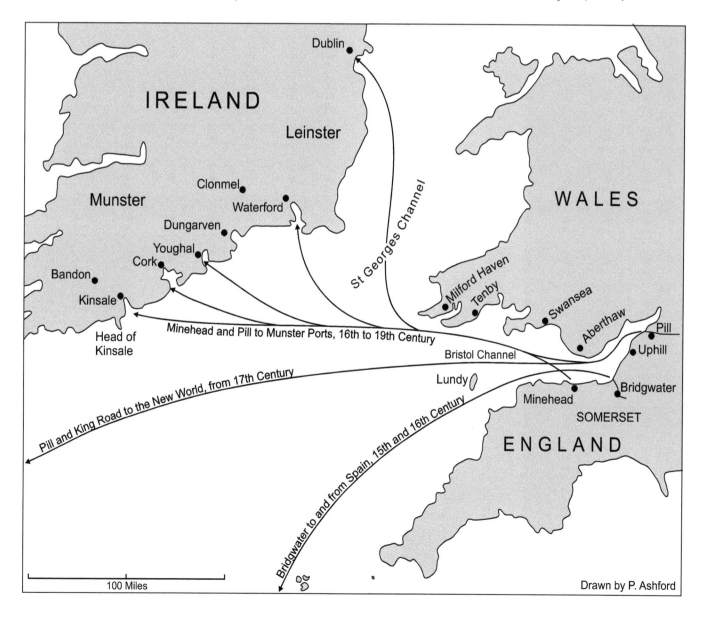

accounts of trips to other European continental destinations are relatively uncommon. Whilst Minehead was an important harbour for departure to Ireland, Pill (on the Somerset side of the mouth of the River Avon), and the anchorage at King Road (in the approaches to the Avon), were main points of embarkation, not only for Ireland, but further afield to North America and the Caribbean.

Economic reasons for travel: business

Prior to Tudor times, there had been animosity between the mariners and merchants of Bridgwater with those of Youghal on the southern Irish coast. Sometime before 1475 mariners from each port had rioted, presumably in each other's towns, and attempts were made in that year to keep the peace. Then, in about 1495, Youghal traders seized goods belonging to Minehead merchants. Subsequently, in 1496, licence was given for Maurice Quilayn, George Donnel, Maurice Quirke and John Philip, all of Minehead and all part owners of Minehead's *Sonday* of 40 tons, to seize ships and goods of Youghal until recompense was made. Perhaps in order to help accommodate resulting financial issues, or to seal an agreement after the problem was resolved, the warden of Youghal travelled to Somerset in 1497, disembarking at Combwich where he met the Bridgwater water bailiff.[1] It is difficult to say how successful this mission was, but it is known, from the next remaining Bridgwater port book of 1511, that seven Youghal vessels made a total of 20 journeys to the jurisdiction of the port of Bridgwater for trade, whereas between 1460 and 1497 only 26 sailings of merchant vessels were recorded as leaving Youghal for Bridgwater, with 13 making the return journey.[2]

In 1482, Richard Chapman, a fishmonger, likely to have been a Minehead man, was aboard the '*Flowre*' of Minehead with John Quirke master, probably in the southern Irish sea, when they were captured by Scottish pirates and taken to Ayr where they languished in prison for some time. Later, in 1501, a Gloucester fish merchant, David Vaughan was in Minehead purchasing white herring and salmon which he had loaded onto the *Kynburgh* of Gloucester for the return trip.[3] The context of these events is that there was a lively trade in fish between Ireland and the Somerset coast in the fifteenth century. Vaughan and Chapman were clearly involved in the marketing of the catches and travelled in the Bristol Channel to pursue their business, but as Chapman's experience shows, travelling by water for business purposes was occasionally precarious during this period.

The practise of merchants being passengers on their own or other master's ships seems to have been a common occurrence in Tudor and Stuart times. In 1502 Dyonisius Dwyn, merchant of Bridgwater and Ireland, was aboard a trading vessel sailing from Bordeaux to the Bristol Channel when he was running short of provisions. Off Belle Isle, France he traded for some cod with an Irish vessel on its way

llustration 1.2: A reconstruction of the *Nao Victoria* which circumnavigated the globe from Seville in 1519-1522 under the captaincy of Juan Sebastian Elcano in the Magellan expedition. Perhaps the merchant Antony from Spain sailed in a vessel similar to this when he was anchored at Steart in 1549. (David Worthy)

to Bordeaux. Two years later, in 1504, Dwyn was again in Bordeaux having shipped woad on board his Bridgwater vessel the *Gabriel*. Later in 1549, Antony, a Spanish merchant, was aboard a ship anchored at Steart. Like Dwyn, he suffered great inconvenience, but this time at the hands of the establishment. The vessel allegedly took on wheat and beans without following the necessary customs procedures. Officials were sent to the ship from Bridgwater and Anthony was brought back to the town before the mayor, John Newport. He was reportedly 'mistreated' and later paid a bribe to the mayor so that he and the vessel of San Sebastian could be released.[4] Early in the seventeenth century, Robert Powlett, 'customer' of Bridgwater and Minehead, in his own words, was engaged in 'service designed for the benefit of his Majesty's customs' by protecting merchants from Minehead as they travelled 'to and from Ireland in pursuance of their trade'.[5] His vessel, the *Dove,* was probably used in convoy duties, but there is an implication that merchants sometimes travelled with their cargoes. In 1605, merchant David Butler was aboard the *Speedwell* of Bridgwater with George Escott as master; they freighted in South Wales and travelled to northern Spain and then back to Minehead where Butler disembarked. He then took a passage across to Wales.[6]

Wealthy Bristol merchants, if not travelling aboard ships themselves, were likely to have had factors or servants who went with cargoes in order to secure the business for their employers. This notion is evident in 1648 when Edward Tarrent of Bristol, shoemaker aged about 60, travelled to Ireland acting as a factor for Robert Bagnoll of Keynsham, clothier. Tarrent sold a bale of Bagnoll's cloth to Thomas Turner of Kinsale.[7] Furthermore, not all factors survived the journey. A sad event occurred in 1681 when adverse winds had been holding up vessels for weeks as they tried to sail down the Bristol Channel; some vessels had been at anchor in King Road for nearly three months. Then, a large vessel, the *Victory*, made it out into the Channel, but was 'cast away' near the Holm islands where three or four seamen and several servants were drowned.[8]

One business event that must not be underestimated in terms of its influence on travel in the Bristol Channel in the sixteenth and seventeenth centuries was Bristol's St James's Fair, which took place each year in late July. This was the peak time when ships, merchants and goods arrived in Bristol from Ireland, Wales and from across the south of England. It was the time when accounts were settled,

credit procured, future business secured and commercial relationships cemented.[9] Given that so many valuable commodities and so much cash was in transit at the time, the summer was also a peak time for piracy in the Bristol Channel. In 1575 some pirates left Pill in a stolen vessel and waited in the Channel to intercept merchants leaving for home after the fair. The enterprise seems to have had some successful results since the pirates abandoned the stolen vessel at The Mumbles, near Swansea, and sold some of the stolen goods to the Welsh, no doubt having also robbed many merchants. On their arrival home, Devon merchants (who had been affected) caused Sir Richard Grenville to seek help from Sir Edward Stradling in South Wales in order to apprehend the miscreants.[10] In the event four who were arrested back in Pill were tried in Bristol on 25 September and subsequently three were hung in Cannon's Marsh near the Cathedral.[11]

In early July 1630 a pirate ship or privateer, possibly a 'Biscaner' (a vessel from the Biscay area), lurked near the mouth of Milford Haven halting merchants, ships and goods leaving for St James's Fair and causing great concern for the impoverishment of Pembrokeshire. This was despite two English warships being in the Bristol Channel, from at least May, to try and suppress the pirates.[12] Two years later a warship commanded by Captain Plumley was dispatched on 10 July for Ireland and the Severn 'where pirates swarm before St James's Fair'.[13] In summer 1633 and 1635 a warship accompanied the fifty or so vessels in convoys from Waterford as they sailed for the fair.[14] In 1635 the event was witnessed by Sir William Brereton who travelled from Waterford via Minehead to Bristol where he found the city full of Irishmen for St James's Fair. Even more insidious, perhaps, was that some of the pirates were 'Turkish', *i.e.* from the African coast and were interested in taking people into slavery as much as seizing goods. This was not an isolated event as on 4 July 1636 good quality first hand intelligence came into Penzance that a 'Turkish' vessel had already taken people from vessels and was about to cruise in St George's Channel, in order 'to take passengers' going to Bristol fair.[15] What is certain is that hundreds of merchants would have been in transit each year, including many from the Somerset ports. The records quoted do not detail how many of those merchants disembarked in King Road or at Pill and walked, or rode, the last miles to the fair, or stayed on board until their vessels arrived at Bristol.

Somerset relied heavily on the wool trade which

caused buyers and merchants to cross the Bristol Channel for business. In 1603 a contemporary Welsh source stated that 'Somerset men' twice yearly travelled to Pembrokeshire to buy wool.[16] No doubt they sailed from Minehead to Tenby, since the latter was the main port of departure for Pembrokeshire wool arriving in Minehead in the late Tudor period; the buyers, probably Minehead and Dunster clothiers, may have even arrived back in Minehead with their purchases. Other merchants appear to have moved residence from Minehead to Ireland in the seventeenth century. Minehead merchant Simon Gibbons migrated from Minehead to Youghal, in 1628 and became the principal wool merchant there in the 1630s.[17] In 1629 George Hayman (or Heyman) followed Gibbons to Youghal where his family subsequently became merchants, probably helped by his marriage to Mary, daughter of Simon Gibbons in 1632.[18] Lord Boyle frequently mentioned these two merchants in his diaries since he did much business with them; on one occasion in 1639 he sent a retainer, Thomas Badnedge, to Minehead from Ireland to transact business with Hayman which also involved Gibbons. Badnedge only took four days to make both legs of the journey before arriving back in Munster with money from Hayman.[19] The link between Minehead and Youghal in the 1630s and 1640s is underlined by the fact that Peter Reynolds of Minehead was allowed to set up as a tradesman in Youghal in 1629 and, furthermore, in 1643 John, son of Thomas Holland a tailor of Minehead, was apprenticed to Thomas Taylor of Youghal, merchant. The apprenticeship lasted an unusually long period of 15 years ending in the late 1650s when John applied to be a freeman of Youghal.[20] Did Thomas Taylor collect his young apprentice from Minehead, in the 1630s, whilst he was in the port on business and then depart for Youghal with him?

Two further Hayman brothers left Somerset for Ireland in 1662, when Robert settled in Clonmel and Samuel settled in Youghal, where in 1670 he bought some of the lands of Sir Walter Raleigh, including a house that Raleigh had built.[21] Other Haymans of Minehead were merchants and shipmasters in the seventeenth century, such as George Hayman, who sailed, on occasion, as a merchant on the *Thomas*. He traded in items including butter and woollen cloth between Minehead and Youghal from 1685 to 1687. George was in Youghal buying goods to trade in October 1685 and in August and October 1686.[22] Amongst others, he traded with Hayman and Crockford relations in Ireland as his in-laws were

Crockfords. In 1681, Thomas Dineley, a traveller in Ireland, met Edward Crockford, then resident in Youghal. Dineley described Crockford as a son of Edward Crockford of Minehead, merchant, and Anne Laundy of Youghal.[23] The Crockford family had traded between Minehead and Ireland for generations and, no doubt, Edward junior functioned at the Youghal end of the enterprise in 1681. Such was their success that Edward became the mayor of Youghal in 1684.[24] Appendix 1.1 shows the prominence of migrants from Minehead in the government of Youghal from 1666 to 1686.

An example of immigration connected to the wool trade occured in 1679. Nineteen year-old Cork Quaker, Joseph Pike traded in wool in Cork the year before, and then came to Minehead for six months where he worked as a trader for his brother-in-law Henry Wheddon. He did this to Henry's 'satisfaction and then made it my business to get [a] full insight into wool, for I delighted in the trade'. For 'a while' Pike formed a partnership with William Alloway, a notable Somerset Quaker, dealing in wool and English goods, *i.e.* mainly cloth related products.[25] Though 19 years of age may appear young for a businessman, Pike had already been to Bristol from Cork in 1677 'on account of trade'.[26] Benjamin, another member of the Alloway family who was engaged in business, moved from Minehead and

Illustration 1.3: A drawing of the *Angel Gabriel*. In 1631 Robert Aldsworth and Giles Eldridge, merchants of Bristol, were granted 12,000 acres of land in New England with another 100 acres for every settler transported to the colony of Pemaquid in the present state of Maine. The initials of their surnames and the year of the patent are found on this seal with an illustration of the vessel that anchored in King Road and embarked passengers, such as the Cogswells, in 1635 in order to take settlers to the plantation.[30]
(http://homepages.rootsweb.ancestry.com/~legends/pequseal. gif accessed February 2013)

settled in Dublin in about 1700.[27]

West of England woollen industry operatives also made transatlantic journeys from the Somerset coast when they emigrated to the New World. In May 1635, John Cogswell, a clothier from Westbury in Wiltshire who ran fulling mills in Frome, sold up his land and with his wife Elizabeth, at least five of their children, and servants, embarked on the *Angel Gabriel* in King Road and sailed for the 'new world' to find their fortune. The ship was wrecked by a 'hurricane' on the American coast but the family, along with most of the passengers survived. The Cogswells set up home in Ipswich, Massachusetts and by all accounts, of which there are many, they thrived economically as the inventory of John's goods in 1670 (made when he died), is considerable.[28] Then, in September 1683, when the New World was far more familiar to British people, William Salway, a Quaker serge maker from Taunton, travelled from Bristol on the *Society*, or the *Samuel and Mary*, in which Sealy owned part of the cargoes of cloth. Sealy landed in Pennsylvania and set up a fulling mill there in 1684.[29]

During the seventeenth century, King Road was the established position within the jurisdiction of the port of Bristol, just off the Somerset coast, for transatlantic departures. In 1603 two small vessels financed by Sir Walter Raleigh left King Road for an exploration of the Cape Cod area, returning with wood for trading.[31] On 5 July 1610 a vessel left King Road with 39 men and Governor elect, Bristolian John Guy, who, armed with a charter from James the First, were due to establish a colony in Newfoundland. Upon leaving King Road, a storm caused the loss of an anchor so the vessel sheltered in Minehead until 11 July. Whilst anchored there for a few days, the party lost one of their 12 goats and the colony's blacksmith disembarked and failed to make the journey. John Guy, his brother Philip, brother-in-law William Colston, and the other men succeeded in establishing the colony and aimed to make money from wood, fishing, furs and mining. The Cupers Cove colony was the first official English settlement in what is now Canada. The following year Guy returned to England and recruited young women for the colony whom he conveyed back to Canada.[32]

1619 was the year when the 45 ton *Margaret* from Bristol set sail from King Road for Virginia with 38 male settlers and Captain John Woodlief at their head and Tobias Felgate as their pilot; this was a year later than had originally been planned as the *Margaret* had

Illustration 1.4: John Guy (1567-1629), whilst on his way to set up the first English settlement in Canada anchored at Minehead for a few days in early July 1610. This stamp was printed to celebrate the 300th anniversary of the colony.

been wind-bound, in Ireland, the previous summer and could not make Bristol early enough in the year to make the journey before winter set in. They were destined to set up an area known as Berkeley hundred for the Virginia Company; Berkeley because they were financed by gentlemen from south Gloucestershire including a member of the Berkeley family, indeed, boatmen from the town of Berkeley brought wheat, amongst other items, down the Severn to King Road to help provision the ship. The *Margaret* weighed anchor at 8 a.m. on 16 September 1619 but southerly winds meant that they made little progress along the Somerset coast. It was over a week until south-westerly winds of a stronger nature allowed the ship to finally escape the Bristol Channel, leaving Lundy behind them. The Virginia Company sent another vessel, the 70 ton *Supply* in 1620, financed by the same Gloucestershire gentlemen. Again boats from Berkeley helped provision the ship and the passengers lodged at Pill before embarkation; this included the captain's wife and children and other women (who had been brought down the Avon from Bristol in a boat), before they were ferried to the *Supply* that was anchored off Pill. Want of wind caused Captain Tracy to nearly run out of money and he wrote to his Gloucestershire backers for more cash to pay his expenses before leaving. After sailing down the Bristol Channel, they were forced into Kinsale because of a leak in the ship where at least

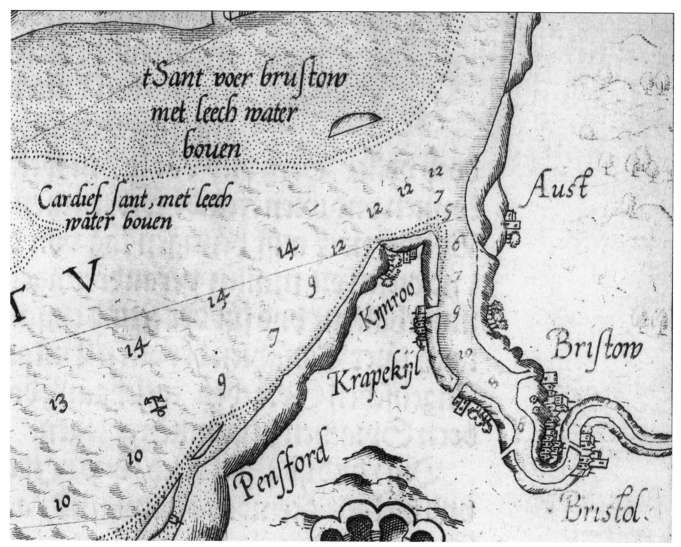

Illustration 1.5: An extract from a Dutch chart published in 1589 showing the north coast of Somerset and the River Avon. Kynroo is King Road, and Krapekyl is Crockern Pill or just Pill. (L. Waghenaer, *Spieghel Der Zeevaerdt* (Leiden, 1589))

five passengers disembarked and did not travel on to Virginia. However, the remainder eventually arrived in Virginia, as did all the men on the *Margaret*. Within three years many of these settlers were killed in an American Indian uprising.[33] Clearly, Pill had a significant role for transatlantic conveyancing of passengers in the early seventeenth century. In 1640 for example, 125 passengers about to travel to New England in the *Neptune* had to make oaths at 'Crocan Pill'.[34] Evidence from the year before when Bristol's *Mary Rose* was licensed to take 120 passengers to New England from the city was that these oaths were in relation to 'Allegiance and Supremacy'.[35]

King Road was a point of departure and arrival of another Bristolian travelling to and from the New World for business reasons in the 1680s. Quaker, Thomas Pearson, who had served an apprenticeship in Bristol, probably as a land surveyor, left Bristol for

Maryland in 1675. In late 1681, he boarded the *Comfort* of Bristol off the Maryland coast and disembarked in King Road on the 20th March 1682. In June 1683, King Road was the point of embarkation onto the same vessel for his third Atlantic crossing, this time to Upland, Pennsylvania. Pearson then married and went on to become deputy surveyor in the state and worked with William Penn in the early administration of the Colony. He did not visit his home city again.[36]

There were also clear business links between west Somerset and Glamorganshire which occasioned interconnecting travel. In 1585, or 1586, it appears that Robert Hensley, probably of Porlock or Selworthy, hired an anvil to Thomas Sully, maybe another Somerset man, but one who then lived at St Athens, Glamorganshire and no doubt plied the trade of a blacksmith, or iron worker, in South Wales. It appears that both Sully and the anvil travelled to Wales from west Somerset and in 1586 Hensley travelled over to Glamorganshire to Sir Edward Stradling, of St Donats, in order to try to retrieve the said anvil in line with the agreement that had been made.[37] The cattle trade also caused merchants, buyers and sellers to travel by sea to Somerset. In 1623 Glamorganshire cattle trader John Williams shipped cattle into Minehead, rather than Bridgwater, because traders could be confident of arriving within one tide. He also bought further stock in Chard and was well known to at least three Taunton butchers.[38] No doubt he travelled with his cattle to Taunton fairs. Other Welsh drovers are recorded to have sold cattle at Taunton fairs in the 1620s and 1630s and they are likely to have come over the Channel with them, probably to Minehead, before selling them in Taunton. Furthermore, in 1632, James Reade from Hutton was stated to have often travelled to Wales to buy cattle, which were again shipped to Minehead from Aberthaw;[39] Hutton is but two miles from Uphill where there had for centuries been a reliable passage available to Wales. The most likely scenario was that Reade took the short trip across to Sulley from Uphill, bought cattle in Wales and then returned with them to Somerset via Minehead. Another agricultural related cross-Channel passenger link is recorded right at the end of the period under study here. On 28 July 1844 the *Picton* of Aberthaw arrived in Minehead 'for harvest men' of Somerset and returned with them from Glamorganshire two weeks later.[40] How many people this involved, how long this seasonal movement of grain reapers had been occurring and where the home towns or parishes of the harvesters were, are all unanswered questions.

A spin off from the cattle trade with Ireland was the availability of transport for general passengers, as well as cattle merchants. In 1639 three Youghal men sold 40 cattle at a Taunton fair, included in their customers were buyers from Stogursey and Staplegrove. It is quite probable that they had travelled over to Minehead with their cattle since Minehead was the main Irish cattle port in the Bristol Channel. Also, in the other direction, Edward Gille of Salisbury, Wiltshire stated that he had often travelled to Ireland to buy cattle to bring back to England. However, in 1639 he reported that a consignment of his cattle had been lost at sea which reduced him to seeking charity.[41] Later in the century, in 1661, Abraham Lawton of Youghal sold £160 worth of Irish cattle in England and was returning to his home town, via Minehead, when customs officials sequestrated his earnings.[42] Since the business link between the Somerset coast and southern Ireland was long established by the seventeenth century, it is understandable why on the 1 April 1636 Thomas Anthony, who had a wife and children living in Bridgwater and so probably lived there himself, was in Minehead seeking a passage to Ireland. By 20 April he was in Kinsale having travelled overland from Youghal. Anthony was a factor for a London ship provisioning firm who was sent to Kinsale to buy stores and cargo for a vessel, the *Abraham*, which was expected to arrive in Kinsale from London and then sail for Virginia.[43]

Wealthy land speculators made the journey from the Somerset coast to Ireland during the seventeenth century, such as Percy Freke of West Bilney, Norfolk, who travelled with his cousin and wife, Elizabeth, from Pill to southern Ireland in 1677. Percy was using his wife's money to purchase land in the Cork area during the last twenty years of the seventeenth and first decade of the eighteenth century, commencing his purchases in 1676 from the second Earl Barrymore with a property near Cork called Rathbarry. The couple's first journey to Ireland was an eventful one. Plots against King Charles the Second meant that only people with permits could travel by sea, but the Frekes had no permit to circumvent the travel embargo. Whilst staying with relatives in Bristol they managed to secure a private boat from Pill, which took them to a ship which may have been lying in King Road. The vessel departed on 25 August but 'tempestuous winds' drove them into Ilfracombe where they stayed from the 26th to the 28th. The wind changed so they sailed again and were a few hours from Waterford when a storm blew them back to Lundy, where they sheltered with four other ships in the lee of the island fearing for their lives. However, the wind abated again and they sailed for and eventually arrived in Ireland.[44] A few years later, in 1683, the Frekes once again departed from Pill to Ireland on 26 July, arriving in Cork three days later. Political difficulties meant they were detained and searched in Cork on the orders of the mayor of the town. On a third business trip from Pill, Percy Freke, travelling alone in June 1702 after undertaking business in London collecting money for new land purchases, travelled from Pill to Waterford and then overland to Cork with over £1,000 on his person.[45]

Quaker businessman James Jenkins, who moved from England to Ireland in about 1771 and was in the grocery trade, travelled from southern Ireland to Minehead early in March 1778 in order to visit Bristol, London and Portsmouth, the latter places which he described as the main ports of entry for Irish butter at the time. Presumably he was developing contacts to try and increase trade. He embarked on the 4 March at 4 a.m. on the *Whitworth*

Illustration 1.6: George Frederick Cooke (1756-1812) a renowned actor who travelled from Cork to Pill in 1800 dressed for his appearance in Richard the Third. (Published in 1818, by Simpkin & Marshall, Stationers Court and Chapple, Pall Mall, London)

about two hours we got out of reach of her guns, when her commander gave up the chase'.[46] Jenkins was more fortunate than the 150 passengers on the *Britannia* in October 1781, en-route from Bristol (probably via King Road) to Cork, who had their vessel captured by a French privateer and were subsequently taken out of their way to Morlaix.[47]

In the first decade of the nineteenth century a troupe of travelling players in Bridgwater heard that many people of society were gathering in Tenby. Their manager proceeded to negotiate their passage with the master of a merchant vessel in Bridgwater about to sail for Wales. The troupe and their props embarked and they were soon performing in Tenby to the intended audience. Upon completion of the tour the troupe embarked for Ilfracombe and continued performances in North Devon.[48] Another passage in the Bristol Channel which was precipitated by a desire to perform in a theatre, took place in October 1800, when an actor George Cooke embarked at Cork for Bristol, disembarking at Pill. He then went on to London and rehearsed for a part in King Richard the Third in Covent Garden theatre where his performances made him famous.[49]

In 1820, tragedy struck a young man going about his family's business of installing lighthouse optics, necessary when navigational lights were improved by replacing coal fired braziers with oil lamps. The Robinson family gained contracts from Trinity House and worked on Flat Holm lighthouse, which was converted to the new oil fired system in 1820.[50] George Robinson, aged 23, was returning from Flat Holm by boat to Uphill during his supervision of the improvements. Sadly, due to the 'upsetting of the boat' he was drowned. His father, also George Robinson, from Norfolk, had an unusual marble tablet, showing Flat Holm, erected in Bristol Cathedral, on a wall now not seen by the general public, in memory of his son describing and depicting the sad event.[51]

Thus business within the Bristol Channel, and further afield to Ireland and the New World, caused many people to travel the breadth, or length, of the Bristol Channel, with most intercontinental journeys commenced, or terminated, in King Road or at Pill. Minehead was an important staging point for business with Ireland. Whilst other landing places along the Somerset coast would have seen some business traffic, they were undoubtedly less significant than Minehead or Pill, places which witnessed thousands of travellers arrive and depart during the period of this study.

with Captain Martin in charge. They left port, probably Waterford, followed by about 'ten other sail', the sight of which was 'both novel and pleasing' to him. He arrived in Minehead about 30 hours later accompanied by Dr John Davis, Godfery, an organ builder of the Strand in London and a young student of the law who was travelling to London to complete his studies at the 'Temple'. Early the following year Jenkins made another business trip, which was eventful for him and the rest of the passengers and crew. The passage to Minehead was, a 'tedious' four days but, during the passage, fear came in the form of a chase by a French privateer. At one time it 'came so close that it fired some shots to bring us to ... some of them went over the deck and fell into the sea beyond the ship'. Fortunately they were not caught because 'by hoisting more sail than usual, in

Illustration 1.7 Flat Holm lighthouse and a shipwreck from a memorial marble to George Robinson aged 23, drowned in 1820 on a passage to Uphill. (Courtesy of the Dean and Chapter of Bristol Cathedral)

Economic reasons for travel: poor migrants

Many poor Irish immigrants (without obvious mercantile interests) arrived in Somerset from at least the late fifteenth century on Irish and English ships. Many were seeking refuge from religious and political upheavals, but there must have been countless others who took the journey in search of work. In 1495 John Thyne was reported at the Minehead manor court for transporting vagabonds from Ireland against the order of the court and Thomas Whyle was presented for keeping vagabonds in the town and refusing to carry them back to Ireland.[52] It is clear that Leyland's famous quote from the 1540s that

Minehead was 'exceedingly full of Irishmen',[53] also reflected the position half a century earlier. Some of these Irishmen would have found work locally in an around the port, such as the three employed to work on a weir in Dunster in 1559, possibly one of the coastal fish weirs.[54] In the seventeenth century poor immigrants who could not find, or were incapable of, work often became a burden on the local parishes and a problem for the local justices,[55] such as the group who were landed clandestinely on Porlock beach in 1622, when the Irish vessel landing them departed very quickly before it could be identified and apprehended.[56]

Three years prior to this event, in 1619, Thomas Bennell, a Lancastrian who had spent time in Dublin as a footman, disembarked a ship in Bridgwater from Ireland. He wandered around for a few days and then had to appear before a justice of the peace for a settlement examination.[57] The disbanding of Charles the First's armies in Ireland in 1629 exacerbated the

Illustration 1.8: The *Matthew*, a reconstruction of a fifteenth-century sailing ship, anchored at low tide in Porlock Bay on 23 May 2010. An Irish vessel which disembarked vagrants in 1622 may well have anchored at a similar position. (Derek Purvis)

problem, with soldiers who had served in Ireland, and their families, wandering around England. Some of these soldiers could have been amongst the people mentioned at the Western assizes in August 1629 when John Paule and George Bond, constables of Minehead, had incurred 'intolerable charges' in deporting 'Irish begars' in accordance with 'the King's recent proclamation'.[58] The problem did not end there, as in 1630 it was reported how 76, mainly poor Irish people, were landed at Portishead Point,[59] probably the occasion when an Irish shipmaster from Waterford, Maurice Kenson (or Keyson) of the *Peter*, said 'as long as there were English in Ireland hee would bring Irishmen to England' after having landed Irish people at Portishead.[60]

The Somerset justices, as well as those in other counties, were able to round up and repatriate many Irish vagrants with no legitimate reason, or business, for being in the country. In 1630 the justices at

Sherborne, Dorset rounded up Treolan McBrean and other Irish people, whom they regarded as 'wandering and dangerous persons' who had forged their passes. The court condemned the group to be whipped at a cart's tail and then sent to Minehead where they were to be shipped back to Ireland.[61] In 1631 the justices at Devizes were interviewing a man from Mallow, in County Cork, who had been 'compelled to leave Ireland and sail to Minehead' because of debts he had accumulated at home.[62] Justices at Salisbury interviewed Richard Whyte who was found wandering with Mourne Treye in the summer of 1633. They had false passports and were not married as they had pretended. Richard was punished and sent to Minehead to be forwarded to Ireland whilst Treye was sent to Bristol for embarkation to Ireland.[63] Presumably; extra punishment was the reason why they were sent to different ports.

The first English Civil War of the 1640s seems to have reduced the problems of Irish vagrants in Somerset, possibly because of a greater fear of travel over the Bristol Channel which was controlled by parliament and, subsequently, there was a greater risk

Illustration 1.9: A close up of the *Matthew* with its twenty-first-century awning in the Floating Harbour, Bristol, 2009. (Adrian Webb)

Illustration 1.10: A small ship heading down the Bristol Channel just about to pass what is now called Battery Point by Joseph Walter, 1835. The bay just behind the small fishing vessels is probably the location where Kenson disembarked 76 Irish people in 1630 and is intriguingly called Kilkenny Bay. The vessel illustrated might have been very like one which the Irish women, adjudged in Somerset as vagrants, were taken back to Ireland from Bristol in 1746. (Courtesy of Bristol Museum and Art Gallery)

of danger because of an increased density of men under arms. On the other hand, it might be that the disruption of the war meant that fewer records relating to the vagrancy were kept. However, in 1640 the Minehead churchwardens' accounts indicates that they gave 6d to a 'poor man out of Ireland', but in 1664 another 'poor Irishman' turned out to be from Wales.[64] During the Commonwealth the problem of Irish vagrancy resurfaced. In 1653 John Laffin and his 'Irish heiress wife' came to Minehead travelling on false passes. Later, in 1654, John was convicted at Ilchester for being 'a wandering person' and then sent back to Minehead so he could be 'transported into Ireland with the first conveniency'[65] and, in 1657, a

poor distressed man who had been granted a pass to Ireland was given charity by Minehead parish.[66] Furthermore, 27 Irish people from six families who had landed in Minehead in 1693 were also sent back.[67] A likely reason why Minehead was often used as a port of departure back to Ireland is that ships' masters would have more difficulty landing vagrants back on the Somerset coast instead of transporting them straightaway to Ireland, something that they would have more opportunity to do if the point of departure was anywhere in the bounds of the port of Bristol.

The problem of Irish immigrants, apparently, had a detrimental effect on other parts of Somerset's economy, not just the ports. According to Taunton woollen industry clothiers and fullers in 1692, many Irish immigrants had been employed 'in charity in the woollen manufacture' where they 'gained such experience therein, as before they never understood; and being returned home, can make and sell their commodities much cheaper than the English', thereby undermining English trade which then needed protecting. Indeed, the merchants, clothiers and fullers of Minehead said that during the reigns of King Charles the First and King James the Second (1660-1688), the trade in serge had become 'dead' due to undercutting from Ireland.[68] As a result, in about 1697, when the trade in Taunton was suffering, Ireland became a destination for at least 50 Taunton and district woollen industry operatives and their families.[69]

The issue of Irish vagrants continued into the eighteenth century. In January 1732 Minehead constables, Thomas Adams and Robert Sprages, incurred expenses by keeping three Irish vagrants in custody for three weeks, presumably awaiting a suitable passage back to Ireland. Probably winds kept ships wind-bound because eventually the vagrants needed to be taken to Ilfracombe for the passage.[70] During the 1740s, the port of departure for Irish vagabonds in Somerset changed from Minehead to Bristol. Presumably the system of removal was robust enough that the risk of vagrants disembarking on the Somerset coast again was minimal or non-existent. For example, in 1744, James Baldung, an Irish vagrant arrested in Chard, was sent to the staging point of St Mary Redcliffe, Bristol before removal to Ireland.[71] In 1746 a group of Irish women, many of whom alleged they were the wives of Welsh Fusiliers who had served in Ireland but were then drafted to other parts of the world, were arrested as vagrants in Taunton. Rose Sinclair, Katherine Lathey, Anna Ridgeway, Susannah Ridgeway, Katherine Howard and their children were all sent to St Mary Redcliffe for the first leg of the journey back to Ireland.[72] It is not unlikely that the women had recently arrived in Somerset from Ireland through Minehead. Somerset Quarter Sessions also dealt with similar cases via Bristol in the late 1740s.[73]

Of course, not all vagrants reaching the Somerset coast were Irish. In 1729 an extended family group (some who may have originated in the north of England), Alexander and Thomas Long, their wives Elizabeth and Susannah and three of Thomas's children had travelled from Anglesey to Cardiff and then took a ship to Uphill. Some of the group were picked up as vagrants in Williton and claimed they were on their way to Launceston in Cornwall.[74] In addition to the above case there are many references in the Somerset Quarter Sessions records from the seventeenth and eighteenth centuries of poor people from Wales receiving settlement, or removal, orders from Somerset. Whilst, most probably, many people either arrived or departed by sea, it is not made clear in the records that this indeed was the situation. However, four cases considered below, from 1733-1751, are ones where it seems most likely that at least one of the journeys was by sea.

Welsh sailors and their families sometimes lived in Bridgwater, possibly arriving on coal boats that were a regular feature at the port. In 1733, John Bowles, his wife Mary and their five children were removed to Pembrokeshire[75] and Evan Evans, his wife Anne and two children were removed from the town to Swansea in 1751.[76] In 1741 the Hollingworth family, this time not recorded as being a maritime family, were removed from Bridgwater to Tenby in Pembrokeshire.[77] In 1748 Hannah Jones and her daughter Rachel were apprehended in Dunster and it was ordered that they be 'carried to Swansea' on their way home to Merionethshire in Wales;[78] it is most likely that Hannah and Rachel were 'carried' in a vessel from Minehead. Similar to Irish vagrants, not all Welsh people removed from Somerset in the eighteenth century left through the West Somerset ports. In 1750, John and Mary Williams and their family were removed from Wellington to Wales through St Mary Redcliffe in Bristol.[79]

As the seventeenth century progressed, Bristol increasingly became the 'gateway to the New World' and many people travelled to the colonies through the port looking for an improved life. Workers were needed in the colonies and mainly younger, poorer, single people, opted to commit to labour for periods of about four years on the other side of the Atlantic. Sadly, for some of these young people, their status was not much better than that of slaves and many died before their term of servant-hood was over. From 1654 their intentions to travel from the port of Bristol were lodged with authorities in the city. This chapter shows that many transatlantic journeys commenced from King Road, so many of these indentured servants would have embarked from Pill, though there are no indications of this occurring within the records of indentured servants. However, one person who boarded near Portbury was the orphaned, runaway apprentice Farwell Meredith, who on 14 October 1653 walked out across the mudflats in King Road to try and board the *Dolphin* of Bristol which was bound to Barbados. He became stuck and was rescued by the crew, taken to Barbados and put to work at a plantation, all of his own will, according to his rescuers.[80]

1659 is used here as a sample year to illustrate the impact of the indentured servant migration from Bristol on Somerset. In that year there were 128 known indentured migrants from the county and possibly many more. 75% of those were male and, where occupations are recorded, many were farmers but others were trained in the cloth industry, or were craftsmen such as smiths, masons or carpenters. Most of the women were spinsters but there was the occasional widow. Over 10% came from the maritime parishes of Bedminster, Easton-in Gordano, Portbury, Portishead and Bridgwater so may well have been familiar with the comings and goings of ships in the Bristol Channel. Half of the servant migrants came from Somerset's main towns with Frome providing 12, Wells 10, Bruton 7 and Bath 6. No servants in this particular year came from west of Bridgwater and Taunton, but whether legal or illegal transfers of servants therefore took place through Minehead is so far unknown. It is worth noting how in June 1657 Arthur Davis of Minehead, yeoman and Joan Harper of Minehead, spinster, possibly an eloping couple, travelled to Bristol to become servants in Barbados, bound to the same person. The migrants dribbled into Bristol throughout the year in ones and twos and it seems likely that some came with a friend, or a sibling, but most came alone from their village. The destination of 116 of the 128 is stated and 68% of these were bound for Barbados and 32% for Virginia.[81] Many of those bound for Barbados would have worked on sugar plantations, whilst those in Virginia would have worked predominantly in the tobacco fields. Both commodities were transported back to Bristol in local ships, thus completing a trans-Atlantic chain of supply and demand for goods and labour.

Though it is clear that there was considerable civic organisation in Somerset, and in Bristol, there were difficulties controlling both nuisance migrations of Irish beggars and indentured servant movements to the New World. There were also concerns at both county and national levels regarding the ease in which Irish beggars came into Somerset and over the exploitation of young people, as it was thought many servants might have been taken abroad against their will in the early 1650s. Therefore, because of the nature of illegal immigration of the Irish and emigration of servants, it is possible that there were many arrivals and departures that were never recorded. Such illegal movements of people could have taken place from any point along the Somerset coast, not just through the main ports, as the records of illegal migrants arriving through Porlock and Portbury show.

Personal reasons including family, friendship, education and health

Travel in order to meet or stay with family members, or friends, was a strong motivation for the movement

of rich and poor alike, though the former have always had a greater financial ability to make the journey. The Stradling family of St Donats, had land and property on both sides of the Bristol Channel in the fifteenth century. In 1449 Henry Stradling, his wife Elizabeth and daughter were sailing across the Bristol Channel from Minehead in their vessel, *St Barbe,* to the family home at St Donats when a Breton pirate, Colyn Dolphyn captured the family, their faithful servant Dewryn and the crew. Dolphyn took them to St Malo until Henry's father, Edward, had raised enough redemption money by selling land in Oxfordshire and Monmouthshire. Upon their release and return in 1451, Henry built a watchtower overlooking the Bristol Channel at St Donats and kept armed men on the lookout for Dolphyn's ship

Illustration 1.11: Katharine Fitzgerald, Countess of Desmond (d.1604) who, with her daughter, sailed in the Bristol Channel to and from Bristol in 1604. Without doubt she was and is the oldest human to have seen the Somerset coast from on board a vessel in the Bristol Channel. (From an engraving in the *Wonderful Magazine*)

WONDERFUL MAGAZINE.

CATHERINE Countefs of DESMOND.
Who lived to the Age of about 140 Years.

since he was a frequently in the Channel at the time. Subsequently the watchtower, in which a fire was lit at night, caused Dolphyn, on another piratical cruise, to beach his vessel on Nash Sands. He and his crew were caught and hanged.[82]

Somerset merchants sometimes sent apprentices or family members abroad to learn a European language at the destination point of their foreign trade, which for the most part would have been France or Spain. These people became factors for the merchants in their trading ports. In 1549, the 15 year old nephew of John White, comptroller of the port of Bridgwater was the servant of Bridgwater merchant John Tyrrel. The teenager had been sent to Spain at the behest of Tyrrel to learn Spanish. Given the trade link between Bridgwater and the northern Spanish coast at the time, it is highly likely that the lad sailed from Bridgwater to San Sebastian.[83] At the completion of his learning he would most likely have been involved with the wine trade from Spain and would have helped sell corn and cloth coming in from Bridgwater.

A remarkable journey from Cork to Bristol took place in 1604 when Katharine Fitzgerald, Countess of Desmond, accompanied by her 90 year-old daughter, sailed from Cork to Bristol. Katharine's age is unknown but historians estimate it to have been between 120 and 140 years. She is known to have danced with Royalty before the end of the fifteenth century. Perhaps, without fear of contradiction, these notes relate the passage of the oldest person ever to travel by ship in the Bristol Channel for all time. Katharine's husband had his lands sequestrated by the English after he had become involved in an uprising against the English in southern Ireland in Tudor times. Much of the land was ceded to Sir Walter Raleigh in the 1580s. Raleigh, who lived in

Illustration 1.12: The province of Munster in the 1580s after Desmond land had been allocated to Sir Walter Raleigh, Sir Christopher Hatton and Sir Richard Grenville who undertook to re-populate the land with English families. (National Maritime Museum E9078)

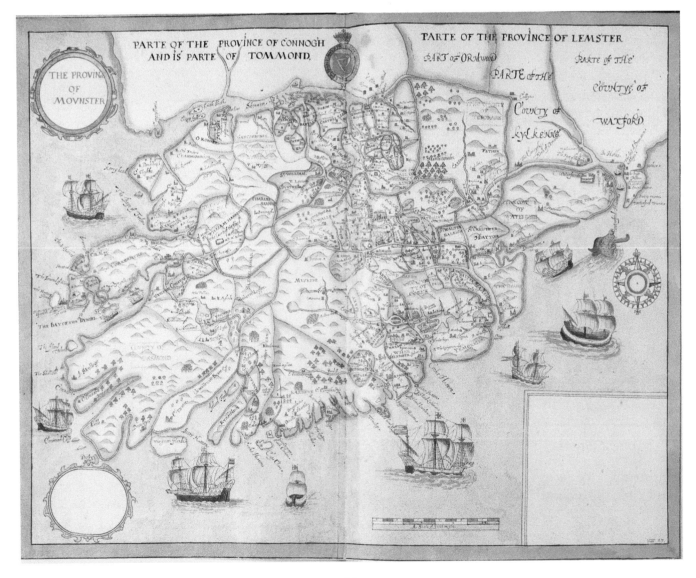

Illustration 1.13: Robert Boyle (1627-1691) the famous scientist, who as a young man was in Minehead in 1635. (From an engraving by John Faber, Jr.)

Youghal for periods in that decade and was mayor there in 1588, had settled 144 English men from the south-west of the country on lands around Youghal and Cork, but he left Katharine with a life interest in a property near Youghal. He must have reasonably expected her to die imminently so his action was not particularly munificent. However, Katharine lived on and Raleigh sold his Munster lands to the First Earl of Cork, Richard Boyle, in 1602. Soon after, Boyle unkindly evicted Katharine and her daughter, so they chose to appeal personally against the decision at the English court. Thus, in 1604, Katharine disembarked within the bounds of the Port of Bristol and then walked to London with her daughter following in a cart. The appeal was made to King James the First and the two elderly women retraced their steps and returned to Youghal. Sadly Katharine died before the end of 1604, not from old age but from falling out of a fruit tree.[84]

Travelling to Ireland in 1625 were Edward Byam, vicar of Dulverton, his wife Elizabeth, and their children. It is most likely the family travelled north to Luccombe where he was born and where the graves of his parents were, taking the opportunity to say their farewells to Edward's brother Henry, who was vicar of the parish. The family travelled to Minehead for their passage to Ireland, as Edward had found preferment as the precantor at Cloyne as well as being made vicar of Castle Lyon near Cork. The main

motivation for travelling was Byam's wish to be able to better provide for his family;[85] see Appendix 1.2. In September 1635, Robert Boyle (who later became a famous physicist), with an elder brother Francis, accompanied by the Boyle's faithful servant Robert Carew, obtained a passage from Youghal; this vessel 'touched' at Ilfracombe and Minehead on its way to Bristol as part of the journey to Eton.[86] It is not clear whether it was unfavourable winds that caused the vessel to visit the intervening ports, or whether it was part of the planned route. These boys were the sons of Lord and Lady Cork and had been too young to travel to England in 1628 with their parents and older sister in what was a most eventful journey (described later in this chapter). Then, in late July 1638, Mary, aged 13, the Boyle brothers' younger sister accompanied her father, George Kildare, and a large retinue of servants and gentlemen in the *Ninth Whelp* from Youghal for a journey to Bristol. On arrival the party went to Stalbridge in Dorset, a house recently bought by Lord Cork.[87]

Other children making the journey from Ireland to Minehead included the offspring of Henry Sprague of Waterford who had been sent to live with

Illustration 1.14: Richard Broklesby (1722-1797) an eminent surgeon who passed through the port of Minehead when a child. (From an engraving in the *European Magazine* of 1798)

Illustration 1.15: A West Indiamen in King Road, 1837. Perhaps Henry De la Beche was a passenger in a vessel looking similar to these when he embarked in King Road for Jamaica in 1823. The north Somerset coast is to the right of the group of vessels in the centre of the painting by Joseph Walter. (National Maritime Museum BCH1194)

their grandmother, Elizabeth Baker of Minehead, probably because of the death of their father in 1690.[88] Also in about 1690 C. Crofts, a 'busy Cork citizen', 'hopped over to Minehead' with his family and had his son 'put to the great school at Tiverton'.[89] Minehead's Quaker mercantile Alloway family, like the Haymans, had family links with southern Ireland as Mary Alloway married a member of the Quaker Brocklesby family who lived near Cork. She became pregnant and subsequently took a passage over to Minehead to visit her relatives and her son, Richard, was born in Minehead on 11 August 1722. Mother and son stayed in Minehead until the lad was three years old, when he went back to Cork to be brought up at his father's house. He later became an eminent military surgeon.[90]

As well as travelling for business, the Freke family also travelled for family reasons. Elizabeth and

Percy's marriage seemed to be a loveless and strained one and she often travelled and lived without her husband for months or years on end, staying with members of her extended family. On 30 April 1682 Elizabeth went to Kinsale with her young son and four servants to await a passage to England. They embarked on a 'man of war' and were relieved to disembark at Pill for the vessel had struck sands on three occasions. Elizabeth had another lucky escape in 1691. She travelled to Bristol, embarked on Captain Pool's vessel and sailed to Cork between the 2nd and 5th of October. Her good fortune was that the day before her arrival two French privateers had entered the outer harbour at Cork and attacked two ships: a captain was killed and passengers were stripped and landed ashore. In October 1692 Elizabeth was once again travelling without her husband. On arriving at Cork harbour at night she was rowed through the buoys and ships but was afraid of a collision and sinking. Upon landing in the middle of the night she could find no accommodation, but a friendly Doctor eventually took her in, although she fell sick for some time with the strain of the journey. In March 1698 Percy Freke and his son Raufe landed at Minehead, presumably from Cork, fortunately 'two howres before a most dreadfull storme' happened; they went on to London where marriage matches were considered for Raufe. Finally, in September 1705, Elizabeth, Raufe, Raufe's wife and son, including their servants, were yet again at Pill awaiting passage to Ireland. They secured births on the *Faversham*, a 'man of war' that departed Pill on 19 September. However, at some point in the Channel they were blown back to Pill and had to wait for three more days before departing again. On this second attempt they had a quick journey to Ireland.[91]

The enlightenment movement of the eighteenth century caused many journeys by land and sea for educational purposes in the age of reason. No doubt there were many who sailed in the Bristol Channel for this purpose. For example, three academics, Messer's Chandler, Revett and Pars returned to England after a two year study of the architecture and antiquities of the Eastern Mediterranean on the commission of a learned society. They had departed from London in 1764 but were brought back by the brig, *Diligence*, which disembarked them in King Road, on 2 November 1766, after a stormy voyage prior to the group's return to London.[92] Then, in November 1823, Sir Henry De la Beche embarked in the *Kingston*, lying in King Road, and sailed to Jamaica to visit family land and to study the geology of the island.[93]

An army General serving in Ireland, William Dyott, managed to obtain three months leave in order to visit friends and family, in December 1786. On the 20 December he found the *Britannia* in Cork bound for Minehead. The ship left on the 21st but went aground a mile down-river from Cork harbour, when he went ashore and waited for the next flood tide. The *Britannia*, Dyott and his travelling companion, Major Thompson of the 57th Foot, were underway on the morning of 22 December and in just over 12 hours were in sight of Lundy. However, the wind turned and they 'beat about' until Christmas day. The crew expected a gale the next day and tried to put into Tenby, Pembrokeshire but could not, so they had to be content with Milford Haven.[94] A later passage, to attend a christening, was undertaken by Col. Stephen Strangways and his 16 year old nephew, who travelled from near Crewkerne in August 1803 to Minehead and then made a crossing to Swansea, travelling on to Penrice on the Gower for the christening.[95]

The Quaker community developed strong and lasting friendships which caused members of the faith to travel long distances over land and sea. William Godfrey of Minehead went to Ireland at least three times, in 1699, 1702 and again in 1714; on one occasion he landed in Baltimore and in 1714 travelled to Connaught. Though he may well have ministered as a Quaker once in Ireland, it was recorded that he 'came chiefly to visit his relations in these parts'.[96] In January 1720 Deborah Bell left Pill and took a passage to Cork to visit various groups of 'Friends'[97] and in 1737 James Gough, who was accompanied on his journey by Dr Rutty of Dublin, made the same journey but arrived at night in the Cove of Cork. Gough went to live with a family of Quakers and became a tutor for two boys.[98]

From Ireland, in September 1777, Catherine Philips embarked at Waterford (travelling with Robert Grubb) for Minehead to visit Robert Davies and his family, who at the time were the last remaining Quaker family in the town. She was met on Minehead beach by a member of the Davies family and despite feeling very unwell and weak from seasickness, walked some way to the Davies' home. Robert was ill but apparently she brought some comfort to him. Two years later, in March 1779, Catherine used the ferry at Pill to cross between Somersetshire and Gloucestershire as she moved between Friends in Portishead and Thornbury.[99] A decade later in 1788 Mary Dudley, accompanied by two Quaker Friends, Robert and Samuel Grubb who lived near Waterford, travelled over to Minehead and visited their friend Hannah, the wife of Robert Davies.[100] On 4 May 1794, a member of the Grubb family left Cork for Bristol (via Cove) before making the passage within two days. The vessel either anchored in King Road or Pill for Grubb was soon breakfasting (opposite Pill) in Lamplighter's Hall, Shirehampton. Subsequently he called on at least four Friends.[101] However, not all Quaker passengers in transit through the Bristol Channel arrived safely.

Sadly, Quaker Joseph Sparrow, likely to have been living near Clonmel, Waterford, drowned on 30 December 1781 when the *Elizabeth* packet from Cork, mastered by Captain Surmister, foundered as he was travelling to Minehead via Bristol to get married. Sparrow first came to Minehead from Ireland to propose to Mary Davies (of Minehead) in January 1781. He visited again in the summer, departing from Minehead to Waterford on 19 July.[102] On his fateful journey, Joseph was travelling with Edith Lovell of Frenchay, Bristol who had been visiting 'Friends' in the Cork area[103] when unfortunately they were both drowned. Apparently the lighthouse which would have guided the vessel was not lit and 'in consequence the vessel was wrecked in a storm on Culver Sands off Burnham'.[104]

This very human tragedy was, in a way, not caused by the storm but by another extenuating human event, as the lighthouse keeper was dying and 'his son was so busy attending his father that he forgot to fire the beacon'.[105] In the late eighteenth century, ships in this area should have been guided by two lights in the Bristol Channel, that on Flat Holm (which had been present since the late 1730s)[106] and at Burnham. The unlit beacon was on Flat Holm, so the master of the packet perceived that Burnham's light must be the one on the island, so steered too southerly a course and struck Culver Sand near the mouth of the Parrett. In the event, Sparrow and Lovell were two of 24 people who perished, but 13 others escaped in a boat. Lovell was too afraid to enter the ship's boat so Sparrow stayed with her and perished, despite being a strong swimmer. Lovell's body was never found but Sparrow's body, identified by his stockings, washed up at East Quantoxhead several weeks later and was subsequently buried in the churchyard with

a simple stone with the initials 'J.S.' engraved upon it.[107]

Culver Sand was the location of a further tragedy in January 1816 when another Cork packet, the *Greyhound*, mastered by Captain Rich, foundered on its way to Bristol with all lives lost. Among the dead were many Cork citizens 'and their connections'.[108] In the following year, another packet, this time travelling to Waterford, foundered in the Bristol Channel. The Pill registered *William and Mary* left its home village at 9 p.m. one October evening and on a clear night with fair weather made the Holm Islands by 11 p.m., but unaccountably hit rocks called the 'Willeys' and sank. Nine people out of about 60 passengers and crew survived, with some of those fortunate enough to live repeating some heart rending tales of families holding on to each other and drowning as the vessel sank.[109] Another report of the same event stated the rocks which the vessel struck were the 'Wolves' and that 25 people survived. Amongst the drowned were 'Captain Mawly and several ladies and gentlemen of respectability'.[110] The following year, shops in Pill still had notices displayed regarding the local widows and orphans caused by the loss of crew members.[111]

Perhaps one of the most tedious trips to visit

Illustration 1.16: An extract from a chart published in 1777 showing Culver Sand in Bridgwater Bay, the location of the drowning in 1781 of Joseph Sparrow and Edith Lovell amongst others. (Adrian Webb)

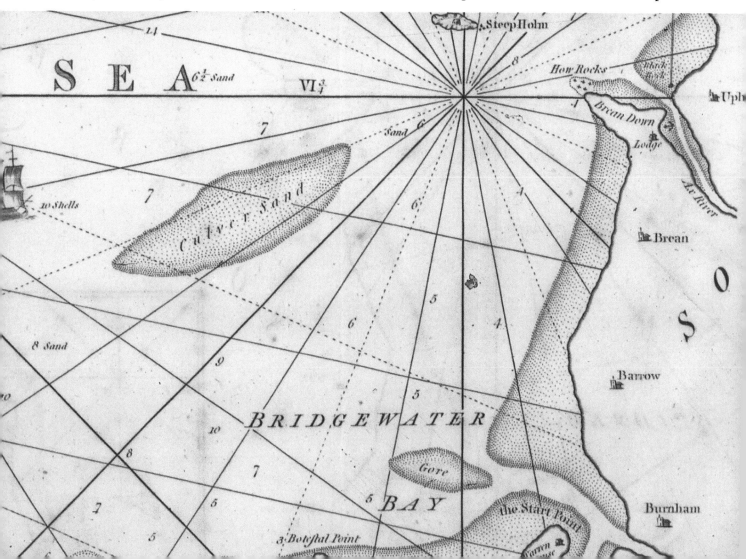

Illustration 1.17: Valentine Greatracks or Greatrakes (1628-1683), also known as Greatorex or The Stroker. He was an Irishman who claimed to be able to cure people by the 'laying on of hands' through God's providence. He sailed into Minehead at least twice in his life, in 1666 and 1668. (From an engraving published by W. Richardson)

family members was that of schoolboy S.C. Hall. He left Pill for Cork, in 1815, and spent 42 days on a Cork packet as he endeavoured to meet up with his family in the city, having to shelter in Ilfracombe and Tenby on the way. Hall described the incommodious cabin conditions of the time in some detail and how most people only packed enough food for three days in their sea chests, including fowls, bread and brandy. Subsequently, when their food ran out, passengers fed on 'salt junk and hard biscuits' for the remainder of the journey.[112]

With regard to health, evidence remains of a 'healer', otherwise termed an 'eminent Irish Doctor', called Valentine Greatracks, who in January 1665/6 was sent for by Lord Conway to come to Ragley in Warwickshire, to attempt to relieve his wife of violent headaches. Greatracks accordingly embarked at Youghal for a passage to King Road, but the adverse winds compelled the vessel to put into Minehead, where the Doctor met many of his previous patients

in the town. Greatracks apparently continued his journey to Ragley, healing as he went, but he was sadly unable to save his principal patient.[113] This episode has prompted one historian to state that during the 1660s, unwell residents of Minehead and neighbourhood 'thought nothing' of travelling to Youghal and a little inland to consult the eminent Greatracks.[114] In 1668 the overseers of the poor in the parish of Stogumber paid for a short coat for James Worth and had him taken to Minehead to meet 'the Irish Doctor'.[115] Greatracks had arrived there on a ship from Bristol upon which he had met Anne Kelly from Windsor, a former patient. It seems likely that whilst in Minehead, on this occasion, Greatracks stayed at the house of Samuel Crockford since the Minehead merchant was grateful to the 'healer' for curing his son in Ireland, in 1665, and was subsequently willing to certify cures performed at his house in 1668. Having said this, Minehead merchants and ship-owners, such as Crockford, had everything to gain from cure testimonials since they would benefit from patients sailing from Minehead to Ireland to consult Greatracks.[116]

People also travelled by sea to Bristol in order to take the 'Hotwells waters'. In 1798, Mary Dudley had been unwell and family discussions led to the conclusion she should sail to Bristol to take the waters at Hotwells. Therefore, she embarked at Waterford with her eldest son and four daughters on a passage to Milford Haven, where she rested for a few weeks and gained her strength. Then they took another passage to Bristol and disembarked at Pill, where they were looked after by friends. Mary went on to take the waters at Hotwells and her health improved. She was more fortunate than another lady, Miss Proby, daughter of the Dean of Lichfield, who was returning from Barbados in ill-health intent on taking the waters of Hotwells, but died aboard the *Atlas* in King Road in 1804.[117]

Since family reasons were and are *bona fide* reasons for travel, it is not surprising that the majority of such journeys involved Pill or Minehead, which were the main harbours in Somerset from which vessels sailed to, and from, Ireland where passages could be conveniently secured. There must have been many more similarly motivated journeys from Somerset to Wales and *vice versa*, but, perhaps because of the relative brevity of the journey, far fewer records of such passages exist.

Avoiding authority

In 1612 John Stokes, having abandoned his wife in

Wales, consorted with women in Dunster, Minehead and Watchet, fathered at least one illegitimate child and 'passed suspiciously' between England and Wales, presumably in an effort to avoid the law.[118] Later, in February 1658, Richard Morton of Ilminster reported that about a year previously he had met Richard Vagge, minister of East Lambrook, in Minehead. The men sailed for Ireland (for unrecorded reasons), but amongst their group was a young woman whom Vagge claimed was his wife, but Morton said to the justices that he knew this was not the truth.[119] It is not known why Morton travelled to and from Ireland but it is possibly clearer why Vagge made the journey.

In the seventeenth century the parish unit was predominantly responsible for the maintenance of orphans, or illegitimate children, if there was no identifiable father or guardian; society could be harsh on the mother of an illegitimate child. Perhaps this was the motivation for Elizabeth Goodman of Wells who, in 1607 when pregnant, travelled to Uphill to 'seek a passage into Wales'.[120] Was she trying to avoid opprobrium in the city? However, her baby was born at Uphill, so the parish overseers repatriated Elizabeth and child to Wells in order that they did not become a burden on their parish. Also in 1607, it was alleged that William Manship from Locking, near Uphill, 'dealt with the placement of bastards in Wales'. No doubt they passed through Uphill. He was known to an ex-churchman of Locking, David Jenkins, who was alleged to have 'harboured fugitives and vagrants out of Wales'.[121] It appears, therefore, that Uphill was a key place for illegal people trafficking between Somerset and Wales in the early seventeenth century. In 1617 Robert Corrocke, a Glamorganshire weaver, 'fled to Somerset' (presumably across the Channel) since he was the alleged father of a base child.[122] Travelling in the opposite direction in 1619 was Andrew Strong of Selworthy, who was 'conveyed to Wales' since he was the reputed father of the base child of Joan Hopkins.[123] No doubt they left to avoid censure or punishment by the local justices.

An account from 1620 describes the journey of John Snow of Marwood in Devon, who followed his pregnant girlfriend, Alice Dolbere, to Minehead and then over to Penmark in Glamorganshire. When their child was born they were removed back to the English side of the Channel, with Snow having to explain his movements to J.P. George Luttrell of Dunster.[124] What torment these people went through is unknown, but it is known that a young child was found under a hedge in the parish of Cutcombe in

1620 and it was ordered that it should be transported to Penmark in Wales where it was born.[125] It seems likely that this was Snow's baby and the knowledge of where it had been born must have come from the interview he had with Luttrell. The correct interpretation of the fact that Agnes Williams, a Welshwoman living at Worthy near Porlock Weir, had her baseborn child buried at Porlock church (after it's death in May 1637), may well be that she had arrived in Porlock by sea, whilst pregnant, in order to avoid censure in Wales.[126] Whilst many infants of this period died in their first month of life, the circumstance makes the child's death more suspicious to the modern observer. Later, in 1692, the Luccombe overseers were keen to return a 'Welsh child' to its home parish. There were considerable expenses incurred by the overseers in attending meetings over the child and then in travelling to Combwich, via Minehead by horse, from where they took a passage across to Wales.[127] Presumably the child did not come from the Newton area where Porlock vessels often travelled to, or Aberthaw where Minehead vessels commonly sailed, but somewhere further east, possibly where small Bridgwater vessels regularly journeyed. Reflecting on the social position in Somerset during the seventeenth century, one author has stated that

> a large number of Somerset girls accompanied by their seducers awaited the delivery of their illegitimate children in Wales. From the west of the county [where] they shipped from Minehead, often to Glamorgan. One girl was accompanied by her seducer and his brother's wife and had received £7 to cover the costs of her stay in Wales.[128]

A similar type of event took place in 1662, when the wife of Benjamin Walters went to Wales with Elinor Harnoke who had become pregnant by her master, Edward James of Kilmersdon near Radstock. James had asked Walters to arrange the place in Wales for Elinor to give birth.[129]

Running away from difficult situations in relation to children, or from contracts and masters, or even to avoid capture if a crime had been committed, must have been a common occurrence. Crossing the sea must have seemed to put a considerable barrier between the person and the event or situation they were running from. However, even in the sixteenth and seventeenth centuries it was not universally easy to 'disappear' by making such a journey. In 1585 Ellis Bagge, a young man without a beard and a maimed left leg, left his master at Cothelstone, contrary to law, and on 18 June 1585 took a boat from Minehead to Wales. Sir John Stowell of Cothelstone wrote to his relations, the Stradlings in Glamorganshire, and asked for help to apprehend the young man.[130]

In July 1668, customs officials in Swansea observed a peculiarly behaved stranger with a 'black complexion', who had come over from Minehead in the *Blessing* dressed in very poor clothing and a black periwig. Upon arrival in Swansea he called for a tailor and liberally paid out £20 or £30 for a new suit in 'vain generosity' and then sailed on to Youghal. Apparently he had claimed to be the eldest son of Sir Henry Dover of Wiltshire, but aroused so much suspicion that the customs officials thought the incident should be advertised in the *London Gazette* in case he was spending ill-gotten gains.[131]

In late 1684 John Halcomb of Taunton ran away from his master. His father, also named John, supposed he had run away to his uncle in Clonmel near Waterford. So, in early December 1684 John the elder went to Minehead and sailed to Ireland to find his son, but unfortunately the journey was wasted because John junior was not found in Clonmel. John senior's return journey involved boarding the *Thomas and Anne* from Cork, which sailed to Bristol under the captaincy of Samuel Lugg with other passengers, and landed in mid-February 1685.[132]

Notorious highwayman John Doyle passed several times between Ireland and England in the years after 1715. On one occasion, after having committed serious crimes in the London area, he made his way to Bristol and boarded a small vessel in King Road that was bound for Waterford. Had fellow passengers been aware of his proclivities, they would have been very afraid. Doyle was hung for his crimes in 1730.[133] In 1737 Henry Nethway arrived at a scene of a crime having been on a sea passage past Steep Holm, and then up the River Axe as far as Berrow Hams. It is at this point that he was alleged to have committed a burglary, taking sheep shears and sheep marking irons from a house.[134] This crime appears to have been opportunistic rather than pre-planned. Some slightly conflicting testimony remains from events that took place in October 1748, relating to a brigantine from Guernsey that was in the Bristol Channel on a smuggling mission. The part of the matter that is relevant here is that John Lake, owner of the *Heart*, a skiff, from Ilfracombe, brought John Campbell and his wife from their brigantine, anchored in Lundy roads, to Porlock, landing the at 5 a.m. on Sunday 27 October. It seems likely that John Campbell discussed running contraband with locals, since in the following days contraband was landed from his vessel on the Somerset/Devon border at Glenthorne and later at Woodspring.[135]

Pill was the point of flight in January 1829 for Rowland Stephenson, M.P. for Leominster and partner in a city bank Remington, Stephenson and Co. of Lombard Street, who gambled considerable amounts of his bank's finances. This financial

Illustration 1.18a: A seal, depicting a ship with mainly reefed sails from a lease of 1685 involving Robert Sulliven of Minehead, mariner. John Halcomb may have sailed from Minehead to Ireland in 1684 in a vessel constructed like this. (SHC, DD\L/1/44/5/22)
Illustration 1.18b. Sketch showing the lines of the ship. (Adrian Webb)

scandal, considered a national disgrace, was reported in *The Times* newspaper and led to an Old Bailey judgement against the banker. Stephenson and his clerk, Lloyd, fled to Bristol, hired a pilot boat from Pill for two guineas a day, and sailed the Bristol Channel looking for an outgoing vessel for the Americas upon which to board. None was to be found, so they were put down in Clovelly, Devon and subsequently hired a skiff that eventually put them aboard a vessel bound for Savannah, Georgia.[136]

In some ways it is surprising that so much evidence remains regarding people travelling along the Somerset coast trying to avoid censure, since many would have wished to remain un-noticed. It seems highly likely that all ports, creeks and landing places along the coast, would have received numerous other passengers over the years travelling by sea in order to make a getaway. However, unless the person had enough money to make private arrangements with boatmen to be taken off relatively deserted beaches, the most obvious places to travel

from would have been Minehead and Pill. The higher frequencies of vessels arriving and departing meant there were larger crowds around the ports in which to hide.

Travel for pilgrimage, Church business, preaching tours and mission

In the early fifteenth century the Pope decided that due to the dangers associated with pilgrimages to Jerusalem, a journey to St Jago (now Santiago) de Compostela in Galicia, northern Spain, would be of equal merit. There, the shrine of the patron saint of Spain, St James the Apostle of Jesus, could be visited. Since this trip was less perilous and cheaper, it appealed to many English people and must have been encouraged by West Country merchants with links to Spain. The motivation for pilgrimage could be different for each individual, but included a desire to receive divine healing, an act of penance, a sense of Christian duty and no doubt for some it was the sense of adventure and danger that was attractive. Details survive of 13 licensed pilgrim sailings from the Somerset coast from 1428 to 1456, which are listed in Table 1 below. Bristol vessels may well have departed from King Road and the most likely point of disembarkation for the pilgrims would have been Corunna. In 1417, Margery Kempe from the east of England, spent six weeks in Bristol awaiting a passage

Illustration 1.19: This view of the moorings at Uphill, and the Bristol Channel beyond in 2011, shows Brean Down to the left of the picture. Steep Holm is directly behind Brean Down and it was from here that in 1737 Henry Nethway sailed. He then passed up the Axe which is to the left of the beached boats, and stole shears from a house on Berrow Hams. (Anne Ashford)

to Santiago de Compostela because of a shortage of ships since Henry the Fifth had requisitioned so many for his summer military campaigns. Eventually she boarded a Breton ship in August, the outgoing journey taking seven days and the return, five days after a two week stay in Spain.[137]

It is also likely that the vessels carried woollen cloth from the city and that the *Catherine* of Minehead, sailing in 1434 with 40 pilgrims, may have had Dunster cloth aboard. West Country woollens were certainly aboard the Bristol cog, the *Anne*, Robert Stormy as master, which left King Road in 1446 with 160 pilgrims prepared to court danger and journey to Jerusalem. Apparently the passengers decided to return to England overland, which is just as well since the *Anne* was lost in the Mediterranean on its return leg.[138]

Table 1.1: Some recorded pilgrim departures to Santiago de Compostela, Spain, from the Somerset coast, 1428-1456

Year	Owner and/or Master	Vessel	Number
1428 March	John Popenham and William Piers	Cog *John* of Bristol	80
1428 July	John Popenham and William Piers	Cog *John* of Bristol	80
1428	Thomas Fysh	Barge *John* of Bristol	100
1428	William Coates, Jordan Sprynge & John Monk	*Mary* of Bristol	100
1428	Philip Richard	*George* of Bristol	100
1434	John Woderufe	*Christopher* of Bristol	80
1434	William Weston	*Trinity* of Bristol	80
1434	John Popenham	*Mary* of Bristol	80
1434	Roger Kyng	*Catherine* of Minehead	40
1445	Henry May	*Mary* of Bristol	120
1445	Walter Fylpot	*Catherine* of Bristol	100
1445	Robert Stormy	*St Anne* of Bristol	200
1456	Robert Stormy	*Catherine Stormy* of Bristol	60

Source: G. Roberts, *The social history of the people of southern England* (London, 1856), 126-34; E. Carus Wilson, *The overseas trade of Bristol in the later middle ages* (New York, 1967), 60-109.

In 1434 there was an investigation as to whether any ships had left the Somerset coast for Santiago without a licence. The outcome of the enquiry is not known. Presumably the vessels listed in the table

above had such licences.[139] Not all Somerset pilgrims sailed from the Somerset coast. There is a record of an un-named Somerset man embarking at Plymouth for a pilgrimage in 1456.[140] There is also a reference that for centuries the port of Bridgwater was often the port of embarkation for the pilgrimage to the shrine of St James, a comment made by a reputable Bridgwater historian, but no supporting evidence is given. The claim is likely to be true given Bridgwater's trade links with northern Spain, prior to the formation to the Church of England, and the decline of Catholic doctrine and practise.[141] The will of Sir John Wadham, knight, proved in 1501 (who was buried at Ilminster), stated that he wished for 'an honest man' to be commissioned by his executors to go on a pilgrimage to St James (of Compostello).[142]

Church officials passed through the Bristol Channel in their particular line of service, though winds often disrupted journeys. In 1450, two officials of the abbey at Tewkesbury passed through Bristol and embarked for South Wales, in order to attend the periodic courts administering abbey land near Cardiff. In this particular year, upon passing Portishead, a storm blew them into Uphill where they had to wait two nights and a day before the weather was suitable enough for them to make the Channel crossing. However, in 1586, Thomas Brown, a spy working for Walsingham's anti-Catholic spying network, seems to imply that the Stradlings, who had bought the Tewkesbury Abbey land in 1543, were recusants. Brown had been to East Brent and visited John Brackenbury, a recusant school teacher, as well as an Irish Catholic priest living within a mile of the village. Brackenbury clearly intended to visit Sir Edward Stradling in South Wales by taking a boat from Uphill and he advised Brown, who obviously was pretending to be a supportive papist, to do the same.[143] In the following century, in 1639, an Irish Catholic priest who landed at Bridgwater was closely questioned by the borough authorities, trying to ensure he would not create difficulty in the county.[144] Another Irish Catholic priest, whilst on a passage from Bordeaux to Cork, was blown by a storm into Minehead on 21 February 1679. Since his presence was not wanted in England, a case was brought before the King's Bench despite his involuntarily arrival.[145]

Church of England officials and ministers also made the passage between Minehead and Ireland, or vice versa, in their line of duty. John Atherton (1598-1640), when incumbent at Huish Champflower, left Minehead for Dublin in 1629, having been made a

Ilustration 1.20: Bishop Atherton, said to have been born near Bridgwater. (*The life and death of John Atherton* (London, 1641))

canon of Christ Church Cathedral. Subsequently he became bishop of Waterford and Lismore in 1636. Sadly, he became notorious for matters that would make headlines in today's tabloid newspapers and was executed in Ireland in 1640.[146] After the Irish Rebellion in Ireland, in 1641, a number of 'distressed' ministers took up residence in Minehead.[147] Presumably they had arrived in the port after making their escape and, perhaps, some were eager to return when conditions were safe enough in order to

resume their calling, so they stayed in and around the port.

In March 1689, the Revd Rowland Davies, Dean of Cork, was required to travel to London on Church business. He travelled in the *Mary* of Cork, with about 140 other passengers from Cork to Minehead, spending a night at anchor in Porlock Bay before continuing to London overland.[148]

Some non-conformist preachers that passed through Minehead, or along the Somerset coast, often left diaries, or other records detailing their movements. These reflect the waves of growth of various non-conformist denominations since the English Civil War of the seventeenth century. Westmorland Quaker, Edward Burrough, who came to Somerset to promote Quaker teaching, held 'great' meetings near Ilchester and at Glastonbury in 1660.[149] In June of that year he sailed from Bristol, rather than Minehead, to Cork to continue his prophetic ministry.[150] In the following year, John Perrot, an intrepid Quaker missionary, who had previously travelled to Rome to 'convert the Pope', returned 'out of Ireland unto Minehead'. Perrot was also renowned for having caused a disturbance in the Quaker community by habitually not removing his hat during public prayers.[151] On 7 March 1664, two prominent Quaker women landed in Minehead following a mission in Ireland; Katherine Evans of Englishcombe, Bath, whose husband John had died in prison in January 1664, arrived back in Somerset

Illustration 1.21: The *Matthew* having anchored in Porlock Bay overnight on 22 May 2010. Culbone woods and Foreland Point are in the left of picture. The Revd Davies could well have spent the night in a very similar location, but did he wake up to such an idyllic morning? (Derek Purvis)

Illustration 1.22: Prominent Quaker George Fox (1624-1691) who disembarked in King Road in 1673. (An engraving after a painting believed to be by S. Chinn)

with Sarah Chevers. Four days later they attended an illegal Quaker meeting at Wiveliscombe, which was broken up by the mayor and J.P. Robert Hawly, who waved his sword over their heads. They were arrested, faced a hearing near Taunton the next day and were committed to Ilchester goal. In May they were taken to the quarter sessions at Taunton where they were fined for illegal assembly, sent back to Ilchester, taken to Bridgwater sessions in August for non-payment of fines and sent back to Ilchester again. Their release came in the next few months, but, sadly, Sarah Chevers died soon afterwards.[152]

In May 1671 it was the intention of Cumberland born John Banks, who was a significant Quaker and gospel preacher, who clearly had visited Ireland, to travel from Cork to Minehead, since 'the harvest was plentiful in the West of England'; it is likely that he fulfilled his intention because he came to live in Somerset in 1677. Even so, he was imprisoned in Carlisle for seven years, from 1684, for non-payment of tithes. In the last 14 years of his life, between 1696 and 1710, he lived at Meare and Street where he

helped grow the local Quaker congregations there, having married Hannah Champion, a Quaker widow from Meare in 1696.[153] On 28 April 1673 prominent Quaker, George Fox returned from Virginia, after spending two years in Jamaica, and the American Colonies preaching to colonists and Indians alike. The ship which conveyed him cast anchor in King Road, and after conducting the last of many services aboard, he was conveyed, probably by a rowed vessel, to Shirehampton where he procured horses for the ride to Bristol.[154]

In June 1698, Quaker William Penn, who had founded the colony of Pennsylvania and lived there between 1682 and 1684, went on a preaching tour of Ireland accompanied by Thomas Story. Upon completion of the tour they boarded the *Jane* of London, at Cork, and in 'a day or two' they disembarked at Minehead and continued overland to Bristol.[155] John Fothergill, another Quaker preacher, toured in the Cork area and returned to Minehead sometime in 1701 and then, in early 1708, again arrived back in Minehead from a preaching tour of New England and Jamaica.[156] Also in 1708, Samuel Bonas, 'a Quaker preacher held in some esteem' obtained a certificate from his monthly meeting and embarked at Minehead for Cork.[157] Samuel was about 32 at the time and, having recently married a Somerset woman, was living in the county after

IIllustration 1.23: Prominent Quaker William Penn (1644-1718) who landed in Minehead in 1698. (David Worthy)

⚓

returning from a missionary trip to America. On arrival in Ireland he went on a preaching tour and 18 weeks later made the return journey.[158] Thomas Story continued his Quaker ministry around England and in early 1716 he was in Bath, where he was encouraged by Samuel Bonas's preaching. On 20 May 1716 Story embarked at King Road for another preaching tour of Ireland which lasted several months. Contrary winds on his outward passage caused his vessel to put into Minehead. This must have been for several days since he did not arrive in Cork until 28 May.[159]

Eighty-five years later, in 1801, Sarah Stephenson embarked at Pill for a passage to New York where she visited Friends at Long Island. Sarah, who was born at Whitehaven, Cumberland in 1738 had been an itinerant Quaker traveller and encourager since the 1760s. She had travelled extensively in the British Isles on her Quaker ministry, visiting Somerset twice in 1774 and 1787 in order to encourage Quakers in various parts of the county. In 1789 she had met Mary, daughter of Robert Davis of Minehead, the young lady whose fiancé had drowned on Culver Sand. They travelled together in Hampshire visiting Quaker meetings. In 1801 she felt the call to go to America and thus with Mary Jefferys (who also gained certificates of commendation from Quaker meetings), boarded the ship *Uncle Toby* which was lying at Pill on 8 July. Also aboard was Samuel Smith of Philadelphia, a Quaker returning to America after a period of ministry in Ireland. Stephenson recorded her experience in the Bristol Channel:

> We staid two nights, but the wind being contrary, we came on shore on the 10th. To a friend's house about two miles distant where we also staid two nights, and then were called up early, the wind being tolerably fair, though the weather was unsettled. The captain, being very anxious to get out, set sail; but in a few hours we had a head wind, and a very rough sea, so that I apprehend we were in considerable danger. On seventh day night, I was very ill, not able to undress but got into my birth. On first day morning the pilot thought it best to run back from the Holmes to King Road, which we reached by noon and then anchored.

Sarah was made quite ill by the experience and was taken ashore, staying at a Friend's house where she recovered. She re-embarked on 17 July and sailed at 11 o'clock in the morning. By 18 July they were off Ilfracombe at anchor waiting for the tide and the next

day they passed Lundy where their pilot left the vessel. Their remaining journey, via the Newfoundland Banks to New York, took several weeks.[160]

Ten years later in 1811, another itinerant Quaker activist, Thomas Shillitoe, with letters from his monthly meeting, boarded a vessel at Bristol on 25 March. He wrote:

> We weighed anchor but the wind soon turned against us; yet, having the tide in our favour, we made our way several miles down the channel; observing that the men were obliged to be frequently at the pump, was discouraging. The tide turning, drove us back to Pill, about twelve o'clock on the Tuesday night.

Two days later they set out again with a fair wind and had sailed quite close to Cork but the wind dropped again. Shillitoe was still concerned because

> Men continued so frequently at the pumps that some of our company manifested alarm on this account. On the Saturday evening a tremendous storm arose; our Captain could not quit the deck the whole of the night. I found it so difficult to keep to my berth that I was obliged to lie on the Cabin floor. The creaking of the vessel as if she would part asunder, and the Pumps being almost continually at work, were truly awful; towards morning the Storm abated. Sunday morning we gained sight of Ireland. About three o'clock in the afternoon I went ashore at Passage and then walked to Black Rock.[161]

In the eighteenth century John Wesley oversaw the rise in Methodism, which eventually became officially recognised as a separate denomination. On Wednesday 18 April 1744 Wesley was in Minehead, when he 'preached near the sea shore to almost all the inhabitants of the place'. The next day, 'having a sloop ready, which came on purpose' he crossed over the channel to Wales landing on a beach near Cardiff. The passage was repeated in the same direction on Friday 14 July 1745. On both occasions the sloop in which he travelled was likely to have belonged to the Robert Jones family of Fonmon, friends of Wesley. Mrs Jones's father, Robert Forest, was involved in cross-Channel trade and had houses in Aberthaw and Minehead.[162] In addition, John Wesley made a journey from Cork to Bristol quay in July 1749, sighting Minehead on the way at 4 a.m. on a Sunday morning.[163]

John Wesley's brother, Charles, the famous hymn writer, after a preaching tour of Cornwall in early August 1744, left to travel to the Barnstaple area and then on to Minehead. He crossed to Wales and then went on to Bristol arriving on 19 August.[164] On 22 July 1750 another notable Methodist preacher, Mr Christopher Hopper, embarked on a vessel in Dublin with 'Mr Wesley' for Bristol. Hopper wrote:

> July 22nd. We sailed about ten in the morning, and in the afternoon came to an anchor.
> July 23rd. We had a vehement squall of wind, thunder, and lightening, between the Welsh Sands and Lundy. We cried to the Lord in our trouble, and he delivered us out of our distress.
> July 24th. The wind was contrary. It blew a storm. The seas ran mountain high. We were tossed in a narrow channel, full of shoals, rocks and sands. We prayed for help; our God heard and brought us safe to Pill.[165]

Hopper was fortunate as the safest course from St George's Channel to Bristol was along the southern shore, rather than near the dangerous sands off the

Illustration 1.25: Wesley's equine statue is to be found in the grounds of the Methodist New Room, Broadmead, Bristol. (Garry Holden)

Welsh coast.

John Wesley was in Ireland again in 1752, having arrived there via Whitehaven, however, on 6 October 1752 he embarked at Cork for a passage back to Bristol. That night he disembarked with others and spent a day or two in Cove. On Sunday the 8th they were called back on board as it appeared the winds were right for their departure and Wesley preached to the passengers, but storms later that day until the Tuesday wrecked several vessels along the coast. Subsequently, they sheltered on the ship in the

Illustration 1.24: John Wesley (1703-1791), who sailed the length or breadth of the Bristol Channel at least four times during his ministry and passed through the port of Minehead at least twice, in April 1744 and July 1745. (R. Watson, *The life of John Wesley* (New York, 1853))

Illustration 1.26: Charles Wesley (1707-1788) who sailed in the Bristol Channel at least twice and went through the port of Minehead at least once in August 1744. (G. Osborn, *The poetical works of John and Charles Wesley* (London, 1868)).

neither could I eat ... the passengers cried out "we are not fit to die" ... on Saturday the wind abated and we arrived in Cork.[167]

Walsh recovered enough to preach for a few more months in Cork and Limerick but died at Dublin in April 1759. In 1801 Lady Anne Erskine related, in a letter to a friend, an event that overtook another Methodist preacher, Mr Finlay, on his way from Pill to Cork, presumably in 1800. The 'lively young man' embarked for Cork in November, but because of 'an unskilful pilot' and a 'dreadful wind' struck a rock, possibly in King Road, and the vessel was badly damaged. Hurried pumping kept the ship afloat and distress signals brought boats hurrying from Pill, which towed the distressed vessel back to their village. Finlay then caught another vessel to Swansea and Milford Haven and then caught a ship bound for Waterford. Just prior to arrival a storm engulfed them for 36 hours, but fortunately the vessel arrived safely in Ireland and Finlay apparently went on to have a successful ministry in Cork.[168]

Pill was also an important point of exit for Methodist preachers travelling to America. Francis Asbury volunteered for missionary work in America at a Methodist conference in Bristol in 1771 and departed from Pill in the same year. He was the only Methodist preacher to stay in the colonies during the American War of Independence, became Bishop of the American Episcopal Church and was called 'the St Paul of American Methodism'.[169] Two years later, Methodist preacher Thomas Rankin departed from Pill on Good Friday, 9 April 1773 in the *Sally*, bound for Philadelphia. He stated 'the wind was fair from Pill and soon brought us down to the Isle of Lundy where our pilot left us' and how 'all the passengers were extremely sick'. Rankin arrived safely in America where he met Asbury and preached to many Methodist congregations for the next five years.[170] Also on board was George Shadford, another prominent Methodist, who had preached in Norwich in the early 1770s; Shadford preached on the Methodist circuit in America for a year before he returned to England, since he could not obtain further travel permits during the war.[171] Three other preachers, Thomas Coke, Richard Whatcoat and Thomas Vasey departed to America from Pill in 1784, after their ordination, in order to help promote the gospel in the newly formed independent country of the United States of America.[172]

The Baptist denomination had its roots in the seventeenth century like the Quakers. Some of England's earliest Baptist congregations were set up

harbour until departing for Bristol on Thursday 12 October at noon. During the passage, which was calm, Wesley read *Pascal's thoughts* which, upon completion, he did not think was a good book. Two days later the ship sailed into King Road which was the conclusion of his 'little voyage'.[166]

Departing from Pill for a passage to Cork in April 1758 was a young Methodist Preacher, Thomas Walsh. Walsh was born in Ireland in 1730 and in his teenage years had decided, after considering his Catholic background, to become a Methodist. He became a well known preacher, both in Ireland and then in London. Aged 28, he arrived in Bristol increasingly unwell with a condition, probably tuberculosis, which caused his death a year later. He preached on the Bristol circuit and then embarked for Ireland on 13 April. He noted how

> The passage was extremely dangerous; insomuch that the mariners themselves looked for nothing less than perishing, so boisterous were the winds and seas. ... I prayed and praised God incessantly for I could not sleep an hour whilst on board; and

Illustration 1.27: Francis Asbury (1745-1816) who at the age of 26 responded to John Wesley's call in the Bristol Methodist meeting house to go to serve Christ and the church in America. Asbury departed for the New World in 1771 from Pill. This fine equine statue of him is in Washington DC. (David Worthington, Manager of the Methodist New Room in Bristol and is reproduced with his kind permission)

in Somerset; Chard in 1653, Wedmore and Stogumber in 1656 and Paulton in 1658. In addition, there appeared to be slightly rebellious Anabaptists, such as Samuel Wade and Samuel Bowers, in Dunster and Minehead in 1667 'almost goading' the authorities to harass their conventicle.[173] The movement grew considerably during the Industrial Revolution, and developed into a missionary church. Baptist minister, Rev. Thomas Lewis, who served a congregation at Bridgwater, moved to Ireland in 1780, first serving at Clough Jordan near Limerick and then from 1785 until 1804 as pastor of the Baptist congregation at Waterford.[174]

The Baptist Missionary Society was set up in the 1790s, and some of its first missionaries used King Road as a point of embarkation on 3 January 1804. The people in question were four recently married young men and their wives, Richard Mardon and John Biss from Devonport, William Moore from Stogumber and Joshua Rowe from Salisbury who wrote a letter to John Sutcliff from the vessel whilst in the Bristol Channel. The ship had been wind bound for a few weeks, so the group stayed in Bristol for a time and made many friends amongst the Baptist community there. So, when the day of departure came 'many of their friends accompanied them to their ship which lay at Kingroad over against Pill and had a most affecting parting not expecting to see their faces any more on earth'.[175] Although they were destined for the Baptist mission in India, they first sailed to Philadelphia; Biss and his wife were accompanied by their young child. On 3 January 1804 'Very Dear Sir,' wrote Rowe later in the day.

> Have but just time to write a few lines, to send on shore by the pilot, who intends leaving the ship much sooner than expected, on account of having such a fine breeze to take us down the

Illustration 1.28: Kenneth Wyatt's illustration entitled 'Offer them Christ' depicting Coke, Whatcoat and Vasey's departure from Pill to America. John Wesley is depicted seeing the trio off but was in fact on a preaching tour when they departed. (Methodist New Room, Bristol)

Illustration 1.29: Memorial at Pill erected in 1984 in memory of the Methodist ministers who departed from this creek. (Garry Holden)

FRANCIS ASBURY IN 1771 AND THOMAS COKE IN 1784
AND OTHER METHODIST PREACHERS
SAILED FROM HERE FOR AMERICA

Erected to mark the Bicentennial of the
Methodist Episcopal Church U.S.A. in 1984.

Sponsored by the World Methodist Historical Society
in memory of George Ruck.

Illustration 1.30: Plaque from the memorial at Pill. (Garry Holden)

channel. ... Friends of both sexes ... accompanied us down to Pill. We stood on the Quaterdeck and sang Mr Saffery's 2nd Hymn. Find it very difficult to please our sisters. On my left hand is Mrs Moore very sick, calling lustily for a pot: bro: Moore holding her head and calling for a bucket. Complains of being sick himself. Mary Biss vomiting upon her mother. Bro: Mardon ascending the ladder for fresh air, but obliged to empty the contents of his stomach before he could get on the deck. Mrs Biss very sick: bro Biss holding her head and very quamish himself. Mrs Mardon sitting on the floor of the state room casting up her accounts . . . Betsy looking pale . . . The vessel begins to heave much now, I do not know what kind of night we shall have . . .

Yours in our dear Lord,
Joshua Rowe[176]

Non-conformists also served the Jamaican

Church with King Road again being the point of embarkation, or disembarkation, but missionary work often cost people their lives. Philip Howell, a seaman and member of the Brethren Church, with his second wife, served as missionaries to Afro-Caribbeans in Jamaica from 1796. Ill health caused them to return in the *Nile* under the command of Mr Marychurch to King Road arriving on 6 July 1805. The death of four seamen *en-route* meant that all were kept aboard under quarantine for about two weeks. Howell, now very unwell, was taken off the vessel on 19 July and was cared for by Brethren members in Bristol until his death from tuberculosis on 13 August 1805.[177] On 30 April 1814 Devonian, Rev. Thomas Trowt, who had studied at the Bristol Baptist academy, boarded the *Commerce* in King Road for missionary service in Java. He was accompanied by Eliza, his wife of less than a month, who was the daughter of a Plymouth Baptist pastor. Initially they found it dull on board waiting for a wind to cause

Illustration 1.31: Richard Whatcoat, Thomas Coke and Thomas Vasey, the three Methodist missionaries who left Pill for America in 1784. (Methodist New Room, Bristol by Garry Holden)

them to sail down the Bristol Channel. However, eventually they did sail and served for two years in Java, baptising new Christians before Thomas died of fever in 1816 aged 32.[178] A few years later Baptist missionary Thomas Godden, commissioned at Frome, and his wife, sailed from King Road in February 1819 to Jamaica to serve the Baptist church there. Godden was also an ex-naval seaman and had endured eight years captivity in France during the Napoleonic wars. He was quickly active, establishing and growing a new church amongst Afro-Caribbeans in 'Spanish-town' near Kingston. However, in September 1819 his wife died after the birth of their son, the following year arson at his house and church nearly cost him his life, he became ill in 1823, was recalled by the Baptist Missionary Society and returned to Bristol where he died at Lawrence Hill leaving an orphan son of five.[179]

Jamaica was also the destination of Methodist missionary, Rev. John Jenkins, who set off from Pill on 1 February 1824 in the aptly named vessel, the *Jamaica* which permitted its pilot to leave at the Holms taking a letter from Jenkins to his parents on the way. A further letter describing severe sea conditions was written at Cork three days later after Jenkins had endured a storm in the St Georges channel.[180] Also in 1824, J.P. Briscoe was sent by the Baptist denomination, via Bristol to Cork, to encourage and grow the congregation in that city, but contrary winds caused him to have to spend over two weeks in Minehead and Milford Haven on the way. He was more than a little apprehensive about the size of the expenses he incurred, compared to what it might have been, had it not been for delays, as well as being a little concerned that he needed to stay at inns whilst waiting for his passage.[181] Such were some of the pitfalls of travelling by water, even if you were on God's work.

Given the importance of Minehead's links with Ireland, it is not surprising that many Quakers used the port in the second half of the seventeenth century, since that was the period when adherence to their beliefs was rapidly expanding. Equally, the Bristol area was a place where Methodism took a strong hold in the eighteenth century, so it is consistent that many eighteenth century Methodists travelled through Pill, especially those on their way to the New World. Otherwise, since church people had legitimate reasons for travel, they would have used the most obvious and convenient points of embarkation, either to or from Somerset, or elsewhere. Apart from pilgrimages, it is the journeys of pastors and missionaries that have been detailed

here, as they travelled between congregations and mission locations. It is unlikely that many regular journeys to Sunday worship by members of congregations took place in the Bristol Channel, though it is known that people travelled to Westonzoyland church by boat in 1633 when the Somerset levels were flooded. Traveling to church by river boat took place on the Somerset waterways until the twentieth century.[182]

Government duty and service

Former Member of Parliament for Southampton, Sir Henry Wallop was appointed deputy treasurer for Ireland in 1579 and on 8 September departed from King Road for Ireland with his retinue of 40 people.[183] It is likely that many important officials mentioned in this section travelled with family members, servants and other officials, though the sources examined do not often record the fact.

In March 1601, after a five month visit to the Cork area, the First Earl of Desmond landed at Minehead, from Ireland, and then travelled to court in London; whilst in Ireland his duties included delivering despatches to the Lord President of Munster, amongst which was a letter from Queen Elizabeth the First.[184] In the same year Richard Boyle, First Earl of Cork, travelled speedily from Cork to Bristol and then by post-horse to London, delivering news of a 'victory' at Kinsale over the Irish and Spanish.[185] On 11 September 1602, the 4th Earl of Thomond, embarked at King Road in order to make his way back to Ireland to take his part in leading the situation there. The mayor of Bristol reported the departure to the Privy Council, but commented that since other vessels had been driven back to Bristol, by contrary winds and storms that day he fully expected Thomond, who was aboard the Queen's pinnace *Merlin*, to be returned to port. Indeed, a biography of Thomond states that he arrived back in Ireland in October 1602. At the same time, 'Clifton', who was clearly engaged in Government business and was entrusted with dispatches from Robert Cecil to the Lord President of Munster, embarked with his papers in a chest on a vessel belonging to John Smythe of Bristol, which was awaiting winds for the passage to Cork.[186]

An eventful passage took place in 1628 when the Boyle family, comprising the Earl and Countess of Cork, their daughter Lettice (aged 18), Joan Hodge Power (a cousin), and Arthur Loftus (Dorothy Boyle's betrothed husband), sailed to Minehead from Youghal to meet with Lord Buckingham, who represented their interests at court. They departed in a 'biskaner', a vessel from present day southern France or northern Spain, at 5p.m. on 7 May. At dawn on the 8th, to their horror, they spied a 'Dunkirker', from the present day Belgian or northern French coast, with two tiers of guns, which they knew was a privateer and they were in great danger. They were chased all day and were nearly overtaken by the privateer near Milford Haven. Unfortunately, the privateer did manage to fire about twenty shots at a following vessel, which contained the Boyle's footmen and horses, which was subsequently over-run. The Boyle's relief on reaching Minehead was palpable, but tinged with great sadness over their loss of the servants and horses. They continued their journey overland to Taunton and then to London. Richard Boyle's diary mentions that the horses were subsequently put ashore in Wales, but he does not mention the footmen again.[187] It is likely that the Corks made similar journeys on several occasions, either for reasons of family, business or duty. In October 1641, the Earl of Cork and his company, including his son and daughter-in-law (Lord and Lady Broghill) and Lady Kinalmeaky, were in Somerset staying at Glastonbury for one night and at Bridgwater the following night. On their return to Ireland they lodged for four nights at the home of Isaac Thornbury, the chief customs official in Minehead whilst waiting for a passage to Ireland. On 15 October they set sail in the 60 ton *Amitie* for Youghal and paid the owner, Mr Jones, £22 for the transit of the group, but the grooms and horses had to await further shipping in Minehead.[188] They disembarked on 18 October and upon arrival Cork attended prayers 'to thank God for our speedy and safe journey'.[189]

In March 1636, an un-named London factor was prevailed upon by the British Government to travel from the capital, to Munster, to supervise the transport of 'indentured retainers' to the Caribbean. These indentured retainers were probably the equivalent of today's political prisoners. When the factor arrived in Bristol for a passage to Munster, there was none available, and he was advised to travel on to Minehead to secure one. This he did with success, but the wind was contrary and he had to wait for 16 days for it to turn. When at last he set out, the journey to Youghal took two days.[190] The problems in Ireland were exacerbated by the English civil wars. On 18 March 1642 Lord Inchiquin,[191] a son-in-law of Munster President William St Leger, landed at Youghal from Minehead and two days later set out to sea for Cork, in order to help in the relief of the siege of the city. The following day, Captain William

Jephson arrived in Youghal, probably also from Minehead, with 200 mounted soldiers, half of them for Inchiquin.[192] In August 1642 Inchiquin went on to defeat Catholic insurgents in south-west Ireland at the Battle of Liscarrol, but he was not made president of Munster after St Leger's death in early July, or even after the August victory.[193]

In February 1646, Philip Sydney, Viscount Lisle, the newly commissioned Lord Lieutenant of Ireland, departed from Bristol, but on the way spent at least a day in Minehead before embarking there and eventually landed at Monkstown, near Cork. His entourage followed in Captain Swanly's vessel from Bristol, which looked into Minehead on the way in case they needed to embark Sydney if he had not found another vessel for the passage.[194] However, attendant political difficulties, partly because of the ambiguity of Inchiquin and the subsequent failure of his lieutenancy, meant that he sailed back from Cork to Minehead on 17 April 1647. The vessel passed through a storm and landed at Minehead at midnight on 21 April with an important entourage, including his brother, Algernon Sydney, the Lord of Valentia, Sir John Temple and Sir Adam Loftus, privy counsellors, Lord Broghill[195] (Roger Boyle) and Major Harrison.[196] Lisle and some of the party continued their journey overland to Bristol, aiming to arrive there by the 24th, probably judging the land route quicker than a trip of unknown time by sea, especially if the wind was unfavourable. However, Sir John

Illustration 1.32: Image of a ship, partly in sail, from a Minehead seal of 1657. Perhaps Philip Sydney, or some of his entourage, sailed back to Minehead in 1647 in a similar vessel. (SHC, DD\L/1/23/3/22)

Temple, Sir Adam Loftus and Sir Arthur Loftus (according to Algernon Sydney), who were also in the party, continued by ship to Bristol and seemingly arrived by the 23rd; Sir Arthur then took the 'Friday evening poste' and arrived in London on the Sunday morning, with letters for parliament.[197]

After the change in Government, Oliver Cromwell subdued Ireland in 1650 and 1651. His son-in law, Henry Ireton was made president of Munster in 1650 and, later in the same year, Lord Deputy of Ireland. Ireton died of the plague in Limerick in 1651, his body was brought to King Road, where it was disembarked, placed on a velvet draped vessel and taken up the Avon for an official reception in Bristol.[198]

Another key contributor to the control of Ireland under Cromwell was Edmund Ludlow, 'commander of the horse'. Ludlow, an Anabaptist and co-signatory of Charles the First's death warrant, was prominent in national affairs during the 1650s and was sent to Ireland again in 1659 in order to help shore up parliamentary authority. With the nation moving towards the Restoration, and finding little support, he returned to England, via Duncanon Fort in lower Waterford harbour, in January 1660. Ludlow and his entourage hired a Dutch vessel with a French master and made for Minehead. Contrary winds, and heavy seas east of Lundy, caused them to make landfall at Ilfracombe, causing Ludlow to have to ride with difficulty over a snow covered Exmoor on his way back to London.[199]

Earlier, in May 1657, Lord Broghill, a protestant parliamentarian and supporter of Cromwell, travelled on Government business from London to Minehead, where he was collected by a Kinsale vessel and landed in Waterford.[200] He returned to England from this particular visit to Ireland with Lady Broghill, their attendants and the Earl of Barrymore with his servants, via Minehead in late December of the same year. The party embarked from Youghal in a Royal Naval vessel under Captain Richard Hodge, even though Broghill was feeling unwell.[201] The poor weather caused the journey to be more tortuous than usual. In a letter written from Orchard Wyndham (near Williton), on 29 December 1657, to a Government official, Broghill described the journey and, even though still unwell, offered himself for further Government business:

> I Only send you this to acquaint you, that havinge recovered as much strength as did make me to use a coach to the ship-side, the first faire winde I sett to sea; and after part of foure dayes and three nights beinge tumbled on it, it pleased God to send us safe to Minhead in Somersetshire. I doe intend for a few dayes to rest at my owne house, to recover the better use of my feet; but if you have any commands for me at London sooner, be pleased to signify them to me by the post, directinge your letters for me to the postmaster of Bathe in Sommersetshire, and they shall, God willinge, be forthwith obeyed . . .[202]

From 1668 to 1676 Broghill, sometimes accompanied by his wife, often travelled through Minehead on his way to and from Ireland. On 15 June 1668 Broghill, now titled, the Earl of Orrery, arrived in Minehead with the Earl of Roscommon and 'several other persons of quality'. They had sailed from Ireland in one of the Kings yachts, the *Merlin* (sometimes erroneously recorded as the *Martin*) and disembarked to a 'warm welcome' when an 'abundance of people got together to see and welcome the Lord President of Munster', *i.e.* Orrery.[203] The yacht that brought over the party had orders to sail to Plymouth for re-provisioning, but, after two attempts, it was returned by contrary winds so it had to sail to Bristol and re-provision there, having damaged a mast in a storm.[204] In July 1669, the Royal yacht *Monmouth* was in Minehead waiting to take Orrery to Ireland, when Government officials joked about how interminably long vessels had to wait for him and that crews would run out of provisions and starve in the wait.[205] Orrery sailed from Minehead to Ireland in late March of the following year[206] and in May 1671 he was conveyed

Opposite: Illustration 1.33: The Boyle Monument in St. Patrick's Cathedral, Dublin erected in 1651. It shows the Earl and Countess of Cork who had 15 children. Richard Boyle, First Earl of Cork (1566-1643) migrated to Ireland in 1588, left from Dingle and sailed to Bristol in 1598 to avoid the Irish revolution. He returned in 1599 to help fight the revolution, was chosen to take news to London in 1601 after the Kinsale victory. He bought much of Raleigh's lands in 1602, settled the lands with armed English colonists, initiated economic development in Munster, became rich and powerful, was created Lord Boyle in 1616, Earl of Cork in 1620, Lord Justice of Ireland in 1629 and Lord High Treasurer in 1631. The Earl, Countess and Lettice travelled in the Bristol Channel to Minehead in the 1628, narrowly escaping pirates. Others, the male 'children' include Burlington and Broghill, as well as Robert Boyle the famous scientist, and the females, Mary Rich and Catherine Ranelagh, all have some of their travel experiences in the Bristol Channel recounted in this chapter. (Image courtesy of St. Patrick's Cathedral, Dublin by David Monaghan)

THE TOMBE OF THE RIGHT
HONORABLE RICHARD LORD
BOYLE EARLE OF CORKE AND
THE LADIE KATHERYNE HIS
WYFE WITH THE ARMES
OF SUCH OF THEIR DAUGHTERS
HUSBANDS AS ARE MARRIED

again from Minehead to Ireland in one of the King's yachts, which had to sail from Falmouth to pick him up.[207] On 7 May 1671 Orrery wrote that he knew the vessel had been waiting at least a week for him.[208] However, the *Merlin* was back in Minehead on 18 May 1671, having delivered Orrery and 'Burlington' to Youghal and was then waiting for the diplomat and secretary of state for Ireland, Sir Robert Southwell.[209] The wait, on this occasion, was at least eight days.[210] Four years later, in June 1675, the *Monmouth* yacht, which had been to Dublin on business, was sent to Minehead to await Orrery,[211] but in late July 1676 it was the turn of the crew of the *Norwich* to wait at least a week in Minehead Road for Orrery and his lady who were due to be taken to Cork.[212]

Broghill's elder brother, Richard, second Earl of Cork and first Earl of Burlington, also travelled between Ireland and Minehead on Government business. In June 1656 his wife, the Countess of Cork, obtained Government dispensation to travel out of Ireland by the first available warship. Captain Richard Cowes, with the *Paradox*, went to Kinsale and took on board the Countess of Cork and landed her at Minehead.[213] Burlington himself was transported from Minehead to Ireland in the *Merlin*, in April 1676,[214] and returned to Minehead a few months later (in early August 1676) in H.M.S. *Norwich,* which had only just arrived in Ireland from Minehead with Broghill.[215] Also sharing the same passage was John Gailhard, who became famous two years later when he published a book entitled *The perfect Gentleman,* and his tutee, the young Sir Philip Percival.

Further members of the aristocracy, who frequently had political and administrative responsibility, often used Minehead as a staging post in order to travel to Ireland. For example, James Butler, the First Duke of Ormond, often travelled in the Bristol Channel, from Bristol and Minehead. When he was a small boy, he was taken by his nurse from London to Bristol and then onwards to Ireland.[216] A few years later his father was drowned on a passage from Ireland to England, near the Skerries off Anglesey. When Ormond was an adult and in Government service, he left London on a Saturday in September 1633 at four o'clock in the morning with two horses and arrived at Iron Acton, north of Bristol, where the family had lands later in the day. He then sent word to King Road where the *Ninth Whelp* was at anchor and was told the vessel would sail the next morning since the wind was set fair. He rose early on the Sunday morning, rode to King Road and was aboard by 8 a.m. Once aboard he ate a hearty breakfast and then slept for eleven

Illustration 1.34: The *Merlin*, an English gallion-rigged yacht built in 1666, was sold by the Royal Navy in 1698. The vessel had five gun-ports on each broadside, a lion figurehead and was 109 tons and 70 feet long. The *Merlin* was in Minehead in 1668 and 1671. (National Maritime Museum, PT2537)

hours. The ship set sail at 9 a.m. and 24 hours later was anchored in Waterford harbour. After disembarking he hired horses from Sir Robert Welch (whom he met in Waterford) and then rode the 16 miles to his house at Carrick where he dined at 3 p.m.[217]

Much later in his life Ormond was made Lord Lieutenant of Somerset at the Restoration, and, whilst at Hampton Court, on 27 July 1665, he asked the Navy Board to provide two frigates, the *Pearl* and the *George* of Bristol, to take himself and his retinue back to Ireland from Minehead. The orders for this were given on 30 July, and the next day Ormond personally ordered a third frigate to Minehead. In the event he may have travelled from Milford Haven, but it appears that at least some of his retinue left from Minehead.[218] The heavy security was required as the transit took place during the Second Dutch War, at a time when Dutch vessels were operating in home waters. The following year a new frigate, the *Harp,* conveyed Butler to Ireland from Minehead. About seven or eight other merchant vessels accompanied the *Harp* since there continued to be a fear of being attacked by French, or Dutch, vessels.[219] Later, on 17 June 1674, the Duke of Ormond was in Bath writing that he was about to depart for Minehead as 'his' ship had lain there for almost two weeks waiting for him to be ready for the journey, which was even longer than Broghill kept vessels waiting. He and his retinue embarked on 27 June and arrived back in Ireland, disembarking from the vessel in the Waterford River the following day. With regard to the journey he stated that it took less than 24 hours from 'setting sail' and that 'Captain Penn's care was much contributory to his safe and quick passage over the sea'.[220]

Additional officials with naval, legal and administrative responsibilities, also made the sea journey between Ireland and Minehead in the seventeenth century. In March 1655 Colonel Robert Sanders, governor of Youghal, and his family were

Illustration 1.35: James Butler, Duke of Ormond (1610-1688), a supporter of the Royal cause and a very prominent peer when in favour especially after the restoration, travelled to and from the port of Minehead on several occasions in the 1660s and 1670s often in Naval vessels. (E. Clarendon, *The history of the Rebellion and Civil Wars in Ireland* (London, 1720))

conducted to Minehead, in the Navy's *Mayflower,* under Captain Peter Bowen. He wrote to the Admiralty, from Minehead Road, to report his accomplished mission, then, in August 1656, it was the turn of Captain Richard Hodges in the *Basing* to conduct Sanders' wife back to Ireland from King Road.[221] It appears that many of the naval vessels did not enter Minehead harbour but anchored nearby and would have transferred passengers by ship's boat or local small boats. In April 1657 the *Paradox,* captained by Richard Cowes, picked up Justice Cook from Kinsale and brought him to Minehead;[222] Cook was one of the senior Judges who heard evidence regarding those heavily involved in the Irish Rebellion in the 1640s. Later, in October 1671, Peter Bronsdon was in Cork awaiting a passage to Minehead. Bronsdon had been in Galway, surveying the woods of Sir Francis Brewster and the usefulness of the standing timber for naval purposes. He was on his way back to London.[223]

Royalty, pursuing their perceived duties for their country, also passed along the Somerset coast. In 1690 King William the Third, who was accompanied by Prince George of Denmark, after campaigns in Ireland, including the Battle of the Boyne, sailed from Duncanon Fort, Waterford, in an English warship to King Road, arriving on 6 September. Upon anchoring at King Road he came ashore at Shirehampton. The King, and his retinue, then went to the house of Sir Robert Southwell at Kingsweston; Southwell was secretary of State for Ireland at the time and had attended King William on his campaign in Ireland. It seems likely that Southwell also accompanied the Royal party and escorted William to his country home, though some sources say he remained in Ireland until October. The following day William was driven through the streets of Bristol in a coach belonging to the Duke of Beaufort and received by the mayor of Bristol, though he did not alight from his transport. Subsequently he was taken to Beaufort's home at Badminton, Gloucestershire, before returning to London.[224]

Clearly, those people travelling on Government business used the most convenient ports, usually accessible by roads fit for carriages. This also meant journeys could easily be made to the large houses where the aristocracy lived, or where they stayed when they were in transit. Journeys often commenced or finished in London. Minehead became a convenient point of embarkation after the development of harbour facilities in the second decade of the seventeenth century. However, the use of some of the King's yachts, in ferrying important

Government officials between Munster and Minehead, may hint that only smaller naval vessels could use Minehead harbour, with larger ones having to anchor in Minehead Road. But, as the seventeenth century wore on, the usefulness of Minehead became more evident. People embarking on Government business in Ireland made more journeys from the port, partly because it was less wind bound than King Road, since when facing contrary winds vessels took longer to beat down from Bristol than leave for Ireland from Minehead.

Troop movements

Queen Elizabeth the First's policies regarding Ireland caused many soldiers to be shipped there, mainly to support the Munster colony by putting down uprisings, such as the Desmond uprising of the early 1580s, and fighting Spanish troops who occasionally landed. Many of those soldiers left through the port of Bristol and no-doubt some boarded in King Road, or were transferred from Pill, as was the pattern in later centuries, though often this is not specifically stated in the sources. Details of troop numbers and specific leaders of the regiments for 1551, 1565-6, and on numerous occasions throughout the 1580s and 1590s, are recorded elsewhere. It is worth mentioning here that the embarkation of 114 horse, under the command of Sir Henry Danvers, for Ireland took place in King Road in March 1599, and the subsequent unfortunate drowning of six of these horses took place at Ilfracombe, after the expedition's ships got into difficulties in a storm.[225] Appendix 1.4 outlines an event in 1596 when twelve Pembrokeshire soldiers were drowned outside Minehead harbour. It is not clear why these troops came to the town.

On 11 September 1602 William Vawer, mayor of Bristol, caused soldiers which had been billeted in the city (under the command of Sir George Thornton), to be embarked for Ireland since the wind appeared favourable. Their embarkation was in King Road on the *Tramontana*, which had been waiting downriver for soldiers since April after being refitted in Bristol harbour as a warship. However, sudden changes in the wind, and stormy weather, meant that the vessels returned the next day. On 30 September 1602, the mayor of Bristol wrote to Sir Robert Cecil stating that the soldiers had been up and down the Channel 'twice or thrice' and still contrary winds prevented the passage to Ireland.[226] Somerset men, of course, were drafted to serve in Ireland and some sailed from Bristol in these shipments.[227] Many troops died in

Illustration 1.36: Sir Henry Danvers (1573-1643) who in 1599 supervised the boarding of 114 horse in King Road for service in Ireland. This illustration is inspired by the full colour portrait of Danvers by Anthony van Dyck. (Kim Stephens)

Ireland, whilst others returned injured and received support from their home parishes. Further men returned fit and lived to an age when they could draw a 'pension' from the community because of their service. There are records of such men who served in Ireland in the late Elizabethan, or early Stuart, periods, including John Crews of Dulverton and James Juckor of Mark (in 1608), John Audy of Odcombe (1611), William Stowey of Cutcombe (1612), Christopher Smalland of Creech St Michael (1614), Henry Pittard of Martock (1620) whose service definitely was in the Elizabethan period, Clement Dodrell of Shepton Mallet and Andrew Phillips of Ubley (1624).[228]

In the autumn of 1627, 700 men of Sir Pierce Crosbye's Regiment arrived in Bristol and stayed for ten days before embarkation for Ireland. Lighters and 'towboats' were hired to 'carrye the soldiers into Kingroad' where they embarked. Soon afterwards another 50 soldiers arrived in the city ready for the same service. Boats were also hired to take them to King Road on two occasions, because their ship was not ready to receive them when they first arrived in the roadstead. When they finally did embark there were drummers to 'warn them aboard'.[229]

Soldiers in their line of duty often passed through

Minehead, such as Richard Power, who arrived there on 4 May 1639 with Lord Dungarvan's 'coronet of horse out of Ireland'.[230] These troops, mounted or otherwise, were just a foretaste of the thousands which passed through Minehead during the Civil Wars, making the 1640s one of the busiest periods in the history of the port in relation to the movement of officials, troops, cavalry and supplies. These movements, although bringing some inconvenience and tension to the town at times, would have brought in much needed revenue to parts of western Somerset.

In response to the Irish Rebellion which broke out in October 1641, and despite quarrels between King and Parliament in England, in February 1642, 200 men left Bristol for Duncannon Fort in Ireland under Captains Wilding and Austin. A further 300 left Minehead, under the command of Captains Pinchback, Manners and Roberts, in order to try and protect English interests.[231] Later, in May 1642, it was reported that 2,000 men were waiting in Minehead to be sent to Ireland but were delayed by the absence of the Lord Lieutenant in Ireland and also their embarkation instructions.[232] Furthermore, in September 1642, the Government ordered ten captains, including William St Leger, to raise two thousand troops in England and Wales to put down the rebellion in Munster, the troops were ordered to leave through Minehead and Bristol.[233] Political developments in England in 1642 saw Minehead and Bridgwater, the two largest of the Somerset ports, declare for parliament. Shortly afterwards, on the 22 September, the Royalist Marquis of Hertford and his men tried to find passage from Minehead to South Wales. To their horror they could only find two vessels, coal barges, and could procure no more due to 'the malicious activity in the country being far more powerful against them'.[234]

The following year, Irish soldiers from Munster, sent by Inchiquin, disembarked at Bristol and Minehead to serve the crown on English soil. Noah Rendall who had been in Minehead reported to soldiers in Bridgwater that about 1,000 'Irish rebels' had been landed there, which caused unrest even amongst Royalist troops in Somerset.[235] There must have been tense scenes as these troops marched through mainly parliamentarian West Somerset. Then, in January 1644, further Irish troops were landed in Bristol to the disquiet of the city and when additional Irish troops were sent to Bristol in March to further the Royalist cause, the pilots of Pill rebelled and refused to bring them up-river to the City. The Bristol authorities then diverted the March

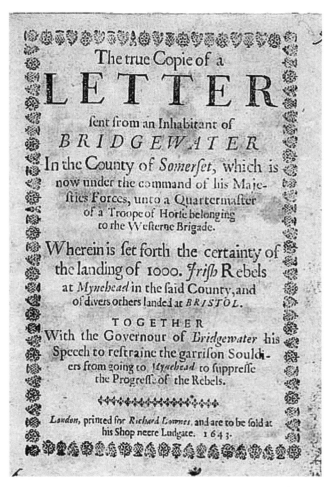

Illustration 1.37: A pamphlet reporting the landing of 1,000 Irish Rebels at Minehead in 1643. (SANHS)

convoy to Bridgwater.[236] In 1644 it appears that even more Royalist soldiers landed in Minehead, Watchet and a further 1,500 at Uphill. These troops gathered in Bridgwater, on 9 July, too late to intervene in the Battle of Langport, which was a parliamentarian victory of some proportion. After the battle of Langport, 1,500 Welsh foot soldiers who had come over the Bristol Channel became prisoners of the parliamentary forces, possibly the same troops that had landed at Uphill. These latter events represent the last significant numbers of Royalist seaborne troops arriving in Somerset during the civil war, since Bristol, and the remaining Somerset Royalist garrisons, were soon to fall into parliamentarian hands. A few days later the parliamentary Navy captured twelve vessels gathering at Steep Holm, which were to have been used to transport other Royalist troops to Somerset;[237] these troops were probably the 1,600 Welsh levies that were due to have been shipped over to Bridgwater from Swansea and Newport by 16 July 1644.[238] Later in the month Pembrokeshire soldiers, stationed at Bridgwater, who had changed sides to parliament after the Battle of

Langport were shipped back to serve parliament in their home county.[239]

In response to Irish soldiers being brought to England to support the Royalist cause, parliament issued an ordnance on 24 October 1644, stating that 'no quarter shall henceforth be given to Irishmen . . . captured on land or sea in England and Wales'. A few weeks later Captain Swanly, a parliamentary naval officer operating with a small fleet in the Bristol Channel, came upon a troop transport off the coast of Pembrokeshire. It was carrying soldiers of Royalist persuasion from Dublin to Bristol. Swanly's interpretation of the ordnance was not dissimilar to those of his peers, on land and sea, who supervised the killing of Irish people in cold blood on several occasions during this period. Of the hundred or more Royalist troops which Swanly found, seventy were classified as being Irish. In addition to two women, these men were tied back to back and thrown into the sea upon his orders.[240] From the perspective of today, it seems outrageous that Swanly was rewarded by parliament for this atrocity.

Irish issues have often been complex and protracted, thus, after hostilities had ceased in England in 1646, troops were still needed in Ireland in furtherance of Cromwell's policies. Thus it is not surprising to find that on 7 July 1646 Colonel Jephson rode from Ashton Court, near Bristol, not to Pill, but to Minehead, via Bridgwater, to make provision for the transportation to Ireland of 'our men and horses'. Inchiquin was also at Ashton Court and intended to make the same journey via Minehead. Whilst at Bridgwater on 11 July, Jephson was informed that 'the Admiral came into Minehead road last night' and stated, 'tomorrow morning we go to him.' Jephson had 100 'horse' with him, but was still waiting for 600 infantrymen from 'Sterling's foot.' The 'foot' must have arrived and embarkation expedited, for on 20 July Jephson stated that he arrived in Cork the day before. He was accompanied his wife, and, in addition, it is explicit that Jephson was using the opportunity to conduct business. He personally knew Mr Robert Quirke, merchant of Minehead, and thus was probably involved in some trade with him.[241] It is clear that naval ships were not the only vessels to transport troops and horses from Minehead to Ireland at this time. Nathaniel Bullock, owner of the *Patience* of Minehead had transported passengers and goods to and from Ireland for thirty years. This experience had led to him being given a warrant to impress Irish ships to take men and horses to Ireland during the civil war. In doing so he fell out with Robert Quirke who allegedly came to blows with men

working for Bullock over the priority of maintaining vessels in Minehead belonging to Quirke and Bullock.[242] Quirke's ships were undoubtedly also involved in moving troops. Further troops followed Jephson, for in 1647 shipping was again ordered to be in readiness to transport Colonel Long's Regiment from Minehead to Ireland.[243]

Two years later, in April 1649, troops of Lieutenant-Colonel Cooke's Regiment stationed at Guildford, in Surrey, drew lots for service in Ireland. The regiment marched to Minehead and were due to set sail on 9 August when a near mutiny erupted due to an apparent lack of pay. *The Moderate*, a broadsheet from August 1649, featured the event as a news item reported from Barnstaple on 10 August:

> Yesterday, Col. Cooke's regiment was shipped at Minehead, though not without some difficulty the governor of Dunstar being forced to send 80 men from Dunstar, and to place them in Minehead church, and at every passage in the town to Stop all stragglers; as also to assist Col. Cooke if there should be occasion. The Governor of Dunstar Castle presently sent for his men to come down to the key, intending to fall upon the mutineers, . . . but when the men came in sight the mutiny was well staid, and they were kept at the seaside till they were all forced aboard, and their ships launched in the channel.[244]

The regiment failed to land in Munster but eventually landed near Dublin on 15 August. A month or so later in the autumn of 1649, Colonel Farr's Regiment of Foot marched from Sussex to Minehead for transportation to Ireland.[245]

Troops were needed by Oliver Cromwell for the subjugation of Ireland, so the Somerset ports also saw troop movements in the 1650s. In early February 1650 letters from Cork detailed how troops travelling from Minehead to Ireland had experienced a horrific journey. Five ships with soldiers aboard were all 'cast away', perhaps because of difficult weather when 'Captain Ensor, Captain Whiting, with 80 horse and 150 foot, and all the seaman drowned except 20 or 30' who managed to swim to shore.[246] Another record of the same event suggests that it took place in 1649 and that it was Minehead vessels that had been lost, not just vessels using Minehead. Quite a number of Minehead crew drowned since they allegedly left about one hundred widows and orphans who became a burden on the parish.[247] Also in 1650, on 4 March, Colonel Solomon Richards embarked 80 men under Major Poole at Pill for

Ireland. There were other soldiers waiting to embark but this was slowed by a lack of finance and unpaid bills which had been run up by the awaiting troops. Richards kept a low profile fearing being 'divided up amongst brewers, bakers and cheesemongers'.[248] Whether there was a realistic chance of being sued or assaulted is not clear.

On 19 February 1651/2 money was ordered to pay Mr Bond in Minehead for organising the transport of 'horse' from Minehead to Ireland.[249] A further 800 troops were quartered in Minehead and moved to Ireland in April 1651.[250] Warrants for the movement of 800 soldiers from Somerset to be shipped to Munster from Minehead were issued on 8 May 1651;[251] presumably these were in addition to the 800 that had been moved in April. Minehead vessels involved in the movement of troops to Ireland in 1651 were often quite small. They included the *Sarah* of 15 tons which could embark 30 soldiers and the sixty ton *Patience* which could carry 200 troops.[252] On 9 January 1652 a warrant was issued for Quatermaster William Cooper 'to sail with his part of Capt. Bagnall's troop of horse from Minehead to Ireland, as soon as possible, taking provisions for horse and men'.[253] This troop had previously set sail from Milford to Ireland, but had been driven back by foul weather into Minehead where the horses and men had received refreshments for several days.[254] Yet another welcome boost to the Minehead economy.

After the 'glorious revolution' of 1688, troops from the Duke of Schomberg's Army passed through Minehead, for Ireland, to serve William the Third in June 1689.[255] In March 1691 a vessel sailing from Cork to Ostend with soldiers was blown into Minehead, but was too leaky to carry on; orders were sought by commanders as to how they were to procure another ship for the journey.[256] March 1692 saw ships designed for the transport of the five battalions of soldiers sailing from Bideford and Minehead to Cork, and Kinsale.[257] In 1698 disbanded Irish soldiers and their families were being transported through Minehead into the 'kingdome of Ireland'.[258] All of which proves how Minehead played a role in virtually all the military campaigns in the seventeenth century involving Ireland.

At some point in the Autumn of 1712, exhausted and depleted regiments returning from service in the American colonies where they had been fighting the French and their Indian allies in what is known as 'Queen Anne's war', arrived back in England. They disembarked mainly at ports on the south coast, but detachments of the second Queen's Royal regiment landed at Minehead before joining their colleagues in Hampshire, where they recovered from their service and long trans-Atlantic journey.[259] In this case, Minehead seems to have been used to help speed the disembarkation of a large task force, which had suffered significantly and who had lost colleagues when some ships of the fleet foundered on the journey. In March 1719, after the raising of Irish regiments to replace English ones, Edward, Viscount Hinchinbroke's Regiment left Ireland for England. The troops disembarked at Minehead and Bristol on the 31 March and found quarters near Bristol, before moving on to Devizes and Warminster, in July, where they waited for further duties.[260] These were part of the 'four battalions' of soldiers from Ireland, that were rushed to the South West of England in order to bolster the region's defences in the face of a Spanish fleet that left Cadiz, in late February, with the perceived intent of invading England. In the event, a violent storm dispersed the Spanish fleet and thwarted any action planned by the Spanish.[261] Sixteen years later tragedy met troops returning from Ireland, when, in February 1735, a vessel foundered somewhere on the west Somerset coast. On the 21st some 19 soldiers, a boy, two women and two children were found drowned on the shore of Dunster parish and were all buried in the churchyard. Another nineteenth-century source states that the event took place in 1736, and the ship in question was the *Lamb*, which was taking soldiers to Waterford from Bristol.[262] Furthermore, 35 men, women and children were buried in Minehead on 22 February in one grave, who had all been victims of drowning. Later tides brought in more bodies and seven men, one woman and a child were buried in Minehead the following day.[263] The minimum death toll from this event seems to have been 67 people. This appears to have been the worst single tragedy along the Somerset coast in the eighteenth century.

Pill continued to be a common location for the embarkation and disembarkation of troops and military personnel in the eighteenth and nineteenth centuries. For example, in 1739 the Treasury was billed for three regiments that were moved from Cork to Pill.[264] Furthermore, in November 1754, about 100 men from the 20th Regiment were drafted from positions around Exeter, marched to Pill and embarked on waiting ships. They were taken to Cork *en-route* to serve in Virginia, as Anglo-French relationships deteriorated and war against the French broke out yet again in North America.[265] On 30 December 1748 horses belonging to troops of Brigadier Richbell's regiment departed for Ireland in

Illustration 1.38: Low tide at Minehead in July 2011. Sodden timbers are visible in the foreground at the exact position of the conjectured site of the wreck of the *Lamb*, as indicated on a map of Minehead's post Medieval archaeological sites. Could this actually be one of the few remains of the stricken *Lamb* where so many people drowned in 1735? (Author)

the *Duke* transport; however the associated troops who embarked on the *Alexander* whilst anchored in King Road could not set sail because of storms.[266]

During the period of the Napoleonic wars there was also considerable troop movements to meet particular contingencies, with 1794 becoming a very busy year for the town of Pill. In June of that year three brigs and four sloops brought the newly formed Cameron Highlanders from Belfast, landing at Pill, who marched to Frome and then on to Southampton where they embarked, initially, for the 'Low Countries'.[267] In September, the Leinster Regiment embarked in five coal transports from Dublin and sailed for Bristol. The disembarkation took place at Pill, after the soldiers had spent a night at anchor waiting for dawn.[268] Oliver Moore (possibly a pen name), a staff officer with the regiment, commented that the soldiers' accommodation in the coal ships was very poor, but the five or six officers occupied a reasonably furnished cabin in the ship he was sailing in. However, the cabin was so smelly that expensive perfumes were used to try and cover up the stench, but to no avail. Two officers were so sea sick that they stayed in their cots between Dublin and Lundy, whilst the others 'contrived to amuse themselves and laugh away the hours till midnight' until the ships got underway. Moore, who was not seasick, stated:

> I felt my time for three days pass very pleasantly on board. We had abundance of fresh provisions, of wine, also cards and backgammon to while away the time between meals. Besides the men, to the amount of nearly one hundred and fifty, we were blessed with the addition of nearly half as many women and children on board, who contracted for their own passage, as a private speculation with the Captain.[269]

Just two months later the 83rd Regiment, County of Dublin, also embarked from Dublin and subsequently landed at Pill. They marched to Bath where they were quartered for the winter, subsequently moved to Poole in Dorset and then on to the Southampton area; the following year they were embarked for the West Indies.[270] Also in 1794, but in the reverse direction, on 4 October, General William Dyott embarked from Pill with the Bristol Regiment, bound for Dublin. They lay wind bound until 13 October, but then eventually had 'a fine passage'.[271] This regiment, which comprised nearly 700 men, was known as the 'Loyal Bristol Regiment', or the 103rd Regiment of Foot under the command of Lord Charles Somerset.[272] A year later, in 1795, two troops of the 13th Light Dragoons, who had been serving in Southern Ireland embarked at Cork and sailed to Bristol prior to travelling to Southampton for embarkation to serve against the French in the West Indies. It may have been these dragoons that were required to charge a regiment of Irish Fencibles, who, in 1795, refused to embark at Pill onto transports which were waiting to take them to Jersey. There were complaints regarding their lack of pay so they had mutinied, threatening to hang two of their officers and in the ensuing fight many soldiers were injured, but they were forced to embark and then imprisoned on their transports.[273] Writing

an anti-war polemic in 1795, Samuel Taylor Coleridge referred to the dehumanising effect that filth and confinement had on an Irish regiment that had 'landed at Pill' in recent times.[274] This topic had clearly been the conversation of Bristolians. The seemingly uneventful passages to and from Pill, mentioned above, should probably be considered in a less than glorious light, especially in terms of the stress it caused to the ordinary foot soldier, let alone the more dramatic events when mutinous troops needed to be managed.

Troop movements of a different kind occurred in February 1797 when 1,400 French troops landed in Pembrokeshire. The four French vessels in which the force was embarked had previously tried to sail

Illustration 1.39: A section from a survey of 1687 of land in West Somerset. Were these ships purely added as an embellishment by the surveyor, or was the Bristol Channel often to be seen with many ships in its waters? Note how some of the ships are of a much earlier period than 1687, suggesting how some ships remained in service for many decades after they were built. (SHC, DD/L1/10/35A)

up the Bristol Channel, reaching Porlock, but the French Commanders found that the flood tide did not help against a strong easterly wind, so they fell back to Pembrokeshire. This invasion quickly came to nothing, but, on 2 March, there was erroneous information circulating in Bristol that more French troops had landed in South Wales and were advancing on the city. All troops available in Bristol, including regulars and the Buckingham Militia, were marched to Pill and embarked on pilot skiffs ready to sail to Tenby to meet the threat. Soon after the embarkation came news that there had been no second French invasion, so the troops were disembarked and marched back to their quarters.[275] On 6 September 1798, 614 men of the North Gloucestershire Militia embarked at Pill for Ireland, when it was recorded that 'every assistance' was spontaneously given by the inhabitants of the village to the troops.[276] In the reverse direction, on 9 October 1799, the Dorsetshire Regiment had landed at Pill from whence they returned to their home county.[277] On the same day the Lancashire Militia, who had been serving in Ireland, embarked at Waterford under Captain Ralph Williamson, disembarking at Pill three days later. Immediately they marched to Chipping Sodbury, Gloucestershire, before nightfall and subsequently marched on to Preston.[278] After the Peace of Amiens, all the naval prisoners at Stapleton, in Bristol, had to be returned to France, the last 417 sailing from Pill on 11 May 1802 on board the *Alfred*, a 390 ton ship belonging to the port of Lancaster, *en-route* for Morlaix in Brittany. The Admiralty, however, grumbled at the delay, saying that this was the last prison in England to be cleared.[279]

As well as being at war with France in the early nineteenth century, British troops were still needed for peacekeeping duties in Ireland. In the first few years of that century, the '4th King's Own' saw action in various parts of Ireland, but, in 1804, some officers were detailed to travel to Launceston, in Cornwall, to raise more troops. Major Wood and Captain Short, accompanied by 27 non-commissioned officers and drummers, embarked in Dublin for Minehead for the first leg of the journey to Cornwall.[280] Irishmen were also drafted into British forces helping an enlarged army fight Napoleon. In 1805, a Dorsetshire shepherd's son, Benjamin Harris, who had been drafted into the army in 1803, returned from a recruiting drive in Ireland landing at Pill. Harris and his compatriots marched to Bristol and then to Ashford in Kent, via Salisbury Plain, where the Irish recruits rioted.[281] Furthermore,

in 1810, Charles O'Neil, an Irish carpenter's son, enlisted in the Louth Militia. By October, Charles and the rest of the regiment were awaiting transports to England in Cork. They embarked in a transport ship, the *Lunar*, sailed to England and disembarked at Pill. They marched to Bristol, then Plymouth, before embarkation for the Peninsula War. O'Neil went on to survive actions in Spain and Waterloo, retiring to Massachusetts.[282] In the reverse direction, in 1813 further numbers of troops, this time from the Oxfordshire Militia, embarked from Pill for the Cove of Cork and then marched on to their barracks at Bandon.[283]

Clearly, the movement of troops to and from Ireland, and the passage of Irish troops through Bristol, caused some problems for the city authorities, especially when impoverished Irish soldiers were trying to make their way home. In 1811 the Bristol Corporation of the Poor bought two small houses at Pill in order to 'aid the shipping home to Ireland of natives' who had served in the British forces, as well as their families. By 1813 'other arrangements' had been made and the houses were no longer needed, so they were sold.[284] For a brief period, these houses would have been the temporary accommodation for soldier families awaiting a fair wind to Ireland.

After the war, in August 1816, Lieutenant Charles Spencer travelled from Bristol to Youghal to be with his regiment. He bemoaned the link with his particular regiment because it had not been posted to Waterloo. Spencer boarded a merchant vessel at Bristol Quay with two other passengers and since it was just about to depart for Youghal; this precluded him having to travel down to Pill to catch the packet. His journey was eventful with a becalming in mid-Channel, terrible sea sickness and a severe storm for a couple of days. At one point, the crew were in conference, asking the most experienced seaman where they were. His reply was "If ye'd only but show me the ould Head of Kinsale I'd tell ye where ye are in a twinkling; but devil a bit of me knows one o' these waves from t'other".[285] Surprisingly, not overly worried about this lack of navigational information, Spencer then slept until they were alongside the quay at Youghal.

Clearly, during the period of this study, Minehead and Pill were the main locations where troops were embarked or disembarked for duties, mainly in the old colony of Munster and, to a certain extent, the 'New World'. Minehead and Pill were the locations that could service bigger transport ships most easily, so, locations such as Bridgwater do not figure in the

Illustration 1.40: The port of Cork in 1811 by Neville Bath. Scenes similar to this were witnessed by many of the travellers through Cork on their way to or from Somerset. This would have been a typical port scene in England as well as Ireland. (UKHO)

process of troop movements. There were some exceptions to this pattern, such as the landing of Royalist troops from Ireland at Watchet and Bridgwater, and Welsh troops at Uphill, but this would have been for tactical reasons. This volume does not claim to have detailed all movements, but no-doubt the records discussed here indicate that hundreds of thousands of troops are likely to have been embarked or disembarked via the Somerset coast between 1556 and 1815, with Minehead's busiest period being the 1640s and 1650s, with Pill's busiest periods being the late Tudor foundation of the Munster colony and the Napoleonic wars of the early nineteenth century. At these times, it was probably difficult enough provisioning troops awaiting passage at Pill, despite its proximity to Bristol, let alone troops cantoned in the Dunster-Minehead area.

It is unknown whether the quay at Minehead made it easy to embark horses at low tide when ships were tied up alongside. However, port workers and mariners at Minehead had great experience loading and unloading animals since Minehead was a location where thousands of cattle, as well as sheep and horses, were landed during many years of the seventeenth century. The facilities at Pill were less developed, but it is likely that vessels were tied up on the mud of the riverbank when troops and horses embarked via planking, rather than being ferried out to vessels in the river Avon. Any troops embarking in King Road needed to be taken to their vessels by lighters and their animals by horse ferry.

Religious, ethnic and political intolerances and difficulties

In December 1533 several people left Uphill for Ireland but were later questioned after they arrived in Scotland, since it was thought they had become involved in a conspiracy against Henry the Eighth. The King faced several rebellions during the 1530s, but this event does not appear to coincide with any of the main ones. James Griffith ap Howell, his wife Alice and daughter Sache were accompanied by a relation, John Morgan, Henry Ellington, a mariner called Lewis, John a Pen Breere, John Beau Teaw, John Owen (gunner) and David Williams. They were first conveyed from Wales to Uphill in a coal boat where they joined a 15 ton pinnace, loaded with beans, with a master and five mariners, which then sailed on to Youghal from where they made their way to Scotland. Ellington claimed that he had travelled to Ireland to buy horses for royalty at Drogheda.[286]

A peasant's revolt known as the Western Rebellion, took place in the summer of 1549 culminating in the siege of Exeter. Once this had been lifted by the authorities, when they regained control, many of the rebels retreated up the Exe valley with engagements, and executions, on the way as the ringleaders were caught. A party of rebels, of unknown size, it is said, retreated as far as Minehead and then took a ship to Bridgwater. They were finally caught and defeated on 27 August 1549 at Kingweston near Langport.[287] In 1577 an Inuit family, Cally Chough and his wife Ignorth with their child, disembarked in King Road from the *Ayde*, a two hundred ton vessel belonging to Queen Elizabeth the First. Martin Frobisher's expedition to find gold in the Arctic and a North-West passage to China, found it necessary to take hostages as some men from his expedition had been taken by Inuit people. The family were taken to Bristol but they died within two months, presumably succumbing to English endemic illnesses. The 'gold' ore, dug up from the Arctic ground by the expedition, proved worthless.[288]

In May 1635 in the lead-up to the English Civil War, Richard Mather of Toxteth, who had non-conformist views over the wearing of surplices, was ejected from his parish. With his family he travelled to Bristol for a passage to New England, whereupon arrival he found freedom of Christian expression. Mather and family boarded their vessel, the *James* of 220 tons, in King Road where they had to wait for over a week, so long in fact that the vessel had to be re-provisioned from Portishead.[289] Also on board were the Reverend Dainial Maud, another Puritan and Daniel Flower. Mather and Maud took turns in taking services on the *James*, and Maud, on arrival in New England became a school teacher at Boston.[290] Another Puritan cleric arriving in New England prior to 1636 was George Moxon. Moxon, chaplain to Sir William Brereton of Lancashire (whose own travels in the Bristol Channel are discussed in detail later), realised he was about to be ejected from the Church of England. In order to avoid the hearings he disguised himself and travelled to Bristol where he found a passage.[291] Moxon became the first minister of a Congregational church in Springfield, Massachusetts.

By 1642 the Royalist vicar of Luccombe, Rev. Henry Byam, had caused enough resentment amongst his parliamentarian neighbours, by raising a regiment of horse for the King, that his wife Susan found the experience unpleasant enough to want to remove herself to Wales. This she did, probably from Minehead, with Susan her daughter and a servant girl. Sadly their vessel foundered and the three were drowned, but Byam served his King faithfully throughout the troubles of the next decade.[292] A further family to leave west Somerset because of Parliamentarian pressure, this time for a home near Youghal, were the Atkin family of Billbrook, Old Cleeve. John Atkin, his wife Jean, his son and five daughters probably left in 1641, for John the elder died in Ireland before February 1642.[293] The rest of the family stayed in the Youghal area where John's daughter, Elizabeth Atkin married Samuel Hayman.[294]

1642 must have been quite a tense year in west Somerset, as elsewhere, and there were several instances relating to Minehead's maritime role which would have increased local concerns. First, Roger Mainwaring, Bishop of St David's, and his young wife were detained under armed guard in Minehead after a passage across from Dublin for preaching on the supremacy of Kings over law.[295] An Army captain, John Pointz, received permission in July 1642 to leave Ireland having raised a company of soldiers in England, presumably to serve parliament. He took a ship in Dublin and sailed for Minehead. Once on board he recognised Mainwaring who was travelling incognito. After Mainwaring's 'preaching indiscretions' he had roamed from alehouse to alehouse in disguise but 'had slipped across to Ireland expecting to find preferment there'. However, Ireland was no less difficult so he tried to 'slip' back to England, but was recognised by Pointz on board ship and was seized by the Army captain. When the ship reached Minehead, Pointz took Mainwaring before Thomas Luttrell, magistrate, of Dunster Castle. Luttrell in turn passed him to the custody of a constable.[296]

Furthermore, in 1642 there were stories circulating, in print, from Minehead concerning a 'bloodie massacre upon five Protestants by a company of papists meeting them as they were going to Minehead to take ship for Ireland'.[297] In addition, a lurid tale was publicised that, on 18 January 1642, a 'speechless damzel' was landed in Minehead from Ireland which exhibited 'Irelands tragical tyrannie'. Allegedly, the young woman had been raped and had

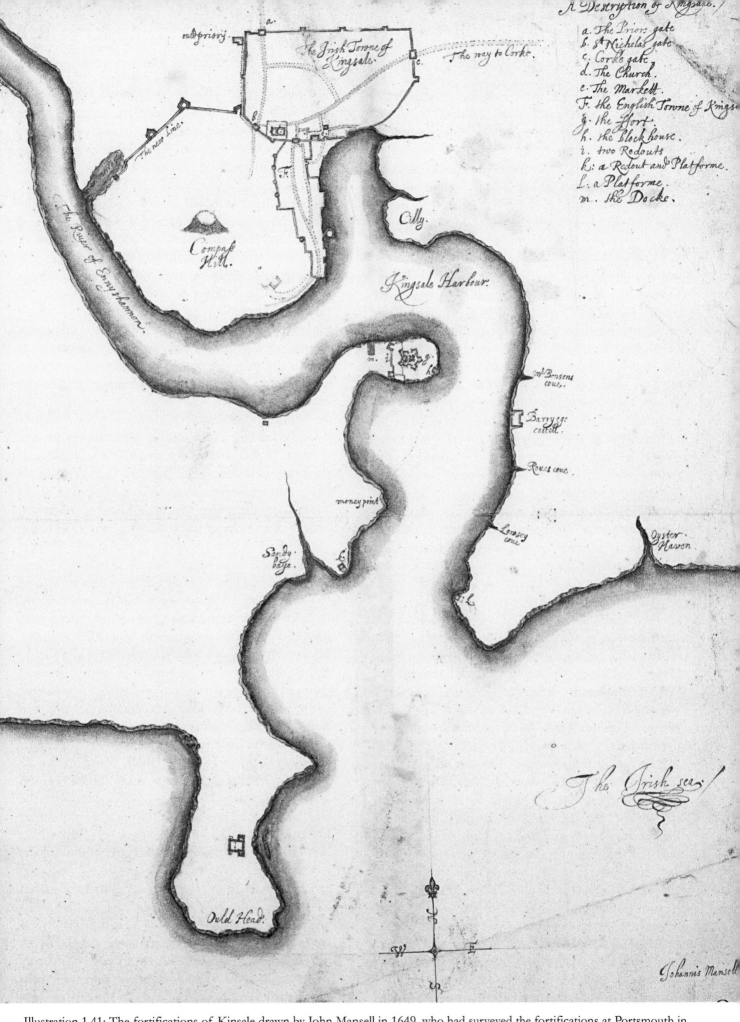

Illustration 1.41: The fortifications of Kinsale drawn by John Mansell in 1649, who had surveyed the fortifications at Portsmouth in 1642. The 'Head of Kinsale' is the promontory to the south. People fleeing the Irish Rebellion in 1642 left this harbour for Minehead (National Maritime Museum, F2042)

her hair pulled off by Irish rebels. Since she resisted, a hand had been cut off and her tongue cut out;[298] sadly, atrocities committed during the civil war in Ireland make this allegation more than a possibility. A few months later, 145 'poor distressed people' who took ship at Kinsale on the 3 April 1642, under the warrant of Captain Kettleby (then serving in the Parliamentary Navy), were set on shore at Minehead; they had been brought there in the *Curteen* of London with John White as master. Passenger traffic was not all one-way, for in September 1642, Arthur Carter, gentleman, travelled from Minehead with money received by friends to help manage the estate of his parents that had been spoiled by rebels.[299]

During the Civil War and 'rebellion' in Ireland in the 1640s 'many poor and distressed' people came out of that country, landed at Minehead and subsequently became a burden on the parish.[300] In response, in May 1642, the House of Commons ordered that all 'mere Irish and papists' in Minehead should be 'sent over again to Ireland', presumably to reduce the likelihood of rebellion coming to Somerset, and that in due time the Government would 'consider of the Relief of the distressed Protestants there'.[301] As part of the relief effort Lord Boyle personally paid for the passage of dispossessed Irish Protestants through Youghal and Waterford to Bristol or Minehead. Mention has already been made of 'distressed' ministers who were amongst the exodus and who stayed on in Minehead. Furthermore, the wives of the aristocracy also came to England to relative safety, compared to being involved in a vicious war in Ireland, such as Lady Fenton, who was Boyle's sister-in-law, and her friends who took houses in Minehead and Taunton.[302] Lady Fenton's husband, Sir William, travelled from Ireland to Minehead in early November 1646;[303] whether his lady was still in Somerset providing the reason for his visit is not known. Mention has already been made that in 1639 a catholic priest from Ireland was questioned by the authorities after landing in Bridgwater. Intolerance towards Catholics continued into the Interregnum for fear of political foment. Two Irishmen, James Patrickson and Arthur Berry, who disembarked in King Road form Cork in the spring of 1655, and whom the authorities considered were 'Romish' priests in disguise, were detained and closely questioned by Government agents.[304]

Persecuted Quakers also travelled via the Bristol Channel. A very early Quaker activist and meeting planter at Cork was Barbera Blaugdone who travelled to Ireland at least twice in the 1650s. In 1658 she was banished from Munster and so took a return passage to England. The vessel in which she was sailing was approaching Minehead when it was met by a pirate ship, which had 'an abundance of men on board'. Blaugdone began to consider whether there was any 'service for me to do among those people'. The trading vessel in which she had taken her passage seems to have accepted its fate without a struggle. The pirates boarded, searched the passengers and carried off their valuables, when Blaugdone had all her property taken, including the coat she was wearing. The pirates were not violent towards her but the captain was taken away as a prisoner until he could pay to redeem the ship and her cargo. It is not clear whether the vessel intended to call in at Minehead, but, after the incident with the pirates, it continued sailing up the Bristol Channel, minus the captain, and with Blaugdone pledged to raise the ransom to free him.[305]

Intolerance towards Quakers waned in Cork but waxed elsewhere in England in the later seventeenth century. In this context Richard and Joan Jacob and their six children (aged 11 and under) rode to Minehead on horseback in 1674, or 1675 and sailed for Ireland. Richard, a typical industrious Quaker of his times, quickly set himself up as a cutler in Cork; the family were the ancestors of the Jacobs who set up the now famous biscuit making firm.[306] Two years later, in 1677, Dublin Quaker Samuel Randall moved to Cork and over the next few years became a friend of Joseph Pike. At the time Quakers in England were undergoing some persecution and their meeting houses often closed. Pike recorded that in 1681 he and Randall travelled to Minehead from Cork and then overland, via Bridgwater, to Bristol to encourage the Quakers there. Their presence and work was noted by the Bristol authorities and they were briefly imprisoned in the city bridewell for their beliefs.[307]

The end of the Second Dutch War came on 31 July 1667. A few weeks later, three Dutch seamen who had been imprisoned in a Cork goal must have rejoiced as they boarded the *Mary* in Cork, with a Dutch captain and a Minehead crew of seven, which was bound for Minehead with cattle and wool. At last they were on their journey home. Sadly, it appears, by 24 September the vessel had foundered somewhere between the ports with all lives lost since no word was heard of her 'but a great cry from the wives and relatives supposing' that all were lost.[308]

In June 1683, as Colonel Henry Owen (brother of prominent Congregationalist minister John Owen) prepared for a passage to Ireland, he was arrested at Minehead by Richard Sandys, the senior customs officer. Owen was allegedly implicated in some way with the Rye House plot, a notorious plan to ambush and kill King Charles the Second and his brother in Hertfordshire. After questioning by the local authorities he was eventually released and may well have travelled to Dublin.[309] The county appeared to be anticipating a plot against the throne in 1683, two years before the Monmouth Rebellion, but not all favoured it. Thomas Read of Bridgwater took as a passenger, a man called Willis, from Bridgwater to Bristol in his barque. Willis appeared to be an ardent Monmouth sympathiser and chatted to Read about alleged preparations for a rebellion. Read evidently did not share Willis's views, as a report of the event came to the ears of Charles the Second's Government.[310]

When the Monmouth Rebellion did materialise, in 1685, it caused many people to travel in the Bristol Channel for a number of reasons. On the one hand there were those who fled the political conflict, such as Christopher Tuthill who was born in Minehead on 24 June 1650. His parents, who lived through the Civil War, must have hoped for more peaceful times but, 'owing to the troubled state of Somerset and Devon' after the Rebellion he travelled, with his wife Mary to Ireland as a merchant; he embarked in the *Happy Return* at Minehead and landed and settled at Youghal on 30 August 1685.[311] However, many Somerset and Dorset Congregationalists were involved in the Rebellion as they were often at odds with the King over his religious views. June 1685 saw Monmouth land in Dorset, but the main engagement took place at Sedgemoor, as is well known. Subsequently 90 rebels who were spared the butchery of the 'bloody assize' were transported to Barbados from the port of Bristol in October 1685. Most of those men had been held in Taunton's bridewell and Bridgwater's goal, but some had also been held in Exeter. Furthermore, many were men of Taunton, Milverton or Bridgwater, with others from villages such as Huntspill, Creech St Michael, North Curry and Westonzoyland. One can picture the weary trudge of the captives under guard as they made their way north to where the ship, the frigate *John*, was at anchor in King Road, the preferred anchorage of men of war for the port of Bristol for hundreds of years. They would have been rowed to the frigate in King Road and taken aboard, and there, rebel Joseph Wickham of Burnham died and was taken ashore and buried. They must have been relieved to have been spared the pain and ignominy of hanging, drawing in the market towns of the county and having their quarters suspended at cross-roads, the fate of many of their comrades. They should have been fearful of

the sea journey to Barbados and the years of slave labour in hot conditions that awaited them. Ten other Somerset men and one each from Dorset and Devon died on the passage to Barbados and were buried at sea, including Justinian Guppy of Taunton, William Mead of Bridgwater and Francis Came of Huntspill.[312]

After the 'glorious revolution' of William of Orange in England in 1688, there was further political turmoil and Protestants feared active Jacobites in Ireland, especially after James the Second landed at Kinsale in March 1689. Dublin was the location of the brief imprisonment of John Heyman (or Hayman), on 7 May 1689, when he and other Protestants were being harassed by James the Second's parliament. John was 'constrained to flee to his relatives in Somersetshire' and since his relatives

Illustration 1.42: St Michael's church, Minehead where, in 1689, the conger eel which saved the *Diamond* and its passengers was hung for a while. The houses surrounding church steps would have been familiar to the Fittons, and many of the other people mentioned in the text, who travelled by sea to and from Minehead. (SHC)

lived in Minehead, it is fairly clear he would have sailed there. Also, his mother and daughter had been buried at Minehead church, so he had strong emotional links with the town. Later he moved back to Ireland and was M.P. for Youghal between 1703 and 1713.[313] Other people who fled from Ireland to Minehead during 1689 because of the persecution of Protestants were Holland Goddard, a Cork shopkeeper, who arrived with all his goods, as did David Gold with 'similar goods'. The Treasury had to decide whether the tradesmen needed to pay customs duty on the 'imports'. Fortunately for the embattled tradesmen they were exempted from duty.[314] It is likely that these three escapees were some of the 400 or so people reportedly landed in Minehead in early April 1689, some of whom subsequently made their way to Bristol where another 500 had landed, including Lady Clancarhy. These refugees had reported to authorities in Bristol that about 50 people escaping in a vessel from Cork had been captured and the story repeated that some were to be forced to serve in James the Second's army.[315] Furthermore, in the summer of 1689, Youghal residents were unsure of William the Third's power to overcome the Jacobites, so some boarded the *Diamond* to make their escape to England, including Richard Fitton, his wife and five year old daughter Ann. The ship was holed and leaky, but, since it was being chased by a Jacobite naval vessel, all aboard decided to continue. It appeared the vessel was sinking off the Irish coast as the pumps were unable to make headway; in fact they were losing the battle to keep the ship afloat despite pumping effort and prayer. Then, suddenly, the rate at which the ship took on water slowed and the pumps saved the ship and the fleeing Protestants. An investigation at Minehead, after disembarkation, showed that a large conger eel had become stuck in the hole. The event was taken as evidence of the providential help of God and the eel was hung in Minehead's parish church for a while. The Fitton family then went to Bristol and were present in the city when King William arrived back from Ireland in early September.[316] No doubt they were elated with news of his victories in Ireland.

Travel for the sake of experience and leisure

A most unusual, and undoubtedly hazardous, sea journey appears to have commenced at midsummer 1590. Richard Ferris, a messenger of Queen Elizabeth's chamber, accompanied by two friends,

Andrew Hill and William Thomas, set off from Tower wharf, London in a small green painted wherry to row to Bristol via Kent and Cornwall. The oars and sail of the vessel were also coloured green. The justification for the trip was that Spanish galleys had not been able to row to invade England, but Englishmen could row along our coast even if the Spanish could not. Therefore the trip was something of a wager. Stopping for rest and refreshment at many ports, they arrived in Ilfracombe on the first day of August and then proceeded towards Minehead. The journey between Ilfracombe and Minehead took place overnight, with an east-south-east wind and choppy seas, when Ferris was the only rower whilst his companions bailed out the vessel. Ferris claimed he was 'constrained to row for life and yet had almost killed myself through the heat'! They stopped, presumably on the second, at Minehead and then rowed again towards Bristol, sailing between the two Holms and arrived at Bristol on 3 August on one tide at six in the evening. After an official welcome they went overland to London, arriving back at court on 8 August hopefully to an appreciative Queen.[317] Has this feat been repeated?

In 1635, Sir William Brereton, who had resigned his parliamentary seat in Cheshire, commenced a 'grand tour' of Scotland, Holland and Ireland.[318] He journeyed from Waterford to Minehead in July 1635 and arranged for his horses to be transferred in another vessel. He wrote of his passage to Minehead on 23 July, 'This day I rested at King's Head (Waterford) and prepared barley water, cordials and perfumes to take to sea to preserve me from fainting'. The next morning he went down to the passage which was so busy with people that he could not find convenient lodgings. He and his party eventually found space in a very noisy public house called the Bell. Although the wind was set fair for the journey, *i.e.* it was in the correct direction, the captain would not take the ship out lest it grounded in the narrow channels of the harbour. However, according to Brereton, two days later on the 25th:

the wind was sufficiently calmed, and stood fair, and they in the *Ninth Whelp*[319] discharged a piece of ordnance to summon us aboard very early, so I was constrained to go aboard without my breakfast. The *Ninth Whelp* is in the Kings books and 215 tons. She carries 16 pieces of ordnance. This ship is manned by 60 men; the captain is Sir Beverly Newcomen. The crew were civilized and well governed men, and diverse of them, I noted, attentive and diligent in prayer. We had (through

God's mercy) a quick, pleasant and dainty passage, for within 26 hours after we parted with Ireland, the utmost point, we landed at Minehead in Somersetshire.

Brereton was also fortunate in the transport of his horses and carriage for which he had no pass. In Waterford he happened to meet a Mr Styles who had a pass for six horses (signed by Ireland's Lord Deputy), though only needed to travel with four, so Brereton bought a third of the allowance for 10s. He then found a loaded cattle barque upon which he had his two horses and carriage loaded; a justice of the peace, Mr Augustine, gave him permission to do this. The fee paid to the barque's master, William Bayley, for the transit of the two horses and carriage was £2 5s, and it cost Brereton a further 2s 4d customs duty when he unloaded his goods at Minehead.

The ship that carried Brereton did not delay by entering the harbour itself since it was a 'Man of War' on convoy duty, instead he was put ashore, perhaps near the present day Greenaleigh Farm to the west of the town. This quiet beach, away from the sight of customs officials, may well also have been a location of illegal landings and smuggling, hence the stories about enchantment and fairies aimed at keeping people away, especially after dark. At mid-day on 26 July he recorded his short journey from ship to shore, stating:

> we left the ship and were carried ashore in the longboat, wherein we were more tossed, and in more apparent danger than in all the passage, the waves swelling and being mighty high and great upon and near the shore, so as we were glad to be landed upon any land, and were set ashore a mile from Minehead upon the sea shore, and near unto an house in Somersetshire, which is said to be enchanted, wherein none dare lodge in the night, so as it is not inhabited. Here we found boys and others attending the orchard which is well furnished with apples, which the faries sufficiently guard in the night-time.

He described Minehead as

> a long straggling built village, whereinto there is great recourse of passengers for Ireland. We lodged at the sign of the Angel and had 6d ordinary (the fixed bill of fare for the day at the inn). Hence I sent by boat, a barque of 80 ton, George Parker, Robin and Will, together with the cloak-bags, who went aboard about 11 hour at night and landed at

Illustration 1.43: Sir William Brereton (1604-1661) who arrived in Minehead from Waterford in July 1635. (J Ricraft, *Survey of England's champions* (London, 1649))

the King Road about 6 hour on Monday evening, who paid 1s apiece for their passage. Here is a high, strong pier, and a good, wide, open haven.

From his description it seems that Brereton, due to the brevity of his stay, only saw Quay Town at Minehead. His description of the Irish link ties in well with Gerrard's description in 1633, where Minehead Quay was described as 'an harbour for ordinary barkes much frequented by such as pas to and from Ireland'.[320] After he landed in Minehead he dispatched his servants to King Road, by another ship, but journeyed to Bristol via Glastonbury and the Mendips. When he arrived in Bristol 'he found the city exceedingly thronged with Londoners, Irish and others' who had travelled for the St James Fair.[321]

The *Ninth Whelp* was on this occasion accompanying a convoy of vessels from Ireland into the Bristol Channel since the whole maritime community was afraid, with good reason, of piracy by the 'Turks' from Algeria or Morocco; this was fuelled by a significant slave raid that had taken place at Baltimore in southern Ireland in 1631.[322] In 1634 several Minehead barques had been plundered *en-route* to Ireland, with passengers and cargo taken,[323] and possibly in the same year there was a night raid on the Somerset coast near Weston-super-Mare when men, women and children were taken from an isolated farm by 'Turks'.[324] Robert Boyle's memoirs also mention the threat from 'Turkish Galleys' when he was journeying from Youghal up the Bristol Channel in 1635.[325] With regard to this threat, Brereton recorded in 1635:

> July 26th. This (The *Ninth Whelp*) is a most dainty steady vessel, and a most swift sailer able to give the advantage of a topsail to any of the rest of this fleet, but they suited their course to the pace of this fleet, whom they waited upon to watch over from Waterford to Bristol fair, and to guard them from the Turks, of whom there was here a fear and rumour that they were very busy upon the coast of France. This day we caused match to be made ready and prepared and looked for them about Lundye next morning, but saw none, only it was the Captain's care to see all the sail before him; for which end staying often, the vessel then tottered and rolled intolerably; this did make me vomit extremely, and much more sea-sick than otherwise.[326]

The threat continued when in 1640 a young Irish clergyman, Devereux Spratt, born at Stratton-on-the-Fosse, Somerset, was taken by 'Turks' on a passage from Cork to Bristol.[327] Later in the century, in 1677, 15 crew members from the *Bridgwater Merchant*, including Captain Charles Reeves, were taken as slaves off 'Argiers' (Algeria) by Algerian corsairs. The ship was taken back into British hands by Sir John Ernley of H.M.S. *Woolwich*, who rescued the three remaining crew members. The following year it was thought that 'Turks' were responsible for the removal of the crew and cargo from the 350 ton *Angel Gabriel* of Bristol, which had been found drifting 20 leagues off the southern Irish coast.[328]

Nine years after Brereton's passage to Minehead, another traveller left a detailed description of a sea journey involving the port, but, on this occasion the traveller had fears other than the threat of 'Turks'. In 1644 a French traveller, Monsieur de La Boullaye Le Gouz experienced a quick passage in an Irish vessel from Bristol to Minehead, then, commencing on 6 May, a longer and more disturbing second leg from Minehead to Dublin. Prior to the sixth he had sailed

> with a fair wind down the Channel and anchored at Migned, where there is a little quay, the most beautiful in the Channel, made of stones extra

large, placed one on another without any mortar. It resists the waves and protects the vessels from the wind.[329]

Whilst in Minehead Le Gouz heard of, and probably witnessed, the strange case of a Welsh bark which ran ashore on the sands of Minehead during his stay there. Her crew had taken to the ship's boat taking one passenger and his moneybag of '200 Jacobins', but this party all drowned when their small boat capsized. An old man and six women had been left to their fate in the bark by the deserting crew.[330] Perhaps this event, if true, was caused partly because of the increased lawlessness and tension during the civil war.

Le Gouz's passage from Minehead was also fraught on a number of counts. Contrary winds in the mornings kept both the vessel in the harbour and its Captain in the public house, who got so drunk he was incapable of giving orders to the pilots when the winds changed around later in the day. They finally set sail at 10 p.m. and Le Gouz recorded:

> This drunkard set sail on a sudden and left many respectable passengers ashore, without giving them any notice, who having lost all hope of him weighing anchor so late, were asleep in their inns.

On the following day, about mid-day, the French traveller experienced a new fear which derived from the appearance of a 40 gun parliamentary ship. He stated

> it was rumoured that the parliamentarians threw into the sea all Irish and those of their party owing to the massacre the Irish had made in their country of the English Protestants. We escaped from them under cover of night.

When the vessel carrying Le Gouz finally approached Dublin, the still less than alert captain gave no navigation orders and the party were nearly wrecked on a sandbank. Only the efforts of passengers and crew, who took in the sails, launched two boats, attached ropes and towed the vessel away from danger saved the situation.[331] The probable reason why the Irish crew had felt uneasy in parliamentary Minehead during their stop-over, related to the experience of the Marquis of Hertford about two years earlier.[332]

An early leisure trip in a newly built pleasure sloop took place in August 1736, when a young Quaker Bristol merchant, Samuel Lloyd, accompanied by other young gentlemen merchants of Bristol, including Mr King and Mr Michael Beecher, sailed from Bristol to Flat Holm, but the trip ended in tragedy. The party picked up a well known pilot, Samuel Rumley, from Pill and headed down the Channel. The group used a small boat to ferry themselves onto Flat Holm and spent some time there. Upon returning to the anchored sloop the passengers all stood up at the same time to board the pleasure vessel. All were tipped into the water and had to swim for their lives. Lloyd and Rumley grabbed the small boat but tipped it up on their heads, subsequently Rumley drowned, Lloyd swam on but was washed away on the flood tide with the party unable to help, and he also subsequently drowned.[333] Another leisure trip, at some time during the 1760s, involved Sir Thomas Stepney, a landowner and mining entrepreneur residing at Llanelli, who sailed from there to Minehead and back with the son of Mrs Montague. It is clear that Montague was living the life of a young gentleman and travelling for experience, who after his journey went off to explore the Welsh mountains. For himself, Stepney may have been sailing for the experience, but may have also used the journey to seal a coal contract in Minehead, for he sold coal throughout the country. The party may have sailed in a yacht, a coal boat or even a fishing 'buss' which Stepney had caused to be constructed for the expansion of the fisheries in the Llanelli area.[334] In 1762 James Woodforde, soon to be installed as curate of Thurloxton (near Taunton), travelled to meet a friend in Bristol. On 31 August they rode to King Road and were probably rowed into the Channel since they boarded two naval ships, the *Tyger* and the *King George* and had a tour of the vessels for which a shilling was paid for the privilege.[335]

In 1792, Julius Caesar Ibbetson and companions, embarked in a sailing boat at Lamplighter's Hall on the North bank of the Avon at Shirehampton. By 1792 this was a place of resort for pleasure seekers, as well as a location for captains whose vessels were lying in King Road. Ibbetson's party packed cold food and were conducted down the Avon, past Denny Island in King Road and as far as Portishead. They disembarked at Portishead and then walked back to Bristol via Easton in Gordano, Pill and Leigh woods, a distance of eleven miles so the party reckoned.[336]

The summer of 1799 saw Mrs Anna Barbauld, a noted educationalist, writer and campaigner, taking time to holiday at Clifton and then in Wales. She took a passage from Glamorganshire to Minehead 'in a

vessel without accommodation'. She stated that the journey should have taken three or four hours, but it took twenty-four because of very bad weather. However, she survived her experience and travelled on to Dulverton, but Anne never set foot in another sea-going vessel, even though friends she met in Clifton invited the Barbaulds to stay with them in Ireland.[337]

In October 1807 a gentleman barrister Richard Fenton and his companion, took a passage from Milford Haven to Minehead. They were travelling for the experience, as well as making genealogical and archaeological enquiries on the way. On leaving Milford Haven, the vessel they had boarded was becalmed, so Fenton was able to be rowed along the coast by the crew where he examined the cliffs and sea life and from where he was able to make several sketches.

Fenton spent the night on board the vessel playing his flute, whilst the captain, who had served in the British Navy in the late eighteenth century, played his violin. About midnight the wind then blew up so the captain

> pleased with my affability, and perceiving me no way disposed to retire, after giving some orders about securing the hatches, reefing, and other preparations to meet the growing storm, charged his pipe anew. I, in my turn, producing my cold

Illustration 1.44: Anna Barbauld (1743-1825) experienced a dreadful crossing from Wales to Minehead in 1799. (David Worthy)

tongue, pickled oysters, and bottled porter, part of our sea stock, pressed him to partake.[338]

Sometime in the early hours the storm abated to a steady breeze and Fenton retired for a few hours, only to be roused and invited on deck at dawn to witness their closing on the Somerset coast under a rose coloured sky. Fenton's travelling companion had not enjoyed the passage and at the first alehouse they could find, after landing at Minehead Pier, he 'cleaned himself from the pollution of the sea voyage' and wrote of his experience:

> With a head that partakes of the fluctuation of that element I have just quitted, I sit down to let you know that I am (thank God) safely landed in the county of Somerset, at Minehead, a miserable looking place, as far as I have yet seen; but had I touched in a nation even of cannibals, I believe I should have felt happy, after what I have suffered at sea, having been out a night and a day, in all of which time I had not ten minutes respite from convulsion.[339]

The two travellers then went to Holnicote (in Selworthy parish) where they stayed for a week or two with the Hon. Mr Fortescue, who had retired after a lifetime at sea, his wife and daughter. Whilst there they took extensive walks in the district and daily ate local Herring which had swum up the Channel that autumn in unusually high numbers.[340] Six years later, in the summer of 1813, a party of English travellers in their own vessel, arrived and anchored in Porlock Bay, disembarked, walked to West Porlock and stayed in the neighbourhood. They soon discovered the woes of the local community, such as the Herring which once provided work for so many in the eighteenth century that had, more or less, abandoned the Bristol Channel; on a previous visit, perhaps years earlier, one of the travellers had witnessed the West Porlock fishermen leaving their houses in the mornings to take their nets down to the beach to fish. After a day or two the party sailed on to Minehead, stayed there a few days and were quite complimentary about the town's environs. Subsequently they moved on and crossed the Channel with the intent of reaching Cardiff, but in about three hours they disembarked at Aberthaw. They travelled by land to explore Cardiff, since the contrary winds would not allow them to reach their intended destination on that day.[341] A few years later, in the summer of 1817, an un-named army officer walked for exercise and pleasure from the neighbourhood of Exeter, to

Illustration 1.45: Richard Fenton (1741-1821), who travelled with a friend from Milford Haven to Minehead in 1807. (Author's collection)

London, York, Bangor, through Wales to Swansea and then to Newport where he embarked for Bridgwater, before walking home again to Exeter.[342] Soldiers of the period were used to covering great distances in campaigns, but, whilst this particular officer had walked distances such as this in the line of duty only a few years before, it was perhaps the first time he had walked so far for pleasure. Hopefully the Bristol Channel crossing was a small rest on the way.

A wealthy American traveller of Dutch descent, George Rapelje, whilst on a European tour, sailed from Cork to Pill in May 1821 in the *Bousford* packet vessel with Captain Cobblestone in charge. Rapelje boarded at 4pm on Tuesday 15 May and recorded his experiences as follows.

> We had a fine fair wind, and four cabin passengers: the ladies were a Miss Gibbs, Mrs Gilmore, two others and a number of poor Irish steerage passengers. Wednesday was a fine clear day. We had run in the night at the rate of six knots an hour, and about that all day. The vessel, though small, had good accommodations for her size; twelve births in the cabin and four athwart ship, against the forward bulk-head. The poor Irish steerage passengers were very filthy, both men and women; the common passengers were so numerous that I could not walk a step on deck.

On Thursday the 17th we got up the River Avon, which is very narrow, to a Place called Pill, about four miles and a half below Bristol. I went on shore and got a Hackney carriage, or kind of stage. The owner, after telling me that I could have it to take myself and another passenger up for half a guinea, wanted to fill it and charge the others two shillings and six pence apiece.

Rapelje went on to tour Bristol and Bath and left interesting contemporary descriptions of the cities.[343]

Just prior to the Victorian era and the age of widespread steam travel, the Acland family of Broadclyst, Devon and Holnicote took to yachting for pleasure. Their adventures began on 9 August 1832 at Porlock Weir when the family boarded the hired *Arrow* for a journey around the south west of England. Only two years later Sir Thomas Dyke Acland purchased a 136 ton yacht/schooner, the *Lady of St Kilda*, named after his wife Lydia who had visited St Kilda in 1810. In that year the family took six weeks to circumnavigate England and Scotland, revisiting St Kilda on the way, starting and ending at Porlock Weir where the yacht was moored for the winter of 1834/5. In the summer of 1835 the family embarked again and this time sailed to the Mediterranean, which involved a visit to Malta.[344]

There were also shorter pleasure trips taking place in the Bristol Channel in the 1820s and '30s, some of which ended in tragedy. In a publication dated 1829 designed for marketing the new resort of Weston-super-Mare, trips from Knightstone into the Bristol Channel were advertised. Apparently local fishermen hired their services for 1s per person per day or 10s 6d for a party. The deck-less vessels could accommodate a considerable number of persons and would take parties around Brean, Steep Holm for rabbit shooting on Flat Holm. Some parties delayed too long on Flat Holm and thus had to stay overnight on the Island, since the vessels used for pleasure could only disembark passengers back at Knightstone at or near high tide.[345] It was stated in 1833 that Flat Holm was visited by many people for the pleasure of its delightful prospects and of the Channel for many miles in extent.[346]

Travelling for leisure reasons is not a modern development, but only the wealthy could indulge in extended travel for pleasure right into the twentieth century. Seventeenth-century travellers, who are documented in this chapter, whilst they recorded their experiences at sea, also recorded their experiences whilst travelling through Somerset on land. It is interesting that Porlock, Weston-super-Mare and Minehead are all mentioned in the 1690s as locations used whilst travelling for maritime leisure, as they are locations which became three of Somerset's contrasting leisure hubs in the twentieth century.

Passages with no known motive

Appendix 1.4 lists numerous people using the port of Minehead, between 1588 and 1624, whose motivations for travel are unknown but who sadly died before embarkation, or died on the journey before arrival at the harbour. In November 1614, writing from Dublin to his father, John Trevelyan of Nettlecombe, George Trevelyan recorded that his 'cousin', Francis Pollard of Nympton in Devon was due to sail from Ireland to Minehead. He asked his father to provide horses at Minehead for Pollard to ride home upon, but acknowledged that the wind may force the vessel that Pollard was to sail in into another port so that may in fact not see his relation.[347] In 1635, as a boy of 10 or 11, John Hull from Leicestershire, departed on the *George,* Mr Nicholas Shaples master, from King Road (presumably with his parents) to New England, settling in Boston after the ship survived grounding on sandbanks before arrival. Eventually he became a recognised goldsmith and silversmith and some of his work survives.[348]

In July 1645 a gentleman, John Willoughby of Leyhill, Payhembury in Devon, who had been staying with his 'cousins', the Steyning family at Holnicote since Easter, took a passage with two of his cousins from Minehead to Aberthaw and returned about four weeks later.[349] Aberthaw merchants commonly traded with Minehead, so there were strong links between the two settlements. However, the only activities that Willoughby is known to have undertaken whilst there was to give charitably to a number of poor people and to loose at a game of bowls! Willoughby was 75 at the time of this journey and became ill afterwards, possibly because of the strain of the sea crossing, or from the stress of trying to be slightly ambiguous in his political position during the Civil War in order to preserve his estates intact whatever the outcome.[350] Equally ambiguous are the reasons why, in about 1649, a Minehead family named Gyles settled in Youghal,[351] and why a poor man with a pass signed by Cromwell, the Lord Protector (who was given charity by the Minehead churchwardens as he awaited a passage to Ireland in September 1657) wished to leave England.[352]

A letter written in 1659 by Lady Ranelagh to Lord

Cork includes details of a traumatic voyage she made from Youghal to King Road in the *Dartmouth* that year. The passage had been going well but soon after the ship passed Minehead the pilot misjudged the tides and the ship violently struck Culver Sand, which scattered everyone in the cabin. The party commended themselves to God, expecting that at any moment they would be swept away by the waves. However, Lord 'Broghill's never failing courage and presence of mind saved their lives'; despite narrowly missing having his 'brains beaten out' by the beam of the detached rudder when he went on deck. Apparently he calmed the terrified crew, forced them to take down sail and then mend the rudder. The rest of the journey was completed in safety.[353]

The Trevelyans of Nettlecombe also had interests in Ireland but a nephew of the George Trevelyan, grandson of John Trevelyan (mentioned above), gave no indication of his purpose for his travel when wrote to his uncle from Cork in June 1663, lamenting the problem of ship availability.

> At my arrivall to Mynhead I found that the Corke ships were all gone so I was forced to imbarque myself in a small vessel bound for Kinsale wherein we had a long and tedious passage being eight dayes before we could get to our port.[354]

The party were more fortunate than the crew and a female passenger in the *Charles* of Watchet, who in December 1677 set sail for home from Swansea laden with coal. Sadly the ship sank in a storm and 'The men all saved themselves with some difficulty in the boat' but the woman passenger drowned. This event presumably occurred near the Welsh coast as the report was written from Swansea.[355] Other deaths in transit past Minehead, to Minehead, or awaiting a passage in Minehead for Ireland, during the 1670s and 1680s inevitably occurred. For example, Mrs Aletheia Brough in transit up the Bristol Channel from Ireland (in a Bristol vessel), passed away and was buried in the churchyard in July 1670, as was gentleman stranger C. Osborne in 1682, who died before embarking for Ireland.[356] A further journey involving Watchet which ended in tragic circumstances occurred in 1822, when Captain Gill, his wife and two sisters, together with a servant boy and two boatmen were sailing from Watchet to Cardiff. Near the Holms the boat capsized and all were drowned.[357]

In August 1681, Richard Pearce of Limerick made his will in Minehead before embarking for Ireland.[358] Whether this was a common practise, given

the likelihood of a maritime accident, is not clear. Two years later, in August 1683, two Quaker sisters (daughters of Quaker Thomas Hurd of Somerton) embarked in King Road for a journey, with other Quakers, to Pennsylvania. On their journey from Somerton to the ship they were accompanied by their sister, Sarah whose suitor, John Whiting, obtained permission to propose marriage to her whilst she was absent accompanying her sisters. John then rode after the girls, visited his friends on the ship in King Road and said his farewells to them with Sarah. He then accompanied his sweetheart home, proposing to her on the way.[359] Though the motive for the sisters' journey with the other Quakers is unknown, it is not unlikely that most were to start a new life in William Penn's colony, responding to a desire to avoid Quaker persecution in England. The vessel that the Quaker sisters sailed in may well have been the *Comfort*, John Reed master, which according to Thomas Pearson, who was a passenger on the vessel, departed King Road on 25 September 1683 and arrived at Upland, Pennsylvania on 28 November.[360]

On 8 June 1687, Captain Henry Boyle wrote that he was waiting at Minehead with Lady Inchiquin for a passage to Ireland. Their ship was ready but had already been waiting for three days because the wind blew strongly from the west. He was still waiting on 14 June since the weather remained very stormy. Word was that the storms would abate the next day 'with a change in the moon' and as there were no reports of 'Argerines' (Algerians) in the Channel, he was hoping for a safe passage. Whilst waiting at Minehead he learned that local merchants were very keen for a re-commencement of the trade in black Irish cattle and sheep, which had been considerable in the 1660s and 1670s. He also noted that several merchants and their families were arriving at Minehead from Cork and Youghal, naming Roger Newenham and Simon Dring from Cork, as well as Ball and Yeates from Youghal, but gave no reason for the small exodus. Intelligence from these merchants was that others would follow.[361]

Further journeys with no known motive remain from the eighteenth century, which provide information on the experience of travel. In 1752 Rev. Murray and his 11 year old son, John, travelled from Pill to Cork. The journey very nearly ended in disaster before it started when the unsupervised lad entered a small boat at Pill and untied it. The flood tide quickly dragged the boat upstream along the Avon, apparently without any adult witnessing what had happened. When the situation was realised, search parties were sent out but failed to find the boy and boat before nightfall as they were all looking too far upstream. Unknown to the searchers, John had managed to tie his boat to another anchored in the river. He was eventually found, extremely afraid, at about midnight and his father, so relieved that he was not drowned, did not severely reprimand him.[362] The situation could have been much worse. If the tide had been falling young Murray would have been drawn out into the Bristol Channel.

Sailing from King Road to Cork and then on to Jamaica, in September 1774, was the *Elizabeth* with Captain Weeks as master. The wind changed in the Channel early in its journey and the vessel headed back, but was too close to the Welsh shore and struck a rock near 'St Dunnels' (presumably St Donats). Only 11 of the 37 crew and passengers survived. Two of the drowned passengers were Captain Sackville Turner of the 33rd Regiment and his wife, who were subsequently buried in each other's arms.[363] A further journey from King Road which was full of fear was made by the American, Mathias Aspden, in September 1798. He embarked on the *Thomas* in King Road, Captain Luscomb as master, on a passage to Charleston. He waited on board between 15 and 22 September, but the vessel took on so much water at the anchorage, and more on the five day journey to Cork, that Aspden disembarked before the Atlantic crossing and made his way back to London.[364] A more peaceful journey took place in 1792, when Lord Stavordale travelled from Cork to Minehead with his wife and children. Presumably, it was quite a calm crossing, because they dined on deck during the passage but the lady was very seasick and they sang songs in the gunroom.[365]

In September 1807 Joshua Stephenson, rector of Selworthy, boarded the *Harriet*, a brig belonging to Mr Fortescue, at Bossington Beach for a passage to Barry Island, the first leg of a trip to Herefordshire.[366] Undoubtedly the *Harriet* would have anchored off Bossington Beach near the lime kilns and a boat would have been sent ashore to pick up Stephenson. Two years later, on 1 June 1809, Mary Sharples and her husband set off from King Road for New York in the brig *Nancy*. There were two vessels in King Road preparing for the Atlantic crossing but the *Nancy* was chosen because she had been 'pronounced well built and perfectly safe and the captain very skilful and of an excellent character'. Prior to the arrival in New York on 20 July, and the port physician arriving on board to undertake a health check before authorising disembarkation, the Sharples had befriended the captain, Wilson Barstow, and spoke warmly of him throughout their lives.[367]

Another Atlantic crossing commenced at Bridgwater in March 1831, when the 400 ton barque, *Euphrosyne* made the crossing to Quebec, Canada in a month of plain sailing. This appears to have been the only sailing to Canada from Bridgwater between 1817 and 1830, so this was possibly a unique event from the Somerset coast. Aboard were at least 40 people from Wiltshire, but there were many more aboard, given the records of how many people were sent to different locations upon arrival in Canada. Included amongst the others were at least one Somerset family, as an infant who had resided near Bridgwater died in transit.[368]

Finally, on 15 March 1827 the sloop, *Thomas* of Bristol, Daniel Bird being the master, was proceeding from Newport to Bridgwater with coal in poor weather and became trapped on Culver Sands. At the next high tide the people of Burnham witnessed huge waves crashing over the trapped sloop until it broke up with the loss of all life. On board were three passengers. Two un-named people were apparently on a journey to Exeter and the third was Mr H. Crossman who kept the Fountain Inn at Taunton, who left a wife and seven children, with the eighth expected. The family were supported by public subscription after the tragedy.[369]

The effect of wind and tide on the passage

Even though this chapter covers 400 years during which time the technology of sailing vessels improved, and the age of square rigged smaller ships came to an end, there appears to be no apparent trend from the available accounts regarding the speed of passage along or across the Bristol Channel. The state of the wind, tidal streams and tide times were the primary influences on all voyages until the age of steam. The state of navigator's knowledge and competence, along with the seaworthiness of the vessels, is rarely recorded. All these factors need to be taken into consideration when judging the relative speed of the passages.

The passage from west Somerset to Wales seems often to have been completed within one day, such as those by John Willoughby passing between Minehead and Aberthaw in July 1645[370] and Colonel Strangways crossing from Minehead to Swansea in 1803.[371] John Wesley's two crossings to a beach near Cardiff from Minehead, in April 1744 and July 1745, both took place in the morning and are recorded to have taken about four hours,[372] but the passage by French travellers between Minehead and Aberthaw in 1813 took only three hours.[373] Some longer passages from Wales were weather affected, including a 24 hour journey, from Glamorgan to Minehead in 1799, by Anna Barbauld.[374] The passage of Richard Fenton, from Milford Haven to Minehead in 1807, which may well have been completed in one day had it not been for becalming; this meant that the bulk of the distance was travelled overnight and also took about 24 hours.[375] Therefore, it is likely that the vast majority of crossings to Wales were made in daylight whenever possible.

One desired passage which did not take place because of high winds, occurred in 1791 when a gentlewoman traveller from Tenby wished to sail to Minehead leaving her husband and daughters behind. The sloop that she wished to travel in was at anchor in Tenby Roads, so the family hired an open rowing boat to take them out to the vessel, where they became soaked to the skin but seemed to enjoy the experience. On arrival at the sloop, which was waiting for a fair wind for Minehead, the mariners on board refused to take the gentlewoman as a passenger, possibly because they considered it too risky to take her aboard in the windy conditions, but also because the captain did not know how long he would have to wait for a favourable wind. It took two hours for the family to be rowed back to shore and the gentlewoman did not make the passage to Minehead on that day.[376]

There appears to have been significant differences in the time taken to sail along the Channel between Bristol and Minehead, and further out to sea from Minehead to Ireland, or from Bristol to Ireland. A passage between Minehead and King Road of 19 hours took place in July 1635, when Brereton servants were sent on ahead of their master.[377] However, a most celebrated and speedy passage between Waterford and King Road was experienced by King William the Third in 1690, when the journey was completed in 27 hours; the brevity of this journey was, no doubt, welcome, but it was not entirely exceptional.[378] Another 'fair passage', between Bristol and Youghal, took place when the Earl of Desmond took 'two days and a night at sea' in the middle of October 1600, a speed which the mariners had never known before for the time of year.[379]

Also brief was the journey of Richard Boyle (first Earl of Cork), from Cork to Bristol in November 1601, when he disembarked at two o'clock in the morning and arrived in Bristol within 24 hours.[380] Perhaps even shorter was the Duke of Ormond's passage, travelling between Minehead and Waterford in June 1674, who stated the passage had been 'safe and quick' and that it took less than 24 hours.[381] In the reverse direction against the prevailing wind, Brereton took just over 24 hours to reach Minehead from Waterford in July 1635, since he described the passage as 'pleasant and dainty'.[382] The same journey took about 48 hours in 1777, when the sea-sick Catherine Phillips sailed the same route between the 12th and 14th of September, despite the sea being very rough near Minehead and the wind turning against them in the final hours.[383] The Cork family's journey from Youghal to Minehead, including a chase by privateers in 1628, may have taken about 48 hours, commencing on 7 May, but their journey in the reverse direction in 1641 took three days in October.[384] In 1681, Dineley commented that the passage from Youghal to Minehead should take about 40 hours with a fair wind, a good vessel and a responsible crew.[385] A passage with a known speed over the water, that of 6 knots, took place in 1821 when George Rapelje sailed from Cork to Pill in two days.[386] Viscount Lisle, travelling from Bristol to Cork in 1646, departed from Bristol on Wednesday 17 February, left Minehead for Cork on Friday the 19th and arrived in Cork on Sunday the 21st, a journey of three or four days with the passage between Minehead and southern Ireland again taking about 48 hours.[387] The Dean of Cork's journey from Cork to Minehead in March 1689 took three days, but the ship had gained Porlock Bay by the end of the second day.[388] The Dean could have been put ashore at Porlock and have ridden to Minehead in an hour or so, but instead spent the night of 10 March at anchor in Porlock Bay, presumably waiting for the next flood tide to take them the last few miles into Minehead. Lisle's return journey from Cork to Minehead in 1647 through an April storm took four days.[389] Newly wedded John and Hannah Hayman departed Minehead on the *Thomas*, on 18 June 1687 bound for Youghal. However, the vessel put back into Minehead two days later, where it had to wait for a further two days until the wind blew from the South-East which enabled it to depart again.[390]

In 1675, John Gailhard wrote a detailed account of a three day passage (from 6 to 9 June) between Pill and Cork, highlighting the effects of wind on the journey.

> We went aboard at Pill at 10 or 11 o'clock and had but an indifferent gale of N.N.E. wind and came near the height of Minehead, but the wind turning somewhat to the west the master of the ship though fit to go back towards Sully in Glamorganshire, where we landed and lay ashore

Illustration 1.46: View of Pill, in the parish of Easton in Gordano by W.W. Wheatley, 1843. (SANHS)

that night. All Friday we had a good sailing with a N.E., but on Saturday, being come to St George's Channel, we found the sea high and rough, it being usual there so to be by the reason of two tides meeting thereabouts, and the wind was good, but somewhat too high, and the vessel making a leak, the master thought of running to St Ives, but wind and sea growing more calm, we sailed directly for Cork, and by Saturday by noon we landed at Cove and went that night to lay at Cork.[391]

Other passages from Pill to Cork which took several days, include that of Thomas Shillitoe in 1811 because of adverse winds and a becalming,[392] as well as Thomas Story's, from King Road to Cork in 1716, that took eight days, including a stay in Minehead because of contrary winds.[393] Furthermore, Deborah Bell's passage took six days in 1720 because the vessel became becalmed on the way,[394] and a tedious passage of ten days, in 1737, due to unfavourable winds, occurred when James Gough made the same journey.[395] Hopper's journey from Dublin to Pill in July 1750 took about 48 hours;[396] whereas Moore's passage from Dublin to Pill in September 1794 took three days and nights.[397]

In the seventeenth century other journeys between Bristol and Ireland, or Minehead and Ireland, lasted weeks: Robert Boyle remembered that in 1635 he had to wait in Youghal for a week for a fair wind and then was beaten back by a storm;[398] a London factor travelling between Minehead and

Youghal in March 1636 was delayed 16 days in Minehead waiting for a fair wind;[399] in 1644 Le Gouz's journey was delayed two or three days by adverse winds, before his drunken captain finally took to the Channel from Minehead;[400] and George Trevelyan's nephew had a tedious eight day journey between Minehead and Cork in 1663.[401] Ten years later, passengers waiting wind bound in Pill for Ireland were in such distress that, on 13 October 1673, some Bristol Quakers, in an act of Christian charity, rode down from the city with £5 to help relieve them.[402] About a century later, wind bound travellers at Pill were hounded out of their lodgings and 'sent away half naked after they had spent their ready money [being] obliged to strip themselves of their clothes … to keep them[selves] from starving'.[403] In 1687 Henry Boyle waited at Minehead for at least ten days for the wind to turn.[404] In 1788 Mary Dudley's vessel put to sea from Waterford on the way to Minehead, but after several hours making no headway the captain put back into port where they spent a further night.[405]

The absence of a fair wind caused extremely lengthy journeys in the eighteenth and nineteenth centuries. For example, in 1708 Samuel Bonas made the trip between Waterford to Minehead in about 48 hours, but not before he had been delayed in Cork for about three weeks waiting for a favourable wind. When he finally set forth with a fair wind it turned against them as soon as they had left Cork harbour. However, rather than turn back the captain just made it into Waterford where they waited for the next helpful wind.[406] A journey of similar length, but from Bristol to Cork, took place in 1823 after Briscoe boarded a ship in Bristol on 13 December. He was detained for eighteen days at Minehead and subsequently at Milford Haven and stated that when a vessel was obliged to put into harbour, on account of bad weather, the passengers were forced to find board and lodging at their own expense.[407]

A long and most infuriating passage of six weeks between Pill and Cork was experienced by S.C. Hall in 1815,[408] but this is eclipsed by the journeys of Benjamin Vaughan in 1738 and the fortunate John Murray, who was nearly lost in the Avon near Pill in 1752. Vaughan was on a passage from Pill to Waterford in September 1738. He stated:

> After being at Pill 10 dayes afterwards putt into Minehead, then into Comb (Ilfracombe) left that and lay under Lundy one night and putt back again to Comb, was in all about seven weeks comeinge over.[409]

Murray was detained for a total of three weeks at Pill, at Minehead and at Milford Haven. He noted how it took

> nine weeks in performing a passage, which is commonly made in 48 hours, and instead of my

Illustration 1.47: John Murray (1741-1815), who as an 11 year old boy in 1752, became lost in a boat on the River Avon at Pill and then suffered a tedious journey with his father to onwards to Cork via Minehead. (J. Murray, *The life of Rev. John Murray* (Boston, 1870))

father reaching Cork before the residue of his family they were there almost at the moment of our arrival.[410]

This evidence supports a generic piece of writing from the mid-nineteenth century regarding Ireland. The author first described the poor living conditions aboard and then stated that the journey commonly could be over in three days, but then went on to state:

> It was once our lot to pass a month between the ports of Bristol and Cork; putting back every now and again to the wretched village of Pill, and not daring to leave it even for an hour, lest the wind should change and the packet weigh anchor. But our case was far less dismal than that of an officer whose two months leave of absence had expired the very day he reached his Irish home.[411]

Perhaps the often protracted journey between Bristol and Ireland was the reason why readers of the *New Bath Guide*, in 1789, were advised to travel to Milford Haven and catch the weekly packet to Waterford, even though this meant crossing the Severn and a long land journey to Pembrokeshire of about 140 miles.[412] Not being able to sail to Ireland from Bristol at all must have been a welcome relief, rather than an inconvenience, for Elizabethan troops in 1595 who were sent home by direct order of the Queen.[413] They had endured a 'nail-bighting' wait for transport but at least they did not die of illness or battle wounds in Munster that year.

Waiting at King Road for a fair wind must also have been an experience that many passengers endured. Richard Mather and his family lived through this frustrating experience in 1635 on the way to the New World. His memoir includes a clear account from the time of boarding the *James* in King Road up until setting sail. On 23 May, when they boarded, there were many disorderly heaps of goods lying on the deck that had not been properly stowed. The following day strong winds in the morning made the ship 'dance' at anchor and many women and children became 'mazy', light headed and seasick. On 25 May they witnessed the *Diligence* of Bristol set sail and move out of sight, so there was anxiety on board regarding any delay, but the mariners still had work to do stowing goods. During the wait for wind, passengers from the *James* and the *Angel Gabriel* visited each other's ships and made friends. Mather wrote in his journal:

> 26 May. The wind being easterly and the decks

being somewhat cleared the mariners began to address themselves for going. At nine o'clock they had taken up one of the anchers but the wind turned against us unto the west, and we were forced to cast ancre again and sit still. This evening the *Diligence* came in again and cast ancre about the same place as she lay before.

27 May. The wind continued at the west, we having sent some of our men a shoar to fech more bread and victuals and more water for the cattel.[414]

4 June. The wind serving for us and the master and all the sailors having come aboard, wee set sayle and began our sea voyage with glad hearts that God had loosed us from our long stay wherin we had been holden.

At this point another vessel weighing anchor was taken by the tide past the *James* and all aboard were afraid of a collision, which was marginally avoided. They managed to sail about twelve leagues before mid-day but then the wind changed to a westerly and the tide went against them, so they were forced to anchor somewhere between Somerset and Wales and wait for the next high tide. Mather wrote:

5 June. The *James* anchored within two leagues of Lundy. This day many passengers were sea-sicke;

Illustration 1.48: Richard Mather (1596-1669) experienced a frustrating wait for a fair wind in King Road in 1635. (Woodcut by John Foster, *c.*1670)

and ill at ease through much vomiting. This day, when the tide turned wee set sail again and so came to ancre under Lundy. Where abiding because the wind was strong against us.

Whilst sheltering under Lundy the master and some of the passengers went for a walk on the island where they found one house, 30 or 40 cattle, 16 or 20 horses, goats, swine, geese and fowl and innumerable rabbits, recording:

Here wee got some milk and fowl and cheese, which things my children were glad of, and so came aboard againe; but the wind being strong against us, especially before night, and the next day, and many of our passengers this evening were very sicke.

The vessel then made Milford Haven and crossed the Atlantic, sighting the Americas on 8 August. Storms were then endured but none of the 100 passengers, 23 crew, 23 cows and heifers, three calves and eight mares lost their lives in the transit.[415]

About a hundred and eighty years later, in 1812, the practise of 'tiding' down the Bristol Channel was described by Mr Godwin, an admirer of Shelley; when winds were very light vessels used the six knot ebb tide to drag them west and then anchor during the flood tide so as not to be taken back east again. The Shelleys had been staying in Lynton, North Devon and Godwin endeavoured to join them. He left Bristol at one o'clock on a Wednesday and arrived off Lynmouth at four o'clock on a Friday, the passage therefore taking 51 hours. On board were 14 passengers and only four births, so he only lay down for a few hours during the whole trip. There was very little wind so the vessel tided down the Channel for six hours and then anchored. The first tide took them to within sight of the Holm islands and the next tide took them off Minehead. There was a threat of bad weather so the captain took them to Penarth. The weather cleared, so they continued to Lynmouth where Godwin was landed by the captain's boat.[416] Whilst other people had sailed this particular route in the past, the journey for one passenger from Bristol to Lynmouth is likely to have been unusual; this must have been concerned with pleasure and taking in the view, rather than making the shortest possible journey.

Not arriving at the designated port of destination because of contrary winds, or storms, was also a common experience. At times, goods in transit would necessarily take longer to arrive at their destination

Illustration 1.49: The harbour at Tenby in 1740, with Caldey Island in the background, by Samuel and Nathanial Buck. It was to here that the Hollingworth family were sent from Bridgwater in 1741, and from here that the gentlewoman failed to be put aboard a Minehead-bound vessel anchored in the bay in 1791 due to rough weather. It was also here that a troupe of players arrived from Bridgwater in the early nineteenth century. (Philip Ashford)

than passengers, mainly because it was difficult to move bulk cargos by road. In a way, depending on the circumstances, once the Irish Sea had been crossed it might have been quicker to travel overland to the final destination whilst the ship lay wind-bound in port. Examples of passengers not reaching their intended destination are numerous: Edmund Ludlow disembarked at Ilfracombe instead of Minehead in 1660;[417] Greatracks, who arrived at Minehead and not Bristol in 1666;[418] Dyott arrived at Milford Haven, not Minehead, on Christmas Day 1786[419] and the un-named travellers who tried to reach Cardiff from Minehead in 1813, but had to be content with making Aberthaw,[420] to name but a few.

Storms in other parts of the world could affect

Illustration 1.50: King Road viewed from the entrance to the Bristol Avon by Thomas Harral, 1824. (Shropshire Archives)

the course of ships looking for re-supply and repair; a Dutch ship, the *Elizabeth* of Flushing, on her way back to Holland, which limped into King Road in December 1651 having been caught in a storm in the West Indies; two shipwrecked French sailors from the West Indies, who had been rescued by the *Elizabeth*, disembarked once the ship anchored in the Road.[421] More inconveniently, contrary winds could blow vessels completely off course. Troops sailing from Milford to Ireland in 1652 were driven back into the Bristol Channel when their vessel needed to take shelter in Minehead, and be re-provisioned, before the journey was completed.[422] In addition, another inconvenient and life-threatening journey took place in February 1669 when two vessels, the *Thomas* and the *John Francis*, plying between Minehead and Cork, were blown by storms south into the Bay of Biscay. After their provisions ran out the crew and passengers alike were close to starvation. The crew of a French vessel declined to help them but crew from a Dutch vessel gave them water, wine and a stone of bread, thus, they had enough strength to make it back to Ireland.[423] Ten years later, in 1679, the *St Saviour*, sailing between Lisbon to Le Havre and Rouen was blown into the Bristol Channel and arrived at Minehead. She had been at sea for six weeks and there was such a scarcity of food on board that two French passengers, Monsieur Contess and Bignion, were but ashore for eight days at an alehouse to recover before re-embarking and resuming their passage. It is only to be imagined what state of starvation they were in.[424] Much later in 1759 a ship bound from the West Indies for Ireland was blown into Minehead by contrary winds, with many passengers including one surnamed 'Hickey'. In Minehead he found Fredrick Caulfield, a distressed Irish seaman whom he clothed and fed, and then the pair returned to Ireland together landing at Waterford. It appears that once they had landed, greed motivated Caulfield to murder, as he was later tried and convicted of killing Hickey and hanged in August 1759.[425]

The strong tides of the upper Bristol Channel/Seven estuary made ferry crossings hazardous on occasions. Some time before 1770, a small group of people were being towed behind a cattle filled ferry across the Severn, from the Chepstow area towards Aust in Gloucestershire. An incident caused the cattle to panic and the ferry to take on water and sink. The towed vessel was detached by its occupants just in time before being dragged under, but then was swept by the tide to King Road, where it eventually made the Somerset

shore and the people were saved.[426]

The plethora of records on journey and crossing times for passages in the Bristol Channel from the seventeenth century onwards is the stimulus for the following table which summarises the findings. The more tentative suggestions are indicated with a question mark. A further conclusion regarding passage times relates to the prevailing wind. The predominant westerly and south westerly winds affecting the Somerset coast, meant that the probability of long delays leaving King Road to sail west through the Bristol Channel was higher than the probability of delay trying to reach Minehead, or King Road, whilst sailing east. Of the accounts here, there are at least twice the number relating to significant delays for vessels trying to sail west, rather than sail east, along the Somerset coast.

Table 1.2: Examples of sailing times in the Bristol Channel, 1600-1820

Route	Shortest time	Common time	Occasional time	Extreme time
Minehead to Glamorganshire or reverse	3 hours	4 hours	24 hours	36-48 hours?
Minehead to King Road/Pill or reverse	Lack of evidence precludes a comment	8 hours?	20 hours	Lack of evidence precludes a comment
Minehead to Waterford or reverse	24 hours	48 hours	10 days	Several weeks
Minehead to Youghal/Cork or reverse	24 hours	48 hours	10 days	Several weeks
King Road/Pill to Waterford or reverse	24 hours	48 hours	Several weeks	Over two months
King road/Pill to Youghal/Cork or reverse	24 hours	48 hours	Several weeks	Over two months

Costs involved in the transits

A fifteenth-century record of a transit charge remains from 1497, when a Government official rode to Minehead (from London?) and then took a passage to Dublin. The total expenses were 13 shillings and 4 pence, but this does not differentiate between hire of a horse, accommodation and passage charges.[427] Abandoned Spanish sailors, left on the island of Lundy by pirates, were presumably given a free passage when they were rescued and taken to Bridgwater in 1534.[428] The Bristol indentured servants of the seventeenth century had their board, lodging and transfer costs to Virginia, or Barbados, paid for them as part of the contract of their period of servitude. The Monmouth rebels also received a 'free passage' to their servitude in Barbados, although given the choice between the gallows or 'slavery' in the West Indies many would have chosen the latter.

Brereton recorded in 1635 that it cost him £2 17s 4d to transport two horses from Waterford to Minehead, including customs duty, with the fare for a person between Minehead and King Road costing 1 shilling.[429] In August 1644, Willoughby was charged 8d for 'diet and horsemeat at Minehead' after he arrived from Holnicote. He stated that 'our passage to Wales' cost 16d, when there may have been three or four people in the party, including two of Willoughby's cousins; their 'diet' in Aberthaw cost 20d and a further 18d was given to 'Mr Spencer and his men' for the passage back to Minehead a few days later. Dinner at Minehead cost 14d and he gave 1s to Nedd Stoare for carrying his cloak-bag back to Holnicote.[430]

On a completely different scale, the charge per person for the 145 distressed people travelling the passage between Kinsale and Minehead in 1642 was only 3s 6d.[431] What is not clear from the source, since the transit was protecting people from what would today be called 'ethnic cleansing', is whether the individuals paid their own transit costs or whether the Navy, Parliament or even Lord Boyle footed the bill.

The aristocracy tended to hire whole ships when travelling. For example, Lord Boyle himself was charged £22 for the transport of his august party from Minehead to Youghal in one vessel in 1641; this did not include the cost of transporting the grooms and horses in a following vessel.[432] Furthermore, a passage from Ireland to Minehead in September 1668 cost Elizabeth, wife of the Duke of Ormond, £65. The price was regarded as a good bargain for the hire of two ships to carry her and her 'equipages' back to England.[433] In this case 'equipages' is likely to have meant baggage, at least one carriage, footman and other attendants. The journey came at the end of the period of her husband's first term as Lord Lieutenant of Ireland, and a year after the end of the Second Dutch War, so the seas were relatively safe for the journey and no naval presence would have been required. Elizabeth stated in a letter to her brother, written on 12 September 1668, that the vessel carrying her coach and horses arrived in Minehead two days later than she had done.[434] The horses were then given a day to recover before being harnessed for the onward journey, so the Lady had a

Illustration 1.51: An advertisement for The Plume of Feathers Hotel in Minehead and the hotel at Blue Anchor which was under the same management. (*Kelly's Directory of Somerset,* 1894)

three day delay in her journey waiting at Minehead.

In 1674, 22 shillings were given by various Quaker Friends for the passage of David Sweet from Glastonbury to Ireland; quite a substantial amount, notwithstanding land travel and accommodation awaiting a passage, possibly from Minehead.[435] This compares with the fact that in 1681, Thomas Dineley, who had been touring Ireland, stated that the passage between Youghal and Minehead was 5s per head, with the use of a cabin being extra.[436] A sliding scale existed for the transportation of horses on the same route, with six horses costing 10s for each horse, four horses 12s and three horses 15s per horse; entry for horses at the Minehead custom house was 2s 6d per horse. The horse transit charges are less than Brereton paid between Waterford and Minehead in 1635 but the customs charge had risen.[437] In the 1740s, Joan Laffan, a servant, paid a 'crown' (*i.e.* five shillings), for her passage from Dublin to Bristol.[438]

An advertisement appeared in Felix Farley's *Bristol Journal* on Saturday 21 June 1788 advertising passages for Swansea and Minehead from Bristol in the *Princess Royal* yacht, Captain John Dickens being the master. The passage was between Lamplighter's Hall, Shirehampton and Swansea, twice a week in each direction. In the advertisement the qualities of the fast-sailing yacht were extolled and the tariff of 10s 6d for cabin passengers and 3s 6d for 'others' stated. Twenty pounds of luggage was allowed free of charge but ½d per pound charge was exacted for excess weight. The passage was clearly via Minehead, but whether such passengers paid less for their passage is not made clear. Minehead travelers could secure their passage by applying at the Plume of Feathers Hotel in Minehead, a business that remained an important Hotel in Minehead well into the twentieth century.

In the early nineteenth century, at Minehead, Colonel Strangways paid 3s for men to carry luggage to a vessel in which he and his nephew were to sail to Swansea, 3 guineas to the captain for the passage, 2s 6d to the men towing the vessel out of the harbour and, once at Swansea, 3s to the men who carried the luggage to an Inn.[439] Whilst the extent of this information is very scant, it does give a little insight into the process of making a passage and the number of different casual workers around the quays that helped travellers and were rewarded, presumably through fees and tips, for their labour. Also, in 1804, the Army was charged £3 3s for the passage of commissioned officers from Dublin to Minehead. The tariff the Army had allowed for the passage of ordinary soldiers on the same route was 6s 6d, but

maybe because of profiteering in wartime, the captain of the vessel in Dublin would not allow soldiers aboard until 10s 6d had been paid for each man.[440]

Conclusion

This chapter has revealed that Minehead and Pill were Somerset's main passenger ports during the period of study, with King Road being a point of departure for larger transatlantic vessels, or naval vessels with no time to sail up the Avon. In terms of the motivation for travel, the political, economic and Christian church developments occurring in Munster, southern Ireland, appear to be the substantial recorded reasons for the passage to and from Minehead. The same considerations both in Munster and on the north-east coast of America seem to have been the main motivations for sea journeys from Pill. Apart from the sailors of different countries mingling in the port towns of Minehead and Pill, the trickle, and sometimes flood, of passengers from other countries must have given these little port towns something of a cosmopolitan flavour. The impact of both Pill and Minehead on the political, as well as economic, development of Munster must not be underestimated, given the number of troops, Government agents and political leaders who passed through the ports for their duties in Ireland.

However, assessing and quantifying the reasons for what must be the great majority of unrecorded passages is clearly impossible, especially across the Channel between Somerset and Wales. These relatively short, quick, and inexpensive passages were so unremarkable that few people left records, in comparison to the many left by people making more significant journeys through the Bristol Channel from west to east, or vice-versa. It can only be tentatively suggested that the majority of cross-Channel passages to and from all the ports, minor creeks and beaches, along the Somerset coast would have been for economic and family reasons. In terms of routes used by the rich as opposed to the poor, it is clear that people of all socio-economic groups used the same routes, and if there was a trans-Atlantic voyage, they would also have used the same ship. However, with regard to travel to and from Ireland, whilst the aristocracy commonly hired whole vessels, presumably the best available, or were transported in naval vessels, the poor used whatever vessels were available at the time. This could mean the poor traveller or soldier being embarked onto coal or cattle boats, or other merchant vessels, especially in the sixteenth and seventeenth centuries, but by the

(Above) Illustration 1.52: A trading brig entering the Bristol Avon in 1838 by Joseph Walter. The beacon, if it is not artist's licence is likely to have been at Battery Point at Portishead. Many Somerset travellers would have arrived at Pill in vessels such as this. (National Maritime Museum, BHC1195)

(Below) Illustration 1.53: The end of the age of sail on the Somerset coast by Joseph Walter, 1835. A steam vessel accompanies various sailing craft as they hurry past Battery Point into King Road on a rising tide before a storm. The fields next to the bay are now the playgrounds and a cricket pitch at Portishead. (Bristol Museum and Art Gallery)

eighteenth centuries the Irish packet service would have taken proportionally more of the travellers.

Delay and seasickness were negative experiences which could strike the sea traveller throughout the period studied to a greater extent than today, because of the delays in waiting for wind and longer journeys sometimes taking place in quite small vessels. Advances in understanding and technology, between 1435 and 1835, may have marginally improved the experience of travel on the routes discussed, although the significant numbers of accounts examined derive from a minute sample of the thousands of vessels which sailed in the Bristol Channel. Seventeenth-century travellers probably had greater rational fears from the activities of pirates and other problems caused by political difficulties of the century, compared to the eighteenth and early nineteenth-century traveller. However, in the hearts and minds of most travellers in the pre-steam era there must have been a greater fear of drowning than most passengers have today, given the fact that few people could swim, the lack of rescue services, the frequency of wrecks (especially during the winter months) and the lack of legislation concerning the seaworthiness of vessels, or the sobriety of the captain, pilots or others in charge.

The age of maritime steam first benefited the Bristol Channel traveller in reducing the impact of contrary winds and, as it developed, proportionally less people would have been delayed. The first steam packet to operate in the Bristol Channel did so from 1823 between Swansea and Bristol.[441] Cross-channel links with Somerset began soon afterwards with a steam packet excursion from Newport to Cardiff, then crossing to Porlock which took place in the summer of 1826.[442] Then, when the steam railways connected up and passengers from London or Bristol could reach Pembroke Dock and Fishguard, the need to use Minehead as an embarkation point for Ireland disappeared. The Great Western Railway began operating its own steam services from Fishguard to Waterford in 1872.[443] No doubt, however, a few fare-paying passengers used sailing vessels to move around the Channel, certainly until commercial sailing ended in the Bristol Channel soon after the end of the Second World War.

Fictional relations of passages in the Bristol Channel also exist. In chapter eight of the 1680 version of the very influential novel, *The English Rogue* (first published in 1666), the hero escapes jail in Bristol by impersonation of someone who was to be collected by a Bristol merchant for service in Virginia. He is placed on a boat and taken down the Avon to

the vessel in King Road in which he is to travel. Whilst half of the crew were sleeping off drink, and the other half were in Pill getting drunk, he escaped with two others in a cockboat and rowed to Portishead, where they walked to Devon via Minehead.[444] Also, an eighteenth-century piece of fiction exists entitled, *T. Ginnadrake* purporting to be the true experiences of Mr Ginnadrake in the late seventeenth century. An early chapter has the hero embarking on an Irish packet at Bristol and being wind bound at Pill with the rest of the passengers (including soldiers) for several days. On departure the passengers had to put up with the captain's agenda, which did not prioritise the needs of the passengers, as there was a person on board with a lady friend at Minehead. They struck shoals near Minehead, abandoned ship and Ginnadrake witnessed some of the soldiers drowning.[445] He recorded that the drowned soldiers were buried in a west Somerset parish and, of course, each and every fictional event detailed could well have been 'true', as the reading of this chapter has shown. However, this chapter shows that in relation to the actual (recorded) experience of the sea passage in the Bristol Channel involving the Somerset coast, truth may not have been' stranger than fiction'. The facts as they have been recorded and related in the chapter have, in many cases, been at least as dramatic as fiction.

Appendix 1.1: Members of Minehead merchant families who had sailed from Minehead to Ireland and went on to hold significant positions in the government of Youghal

Year	Bailiff	Constable of the Staple	Mayor of the Corporation	Mayor of the Staple
1666	Samuel Hayman			
1667		Samuel Hayman		
1670			Samuel Hayman	
1671				Samuel Hayman
1674	John Atkin			
1675			John Atkin	
1676				John Atkin
1677	Edward Crockford			
1678		Edward Crockford		
1683			Edward Crockford	

Source: J. Ohlemeyer and E. O'Ciardha (eds), *The Irish statute staple books 1596-1687* (Dublin, 1998), 313-15, 342-44; R. Caulfield, *The council book of the corporation of Youghal 1610-1659* (Guildford, 1878), 208, 312.

Appendix 1.2: The family of Edward Byam of Luccombe, Dulverton and Castle Lyon, Ireland 1574-1644 and their reasons for travel in the Bristol Channel

A relation of some of the history of this family in the first half of the seventeenth century illustrates several reasons for travel in the Bristol Channel at the time, as well as the underlying links that West Somerset had with southern Ireland. Furthermore, it illustrates something of the trauma that families lived through during the Civil War and the Irish Rebellion of 1641. Lawrence Byam became vicar of Luccombe in 1574/5. He and his wife Agnes had six children, including Henry, the eldest, who followed his father and became Luccombe's vicar in 1615. The third son, Edward, was born in Luccombe in 1584 and studied at Oxford from 1600. In 1612, he became vicar of Dulverton and then married Elizabeth Eaglesfield at Walton, near Street, soon afterwards; they had six sons and five daughters, some in Dulverton and others in Ireland after they moved there in 1625. John Byam, Edward's brother, who was rector of Clatworthy, succeeded Edward as vicar of Dulverton. Edward died in 1639 and was buried at Castle Lyon near Cork. Elizabeth suffered in the 1641 uprising and became one of the many 'despoiled and impoverished Protestants'.

Edward's second son, William, was apparently born at Luccombe, but was educated at Lismore in Ireland and then in 1639, when he was 18, entered Trinity College Dublin. However, after his father's death he entered the army. As a Royalist he would have longed to serve his King and came over to England to do so. Did he arrive in Somerset with Inchiquin's Munster regiments? It is known that in 1644 he was captain of Horse at the siege of Bridgwater and was also promoted to the rank of major. Was he accompanied by another brother, John? John, William's brother, was buried in Bridgwater in 1644. The royalist cause foundered and William surrendered and became a prisoner of war in 1645 but then left for the Caribbean. William's elder brother, Lawrence was an officer in the garrison at Youghal in 1644. Three other younger brothers of William, Henry, Barry and Arthur were supposed to have died in the Irish Rebellion in 1641, but at least four of the five sisters appear to have survived the

troubles. William's aunt, Susan, wife of Henry vicar of Lucombe drowned in the Bristol Channel along with his cousin Susan, probably in 1642, trying to escape parliamentary persecution.[446]

Appendix 1.3: Reasons given for travel by passengers, only some of whom had Somerset connections, who sailed from Cork to Bristol in 1685

13 February 1685.
Bristol. The examination of several persons landed out of the ship *Thomas and Anne*, Samuel Lugg, master, from Cork.

Jasper Farmer says that he is an inhabitant of the parish of Grankimfeke [*sic*] between Cork and Youghall. Last year he carried several servants to Pensylvaina and there settled them. He designed again for Pensylvaina, and came to this city to travel to London to William Penn to purchase land for the settlement of himself and servants. William Robinson now in company with him is his servant and came to wait on him and is to return with him.

Nathaniel Pierce says that he is a silkman in Cork and came over to buy goods in London. He served his apprenticeship with Nathaniel Crabb in Fryingpan Ally near Spittle Feilds and intends to return to Cork to his wife and business there.

Charles Sinderby says that he was formerly a cooper in Bristol and now lives and follows that trade in Cork. He came hither to buy hoops. He has some friends here, viz., Jane Flower, widow, and Christopher Butcher, baker, here present, who married [Jane] Flower's daughter.

Isaack Dickenson says that he is son of William Dickenson [of this] city, keelmaker, and came with his master, Richard Hanslop.

Richard Hanslop says that he sailed in December last out of Bristol with Mr John Neads for Ireland to take possession of a ship which he was to go master of, but finding her not fit to go to sea he was journeying to London to inform his owners, who are James Robinson [of Ratc]liff Cross, London, Hugh Aldworth, cooper, in B... near Bread Street, Charles Durgill, silk d..... Queen's Arms in Spittle-Feilds and others . . .

Richard Cassy says that he came from Eniskene, co. Corke, and designs for London to buy goods. He is a tenant of Lord Corke's and expects a lease to be signed by him in London. He has a bill of exchange of £30 on James Freeman of this city, apothecary, and another of £33 on Mr Francis Burke, merchant in London. Richard White, esquire, near Temple

Barr, is his uncle.

Benedix Markes says that he is a housekeeper in Dukes Place in Rose Ally, London. About five months since he went to Ireland to kill beef for merchants, viz., Samuel Docasirers, a Jew, in the Broad Court in Dukes Place, Mr Greenwood and others, partners.

Simon Harrison says that in May last he went to Ireland to receive money due to him there. He received about £24, for £20 of which he has a bill on Mr Robert Smith, merchant in Bristol. His habitation is at Hudgwell near Richmond, Yorks, where he was now returning.

John Halcomb says that his habitation is at Tanton, (Taunton) Somerset. About eleven weeks passed he sailed out of Minehead for Corke and thence to Clemmell [? Clonmel] to seek his son Jonathan Halcomb, who ran away from his master and, he thought, might have been at Clemmell with an uncle, but finding him not came hither to go back to Tanton. He knows several persons in Bristol.

Robert Berry says that about twenty years since he lived at Felversham, Beds. He went to Ireland a soldier under the command of Sir St. John Bradrig, and became a farmer there and afterwards a tide-waiter in Corke. Being turned out of his office, he was travelling to London to his brother Daniel Berry, woodmonger in Dowgate Wharfe.

Hosea Beldriaw says that his habitation is in Corke, where he married the daughter of Jonathan Perry, notary public. He was travelling to London to see his brother and Mr Daniel Huger, merchant. He well knows Mr Trego here present.

Malcher Scult says that he is a tailor and has [lived] half a year in Corke, having married a [woman of] Flanders who formerly lived in Dublin. He cannot well maintain himself and wife and was travelling to London in hopes of getting work there.

Edmond Demigham [?] says that he is an inhabitant of Ordort [? Ardfort], co. Kerry, and was once a farmer but lost all his stock. His design is for London to wait on Patrick Trant, who lives at new Southampton buildings, to whom he is recommended and hopes to get some business under him or by his means.

John Callohan says that he is a glover. His habitation is in the county of Corke. His design is for London to see his uncle Owen Callohan and John Mackunny, who do or did lately belong to the abovesaid Mr Trant.

John Neate says that his habitation is in Dublin, where he was born. Twelve months since his Aunt Mary, wife of Joseph Sparrow, packer in Coleman Street in Swan Ally, London, sent for him and he was now going to her.

Morton Crompton says that his habitation is in [Borrisokane], co. Tipperrary, where he is tenant to Captain James Stopford, now in London. His business is to wait on Stopford at Somersett House to renew his lease and take more land, but he before designed for Curry Mallett in Somersetshire to receive a legacy left him by Ma..... Hutchenson there lately deceased.

Jeramy Snow says that his father Nathan Snow [of] ..... near Stroadwater, Gloucs., about thirteen years [since] carried him to Ireland and stayed there some time, but finding not things to his satisfaction returned. He was recommended to one Ruffate, a joiner in Nicholas Street here, for his directions to his fa[ther at] Stroadwater, where he now designs.

Benhajah Rossiter says that his mother Dorothy Rossiter, widow, is now (as he hopes) living at Comb St. Nicholas in Somerset. He was now going thither, where he hears his father left him something; which as soon as taken care of, his design was to return to Corke, where his wife and family are.[447]

Appendix 1.4: Some maritime burials relating to Minehead, 1588-1624

During this period, the Minehead parish clerks were more than usually generous with their annotations when recording many burials in the parish register. As well as the incidents detailed below there are many other references to fishermen being drowned, sailors and ships masters being buried, people falling off the quay or trying to swim in the harbour, and drowning, as well as many records (in the 1620s and 1630) of 'Irish beggars' or 'poor Irish travellers' being buried. Since they do not relate specifically to passenger travel at sea, they have been excluded from this appendix. Other events recorded in the Minehead registers such as the marriage in 1654 of William Evan from Margam, Glamorganshire to a Minehead widow and the baptism in 1664 of the daughter of Richard Edwards of Youghal, undoubtedly were also linked to passages into Minehead, but are omitted from the list below. Sadly, few entries in the registers after 1624 are so informative and the two that remain from the 1670s and 1680s are found in the main text. Another source indicates that in 1618, George Cooke of Ballingarie, Limerick in Ireland was due to marry Silvia Fugars, widow, of Minehead in the town. Undoubtedly, this involved at least one sea journey.[448] The parish registers of both Portishead and Easton in Gordano remain from a similar period but the clerks made no helpful comments linking burials with events involving ships' passengers.

1588, 17 November. John and Edward Soize 'with divers others cast awaie with the boat of Newton without the Kay'. (It is not clear whether these were passengers or crew, or both. However, it is likely that the named people were crew and known the people around the quay at Minehead and the 'divers others' were unknown passengers.)

1596, 2 December. Twelve Pembrokeshire soldiers 'drowned without the Key by the oversight of the weight of the barke'.

1598, 29 September. 'Michlemas day buried six men who were cast away at the ridges out of a Gersey barke of whom one was an Irish merchant'.

1599, 24 January. Thorne, 'an Englishman coming out of Ireland, a soldier'.

1602, Thomas Isle, 'a stranger coming forth from Ireland'.

1617, 8 September. Eight 'strange castaways in the reck of a ship coming out of Bristol. Buried seven, five women and three men', (exact quote). The most 'notable' burial was that of Mrs Margaret Goldswell of London and it is not clear from the text whether Mrs Johnson, wife of the controller of Cork, was a survivor or a victim.

1618, 16 November. David Ronoe, 'died on Lundy coming from an Ireland voyage'.

1619, 20 April. Mary David, daughter of Hugh David of Wiveliscombe, a passenger for Ireland.

1621, 30 July. Thomas Horne, a passenger for Ireland.

1623, 23 November. William Thomas, David Keich, James his son, his two apprentices, 'Matthew Lucas a sayler of Comage with divers other passengers were cast away with the *Hope* coming from Ireland between Michlemas and Allhallows tide'.

1624, 3 May. Thomas Martin, a passenger for Ireland out of Taunton.

26 August, John, an Irish youth, a passenger for Ireland.

11 October, Thomas Smith 'of Andov' (Andover), 'a passenger for Ireland, a smith'.[449]

Acknowledgements

I am extremely indebted, in no particular order, to Lucy Stewart and Kieran Burke at the Cork City Library and Maire Ni Chonallain at the National Library of Ireland, Dublin for help in finding and accessing some of the information regarding the link between Minehead and southern Ireland. Louis Parminter, manager of St Patrick's Cathedral, Dublin and David Worthington, manager of Wesley's New Room in Bristol helped secure significant illustrations for the chapter, as did Dr Adrian Webb. Garry Holden took some magnificent photos in Bristol which are used here, as did Derek Purvis of Porlock Bay. Shropshire County Council authorised the use of their image of King Road, SA-IMG 58705, The National Maritime Museum authorised the use of five illustration and Bristol Museum gave permission for the use of two others. Thanks are also due to Steve Popham for help with French translation and to Ed and Emily Ashford for technical support. Also, to Dr Adrian Webb for supplying numerous references and for editing this chapter.

Chapter 1
Notes

1 R. Dunning, *Bridgwater borough archives 1468-1485,* Somerset Record Society (hereafter SRS) 70 (1971), 24; J. Black, *Calendar of Patent Rolls, Henry VII,* 2 (1916), 41; J. Lawrence, *A history of Bridgwater* (2005), 60.

2 The National Archive [of England and Wales] (hereafter TNA), E 122/271, Bridgwater port book for 1511. I am grateful to Dr Duncan Taylor, who has transcribed Bridgwater's sixteenth-century port books, for this reference. See also W. Childs, 'Irish merchants and seamen in Late Medieval England' in *Irish historical studies* 32 (2000-1), 25.

3 E. Carus-Wilson, 'The overseas trade of Bristol' in E. Power, *Studies in the history of English trade in the fifteenth century* (1933), 194; R. Latham, *Calendar of Close Rolls Henry VII,* vol. 66 (1955), 20-1.

4 J. Vanes, *The overseas trade of Bristol in the sixteenth century,* Bristol Record Society (hereafter BRS) 31 (1979), 101; F.W. Weaver, *Somerset medieval wills 1501-1530,* SRS 19 (1903), 63-4. For the 1549 Bridgwater affair, which also details the possible illegal exportation of grain from Bridgwater, which allegedly caused the market price of wheat at local markets to rise from 14d a bushel to 20d, and even 30d in the subsequent weeks and months, much to the concern of local consumers, see TNA, E 111/38/4. Other evidence of Somerset merchants having servants aboard vessels, probably in charge of delivering and/or selling goods comes from 1486-1493 when Thomas Hopar, the servant of Alexander Towys of Taunton, merchant, was captured at sea and taken to Spain by the Lord of 'St Jermayn'; Thomas Smyth of Bridgwater, merchant was also involved in the case (TNA, C 1/108/1). Furthermore, in 1581, Bridgwater and Taunton merchants returned from a business visit to San Sebastian and Bilbao on an English ship which called in to Barnstaple on the way home (J. Jordan, *The history of Dunster church and priory* vol. 1 (2007), 213).

5   J. Bruce (ed.), *Calendar of State Papers Domestic* [hereafter *CSPD*] *Charles I, 1634-5* (1864), 33.

6   D.W. Rice, *The life and achievements of Sir John Popham, 1531-1607* (2005), 206-7; M. Giuseppi (ed.), *Calendar of Cecil papers in Hatfield House* vol. 17 (1938), 394.

7   H. Knott, *The deposition books of Bristol vol. 2 1650-1654*, BRS 13 (1935), 35. This volume has other references to passengers aboard Bristol ships but there is no apparent link with the Somerset coast.

8   P. McGrath, *Merchants and merchandise in seventeenth century Bristol*, BRS 19 (1955), 220. This volume also has other references to passengers aboard Bristol ships but with no apparent link with the Somerset coast.

9   D. Hussey, *Coastal and river trade in Pre-industrial England: Bristol and its region 1680-1730* (2000), 47-8.

10   J. Montgomery Traherne, *Stradling correspondence* (1840), 179-80.

11   Revd S. Seyer, *Memoirs historical and topographical of Bristol and its neighbourhood* (1823), 246. Sir Richard Grenville was born in Bideford and had lands in Munster alongside that of his cousin, Sir Walter Raleigh. Grenville's adventures and trading activity was instrumental in the economic development of the Devon port.

12   J. Bruce (ed.), *CSPD Charles I 1629-31* (1860), 227, 268 and 308.

13   J. Bruce (ed.), *CSPD Charles I 1631-33* (1862), 377.

14   J. Bruce (ed.), *CSPD Charles I 1633-34* (1863), 183; E. Hawkins, *Remains historical and literary connected with the palatine counties* vol. 1 (1844), 158.

15   J. Bruce (ed.), *CSPD Charles I 1636-37* (1867), 52.

16   D. Miles (ed.), *The description of Pembrokeshire: George Owen of Henllys* (1994), 60.

17   M. MacCarthey Morrough, 'Credit and remittance, monetary problems in early seventeenth century Munster' in *Irish Social and Economic History* vol. 14 (1987), 12.

18   W.M. Brady, *Clerical and parochial records of Cork* vol. 2 (1864), 31.

19   A.B. Grossart, *The Lismore papers of Richard Boyle, first and 'great' earl of Cork* (1886), 81-2.

20   R. Caulfield, *The council book of the corporation of Youghal 1610-1659* (1878), 208, 312.

21   J. Burke, *A genealogical and heraldic dictionary of the landed gentry part 1* (1847), 555.

22   Somerset Heritage Centre (SHC), DD/X/HYN/1.

23   National Library of Ireland, Dublin, The diary of Thomas Dinely.

24   S. Hayman, *Notes and records of the ancient religious foundations at Youghal* (1854), 20.

25   R.S. Harrison, *Cork City Quakers: a brief history 1665-1939* (1991), 16. The author quotes from Pike's own autobiography, a photocopy of which is held in Cork City Library.

26   W. Evans and T. Evans (eds), *The Friends Library* vol. 2 (1838), 364.

27   Sir B. Burke, *A genealogical and heraldic dictionary of the landed gentry of Great Britain and Ireland* (1858), 13.

28   K. Hall, *John Cogswell, 1592-1699*, http://kristinhall.org/fambly/Cogswell/John1Cogswell.html (accessed December 2010). At the time of sailing John's sons were William aged 14, John aged 12 and Edward aged 6. One of the family servants who travelled on the *Gabriel* was Samuel Haines who returned to England after a few years for his master, sold up his goods and went to New England again. A further passenger, who may have been a servant of the Cogswells, was William Furber who worked for the family in New England. Other passengers included John Bailey senior and junior. All these would have embarked in King Road. Cogswell exported two horses and two cattle via Southampton and they arrived separately in New England. Had they travelled with the family they would have perished with the other livestock in the ship. The *Angel Gabriel* itself was about 240 tons and had 12-16 guns. The port holes appear to be illustrated in the seal in the text, as does a group of people approaching the ship in a rowing vessel, the method of embarkation in King Road (*New England Historical and Genealogical Register* 23 (1869), 152-3).

29   P. Ashford, 'The West Somerset woollen industry 1500-1714' in *Proceedings of the Somerset Archaeological and Natural History Society*, 150 (2007), 174.

30   W. Sainsbury (ed.), *Calendar of State Papers Colonial, America and the West Indies, 1574-1660* (1860), 141.

31   T. Prince, *A chronological history of New England* (1826), 102.

32   W. Gilbert (ed.), *John Guy to Sir Percival Willoughby*, http://www.crossroadsforcultures.ca/index.php?var=transcriptions&var2=view&transid=11&selection=letter&language=en (accessed December 2010). S. McLeod, *First British settlement in Canada at Cupars Cove, Newfoundland*, http://www.suite101.com/content/first-british-settlement-in-canada-at-cupers-cove-newfoundland-a275675 (accessed December 2010). Others who travelled with Guy from King Road were Richard Fletcher, master pilot, Thomas Percy and Thomas Stone. There does not appear to be a record of the name of the vessel that Guy sailed across the Atlantic in.

33   S. Kingsbury *et al*, *The records of the Virginia company of London*, vol. 3 http://xtf.lib.virginia.edu/xtf/view?docId=2005_Q3_2/uvaGenText/tei/b002245360.xml (accessed December 2010). Specifically see numbers 48, 66, 70, 72, 78, 122, 132, 134, 135, 137, 140, 141, 142, 148.

34   H. Nott (ed.), *The deposition book of Bristol* vol. 1, BRS 6 (1935), 28.

35   P. McGrath (ed.), *Merchants and merchandise in seventeenth century Bristol*, BRS 19 (1955), 236.

36   H. Hayden, *Virginia genealogies* (2004), 354.

37   Traherne, *Stradling correspondence*, 305-6.

38   TNA, E 134/21/Jas1/Hil/15.

39   J.H. Betty, 'Livestock trade in the West Country in the

⚓

seventeenth century' in *Proceedings of the Somerset Archaeological and Natural History Society*, vol. 127 (1983), 123-4.

[40] M. Williams, 'Some aspects of Glamorgan farming in pre-industrial times' in *Glamorgan historian*, vol. 2 (1965), 178.

[41] Betty, 'Livestock', 125.

[42] W. Shaw (ed.), *Calendar of Treasury books, volume 1: 1660-1667* (1904), 318.

[43] K.R. Andrews, *Ships, money and politics* (1991), 84, 93.

[44] R. Anselment (ed.), *The remembrances of Elizabeth Freke 1671-1714*, Camden Fifth Series 18 (2001), 49-50.

[45] Ibid, 75-6, 217-8.

[46] J. Jenkins and J. Frost, *The records and recollections of James Jenkins* (1984), 99-100, 127.

[47] *The Scots Magazine* vol. 43 (1781), 555.

[48] H. Lee, *A manager, or life's stage with new scenery* (1830), 176-80. The precise date of the journey is uncertain as the reminiscences are written without a chronology. Two events mentioned in the text are the battle of the Nile, 1798, and the end of the American war with Britain in 1815, so the transit from Bridgwater to Tenby may well have taken place between these two dates.

[49] W. Dunlap, *Memoirs of George Fred. Cooke* vol. 1 (1813), 110-11.

[50] K. Tretheway, *How lighthouses work: oil additional material*, http://www.btinternet.com/~k.trethewey/Lighthouses/HowLighthousesWork/oil_additional.htm; Trinity House, *Flatholm* http://www.trinityhouse.co.uk/interactive/gallery/flatholm.html (accessed April 2010).

[51] Information from the marble memorial to George Robinson in Bristol Cathedral. My thanks go to the Dean and Chapter of Bristol Cathedral for allowing me access to this memorial.

[52] M.K. McKintosh, *Controlling misbehaviour in England 1370-1600* (2002), 141-2.

[53] R. Trench, *Travellers in Britain* (1990), 42. Bristol also would have been full of 'Irishmen' in the sixteenth century, not least because it is known that between 1532 and 1565 about ten apprentices from Ireland each year were bound to Bristol tradesmen. They were mainly from Munster and about 10% had mariner or fishermen fathers, who, in some way or another, were likely to have been involved in the lively trade between Bristol and Ireland in the sixteenth century. Reference to these volumes show that in 1539, Minehead mariner William Flynn, who by his name might also have come from Ireland, apprenticed his son to a Bristol tradesman, as did William Lye, mariner of Minehead in 1552 and John Hill of Minehead, mariner, in 1553. According to the records, these were the only Minehead families who provided apprentices for Bristol during this period and it is likely that the boys travelled to the city by ship (D. Hollis (ed.), *Calendar of the Bristol Apprentice book 1532-1564 part 1 1532-1542*, BRS 14 (1949); E. Ralph and N. Hardwick (eds), *Calendar of the Bristol Apprentice book 1532-*

1564 part 2 1542-1552, BRS 33 (1980) and E. Ralph (ed.), *Calendar of the Bristol Apprentice book 1532-1564 part 3 1552-1556*, BRS 43 (1992)). The sixteenth-century Irish trade with Bristol, some of which took place in Minehead vessels, is detailed in S. Flavin and E. Jones (eds.), *Bristol's trade with Ireland and the Continent 1503-1601*, BRS 61 (2009).

[54] SHC, DD/L P14-6. I am indebted to Mary Siraut for this reference.

[55] A.J. Webb, *An index to Somerset settlement and removal cases in Quarter Sessions 1607-1700* (1997), viii-xiii.

[56] E.H. Bates Harbin (ed.), *Quarter Sessions records for the county of Somerset vol. 1 1607-1625*, SRS 23 (1907), 318.

[57] SHC, Q/SR/34/96.

[58] J.S. Cockburn, *Western circuit assize orders* (1976), 6.

[59] SHC, Q/SR/62/38-42. Some of the Irish that landed are named in these proceedings.

[60] Webb, *Settlement*, viii-ix.

[61] G. Roberts, *The social history of the people of the southern counties on England* (1856), 188.

[62] P. O'Sullivan, *Patterns of migration* (1992), 21.

[63] P. Slack, *Poverty in early Stuart Salisbury*, Wiltshire Record Society vol. 31 (1975), 61.

[64] O'Sullivan, *Patterns of migration*, 17.

[65] Webb, *Settlement*, x.

[66] J. Savage, *History of the Hundred of Carhampton* (1830), 592.

[67] Webb, *Settlement*, xiv records that the following persons were judged to have been born in Ireland, were not merchants and did not have business of any sort in England, did not have passes from the Lord Lieutenant of Ireland and had been in the country several days against several proclamations and laws of the country: Henry Knight, his wife and two children; Humfry Chard, his wife and child; Elianor Turner and her two daughters; Thomas Carter; Samuel Tumonth, his wife and five children; Moses Good, his wife and four children; Henry Fisher, his wife and his apprentice.

[68] *House of Commons Journal vol. 10, 1688-1693* (1802), 611.

[69] D. Douglas, G.M. Young and W.D. Handcock, *English historical documents* (1996), 453.

[70] SHC, Q/SR/300/128.

[71] Ibid, Q/SR/312/192-93.

[72] Ibid, Q/SR/314/252-63.

[73] Ibid, Q/SR/316/2/53, 3/59, 3/60, 317/2/53.

[74] Ibid, Q/SR/297/19 and 21.

[75] Ibid, Q/SR/301/59-60.

[76] Ibid, Q/SR/319/2/13.

[77] Ibid, Q/SR/309/126.

[78] Ibid, Q/SR/316/1/52.

[79] Ibid, Q/SR/318/2/79.

[80] D. Sacks, *The widening gate* (1991), 252-7.

[81] C. Shifflett, *Registers of servants sent to foreign plantations 1654-1686*, http://www.virtualjamestown.org/indentures/search_indentures.html. There remain a few records of Somerset

indentured servants leaving for the New World from Lyme Regis in the 1680s (Dorset History Centre, DC/LR/m/9).

82 T. Williams, *The doom of Colyn Dolphyn* (1837), Preface, 88-91. Also http://pages.prodigy.net/rodney.broome/pirlundy.htm (accessed 10 April 2010). This latter source says that that Dolphyn was operating from Lundy at the time and the Stradlings were kept for two years aboard his barque, *Sea Swallow*.

83 TNA, E 111/38/3-6. John Tyrell, of Bridgwater merchant, clearly had a business with the Iberian Peninsula. In the 1540s he was in a dispute with a Portuguese merchant over woad (D. Taylor, *The overseas trade of mid-sixteenth century Bridgwater* (University of Bristol M.A. thesis, 2006), 12.

84 Anon, 'The old Countess of Desmond' in *The London Quarterly Review* vol. 92 (New York, 1853), 187; R. Trevelyan, *Sir Walter Raleigh* (2002), 142-3.

85 W.M. Brady, *Clerical and parochial records of Cork* vol. 2 (1864), 306-8; S. Urban, *The Gentleman's Magazine*, January 1848, 40.

86 E. Creasy, *Memoirs of eminent Etonians* (1850), 123-4. The boys were also accompanied by Mr Badnedge on this journey.

87 C. Fell-Smith, *Mary Rich, Countess of Warwick 1625-1678: her family and friends* (1901), 48.

88 Webb, *Settlement*, xi.

89 T.Barnard, *A new anatomy of Ireland: the Irish Protestants 1649-1770* (2004), 171.

90 Sir D. Brewster (ed.), *The Edinburgh encyclopaedia 1781-1868* (1999), 753; A. Chalmers, *The general biographical dictionary* vol. 7 (1813), 34. Mary Alloway married Richard Brocklesby in 1716/17, presumably in Minehead and may well have sailed to Ireland with her new husband. A Hannah Brocklesby (sister of Richard?) married Minehead Quaker Robert Davis in 1727 (SHC, DD\SFR.w/66); this latter marriage possibly took place in Ireland as the Davis family later resided in Minehead and are referred to elsewhere in this chapter. It is likely that the courtships caused various passages to take place between Minehead and Cork, as would family visits after marriage.

91 Anselment, *Remembrances*, 48, 60, 83, 235-6.

92 R. Chandler, *Travels in Asia-Minor and Greece* vol. 1 (1817), 1, 343.

93 S. Donovan (ed.), *Jamaican rock stars 1823-1971: The geologists who explored Jamaica* (Boulder, Colorado, 2010), 13. Sir Henry De la Beche was elected a fellow of the Royal Society in 1819 and wrote a *Report on the Geology of Cornwall, Devon and west Somerset* (1839).

94 W. Dyott, *Dyott's diary* vol. 1 (1907), 18-19.

95 J. Martin, *Wives and daughters: women and children in Georgian society* (2004), 313.

96 T. Wright, *A history of the people called Quakers in Ireland* (1751), 354-5, 357; *Journal of the Friends Historical Society* vol. 10 (1913), 166.

97 W. Evans and T. Evans (eds), *The Friends Library comprising doctrinal theses and other writings* vol. 5 (Philadelphia, 1841), 20.

98 W. Evans and T. Evans (eds), *The Friends Library* vol. 9 (1845), 26.

99 C. Phillips, *Memoirs of the life of Catherine Phillips* (1797), 237-49.

100 W. Evans and T. Evans (eds), *The Friends Library* vol. 9 (1850), 291.

101 *The Journal of the Friends Historical Society* vol. 15 (1918), 3.

102 *The Friends monthly magazine* vol. 2 (1831), 14-20.

103 For information on the home and fate of Edith Lovell see *The Annual Monitor or obituary of the Society of Friends* (1858), 95; W. Evans and T. Evans, *The Friends Library* vol. 11 (1847), 66-7.

104 *The Journal of the Friends Historical Society* 20 (1923), 124; W. Toone, *The chronological historian of a record of public events,* vol. 2 (1826), 312-13. A description of Culver sands made on 24 October 1771 is found in *MHS* vol. 1, 95.

105 The second quotation is taken from *The Journal of the Friends Historical Society* (1903), 116.

106 SHC, DD\DN/189 and 201.

107 *The Friend's monthly magazine* vol. 2 (1831), 14-20.

108 E. Burke, *The annual register* (1817), 6.

109 E. Burke, *The annual register* (1818), 106.

110 *The Literary Gazette* no. 41 (1817), 285.

111 P. Egan, *Walks through Bath* (1819), 254-5.

112 S.C. Hall, 'Something of what the Queen will see and will not see in Ireland' in *St James's Magazine* vol. 2 (1861), 235.

113 J.B. Burke, *Family romance, of episodes in the domestic annals of the aristocracy* (1853), 167.

114 W. Lewis, *et al, The Oxford history of the British Empire* (1998), 322.

115 SHC, D/P/stogm/13/2/1 Stogumber overseer's account 1668 quoted in D. Taylor, *Poor relief* http://www.jamesbarton.co.uk/poorrelief.htm (accessed 10 May 2011).

116 P. Elmer, *The miraculous conformist: Valentine Greatrakes* (2012), 106, 187 and 194.

117 E. Dudley, *The life of Mary Dudley* (1825), 47; S. Urban, *The Gentleman's Magazine*, vol. 96 part 2 (1804), 790.

118 SHC, Q/SR/14/26.

119 Ibid, Q/SR/98/83.

120 Bates Harbin, *Quarter Sessions 1607-25*, 9.

121 SHC, Q/SR/2/90-91.

122 Ibid, Q/SR/27/81.

123 Bates Harbin, *Quarter Sessions 1607-25*, 263.

124 SHC, Q/SR/34/18.

125 Bates Harbin, *Quarter Sessions 1607-25*, 273.

126 T.J. Stoate, *Porlock parish registers* pt. 2 (1995), 92.

127 C. Chadwyck-Healey, *The history of part of West Somerset* (1901), 168-9.

128 G Quaife, *Wanton wenches and wayward wives* (1979), 98.

129 SHC, Q/SR/101/32.

130 Traherne, *correspondence*, 256.

131 M.A.E. Green (ed.), *CSPD Charles II, 1667-8* (1893), 495.

[132] E. Timmings (ed.), *CSPD James II, 1685* (1960), 12-14. Appendix 1.3 details the names and reasons for travel of the other passengers on the vessel including some with Somerset connections.

[133] A. Hayward (ed.), *Lives of remarkable criminals* (1927), 543-52.

[134] SHC, Q/SR/305/208. The place of residence of Henry Nethway is not recorded in this document.

[135] J. Travis, *Smuggling on the Exmoor coast 1680-1850* (Dulverton, 2001), 34-7. In 1758 four Neath women travelled to Bridgwater, presumably by sea, in order to buy smuggled tea to take back to Briton Ferry, probably under their clothing. It is likely that this practise and the smuggling of tea, increased after tea duty was raised higher in 1759 in order to help finance war (R. Platt, *Smuggling in the British Isles: a history* (2011), 25 and 129).

[136] W. Lawson, *The history of banking* (1855), 252-5.

[137] B. Cummings (ed.), *Cultural reformations* vol. 2 (2010), 141; I. Bradley, *Pilgrimage, a spiritual and cultural journey* (2009), 57.

[138] G. Roberts, *The social history of the people of southern England* (1856), 126-34; E. Power, *Studies in English trade in the fifteenth century* (1966), 226.

[139] D. Webb, *Pilgrims and pilgrimage in the medieval west* (2001), 194.

[140] D. Englander (ed.), *Culture and belief in Europe 1450-1600* (1999), 20.

[141] A Powell, *The ancient Borough of Bridgwater* (1907), 206.

[142] F. Weaver, *Somerset medieval wills 1501-1530*, SRS 19 (1903), 30.

[143] W. Rees (ed.), *Accounts of the rectory of Cardiff and other possessions of the Abbey of Tewkesbury in Glamorgan for the year 1449-1450*, South Wales and Monmouth Record Society vol. 2 (1950), 158-9; H. Foley, *Records of the English province of the Society of Jesus* vol. 3 (1878), 431-2.

[144] P. Marshall, *Mother Leakey and the bishop* (2007), 27.

[145] Sir Thomas Raymond (ed.), *Reports of divers special cases ajudged at the courts of the King's Bench* (1803), 377.

[146] J. Sharpe, *Mother Leakey and the Bishop* (Review), http://www.timeshighereducation.co.uk/story.asp?storyCode=208216&sectioncode=22 (accessed 29 June 2008); W. Davage, *Mother Leakey and the Bishop* (Review), http://trushare.com/0148SEP%202007/2528book_reviews.htm (accessed 29 June 2008).

[147] SHC, D/P/m.st.m 4/1/1. I am indebted to Mary Siraut for this reference.

[148] R. Davies and R. Caulfield (ed.), *Journal of the Very Reverend Rowland Davies* (1857), 1.

[149] S. Morland (ed.), *The Somersetshire Quarterly Meeting of the Society of Friends 1668-1699*, SRS 75 (1978), 61.

[150] R. Greaves, *God's other children* (1997), 271.

[151] K. Carroll, *John Perrot: early Quaker schismatic* (1971), 61.

[152] J. Whiting, *Persecution exposed relating to the suffering of Quakers in the west of England* (1791), 467-76.

[153] W. Evans and T. Evans (eds), *The Friends Library* vol. 2 (1838), 2-20; Morland, *The Somersetshire Quarterly Meeting*, 45-6.

[154] G. Fox, *A journal of the life, travel and sufferings of that ancient eminent and faithful servant of Jesus Christ, George Fox* vol. 2 (1831), 142-3.

[155] T. Clarkson, *Memoirs of the private and public life of William Penn* (1827), 68, 71-2.

[156] W. Evans and T. Evans (eds), *The Friends Library*, vol. 9 (1845), 87.

[157] W. Evans and T. Evans (eds), *The Friends Library*, vol. 8 (1849), 361, 367; S. Bownas, *The life, travels and Christian experiences of Samuel Bownas* (1805), 178, 181.

[158] J. Gough, *A history of the people called Quakers* vol. 4 (1790), 399-400.

[159] W. Alexander, *The life of Thomas Story* vol. 2 (1839), 90.

[160] S. Stephenson, *Memoirs of the life and travels of Sarah Stephenson* (1807), 11, 43-4, 119-23 and chapter 9.

[161] W. Evans and T. Evans (eds), *The Friends Library* vol. 3 (1839), 130-1.

[162] Sloop ownership, D. Pike, *Welldigger*, http://daibach-welldigger.blogspot.com/2011/03/john-wesley-in-cardiff-part-1-1739-1746.html (accessed 24 April 2011).

[163] J. Emory, *The works of the Reverend John Wesley A.M.* vol. 3 (1840), 314, 344, 460.

[164] J. Whitehead, *The life of the Rev. John Wesley with the life of the Rev Charles Wesley* (1845), 163-4.

[165] J. Wesley, *The experience of several eminent Methodist preachers* (1837), 99.

[166] J. Wesley, *An extract of the Rev. Mr John Wesley's journal Nov 1751-Oct 1754*, vol. 9 (1788), 39-40.

[167] T. Jackson (ed.), *The lives of early Methodist preachers written chiefly by themselves*, http://wesley.nnu.edu/wesleyctr/books/0301-0400/HDM0377.PDF (accessed 24 April 2011). The piece quoted and referred to clearly comes very near the end of the section of Walsh's life.

[168] *The Countess of Huntingdon's new magazine* (1850), 39.

[169] Salisbury Methodist Church, *Francis Asbury, the founder of American Methodism*, http://www.salisburymethodist.org.uk/francis.htm (accessed 24 April 2011); Church history *Christian churches in Pill, Portbury and Easton-in Gordano*, http://www.pillchurches.org.uk/site/64.asp (accessed 24 April 2011).

[170] T. Jackson, *The lives of early Methodist preachers chiefly written by themselves* (1866), 185-90.

[171] D. Maxey, *A memoir of Mr George Shadford*, http://wesley.nnu.edu/wesleyctr/books/0601-0700/HDM0669.PDF (accessed 24 April 2011). The accounts/memoirs of Rankin and Shadford slightly differ in detail including the name of the captain of the vessel which took them to America. Rankin's memories are quoted above.

[172] H. Hayes, *Sacred destinations: Wesley's new room, Bristol*, http://www.sacred-destinations.com/england/bristol-

wesleys-new-room.htm (accessed 24 April 2011).

[173] *Primitive Church (or Baptist) Magazine* new series vol. 19 (1862), 237; M. Green (ed.), *CSPD Charles II, 1667* (1866), 420; M. Green (ed.), *CSPD Charles II, 1667-8* (1893), 69. Later, in 1672, the house of Stephen Lanclark of Minehead was licensed for Baptist worship (P. Daniel (ed.), *CSPD Charles II, 1672-3* (1901), 176).

[174] *The Baptist Magazine for 1839* (1839), 330.

[175] E. Afoux, *History of the Baptist Missionary Society 1792-1842* (1845), 67. The quote is from *The Evangelical and Missionary Chronicle* vol. 12 (1804). William Moore married Eleanor Hurford in Stogumber on 9 November 1803 (SHC, DD\X\BRKS/1).

[176] T. Whelan (ed.) *Baptist autographs in the John Rylands University Library 1741-1845* (Macon, Georgia, 2009), 117-18. The Mr Saffery alluded to in the letter was John Saffery (1763-1825), who was minister of Brown Street, Salisbury, a supporter of the Baptist Missionary society and a popular hymn writer of the time (Ibid, 142).

[177] *Periodical accounts related to the mission of the church of the United Brethren established amongst the heathen* vol. 18 (1846), 70-2.

[178] Anon, 'Memoir of the Rev. Thomas Trowt, missionary at Samerang in Java' in *Missionary Register for 1821* (1821) 265-70; B. Stow, *A history of the English Baptist mission to India* (1835), 196-200.

[179] The *Baptist Magazine for 1819* vol. 11 (1819), 410; K. Ingram, *Manuscript sources for the history of the West Indies* (2000), 99; J. Clarke, *et al*, *The voice of Jubilee, a narrative of the Baptist mission, Jamaica* (1865), 166-70.

[180] G. Jackman, *A memoir of the Rev. John Jenkins* (1832), 41-2.

[181] *The Baptist magazine for 1824* (1824), 173.

[182] SHC, D\D/cd/75; M. Smylie, *The boats of the Somerset levels* (2012), 26 and 98.

[183] H. Hamilton (ed.), *Calendar of State Papers Ireland 1574-85* (1867), 186.

[184] D. Townshend, *The life and letters of the great Earl of Cork* (1904), 27. James FitzGerald, First Earl of Desmond, an Irish Peer who spent most of his life in captivity, was for political reasons taken to Ireland from Bristol in the autumn of 1600. Extreme sea-sickness caused him to be landed at Youghal, rather than Cork. His mission was not a great success and he was withdrawn the following year through Minehead.

[185] Lady Chatterton, *Rambles in the south of Ireland.* 2 (1839), 289-95.

[186] R. Roberts (ed.), *Calendar of the Cecil Papers in Hatfield House vol. 12: 1602-1603* (1910), 252-276 and 366-389.; Anon, *Donough O'Brien*, http://en.wikipedia.org/wiki/Donogh_O%27Brien,_4th_Earl_of_Thomond (accessed 5 May 2010). Donogh O'Brien, 4th Earl of Thomond (*c.*1555-1624) was a protestant Irish nobleman with strong allegiance to the English Crown. He was extensively involved in military affairs in Munster and was present at the siege of Kinsale.

He had been at Elizabeth's court in the 1570s but, later, returned to Ireland. He made two further visits to London, via Bristol in 1601 and 1602, when his primary concern was to cause his home county, Clare, to be recognised as part of Munster and not Connaught. He achieved this aim and became president of Munster in 1605. Note: The pinnace *Merlin* should not be confused with the Royal yacht *Merlin* mentioned elsewhere in the text.

[187] Townshend, *The life and letters*, 160-1.

[188] A. Grossart, *The Lismore papers of the first great Earl of Cork* vol. 5 (1886), 199.

[189] Townshend, *The life and letters,* 375.

[190] C. Brady, *Natives and newcomers: essays on the making of Irish colonial society 1534-1641* (1986), 174.

[191] Murrough O'Brien, First Earl of Inchiquin (1614-1674), son of the 5th Baron Inchiquin, married Elizabeth, daughter of Sir William St Leger, president of Munster in 1635. In August 1640 he was made Vice President of Munster. He defeated Catholic insurgents in 1642 and subsequently sent Munster troops to support Charles the First in England. Since Charles the First did not make him president of Munster in 1644, the enraged Inchiquin returned to Ireland and declared for parliament, but switched allegiance back to the King in 1648. He fled Ireland and Cromwell's New Model Army in 1650 but returned after the Restoration to be made vice president of Munster (again) in 1664 (J. Wroughton, *The Stuart age, 1603-1714* (2006), 208; D. Plant, *British civil wars, commonwealth and protectorate 1638-1660*, http://www.british-civil-wars.co.uk/biog/inchiquin.htm (accessed April 2008).

[192] J. Buckley, 'The Siege of Cork 1642' in *Cork Historical and Archaeological Society* vol. 12 (1916), 15.

[193] D. Plant, *British civil wars, commonwealth and protectorate 1638-1660*, http://www.british-civil-wars.co.uk/biog/inchiquin.htm (accessed April 2008).

[194] G. Meadley, *Memoirs of Algernon Sydney* (1813), 307-9; W. Page (ed.), *Report on the manuscripts of the Earl of Egmont*, vol. 1 part 2 (1905), 362.

[195] Roger Boyle, Lord Broghill (1621-1679), son of Richard Boyle, first earl of Cork, created Baron Broghill in 1627. A dowry upon his marriage in 1641 allowed him to purchase an estate near Frome in Somerset in early 1641. After returning to Ireland to help defend family land, in October 1641, he became second in command in Munster at the start of the rebellion. In October 1649 he once again sailed for Munster to help secure the southern ports for parliament and helped defeat Catholic and Royalist forces in Ireland in 1650-51. He was M.P. for Cork in 1654, was in favour of the Restoration in 1660, was created Earl of Orrery in 1660 as well as Lord President of Munster and Lord Justice of Ireland in the same year (J. Wroughton, *The Stuart age, 1603-1714* (2006), 174; D. Plant, *British civil wars*).

[196] R.W. Blencowe, *Sydney papers: a journal of the Earl of Leicester*

⚓

and original letters of Algernon Sydney (1825), 17-18.

197 Meadley, *Memoirs*, 312.

198 J. Corry, *A history of Bristol* vol. 1 (1816), 323; Wroughton, *The Stuart Age 1603-1714*, 197.

199 Anon, *Memoirs of Edmund Ludlow* vol. 2 (1751), 318.

200 A. Clarke, *Prelude to restoration in Ireland: the end of the commonwealth 1659-1660* (1999), 24. It appears that Hodge, Captain of the *Basing*, had conducted Broghill, his wife and family and General Pen, his wife and family from King Road to Ireland in late August 1656 (M. Green (ed.), *CSPD Interregnum 1655-6* (1882), 408).

201 M. Green (ed.), *CSPD Interregnum, 1657-8* (1884), 493.

202 T. Birch (ed.), *A collection of the State Papers of John Thurloe, vol. 6: January 1657 - March 1658* (1742), 711.

203 M. Green (ed.), *CSPD Charles II, 1667-8* (1893), 441. Orrery had requested permission of Ormonde, by letter in March 1668, to leave Ireland for a few months and to use one of the King's ship for this journey to Bristol or 'Miniard' (Minehead) (T. Morrice, *A collection of the state letters of Roger Boyle* (1742), 325-6).

204 M. Green (ed.), *CSPD Charles II, 1667-8* (1893), 475.

205 M. Green (ed.), *CSPD Charles II, 1668-9* (1894), 413-14.

206 M. Green (ed.), *CSPD Charles II, 1670* (1895), 144.

207 F. Daniel (ed.), *CSPD Charles II, 1671* (1895), 213.

208 Ibid, 222.

209 Ibid, 246.

210 Binding and Stevens, *Minehead*, 106.

211 Anon, *Letters written by Arthur Capel, Earl of Essex, Lord Lieutenant of Ireland in the year 1675* (1770), 385.

212 F. Daniel (ed.), *CSPD Charles II, 1676-7* (1909), 251.

213 Green, *CSPD Interregnum, 1655-6*, 571.

214 F. Daniel (ed.), *CSPD Charles II, 1676-7* (1909), 89.

215 Percival and Gailhard had made the passage from Pill to Cork in June 1676 and a detailed account remains of the events, including wind directions, storms and an overnight stop at Sully, Glamorganshire. W. Page (ed.), *Report on the manuscripts of the Earl of Egmont* vol. 2 (1909), 44 and 50.

216 James Butler, first Duke of Ormond (1610-1688) succeeded to the earldom of Ormond in 1632, moved to Ireland in 1633 and was appointed Lieutenant-General of the King's forces in Ireland in 1641 once the rebellion had started and made Lord Lieutenant of Ireland in 1644. He surrendered Dublin to Parliament in 1647. After the Restoration was created Duke of Ormond in 1661 and re-appointed Lord Lieutenant of Ireland, a position which he held from 1661-1668 and 1677-1685 (J. Wroughton, *The Stuart age, 1603-1714* (2006), 176-7). Ormond (or Ormonde) was also Lord Lieutenant of Somerset from 1660-1672.

217 The Right Hon. Lord Mountmorres, *The history of the principal transactions of the Irish parliament from 1634-1666* (1792), 204, 217-18.

218 E. Edwards, *Carte calendar vol. 42, July-December 1665* (2004) citing letters written on 27th, 30th, 31st July and 9th August

219. Green, *CSPD Charles II 1665-6* (1864), 472, 529 and 546. The *Harp*, like other vessels, would have anchored in Minehead Road and embarked or disembarked passengers from outside the harbour, so as not to waste a tide. It was national news, via the *London Gazette*, when a westerly gale on 16 August 1666 forced the *Harp* into Minehead harbour to shelter (*London Gazette* No. 81, 20-23 August 1666).

220 E. Edwards, *Carte calendar vol. 52, 1673-1674* (2005) citing letters written on 17 June and 1 July 1674.

221 M.A.E. Green (ed.), *CSPD Interregnum, 1655* (1881), 73; Green *CSPD Interregnum 1655-56*, 404, 408.

222 Green, *CSPD Interregnum, 1656-7* (1883), 532-55 citing 'Letters and Papers relating to the Navy, &c.: April 1657'. Two of His Majesty's yachts that served in the Bristol Channel during the seventeenth century include the *Merlin* (109 tons), built in 1666, and *Monmouth* (103 tons), both of which were 70 feet long, 20 feet beam, drawing 9 feet of water and armed with 8 guns (*MHS* vol. 1, 91-2). Other naval vessels include the *Harp* (8-10 guns) from 1656 to 1671, the *Mayflower* (14-20 guns) from 1649 to 1656, *Norwich* (24-30 guns) from 1665 to 1682, *Paradox* (12-14 guns) from 1649 to 1667, and the *Pearl* (22-32 guns) from 1651 to 1697 (Anon, *Rulebritannia*, http://rulebritannia.pbworks.com/ Smaller-ships (accessed 12 April 2010).

223 F. Daniel (ed.), *CSPD Charles II, 1671* (1895), 523.

224 Rev. S. Seyer, *Memoirs historical and topographical of Bristol and it neighbourhood* (1823), 542-3.

225 Ibid, 241-3; H. Hamilton (ed.), *Calendar of the state papers relating to Ireland 1509-1573* (1860) 112 and 308. 114 horse under the command of Sir Henry Danvers were at King Road in 1599 (Roberts, *Cecil Papers, vol. 9: 1599* (1902), 16-31, 107-26). Sir Henry Danvers (1573-1644) was Lieutenant-General of the horse in Ireland in 1599 and served with some distinction. He was Lord President of Munster from 1607 to 1615 (H. Kearney, *Strafford in Ireland 1633-41* (1989), 26).

226 Roberts, *Cecil Papers, vol. 12: 1602-1603* (1910), 93-109, 366-389, 389-413, 631-60. The *Tramontara* also brought pirates back to King Road from Cork under guard in February 1603 (Ibid).

227 C. Falls, *Elizabeth's Irish wars* (1997), 61-2, 289. In 1580, 200 Somerset levies were ordered to Bristol to be shipped to Ireland, whereas 100 levied from Somerset in 1601 were ordered to Barnstaple for transportation.

228 SHC, Q/SR 3/22, 4/96, 11/10-11, 15/82-3, 19/42-3, 35/88, 39/102 and 49/51 respectively.

229 D. Livock, *City chamberlains' accounts*, BRS 24 (1966), 128-9.

230 Townshend, *Earl of Cork*, 330.

231 Seyer, *Memoirs*, 295. The *Fellowship* of Bristol, under Captain Thomas Powell in the King's service, left King Road and stood into Minehead, on 22 February 1642, on the way to help blockade southern Ireland in order to restrict help

arriving for the Catholic rebels. Powell ascertained that troops destined for Ireland had left the port of Minehead on 20 February, so rather than having to pick any up, he hastened towards his station off the southern Irish coast (D. Edwards, 'The ships journal of Captain Robert Powell 1642', in *Analecta Hibernica* 33 (1998), 258).

232 House of Lords Journal, 3 May 1642, http://www.british-history.ac.uk/report.aspx?compid=34788 (accessed 21 October 2009).

233 House of Lords Journal, 10 September 1642, https://www.british-history.ac.uk/report.aspx?compid=34897 (accessed 21 October 2009).

234 J. Wroughton, *An unhappy Civil War* (1999), 17-18. Minehead shipping had been involved with transporting troops from Bristol to Ireland in 1642. For example, it cost £180 5s 4d for the *John* of Minehead to transport troops on this route in 1642 (T. Garrard, *Edward Colston the Philanthropist* (1852), 73).

235 M. Wankyn and F. Jones, *A military history of the English Civil War* (2004), 133. Noah Rendall's testimony is published in J. Lynch, *Bristol and the Civil War* (2009), 107.

236 J. Latimer, *The annals of Bristol in the seventeenth century* (1900), 190.

237 J. Sanford, *Studies and illustrations of the great rebellion* (1858), 626-8; Lynch, *Bristol*, 141-2.

238 M. Stoyle, *Soldiers and strangers: An ethnic history of the English Civil War* (2005), 164.

239 Ibid, 169.

240 C. Carlton, *Going to the wars: the experience of the British civil wars 1638-1651* (1994), 260.

241 Great Britain Royal Commission on Historical Manuscripts, *Report on the manuscripts of the Earl of Egmont* (1905), 297-300. Some additional information remains from 1649 regarding the movement of military horses from Bristol to Ireland. They were placed in slings and hoisted aboard, then they were tied to ringbolts, which were attached to the ship's woodwork and watered via buckets from the ten days supply of water that had been stowed (Lynch, *Bristol*, 169).

242 SHC, Q/SPET/1/74.

243 Binding and Stevens, *Minehead*, 103.

244 S. Rabbitts and T. Gordon, *The history of the cittie of London trained bands*, http://www.blews-ltb.co.uk/history/tichborn History.asp (accessed 12 April 2008).

245 Binding and Stevens, *Minehead*, 104.

246 D. Murphy, *Cromwell in Ireland: a history of Cromwell's campaign* (1905), 374.

247 SHC, Q/SPET/1/75.

248 J. Nalson, *The manuscripts of his Grace the Duke of Portland* (2009), 560.

249 M. Green (ed.), *CSPD Interregnum, 1651* (1877) 544.

250 Binding and Stevens, *Minehead*, 105.

251 Green, *CSPD Interregnum, 1651*, 185.

252 E. Murphy, *Ireland and the war at sea 1641-1653* (2012), 82.

253 M. Green (ed.), *CSPD Interregnum, 1651-2* (1877), 548, 605.

254 Green, *CSPD Interregnum, 1651-2*, 97, 550.

255 Binding and Stevens, *Minehead*, 112. On 27 January 1689 the Admiralty commandeered six Minehead vessels for a month, or longer if their Majesties required. The vessels were the *Expedition* (85 tons), the *Merchant Adventure* (75 tons), the *Thomas* (75 tons), the *Mayflower* (75 tons), the *Phoenix* (60 tons) and the *Reformation* (50 tons). These vessels were to be used to help the movement of troops and supplies to Ireland (TNA, ADM 1/3560 folio 377). I am grateful for Adrian Webb for this reference. It is not unlikely that some, or all, of these vessels helped move Schomberg's troops from Minehead to Ireland in July 1689.

256 W. Hardy (ed.), *CSDP: William and Mary, 1690-1* (1898), 310.

257 W. Hardy (ed.), *CSDP: William and Mary, 1691-2* (1900), 172.

258 Webb, *Settlement*, xi.

259 J Davis, *The history of the second Queen's Royal Regiment* vol. 2 (1895) 404-5.

260 C.T. Atkinson and D.S. Daniel, *The Royal Hampshire Regiment* (1950), 47.

261 Dr J. Campbell, *Lives of the British Admirals* vol. 4 (1812), 378-9.

262 Savage, *Carhampton*, 591; J. Page, *An exploration of Exmoor* (1895), 184. The wreck of *The Lamb* was seen in 1975 as a 'coherent vessel structure' and thus of archaeological interest. It is revealed at low tide and is about half a mile south-east of Minehead harbour (C. Gathercole, *An archaeological assessment of Minehead*, http://www1.somerset.gov.uk/archives/hes/downloads/Somerset_EUS_Minehead.pdf (accessed 14 April 2011); http://www1.somerset.gov.uk/archives/hes/downloads/Somerset_EUS_MineheadMapF.pdf (accessed 14 April 2011). A letter to the Admiralty from Bristol, at the time, explains that the *Lamb* Brigantine was one of the vessels carrying Brigadier Hargraves's Regiment to Waterford (presumably from Bristol) and that it's stranding, which resulted in the drowning of 'several men', was the fault of the ship's master (TNA, ADM 106/879/21).

263 J. C. Cox, *The parish registers of England* (1910), 137.

264 W. Shaw (ed.), *Calendar of Treasury books 1729-1745* (1901), 193.

265 L. McCardell, *Ill-starred general: Braddock of the Coldstream Guards* (1986), 136.

266 TNA, ADM 354/140/103.

267 E. Mackenzie, *Historical records of the Queens Own Cameron Highlanders* (1909), 12.

268 O. Moore, *The staff officer* (Philadelphia, 1833), 195-7.

269 Ibid, 196.

270 Anon, *Memoirs and services of the 83rd Regiment, County of Dublin 1793-1907* (1908), 14.

271 Dyott, *Dyott's diary*, vol. 1, 77.

272 J. Penny, *A military history of Bristol*, http://fishponds.org.uk/revwar.html (accessed 5 April 2009). The website of the

⚓

Fishponds Local History Society.

273 R. Cannon, *Historical records of the British Army* (1842), 28; *The Scots Magazine* vol. 57 (Edinburgh, 1795), 536. Certainly the Northamptonshire Militia were turned out to quell the insurrection at Pill (A. Randall (ed.), *Markets, popular culture and popular protest in eighteenth century Britain and Ireland* (1996), 106).

274 S. Coleridge (ed.), *Essays on his own times* (1850), 51.

275 J. Latimer, *The annals of Bristol in the eighteenth century* (1893), 520-1; Penny, *A military history of Bristol* http://fishponds .org.uk/revwar.html (accessed 5 April 2009).

276 Sir J. Steel-Graves *The Royal North Gloucester: being notes from the regimental orders of the Royal North Gloucester militia* (1875), 70.

277 C. Atkinson, *The Dorsetshire Regiment* (1947), 11.

278 J. Whalley, *Roll of officers of the old county regiment of Lancashire Militia* (1889), 115.

279 Penny, *A military history of Bristol* http://fishponds.org.uk/ revwar.html (accessed 5 April 2009).

280 A. Pollock, *United Service Magazine* (1879), 220-1.

281 J. Gildi, *Roads to Power* (2012), 156.

282 C. O'Neil, *The military adventures of Charles O'Neil* (1851), 27, 135.

283 J. Davenport, *Oxfordshire Militia, sketch of the history of the regiment* (1869), 14.

284 J. Johnson, *Transactions of the corporation of the poor in the city of Bristol* (1826), 85.

285 *The London University Magazine* vol. 1 (1829), 185-7.

286 J. Gairdner (ed.), *Letters and Papers, Foreign and Domestic, Henry VIII: 1533* (1882), 625 and 649.

287 J. Cornwall, *The revolt of the peasantry 1549* (1977), 200.

288 J. Evans, *A chronological outline of the history of Bristol* (1824), 155-6; C. Officer, *A fabulous Kingdom: the exploration of the Arctic* (2012), 50.

289 R. Asland (ed.), *The Christian reformer* (1862), 481-90.

290 J. Felt, *The ecclesiastical history of New England* (1885), 226-7.

291 Ibid, 252, 313.

292 Chadwyck-Healey, *West Somerset,* 180.

293 B. Burke, *A genealogical and heraldic dictionary of the landed gentry part 1* (1862), 33.

294 P. Ashford, 'The Hayman family of Somerset and Ireland' in *SDNQ* (September, 2012), 248-52.

295 Anon, *New intelligence from Ireland with the arrival of the Bishop of St Davids at Minehead* (1642).

296 W. Pickering (ed.), *Archaeologia Cambrensis,* vol. 96 (1881), 254; Parliamentary Archives, HL/PO/JO/10/1/127.

297 Anon, *Strange and bloody news from Minehead* (1642), 1.

298 E. Green, *Bibliotheca Somersetensis* vol. 2 (1902), 242.

299 W. Coates, *et al, The private journals of the long parliament* (1992), 406, 432.

300 SHC, Q/SPET/1/75.

301 *Journal of the House of Commons: vol. 2: 1640-1643* (1802), 577-8.

302 Townshend, *The life and letters,* 384.

303 Great Britain Royal Commission on Historical Manuscripts, *Report on the manuscripts of the Earl of Egmont* (1905), vol. 1, 328 and vol. 2, 338.

304 T. Birch (ed.), *A collection of the State Papers of John Thurloe, vol. 3: December 1654 - August 1655* (1742), 450-461.

305 M. Brailsford, *Quaker women 1650-1690* (1915), 198-9. There was a report that Scilly pirates took a ship near Minehead in 1650, so perhaps this incident in 1658 was also perpetrated by sailors of the same origin (B. Whitelock, *Memorials of English affairs* (1732), 478).

306 S. O'Maitiu, W. & R. Jacob, *Celebrating 150 years of Irish biscuitmaking* (2001), 3.

307 W. Evans and T. Evans (eds), *The Friends Library* vol. 2 (1838), 364-5.

308 M. Green (ed.), *CSPD Charles II 1667* (1866), 480. Passengers on ships in the Bristol Channel during the Dutch war were not entirely safe during their travels, even if the weather was fine. For example, in June 1666, ships sailing near Swansea witnessed a French Pickaroon chase a vessel from Bristol bound for Ireland with many passengers aboard. The French vessel, on this occasion, failed to catch its prey (*The London Gazette* No. 66, 28 June-2 July 1666).

309 R. Greaves, *God's other children* (1997), 126; Binding and Stevens, *Minehead,* 108.

310 F. Daniel (ed.), *CSPD Carles II 1683-84* (1938), 36.

311 W. Bannerman (ed.), *Miscellanea genealogica et heraldica: fourth series* vol. 3 (1910), 116. Christopher Tuthill had married Mary Hall in May 1685 and in his commonplace book, now held in the William Andrews Clarke Memorial Library of the University of California in Los Angeles (MS. 1977.003), there is mention of the goods sent across to Youghal from Minehead prior to 1688, including damask napkins and Holland pillowcases belonging to his wife Mary must have travelled across to Youghal with Christopher. The same source also mentions that Tuthill became a persecuted protestant whilst in Munster, and imprisoned for short periods in 1689 and 1690 (K. Harvey, *The little republic* (2012), 119-21).

312 J. Hotten (ed.), *The original lists of persons of quality, emigrants and apprentices 1600-1700* (1874), 332-6. See also W. Wingfield, *The Monmouth Rebels 1685,* SRS vol. 79 (1985).

313 The reference to John Hayman is found in B. Burke, *A genealogical and heraldic dictionary of the landed gentry* part 1 (1862), 674, but the mention to his daughter being buried in Minehead is incorrect. His mother was likely to have been buried in Minehead where his wife and infant son were buried under the floor of St Michael's church, Minehead.

314 J. Redington, *Calendar of Treasury Papers, 1557-1696* (1868), 52.

315 BRO, 12964/1/folios 6 and 7.

316 Anne Fitton's story was passed through the generations to her grandson who wrote it down in 1798. A descendent of

the grandson, John Pratt, published the story in 1924 under the title 'Escape of Protestants from Youghal' in *Notes and Queries*, vol. 147, July-December 1924, 398. A question remains as to whether the tale was mere protestant propaganda, but, given that the story was privately passed down rather than printed at the time lends a little to its veracity.

317 E. Arber, *An English garner* (1909), 101-14. See also M. Manous, *You served God he set you free: self, nation, and celebration in the wager-voyaging adventure of Richard Ferris* http://www.britannica.com/bps/additionalcontent/18/27402841/You-serued-God-he-set-you-free-Self-Nation-and-Celebration-in-the-WagerVoyaging-Adventure-of-Richard-Ferris (accessed February 2008).

318 E. Hawkins (ed.), *Remains historical and literary connected with the palatine counties of Lancaster and Cheshire*, The Chetham Society vol. 1 (1844), 165-70.

319 The *Ninth Whelp* was a 14 gun warship of 140-190 tons built in 1628 (N.A.M. Rodger, *The safeguard of the sea* (1997), 482).

320 G. Farr, *Somerset harbours* (1954), 145. The *Angel* was on the east side of Frog Street in the centre of Minehead, now called Holloway Road.

321 Hawkins, *Remains*, 163-76.

322 Rodger, *The safeguard of the sea*, 384.

323 N. Matar, *Islam in Britain 1558-1685* (1998), 7.

324 Binding and Stevens, *Minehead*, 98.

325 Creasy, *Memoirs*, 123-4.

326 Hawkins, *Remains*, 163-76.

327 Rodger, *The safeguard of the sea*, 385.

328 *The London Gazette* no. 1288, 21st -25th March 1678 and no. 1452, 16th-20th October 1679. I am indebted to Adrian Webb for these references.

329 Farr, *Somerset harbours*, 145.

330 Ibid.

331 T. C. Crocker (ed.), *The tour of the French traveller, M. De La Boullaye Le Gouz in Ireland in 1644* (1837), 1-5.

332 J. Wroughton, *An unhappy Civil War* (1999), 17-18.

333 *The Journal of the Friends' Historical Society* vol. 53 (1972), 258.

334 E.R. Montague, R. Blunt and E.J. Climenson, *Mrs Montague 'Queen of the Blues': her letters and friendships from 1762 to 1800* (1923), 117; Lanelli history, http://www.llanelli-history.i12.com/peoplestepney_family.htm (accessed November 2008).

335 J. Beresford (ed.), *The diary of a country parson 1758-1802* (1999), 9-10.

336 J.C. Ibbetson *et al*, *A picturesque guide to Bath, Bristol and Hotwells* (1793), 192-3.

337 E. Rickards, 'Mrs Barbauld and her pupil' in *Murray's Magazine* (1891) 706-10; W. McCarthy, *Anna Letitia Barbauld* (2008), 399.

338 R. Fenton, *A Tour in quest of genealogy through parts of Wales, Somersetshire and Wiltshire* (1811), 77-121, the quote coming from 95.

339 Ibid, 99.

340 Ibid, 101, 121.

341 R. Ayton, 'Voyage le long de la cote de la partie meridionale du Pays de Galles en 1813', in *Nouvelles annals des voyages de la geographie et de l'histoire ou recueil* (1824), 65-74.

342 A. Horseman, 'Superior pedestrianism of Great Britain' in *The Sporting Magazine*, vol. 3 no. 13 (October 1818), 158.

343 G. Rapelje, *A narrative of excursions, voyages and travels* (1836), 74.

344 A. Acland, *A Devon family: the story of the Aclands* (1981), 61-4.

345 J. Rutter, *The Westonian guide* (1829), 24-5, 69-73.

346 J. Gorton, *A topographical dictionary of Great Britain and Ireland* vol. 2 (1833), 35.

347 M. Siraut (ed.), *The Trevelyan papers to 1840*, SRS 80 (1990), 103. The George Trevelyan mentioned in this paragraph was second son of John Trevelyan of Nettlecombe. George had travelled to Ireland in 1604 to serve under his Uncle, Sir Arthur Chichester. He died in 1620 after being elected M.P. for Belfast and receiving a knighthood. He was survived by a wife and son. His father, John, supported the Royalist cause during the civil wars and lost much wealth as a result. Family fortunes were restored by John, eldest son of John, marrying into the Willoughby family of Pahembury, Devon. John Willoughby's travels are mentioned in this text. John Trevelyan the younger's son, also George, is mentioned in this text in a letter relating to 1661 (R. Bush 'Nettlecombe Court: Trevelyans and other residents of the court' in *Field Studies* vol. 3 (1970), 280-2).

348 K. Buhler, 'The Robert Sanderson tankard' in *Bulletin of the Museum of Fine Arts* vol. 35 (1937), 33.

349 T. Gray, *Devon household accounts 1627-59: part one*, Devon and Cornwall Record Society vol. 38 (1995), 258. I am grateful to Adrian Webb for this reference.

350 M. Wolfe, *Gentry leaders in peace and war* (1997), chapter 11 especially page 247.

351 I. Fletcher, *W.B. Yeats and his contemporaries* (1987), 169. One member of the Gyles family became an ancestor of the poet, W.B. Yeats.

352 Savage, *Carhampton*, 592.

353 B. Dobree, *Of books and humankind* (1964), 28, 33. Lady Ranelagh and Mary Rich were two of the first Earl of Cork's daughters. Broghill was their brother and the letter in this case, addressed to their elder brother, Richard, Second Earl of Cork.

354 J. Collier, *et al* (eds), *Trevelyan papers* (1872), 290.

355 F. Daniel (ed.), *CSPD Charles II, 1677-8* (1911), 519.

356 Savage, *Carhampton*, 591.

357 *The Monthly Magazine or British Register* 54: 2 (1822), 571.

358 E. MacLysacht, 'Survey of documents in private keeping', *Analetca Hibernica* 15 (1944), 87.

359 Whiting, *Persecution exposed*, 184-5.

360 H. Ashmead, *History of Delaware County* (1884), Chapter 4.

361 E. MacLysaght (ed.), *Calendar of the Orrery papers* (1941), 329-30.

362 J. Murray and L. Everett, *The life of Rev John Murray* (1858), 1, 16-17.

363 *The Annual register* (1778), 146.

364 M. Aspden, *Letters and other documents* (1837), 207-8.

365 J. Martin, *Wives and daughters*, 322.

366 M. Bouquet, *No gallant ship* (1959), 24.

367 J. Walter *et al*, *Memorials of Washington* (1887), 2.

368 S. Swiggum, *The Ships List*, http://www.theshipslist.com/ships/passengerlists/euphrosyne1831.htm (accessed March 2009).

369 SHC, A\AZF, *Somerset inquests and murders 1825-30*, information taken from the *Taunton Courier*. These sources also record the death of other passengers in the Bristol Channel between 1825 and 1830. Furthermore they detail the loss of merchant vessel crews and pilots in accidents, often in relation to Minehead and Bridgwater.

370 Gray, *Devon household accounts*, 258.

371 Martin, *Wives and daughters*, 313.

372 Emory, *John Wesley*, vol. 3, 314, 344.

373 Ayton, *Voyage*, 65-74.

374 Rickards, *Mrs Barbauld*, 706-10.

375 Fenton, *A Tour*, 77-121.

376 E. Clarke, *A tour through the south of England, Wales and part of Ireland in 1791* (1793), 223-7.

377 Hawkins, *Remains*, 170.

378 Seyer, *Memoirs*, 542-3.

379 Chatterton, *Rambles*, 284-5.

380 Townshend, *The life and letters*, 27.

381 Edwards, *Carte Calendar* 52, 17 June and 1 July.

382 Hawkins, *Remains*, 165-69.

383 Phillips, *Memoirs*, 237-49.

384 Townshend, *The life and letters*, 160-1.

385 The National Library of Ireland, Dublin, The diary of Thomas Dinely.

386 Rapelje, *A narrative*, 74.

387 Meadley, *Memoirs*, 307-9.

388 Davies, *Rowland Davies*, 1.

389 Meadley, *Memoirs*, 312.

390 SHC, DD/X/HYN/1.

391 W. Page (ed.), *Report on the manuscripts of the Earl of Egmont* vol. 2 (1909), 44.

392 *The Friend's library* 3, 130-1.

393 Alexander, *Thomas Story*, 90.

394 *The Friend's library* 5, 20.

395 *The Friend's library* 9, 26.

396 Wesley, *The experience*, 99.

397 Moore, *Staff officer*, 196.

398 Creasy, *Memoirs*, 123-4.

399 Brady, *Natives and newcomers*, 174.

400 Crocker, *The tour*, 1-5.

401 Collier, *Trevelyan papers*, 290.

402 R. Mortimer (ed.), *Minute book of the men's meeting of the Society of Friends in Bristol 1667-1686*, BRS 26 (1971), 79-80.

403 Mrs Clarke, *A narrative of the life of Mrs Clarke* (1829), 136. Though writing towards the end of her life in the early nineteenth century, the author seems to be referring to a time she spent in Pill sometime prior to 1755, when she described the business people in Pill as 'cannibals' and 'beasts of prey' because of their poor treatment of wind-bound passengers.

404 Maclysaght, *Calendar of Orrery papers*, 329-30.

405 *The Friends Library* 9, 291.

406 Gough, *A history*, 399-400.

407 *The Baptist magazine* 1824, 173.

408 Hall, *St James's magazine*, 235.

409 *Journal of the Waterford and South-East Ireland Archaeological Society* 8 (1902), 88.

410 Murray, *Life of Murray*, 17.

411 S. Hall, *Ireland: its scenery and character* (1841), 1.

412 Anon, *The new Bath guide* (1789), 78.

413 Falls, *Elizabeth's wars*, 194.

414 Portishead was the most likely provisioning point for ships lying in King Road.

415 R. Asland (ed.), *The Christian reformer* (1862), 481-90.

416 J. Shelley (ed.), *Shelley memorials: from authentic sources* (1859), 51.

417 Anon, *Memoirs of Edmund Ludlow* 2, 318.

418 Burke, *Family romance*, 167.

419 Dyott, *Dyott's diary* 1, 18-19.

420 Ayton, *Voyage*, 73-4.

421 H. Nott (ed.), *The deposition book of Bristol* vol. 2, BRS 13 (1947), 70-2.

422 Green, *CSPD 1651-2*, 97 and 550.

423 M. Green (ed.), *CSPD Charles II, 1668-9* (1894), 184. *The London Gazette* No. 338, 8-11 February 1668, reported that the two vessels left Minehead on 2 January and after 15-16 days beating about at sea they made it back to Youghal. Other details reported are broadly similar to those recorded in the State papers.

424 W. Shaw (ed.), *Calendar of Treasury books vol. 6 1679-80* (1913), 109.

425 *The terrific register* vol. 2 (1825), 819.

426 W. Gilpin, *Observations on the River Wye* (1800), 135-8.

427 D. Quin, 'Guide to English financial records for Irish history', *Analecta Hibernica* vol. 10 (1941), 65.

428 J. Gairdner (ed.), *LPFD Henry VIII* vol. 7 (1883), 24. The owners of the vessel whose mariners were left on Lundy were from San Sebastian. Since the majority of Bridgwater's trade with northern Spain in the sixteenth century was with San Sebastian it is likely that the sailors were returned to their home before many weeks had elapsed.

429 Hawkins, *Remains*, 163-76.

430 Gray, *Household accounts*, 258.

431 Coates, *Private journals*, 406.

432 Grossart, *Lismore papers*, 199.

433 W. Burghclere, *The life of James, first Duke of Ormonde* (1912), 153.

434 J.B. Ormonde *et al, Calendar of the manuscripts of the Marquess of Ormonde* (1904), 437.

435 Morland, *Quarterly meeting*, 105.

436 E. Shirley, 'Extracts from the Journal of Thomas Dineley (Dingley)' in *The Journal of the Kilkenny and South-East of Ireland Archaeology Society* New Series 1 (1856-57), 146. Also, information from the original diary held in the National Library of Ireland, Dublin.

437 Ibid.

438 Anon, *The trial at bar between Campbell Craig lessee of James Annesley and Richard Earl of Anglesy* (1744), 43.

439 Martin, *Wives and daughters*, 313.

440 Pollock, *United Services Magazine 1829*, 220-1.

441 H. Binding 'Notes By The Way' in *The West Somerset Free Press* (September 2001). The Ernst family of Somerset travelled on the packet in both directions in 1824 and Mrs Ernst has left a description of the passages in her diary (SHC, DD/SWD/10, diary 7).

442 *Cambrian Newspaper*, 5 August 1826.

443 Anon, 'Irish Services', http://www.simplonpc.co.uk/GWR1.html (accessed February 2008).

444 R. Head, *The English rogue* (1666).

445 F. Fleming, *T. Ginnadrake* (1771).

446 W.M. Brady, *Clerical and parochial records of Cork* vol. 2 (Cork, 1864), 306-8; Chadwyck-Healey, *West Somerset*, 162-70; E.S. Byam, 'General W. Byam of Antigua' in *The Gentleman's Magazine, January 1848*, 39-42.

447 E. Timings, *CSPD: James II, 1685* (1960), 12-14.

448 SHC, H. Phipps, *Bath and Wells marriage licences* vol. 1, 2.

449 SHC, T\PH|lanc/10 burials, 1548-1638.

Chapter Two

"Oh, I do like to be beside the seaside …": An Account of the Development of Somerset's Seaside Resorts

Sue Berry

Introduction

JUST AS THE wealthy inhabitants of Imperial Rome were accustomed to spend a portion of the year on the shores of the Mediterranean Sea for the purpose of renovating their vital powers, exhausted by over-attention to study, business, or the claims of luxury, so in our own age of rush and worry it is becoming more and more fashionable to sojourn for a while at the seaside and 'Thousands bathe who never bathed before, while those who always bathed, now bathe the more".[1] So wrote the editor of the *Clevedon Borough Guide* some time around 1900A.D. in a rather optimistic comparison of his town with resorts on the Bay of Naples 1,800 years before.

By 1900 the annual seaside holiday, whether a week's stay or only a day trip, was a fact of life for millions of Britain's urban population. The great resorts of Blackpool on the west coast and Scarborough on the east drew their holidaymakers from the factories of the industrial north; those of the south coast, such as Brighton, attracted theirs from the metropolis of London and other towns of the southeast. In Somerset, the popular resorts of Weston-super-Mare, Minehead, Burnham and Clevedon, enticed their visitors from Bristol and the towns of South Wales, as well as from the population of Somerset itself.

But why was the seaside holiday so popular in Britain? Geography played a part, in that no great centre of population was further than 70 to 80 miles from the sea, and, once the transport systems were in place to move people rapidly from urban centres to the coast, mass travel became possible. There may also have been an element of emulation whereby the rising middle classes, such as the merchants of Bristol, saw the upper classes visiting the seaside and wished to do the same. In 1788 it was stated 'wherever the people in high life take the lead, the next class eagerly follows'.[2] Factory workers and shopkeepers followed the middle classes, assisted by the introduction of Sir John Lubbock's Bank Holiday Act in 1871 and by the growth of disposable income throughout the nineteenth century.

The origins of the seaside visit go back well into the eighteenth century, although it may be misleading to think of many of the early visitors as holidaymakers in the modern sense; they were seeking not a good time, but good health. Spa bathing had long been believed to be good for the health; the Romans had developed *Aquae Sulis*, or Bath as it became known, into a spa before the fourth century. The historian Nennius wrote of the bath there as still being used in the ninth century and shortly after the suppression of Bath Priory in 1539 it came under the control of the Corporation. By 1542 John Leland could write of the Cross Bath as 'much frequented of people diseasid with lepre, pokkes, scabbes and great aches, . . .' and as this bath and the Hot Bath were joined to St John's Hospital 'it may be thought that Reginalde Bisshop of Bathe made this hospitale near these 2 commune bathes to socour poore people resorting to them'.[3] In the early eighteenth century no less a personage than Queen Anne visited the city twice causing the New Bath to be renamed the Queen's Bath in her honour[4] and there is local evidence that the reputation of the baths was widespread among more humble folk who thought bathing in the waters might help them. John Elsworthie was one such visitor. A tin miner from Cornwall, he was detained at Dunster in March 1616/17 suspected of being an incorrigible rogue due to a mark on his shoulder thought to be a brand. However, it was, he said, the scar left "by the fall of a tin work" and he was travelling to Bath 'hoping there to receive some remedy and help for the bruises of his body in working in tin works'.[5] The first national advertisement for the baths was placed by the city's Mayor in 1664;[6] it described the construction of a covered bath which could be used throughout the year thus extending the visitor season. In 1698 Celia Fiennes visited the city and wrote of her experiences in the baths that 'Some will keep on their wet garments and let them drye to them and say its more beneficial, but I did not venture it: I dipp'd my head quite over every tyme I went in and found it eased a great pain I used to have in my head, and I was not so apt to catch cold so much as before . . .'.[7] By the middle of the eighteenth century, the town had become the place to go for the aristocracy and gentry looking for both health and recreation.

The concept of bathing in seawater for health reasons started to develop at the beginning of the eighteenth century and it was seen as an extension of the inland spas. Many in the medical profession believed in the efficacy of sea bathing and published works in support of their theories. In 1753 Dr Richard Russell published his *Dissertation concerning the use of sea water in the diseases of the glands* and in 1769 William Buchan's *Domestic medicine* advocated sea bathing. 1795 saw the publication of Dr John Anderson's *A practical essay on the good and bad effects of sea-water and sea-bathing* and Dr Alexander Peter Buchan published his *Treatise on sea bathing, with remarks on the use of the warm bath* in 1801. Devotees ranged from the poet Samuel Rogers to the author Sir Walter Scott, not forgetting King George the Third and other members of the Royal family. The King himself made 14 visits to Weymouth between 1789 and 1805 during the summer or autumn seasons, making Weymouth one of the most fashionable Georgian era sea bathing resorts. As well as using one of the public bathing machines available there, he also had plans drawn up for his own 'floating baths' by John William Hiort, an architect at the Office of Works.[8] Even after the advent of the

day-tripper in the 1840s looking for an entertaining break from work, many of the published guides to seaside towns emphasized above all the benefits to health of a visit to their resort. The Revd W. Jackson in his 1877 *Visitors' handbook to Weston super Mare and its vicinity* devoted a whole chapter to 'Modern Weston as a Health Resort' and discussed the 'extraordinary vitality' of the air, the quality of the water and the 'very important subject of sewerage'.

Development of the seaside resorts

In Somerset, Minehead was the first resort to develop. Edmund Rack commented in the early 1780s that 'the climate is mild, and by the sea breezes the air is renderd so salubrious that vegetation is earlier by near a month than in the inland parts of the county'.[9] In 1794 it was said of the town that 'on account of the pleasantness of the situation and salubrity of the air, a number of persons of fashion have been induced to visit it as a bathing place in the summer season'.[10] By 1797 there is evidence of there being at least some provision for the intrepid bather

Illustration 2.1: Watercolour sketch of Minehead beach by J.F. Doveton, showing a bathing machine on the far right of the picture, 1797 (SHC, DD\DP/21/2)

on Minehead's beach. In that year, John Frederick Doveton of Blagdon, who was on a walking tour of Exmoor, arrived at a point where he could see the prospect of Minehead's North Hill with, in the foreground, the harbour and the beach. He sketched the scene, showing on the beach, at the edge of the water, a small wooden hut on wheels with steps leading up to a door at one end allowing access to the water, a bathing machine.[11]

The Revd Richard Warner of Bath who visited Minehead in 1799 wrote 'Some appearance of cheerfulness and animation has been given it, till within these few years, by the company which resorted hither in the summer season for the purpose of bathing'. However, he implied that the number of visitors had fallen and he was at a loss to understand why:

> The shore is hard and fine; the machines commodious; the lodgings reasonable . . . and though the access be rendered easy by an excellent turnpike road, which runs to Bristol, yet its distance from the metropolis and the populous parts of England, is sufficiently great to prevent those *felicity hunters*, the teasing insects of fashion, from disturbing with their impertinent buzzings the pensive or rational pleasures of them who choose to enjoy Nature at Minehead.[12]

James Savage in his *History of the Hundred of Carhampton* written 30 years later agreed with Warner that the visitors who came to Minehead would 'not be annoyed by the company of the frivolous part of the fashionable world, of whom so many are to be found in some of our watering places . . .'[13] but by this time it seems that the visitor numbers had increased to the extent that they 'in no small degree' contributed to Minehead's support and welfare.[14] Minehead's position on the fringes of Exmoor played a part in attracting visitors, combining as it did the benefits of sea bathing with the newly discovered joys of romantic scenery as celebrated in the poetry of Wordsworth and Coleridge.

On his way to Minehead, Warner had stayed at the inn at Blue Anchor and noted, that even in this small place, the innkeeper had decided to build a house for lodgers and 'fit up a bathing machine for their use'.[15] It was probably to Blue Anchor that the Revd William Holland of Over Stowey took his boys one day in July 1805. He wrote in his diary that 'When we got to the seaside we got out of our car[t] & the boys ran to the seaside & began a looking for periwinkles and limpets & some took off their shoes

and stockings & were highly delighted'. Holland himself sat in the cart and read his newspaper. Later, while they picnicked on a fine 'lamb pye' and bottles of cider, the haze lifted and they could see Minehead and Minehead Point very clearly in the distance.[16]

Weston-super-Mare began to attract a similar type of visitor from the end of the eighteenth century. The *Gentleman's Magazine* of December 1805 said 'This village is much frequented of late in the Summer and Autumn for the benefit of sea air and bathing'. In 1819, two years before her death at the age of 80, Mrs Piozzi visited Weston and wrote of it 'This little place is neither gay nor fashionable yet full as an Egg . . .'. She had been used to moving in aristocratic and literary circles; her view of Weston's visitors was that they were 'insipid as the white . . .'.[17]

The first guide book to Weston was published as early as 1822. According to the author of this work, there were by this date three bathing machines on the beach with hot and cold baths on Knightstone Island and a hot bath in Somerset Place. The charge for a hot bath was 3s while a cold one was just 1s.[18] In 1829 when John Rutter published his *Delineations of North West Somerset* he included an engraving showing a view of Weston from the sea, with a few houses, two bathing machines and about a dozen people on the beach. However, as Rutter wrote that the 'number of lodging houses is now upwards of 150' and 'the public promenade is now almost unrivalled, and forms one of the finest in the kingdom', possibly the young artist, John Watkins Brett of Bristol, exercised a little licence in his drawing. By this date although 'in fashionable and public amusements, Weston must be acknowledged to be deficient' and 'health not dissipation is the lure it presents', the town could boast 'a good library and a convenient reading room' as well as 'sedan and wheel chairs for invalids'.[19]

By 1832 it was possible to hire either a pony or a donkey to ride on the sands, but when the Revd John Skinner's son and daughter did so in July that year both animals 'were not of the most delightful description'. The day after the ride they all took a boat trip around the bay, noting that had there been more wind 'we should have enjoyed our two hours' excursion much'. Nevertheless, at the end of their time at Weston, Skinner wrote that his son Joseph, who had consumption, was 'evidently the better for the air and amusement he has found at Weston; but we all agree it is a wretched place to continue in for any length of time'.[20]

Closer to Bristol and thus easier to reach than Weston, the resort of Clevedon doubled in size between 1821 and 1831. In his 1829 guide to the resort John Rutter described it as a picturesque place suitable for those invalids who required pure air and the opportunity to take moderate exercise. He stated there were 'delightful walks' in the vicinity, one of the pleasantest being that to the ruins of Walton Church and Castle. However, he added in a somewhat acerbic footnote 'It is much to be regretted that the lessee of the surrounding farm, feels so little disposition to afford accommodation to those who are inclined to explore these interesting ruins'. In his description of Clevedon's recent development he mentioned the 'handsome hotel . . . where comfortable accommodations are combined with reasonable charges'. There were also 'several pleasantly situated lodging houses, recently erected' while on the beach there were three bathing machines which were 'let down and drawn up by windlasses'. Plans for a pier had been approved 'with a view to its immediate execution' and although the state of the existing roads was not good 'a new road, fifty feet wide, is in progress from the hotel to the church'.[21] The frontispiece to the *Guide* shows a prospect of the bay with visitors strolling on the paths and stopping to admire the view out to sea. One young lady has set up her folding camp stool and is sketching the scene. A drawing (illustration 2.2) of the late 1830s or early 1840s shows four bathing machines on the beach although there is no sign of the windlasses referred to by Rutter and they may have been horse drawn. The modesty hood or canopy at the end of the machines can be clearly seen in this drawing: it enabled the bather to enter the water and bathe unseen and is said to have been invented by Benjamin Beale, a Quaker from Margate.

By 1852 it was said 'In the season Clevedon is much frequented as a watering place. The hotels, lodging houses and villas for the accommodation of visitors, as well as the houses of the resident gentry, are principally in the upper part of the village, on the hill. Upper Clevedon, as this part of the village is called, has all been built within the last thirty years'. The town had no industry as such, apart from agriculture, and it was claimed that 'the town almost entirely depends upon visitors in the summer and autumn, but owing to the mildness of climate and the cheapness of lodgings in winter there are some visitors even at that season'. In 1851 the permanent population was 1905 but in the summer the number of visitors brought the numbers to about 2,300 and even in the winter to nearly 2,000.[22]

Burnham was the only Somerset seaside resort to have mineral springs and could thus call itself a spa in the sense of Bath or Harrogate in Yorkshire. The two springs were not discovered by the vicar, Revd Davis, until 1830 and as a result the resort developed later than the other Somerset ones. It was described by a visitor in 1843 as having 'on the whole a very forlorn and unattractive appearance, especially at low water'. The new buildings that it did have were 'on a small scale' and its beach consisted of 'heavy drifts of sand with puddles of water'.[23] However, by 1859,

Illlustration 2.2: A drawing of Clevedon beach with four bathing machines by 'G.M.', *c.*1840 (SANHS, Braikenridge Collection A\DAS/1/102/2 item 3)

according to the author of a guidebook published that year, 'The sea-beach of Burnham is of firm and fine sand . . . It is admirably adapted for the recreation of children, . . . It is impossible that a more delightful or invigorating walk, ride, or drive, could be had anywhere on our English coast'.[24] In 1872 an advertisement for the Clarence Family and Commercial Hotel emphasized its position as being 'in the immediate vicinity of the Baths and Medicinal Springs' and described Burnham itself as 'one of the healthiest watering places on the coast'.[25]

Bathing machines

Bathing machines were an essential part of sea bathing, especially as both sexes bathed naked to begin with and men were not legally obliged to wear a costume until 1880. Women were enveloped in bathing costumes which covered them practically from head to foot earlier than this.

Although bathers were segregated by sex and bathed from different areas of the beach, it was considered essential that they should not catch sight of each other out of the water and bathing machines enabled them to enter the water without being seen from the beach. The author Tobias Smollet described the use of a bathing machine in one of his novels:

> Imagine to yourself a small, snug, wooden chamber, fixed upon a wheel-carriage, having a door at each end, and on each side a little window above, a bench below – The bather, ascending into this apartment by wooden steps, shuts himself in, and begins to undress, while the attendant yokes a horse to the end next the sea, and draws the carriage forwards, til the surface of the water is on a level with the floor of the dressingroom, then he moves and fixes the horse to the other end – The person within being stripped, opens the door to the sea-ward, where he finds the guide ready, and plunges headlong into the water – After having bathed, he re-ascends into the apartment, by the steps which had been shifted for that purpose, and puts on his clothes at his leisure, while the carriage is drawn back again upon the dry land; so that he has nothing further to do, but to open the door, and come down as he went up – Should he be so weak or ill as to require a servant to put off and on his clothes, there is room enough in the apartment for half a dozen people.[26]

Not everyone shared Smollet's view of the bathing machine. An anonymous poet was moved to compose an ode, *To The First Bathing Machine (After Wordsworth)* part of which read:

> So gentle looking a machine,
> Infernal one thou art!
>
> I, grasping tightly, pale with fear,
> Thy very narrow bench,
> Thou, bounding on in wild career,
> All shake, and jolt, and wrench.
>
> Till comes an unexpected stop;
> My forehead hits the door,
> And I, with cataclysmic flop,
> Lie on thy sandy floor.
>
> Then, dressed in Nature's simplest style,
> I, blushing, venture out;
> And find the sea is still a mile
> Away, or thereabout.[27]

As noted above, Minehead had at least one bathing machine as early as 1797. In the mid 1820s a local poet wrote of its three horse drawn bathing machines and recorded the price charged, one shilling a dip. A photograph taken in the early twentieth century shows four wheeled machines although with no sign of any horses, and three other small changing huts in a row on the beach.[28]

In 1829 the bathing machines at Weston were 'well built and are kept clean and neat…females being accompanied, if required, by careful and experienced bathing women'. The numbers of those wishing to take advantage of this facility was, in fact, so great that despite more machines being provided they 'were not, even yet, sufficiently numerous' to prevent bathers having to wait their turn at the busiest times.[29] By 1836 at Burnham 'for the accommodation of those individuals who may prefer bathing in the sea at high water' a number of suitable machines were in existence with 'proper attendants'.[30] In 1864 *The New Handbook of Clevedon and the Neighbourhood* described the bathing machines there as 'recently constructed' and

> perfectly safe and clean. Those for Gentlemen are kept at the South end, and those for Ladies at the North end of the Beach.

In 1854 Weston's beach was described as

> well supplied with commodious and strongly-build bathing machines, which are kept extremely clean

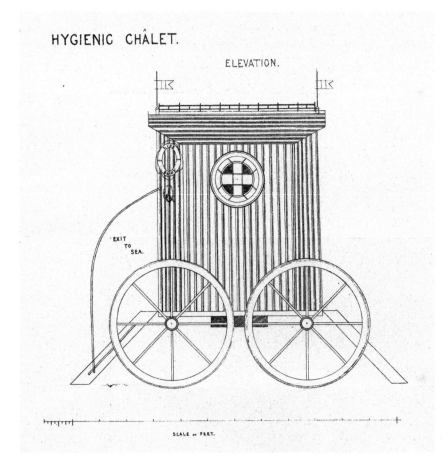

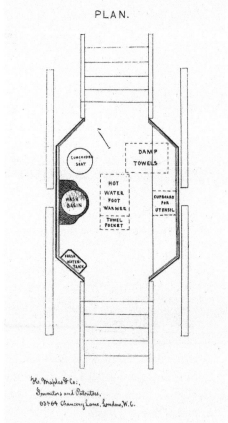

and neat. Experienced female attendants for the ladies are always at hand. The cost of a machine on a single occasion is sixpence.[31]

However, there were those who preferred to bathe as nature intended and who spurned the use of bathing machine and costume alike. In September 1872 the Revd Francis Kilvert, visiting Weston with his mother and sister, made use of a bathing machine on the first morning but only, as he wrote in his diary, because 'I had brought down no towels of my own'. The following morning he

> was out early before breakfast bathing from the sands. There was a delicious feeling of freedom in stripping in the open air and running naked to the sea.[32]

In March 1887 *The Sanitary Record* reported on the The Hygienic Châlet Sea Bathing Company's plans for a new and improved bathing machine: 'The advantages, briefly summarised, are that it provides bathers with a warm room on returning from the sea, hot and cold water, hot towels and a dry floor — hygienic comforts that should render its general

adoption a question of only a short time'. The patentees, H. Maples and Company, circulated their prospectus to seaside resorts, including Weston, in the hope of persuading the towns to buy the new improved machine.[33]

The use of bathing machines continued into the twentieth century, but when over 100 on the beach at Weston were destroyed by a fierce storm in September 1903 they were not replaced. Some machines at Glentworth Bay did survive,[34] although damaged, and a postcard of some of them showing a few local boys sitting on the roofs was published. One copy of this card was sent to a Miss Maude Mattock in Ontario Canada with the comment

> Quite an amazing sight, is it not? But I scarce like to laugh because of the loss it means. They appear like a group of intoxicated men. They were some way away from where the worst of it was or they would have been washed [and] smashed to splinters.

Nevertheless, as late as 1935 the use of bathing machines and the wearing of appropriate costumes on the beach became a *cause celebre* at Minehead. The

Illustration 2.3: The exterior of the Hygienic Châlet bathing machine, 1887 (SHC, A\AKH/6/3/1)
Illustration 2.4: The interior of the Hygienic Châlet bathing machine with all modern conveniences, 1887 (SHC, A\AKH/6/3/1)

THE MINOR ILLS OF LIFE

Portrait of a gentleman attempting to regain his tent
after the morning bath

Illustration 2.5: What the well dressed male bather was wearing
on the beach *c.* 1906 (*Mr Punch at the seaside*)

Daily Express reported in July that year how Somerset
County Council had ordered notices to be put up in
the resort to the effect that

> Persons bathing near the esplanade must use a
> machine, tent or other effectual screen. Further,
> they must wear some garment in such a manner as
> to prevent improper exposure.

Some local people saw both the humorous side of
this and the commercial opportunity it presented. A
local newspaper carried the following advertisement
on 10 August

> Bathing without costumes on Minehead Beach
>
> In view of the fact that the above sport, pastime
> or recreation is strongly forbidden, we ask all
> bathers not to express their pleasure, or displeasure,
> by appearing on the beach in weird, grotesque or
> fantastic costumes. You owe it to yourself to see
> that your Bathing Suit garbs you as in a mantle of
> the valiant. Unless you have visited, and seen, and
> been fitted with your costume at F.H. Cornish &
> Son you have not done the duty you owe to
> yourself as A MAN.[35]

Some visitors decided a bathing costume was
superfluous if they were only going to paddle in the
sea, their trousers needing only to be rolled up to the
knees and their shirt sleeves to the elbows.

The Town Council took the situation more
seriously. It met on 12 August to discuss the County
Council's action and a motion was put forward

> that as practically all other British Seaside Resorts
> permit undressing on their beaches, the Council
> requests the persons responsible for the recently
> imposed restrictions to remove them, as in the
> opinion of the Council they are quite
> unnecessary and do not further the interests of
> a progressive Seaside Resort.[36]

The motion was not carried, which may suggest that
a majority of the members of the Council thought
that possibly Minehead should not be quite so
progressive as all that. It may have been a co-
incidence but it was only the following year that the

Illustration 2.6: *Dea Ex Machina.* A Du Maurier cartoon
illustrating a typical bathing costume of the 1890's. (*Mr Punch
at the seaside*)

DEA EX MACHINA!
(*A Reminiscence*)

Illustration 2.7: A visitor and his daughter dressed for the beach at Minehead in the 1930s (M.F. Webb)

Luttrell family paid for the building of a state-of-the-art swimming pool on the foreshore with a magnificent diving tower, terraces for sun bathing and a café. It claimed to be the only Olympic size pool in the country.

Seawater baths

There was an alternative to waiting for an available bathing machine and braving the cold water of the sea and this was the seawater bath, either hot or cold. Baths were first built on Knightstone Island at Weston in July 1820 by Mr Howe. Lodgings were built for those who wished to stay on the island rather than face a daily boat crossing from the town and there was a refreshment room and a reading room. In 1824 Howe sold Knightstone to the Revd Thomas

Pruen who had the causeway connecting the island and the mainland built. Four years later in 1830 Knightstone was purchased by Dr Edward Long Fox of Bristol who developed the facilities on the island and built an elegant new bath house for visitors, turning the existing bath into the Superintendent's house. Twenty years later when Knightstone was put up for sale, a sale catalogue was produced which contained several illustrations of the buildings on the island as well as a plan of the baths and the following description of them:

> Lot 4. All those excellent and well arranged BUILDINGS, comprising "THE BATH HOUSE" and Superindentent's House, with the residue of the ISLAND OF KNIGHTSTONE, including the Causeway leading thereto, several valuable BUILDING SITES and the PIERS, PROMENADES etc.
>
> THE BATH HOUSE was built a few years since at an unsparing expense, and is admitted to be as complete a Bathing Establishment as any in the West of England.
>
> On the ground floor it contains a Reading-Room and two Waiting Rooms, 6 Warm Baths, 2 Plunging Baths, 2 Shower Baths, and Vapour and Sulpher Baths. The Entrance Hall leads to the Baths on

IIlustration 2.8: A view of the Bath House on Knightstone Island from the landward side, 1850 (SHC, DD\X\VZ/5)

Illustration 2.9: A poster for Minehead's new swimming pool showing the 33' high concrete diving tower, *c*.1936 (SHC, DD\X\WBB/23)

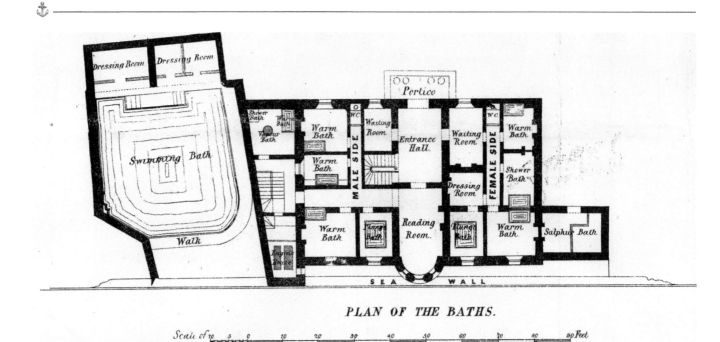

PLAN OF THE BATHS.

Scale of ...

Illustration 2.10: A plan of the baths on Knightstone Island, 1850 (SHC, DD\X\VZ/5)

each side, which are so arranged for the accommodation of Gentlemen and Ladies as to keep them perfectly distinct; and attached to the Gentlemen's side of the House is a large SWIMMING BATH, capable of holding 1400 Hogsheads of Water, supplied through Reservoirs direct from the Sea.[37]

Clevedon had some public hot baths by 1829, described by Rutter as having 'been built by an industrious speculator, who intends also to erect some lodging houses in connection with them'.[38] This was Samuel Taylor of Hutton who, according to a deed of 1829, had 'some time since' built a tenement with 'warm and cold water baths'.[39] He may well have noted the success of the baths at Weston and thought that Clevedon should also provide such a facility. By 1864 when Sir Arthur Elton bought the property, then called Clevedon Park Marine Baths, they were described as 'now void'. Elton sold them in 1876 to a Clevedon builder, John Vickery, and a new bath was built two years later which included some parts of the earlier building. In 1896 the newly formed Urban District Council considered a proposal to obtain an estimate for the restoration and renovation of the baths. This was to include all the materials and the equipment for hot and cold bathing; a town museum was to be incorporated in the same building. This proposal, however, was not carried, presumably due to the expense involved.[40]

Burnham's bathhouse was built by Revd Davies in 1830 in order to attract visitors to the town. In 1836 they were described as a 'spacious building', one part of which had been fitted out with sea water baths, both hot and cold, and also with a bath using the water from the sulphurous spring which Davies had discovered nearby. The other part of the building was 'arranged for the reception and accommodation of such invalids, as may think it expedient, during a course of warm bathing, to avoid all risk from exposure in returning to their residence'. The way in which the machinery that pumped the sea water into the baths was arranged led to its adaptation as a nursery for raising oysters. It was thought that 'the constant supply [of oysters] . . . cannot fail to be a great acquisition to the neighbourhood, and in particular to invalids, to whom it is a nutricious article of diet, and a restorative in emaciating diseases'.[41]

The road to Somerset

Despite all the efforts of these entrepreneurs, the Somerset seaside resorts never became as fashionable in the early part of the nineteenth century as resorts such as Brighton or Scarborough. One reason may have been the fact that they were some distance from any centre of large population, such as Bath, that was patronised by the aristocracy and landed gentry. These tended to go to Weymouth if they wanted a stay by the sea, particularly after the resort was visited by George III and other members of the royal family between 1789 and 1805. Would-be visitors to the Somerset resorts would also have experienced some difficulty in reaching the coast as the majority of the roads in the county were poor and not conducive to comfortable travel. C. and J. Greenwood's 1822 map of Somerset shows the turnpike roads in place at that time.[42] It was possible to get from Bristol to Minehead on turnpiked roads, via East Brent, Bridgwater, Cannington and Watchet, and from Bath to Minehead via the London-Exeter mail coach route as far as Bridgwater and then on the Cannington-Watchet route. What was not possible was to get from either Bristol or Bath to any other Somerset seaside resort without using the parish roads for at least part of the journey. There was no turnpike road to the west of a line between Bristol-East Brent-Bawdrip, apart from a spur from Bristol to Brockley via Flax Bourton.

In his research notes for the Revd John Collinson's *History of Somerset*, Edmund Rack commented on the state of the 'cross' or non turnpike roads in the county. Unfortunately, his notes for the Hundreds of Portbury and Winterstoke containing Clevedon and Weston respectively are not available, but in the Hundred of Carhampton he wrote that:

> The roads (except the turnpike from Dunster to Porlock, and that to Dulverton) are intolerably bad, being only deep narrow paths worn in the natural bed of rock and filled with loose rough stones. This, together with their steepness, renders travelling on horseback very dangerous.

In Carhampton the roads were 'very rough and bad', while Culbone could not be

approachd on horseback without great difficulty and even danger, the road from Porlock being only narrow paths about 2 ft wide winding in a zig zag direction along the slope of those vast hills . . . These narrow paths in the rocks are filld with large loose stones and the roots of trees.

In Luxborough 'The roads . . . are impassable for any wheel carriage and dangerous even for horses, being very steep, narrow channels washd into a kind of broken stairs and coverd with great loose stones and fragments of rock' and in Stoke Pero they were 'impassable for any carriage, being very steep, narrow, and so incumberd with great loose stones that it is dangerous even for horses'.[43]

It was not just in the west of the county that the roads were poor. In 1830 a resident in the Martock area wrote to the Clerk of the Peace complaining of the state of the roads in his locality:

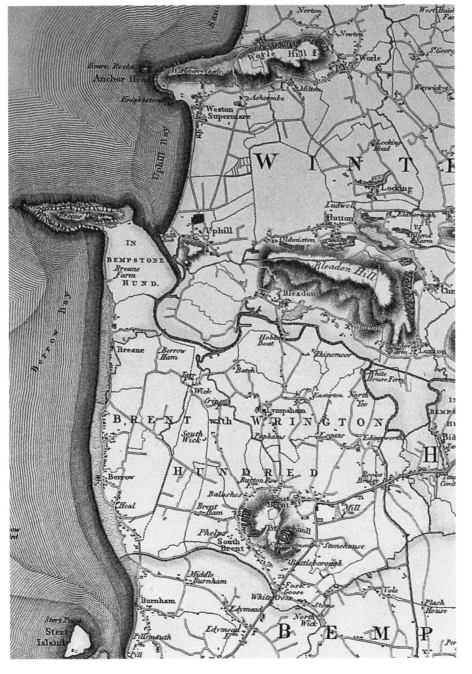

Illustration 2.11: Part of Greenwood's map of Somerset showing the Burnham and Weston area, 1822 (SANHS)

It was but yesterday that the most sure footed horse I ever crossed, (and I have ridden many hundreds of leagues in the most precipitous countries without an accident) was thrown violently forward upon his head and knees . . . by having put his fore foot into a hole, filled with water and loose clay, which might with ease have contained a sheep; and but for Gods mercy and my wary extrication of the stirrups I might have been killed on the spot . . .[44]

Any invalids intending to visit a resort for health reasons and having to travel through this part of the county to reach the coast may well have decided to abort their trip. As late as 1836 Burnham was

only accessible from the turnpike road. For as the Berrow road consists of sand alone, it acts as a prohibition to travelling . . .[45]

Population explosion

Another reason for the lack of fashionable patronage at the beginning of the nineteenth century may have been a dearth of suitable accommodation in the resorts themselves due to their comparatively small populations. Whereas Brighton had a population of around 7000 in 1801, the populations of the Somerset seaside resorts ranged from 1168 in Minehead to only 138 in Weston. Minehead in fact, according to Edmund Rack, had lost a third of its population between 1705 and *c.*1783 and the number of houses had fallen from 318 to 284, many of which 'still remaining being now uninhabited and falling to ruin'.[46] In 1821 Weston's population was still under 1000 and it was not until 1841 that it outstripped those of Burnham and Minehead and began to grow far faster for the rest of the nineteenth century.

By the middle of the nineteenth century, Somerset's resorts, particularly Weston, had grown to the extent that by 1851, in a list of 71 seaside resorts in England and Wales, Weston-super-Mare was ranked 28th with a population of 4,034, Clevedon was 48th with 1,905, Burnham 49th with 1,701 and Minehead 51st with 1,542. In the years between 1801 and 1851, out of 68 resorts Weston had the biggest growth in population, bar one, with a percentage growth of 2,808.7%, Clevedon was 6th with a growth rate of 470.4%, Burnham 32nd with 160.5% and Minehead 63rd with 32.1%. Weston and Clevedon's growth rates were, however, distorted by the fact that their populations in 1801 were so small.

By 1881 their relative positions by population in

a table of 106 resorts were Weston 21st, Clevedon 41st, Burnham 56th and Minehead 82nd and their positions in percentage growth rates between 1851 and 1881 were Weston 14th, with a growth rate of 220%, Clevedon 20th, with a rise of 155.6%, Burnham 28th, with 114.3% and Minehead 81st, with 15%. A few years into the twentieth century Weston was placed 19th out of 145 in size with a population of 23,235 in 1911; Clevedon, the next largest resort in Somerset, was 59th, its population of 6,111 falling some way behind Weston's.[47]

Table 2.1: Population figures for Burnham, Clevedon, Minehead and Weston, 1801-1901

Year	Burnham	Clevedon	Minehead	Weston
1801	653	334	1,168	138
1811	742	455	1,037	163
1821	920	581	1,239	738
1831	1,113	1,147	1,481	1,310
1841	1,469	1,748	1,489	2,103
1851	1,701	1,905	1,542	4,034
1861	2,252	2,941	1,582	8,038
1871	3,257	4,039	1,605	10,568
1881	3,645	4,867	1,774	12,884
1891	4,200	5,412	2,073	15,524
1901	4,922	5,900	2,782	18,275

Source: 1801-1901 census returns

What had led to this great growth in seaside towns' populations? Not all of these people were visitors; after all, the census returns which provide these figures were taken in April or May, whereas one would expect the greatest number of visitors to be staying at the seaside between June and September. Some of the resident population would be born and bred locals such as fishermen and shopkeepers, others would be the retired who had moved to the seaside for the benefits of the sea air, or the young who were enrolled in the many private schools established in these towns. Then there were those who had settled in the seaside towns to cater for the visitors, providing places to eat, places to sleep, and a variety of entertainments. The influx of visitors brought by the steamers and the railways led to a growth in the permanent population, many of whom earned their living catering for holidaymakers; in turn, the growth in accommodation and other facilities provided by the permanent population led to a greater number of visitors arriving to take advantage of these facilities.

Accommodation for visitors

Entrepreneurs in the early part of the nineteenth century realized that comfortable accommodation was essential if middle class visitors were to be attracted to their towns, although hotels built specifically for holidaymakers were a later nineteenth century development. The Revd Warner commented in 1799 that the lodgings in Minehead were reasonable, although whether by this he meant in price or in the accommodation they offered he does not make clear. In 1820 the Wellington Hotel, which described itself as a family as well as a commercial hotel was built, but the majority of the other inns in the town probably did not cater for the fastidious family. James Savage wrote in 1830 that 'To certain classes who wish to visit the sea-side, Minehead offers many advantages; lodgings are low, provisions are good and cheap'[48] but 20 years later, according to the evidence of the 1851 census returns, very few people kept what were described as 'lodging houses'. As Hilary Binding and Douglas Stevens pointed out 'By 1851 only eight people described themselves as lodging-house keepers and only one had a lodger' and ten years later only five lodging houses were listed in the census.[49]

The wealthier visitor in the late eighteenth and early nineteenth centuries who brought not only his family but often also his own servants, would rent an entire house for a stay of several weeks. As the numbers of visitors increased, a shortfall in accommodation meant that it became common for a suite of rooms in a house, where a resident landlady with her own servants was willing to cook and clean for the visitor, to be rented by the less affluent. For those whose means could not stretch to a suite, just one room in a lodging house or private house could be rented and the money paid was regarded as an addition to the household's main income. In Clevedon, for example, in 1866 there were nine lodging houses listed whose owners had other occupations[50] and in Burnham, in the same year, two pilots and a fisherman were also lodging house keepers.[51] In April 1861 Portishead had eight lodging houses, all of which, with one exception, were kept by widows; only one had a lodger resident on the night the census was taken.

Some landowners were quick to realise the advantages of building properties which could be either rented out to visitors or sold to those who

wished to settle in seaside towns. In Minehead, the Luttrell family built new houses on part of their estate to rent to 'respectable families'. In Clevedon, William Hollyman was advertising building plots by 1825 and the following year a Bristol newspaper carried an advertisement for a 'new built house' there which had four parlours, 11 upper rooms, two kitchens and excellent views of the sea. In 1859 a Burnham guidebook carried an advertisement for houses in Catherine Terrace which described them as 'new and substantially built . . . well adapted for GENTLEMEN'S RESIDENCES, or LODGING HOUSES'. The same publication also had an advertisement for Reed's Hotel, close to the railway station and pier 'in every way suitable for the reception of a Nobleman's Family'.[52]

In December of 1805 'GB of Axbridge' following 'my sojourning in the parish with my family last autumn for the benefit of the sea air' wrote to *The Gentleman's Magazine* that several good lodging houses had been built in Weston 'for the reception of company'[53] and, in 1811, a new house there was advertised for sale which had two lodging rooms on the second floor and five in the attic. It also had two kitchens and three parlours and may have been built as a lodging house. The anonymous author of the town's first guide listed the accommodation available in 1822, including Fry's Hotel where Mrs Fry's attention to her guests afforded 'universal satisfaction', The Eagle House which could be rented for five guineas a week, North Parade 'a handsome row of new houses, with accommodation for large families' and other smaller terraced houses available to rent from two to three guineas a week.[54] However, when John Skinner stayed in a hotel there in 1832, he found to his horror that his daughter had been put into a small bedroom which had been divided into two by a thin partition and that two young men had been given the room on the other side. He felt obliged to give her his own room and when he left he lectured Mr Reeves, the proprietor, 'respecting the great impropriety of putting young men in the room contiguous . . . where . . . after having taken too much wine, [they] might have said and done things very improper for a modest girl to hear or be privy to'.[55] A directory of 1830 listed 13 lodging houses in Weston,[56] by 1850 the number had risen to 61.[57]

In 1866 the four towns of Burnham, Clevedon, Minehead and Weston boasted 12 hotels between them; by 1914 the number was only 21 although it had risen to 33 by 1935. These figures are taken from county directories and may not be complete, but the

(Above) llustration 2.12: An engraving of the newly built Catherine Terrace on the Esplanade at Burnham (J. Salisbury's, *A Guide or Handbook to Burnham and its Neighbourhood* (1859))

(Below) llustration 2.13. Reed's Hotel, Burnham, from *The Queen's Album* published by Rock Brothers and Payne, *c.*1859. (SHC A/DQO)

general impression is that the vast majority of visitors stayed in lodging or boarding houses and what were later described as 'private hotels', *i.e.* houses with only a small number of rooms for visitors. In the second half of the nineteenth century, guidebooks and county directories began to carry advertisements for this type of small family hotel.

Larger hotels also advertised themselves in the directories, often with full page illustrated adverts. The Royal Claremont Hotel in Weston said it was the only one in the town 'in close proximity to the Sea' with its own private sea baths while Huntley's Beach Hotel was happy to accept day trippers in large numbers. Although only having 20 rooms it boasted of its five dining rooms which could seat between 40 and 200 and it made a point of being able to seat Sunday School outings of up to 670 children. The Royal in Clevedon emphasised its domestic comforts with a 'charming view of the Sea, the Welsh Coast, and the Mendip Hills'. It also set out its tariff of charges; the cost of board, lodging and attendance in the coffee room ranged from £2 15s to £3 3s a week, which included three meals a day. Visitors who brought their own servants with them could expect to pay 4s a day or 25s a week for their board. Minehead's biggest hotel, the Metropôle, hoped to attract a clientele of the hunting, tennis and croquet playing type who would arrive either in their own carriages or by train in small enough numbers to be met at the station by the hotel's own omnibus. It also boasted of not having a public bar so that those who stayed there would not be disturbed by the ubiquitous day tripper or indeed by any of the native inhabitants. In 1902 Hopcott's private hotel, also in Minehead, offered stabling for those who came for the hunting and a darkroom for those photographers who wished to develop their own material. It boasted of its 'Perfect drainage, and an abundant supply of pure water'. It even had its own dairy to ensure the purity of the milk at breakfast and afternoon tea.

Increasing numbers of visitors after the First World War led to a large choice of accommodation at differing costs. Minehead's official guidebook published around 1935 stated that

> Charges for apartments range from £1 per room per week at houses of the cottage type . . . to £2 2s. per room per week at houses with up to six or more bedrooms. Charges vary slightly in accordance with proximity of accommodation to the Sea front . . .

A copy of 'an Accommodation List, containing about 300 addresses of hotels, boarding houses, apartments and farmhouses in Minehead and neighbourhood . . .' could be obtained from the Secretary of the town's publicity association. As today, the price of accommodation could vary according to the date the holidaymaker wished to stay. Mrs Sage, the proprietress of 'Bactonleigh' which was one minute from the sea, the town and the railway station, as well as being central for all sports, charged two guineas in June, two and a half and three in July, and three in August and September. Other advertisers in the Guide merely described their terms as moderate. The owner of the Carlton Hotel, which overlooked the Winter Gardens, offered Special Winter Terms in the hope of attracting visitors during the 'off season'.[58]

The coming of the railways

A growth in the amount of accommodation available is not enough to explain the great rise in the number of people visiting the seaside from the middle of the nineteenth century. This rise came with the development of the railway system when it became possible for people to reach the coast with comparative ease, not only for those families coming to stay for a week or more but also for the day trippers, the works outings and the Sunday School excursions, who could, and did, arrive *en masse*, a fact not always appreciated by the local inhabitants who were far outnumbered by their visitors. Later, the development of the internal combustion engine led to visitors arriving by charabanc, bus and then the private car. Laurie Lee recalled in *Cider with Rosie* a visit by charabanc to Weston from Slad, near Stroud, a journey of some 50 miles: 'With the help of the powerful new charabanc we even got out of the district altogether, rattling away to the ends of the earth, to Bristol or even further'.[59]

The railway arrived in Weston in 1841. Only three years later it was estimated that over 20,000 holidaymakers a year were arriving by rail, at a time when the permanent population of the town was less than 3,000. Factories in Bristol organised cheap excursions for their workers and up to 2,000 people would descend on the town in a day. It was inevitable that amongst this number there would be some whose behaviour was regarded as unsuitable for the select resort that Weston considered itself. The *Weston Mercury* commented in 1856 'If these conditions continue the future of Weston super Mare as a fashionable resort is at stake'. Showing that the paper still thought of the town as a place patronised by

H. J. HUNTLEY,
Proprietor.
Trading as Huntley & Co.

Telegraphic Address:
"HUNTLEY, BEACH RESTAURANT."

Nat. Tel. 0255.

Huntley's Beach Hotel
(Temperance),

and Restaurant,

Regent Street and Marine Parade,
(FACING
NEW GRAND PIER), **WESTON-SUPER-MARE.**

This Restaurant

contains **5** Dining-rooms,
accommodating from **40**
to **200** in each, ensuring
EVERY convenience for
Large or Small Parties.

This Hotel

contains **20** Bedrooms,
Dining-room & Drawing-
room The comfort of
Visitors has been specially
studied.

HUNTLEY & CO. wish to draw the attention
of **Clergymen, Ministers, Superintendents,**
and **Secretaries** of Sunday Schools, also
Choirmasters and **Heads of Firms,** that they are
in a position to cater for any number on the
Shortest Notice.   They can also accommodate
about **670** children in their spacious DINING-
ROOMS, including **300** in the **Large Room** on the
Ground Floor, and **120** in another Room, whilst
250 can be accommodated in their **Upstairs Rooms.**

Unsurpassed Sea View.

**Clergymen, Ministers, Superintendents, and
Secretaries** of Sunday Schools will find these
Rooms very desirable for School Teas, as they
are close to the Beach.

— SPECIAL. —

A LARGE number of well-appointed Bedrooms
have just been added, also Drawing and
Dining-rooms, *exclusively* for the use of
Visitors staying in the house. This will now be
found one of the most complete and comfortable
Private Hotels and Restaurants in the town.

Boarding Terms given if desired.

Send for Tariff.

Illustration 2.14 An advertisement for Huntley's Hotel, Weston-super-Mare, 1906 (W. Mate & Sons, *Somerset: descriptive, pictorial. An historical guide to the business centres, health and pleasure resorts, and places of interest in the county. Profusely illustrated with specially prepared photographic views* (Bournemouth, 1906)).

those who came for health reasons, it continued 'What invalid would dare to emerge from lodgings on such a day?' However, nearly 40 years later the Board of Health who were running Weston had no doubts about the importance of the railway to the economy of their town. On the 9th of March 1892 it was recorded in the minute book that the Clerk was to thank the Great Western Railway Company not only for 'the stopping of some of the fast trains at Weston super Mare' but also for 'the insertion of the name of our Town in their Book for American travellers'.[60] By the early twentieth century the battle was well and truly lost and the numbers of visitors was such that one author remarked

> I do not know what the motto of Weston-super-Mare may be, nor even indeed if it has one. If not already furnished in this respect, it might well be 'Let 'em all come'.[61]

One visitor who did come by train in July 1895 was Henry Peerless. He caught a train from Paddington at 8.27am and arrived in Weston four hours and 23 minutes later, having stopped at 41 stations *en route*, all of which he listed in his diary.[62]

A branch line of the Bristol and Exeter railway from Yatton to Clevedon opened in 1847 and 20 years later a branch line ran to Portishead, thus enabling visitors to reach those towns more easily. The Weston, Clevedon and Portishead light railway, originally planned as early as 1844 as a tramway to link the three towns, finally opened in 1897 linking Weston and Clevedon; an extension to Portishead opened ten years later. It did mean that visitors arriving at Weston, either by train or by steamer, could transfer to either of the other two without difficulty but as a 1930s advertisement shows, it seems to have been considered more as a picnic and excursion line for those already staying in one or the other of the resorts. Clevedon's visitors were more likely to arrive by train from Bristol and in March 1896 the town's urban council members requested their clerk to write to the railway company 'asking for more through trains in the summer months' to increase the number of visitors.[63]

The railway reached Burnham in 1858 and is said to have been built for the purpose of meeting paddle steamers from South Wales and transporting their passengers from Burnham to the seaside resorts on the south coast of England. The Somerset Central Railway Company even built a 900 foot pier for this purpose and set up their own paddle steamer service in 1860, but it was never very successful and the

service lasted less than thirty years. The pier continued to be used by other paddle steamer companies who brought Welsh holiday makers across the Bristol Channel, most of whom were content to stay in Burnham itself.

Minehead was the last of the resorts to be reached by rail; the West Somerset Railway from Taunton reached Watchet in 1862 and passengers for Minehead could disembark at Williton where a coach service would carry them on to the town. In 1871 an extension of the line to Minehead was begun, it took three years to build and was opened in July 1874. At the lunch held to celebrate its opening Michael Castle, the Vice Chairman of the Bristol and Exeter Railway, was reported to have said "We have long wanted to get a watering place where the water is a little more blue than it is at Weston super Mare and where it is a little nearer the ocean".[64] The extension brought immediate results in the increase in numbers of visitors not all of whom, however, were quite what the town wanted to attract. The official opening was on 16 July; on the 25th some 800 people, employees of the Bristol Waggon Works and their friends, arrived on a day trip. One Minehead resident was moved to write to the *Western Daily Press* stating 'It is greatly to be regretted that [some] should have made themselves so obnoxious . . . by making raids upon the orchards and gardens, breaking down garden fences and shrubs, and robbing apples, pears and flowers, also by using little whips with heavy handles upon the hats and heads of a few of the Minehead lads'. Had it not been for prompt action by the police, the writer feared that a general 'hand to hand battle' would have ensued. He also knew where to lay the blame, stating, 'England's greatest curse, alcohol, the effects of which could be seen in men and women, boys and girls, actually lying down in the fields and roads – drunk'.[65]

Excursionists were still proving a problem as late as 1907 although by this time it was more to the regular train users than to the places they visited. A correspondent to *The Times* in June of that year wrote

> Many of our English railway companies [issue] on the Friday or the Saturday, so-called 'Week-end tickets' as an incentive to visit the country or the sea-side for a brief holiday . . . with the proviso attached that the return half of the ticket may only be used on the Sunday, Monday or Tuesday next . . . It is scarcely necessary to point out that on some lines the use of these tickets leads to much inconvenience and over-crowding . . . and is a sad nuisance to the regular passengers. I venture to call

A BANK HOLIDAY SKETCH

(Above) Illustration 2.15: 'Change 'ere, 'ave we? Then kindly oblige me with a sardine-opener!' A humorous view of the numbers travelling by train on a Bank Holiday (An R. Carter cartoon from *Mr Punch's railway book, c.*1907)

(Below) Illustration 2.16: Excursionists rushing for their seats on a train (A Wallis Mills cartoon in *Mr Punch's railway book, c.*1907)

Our Artist (who has strolled into a London terminus). " What's the matter with all these people? Is there a panic ? "

Porter. " Panic! No, this ain't no panic. These is excursionists. Their train leaves in two hours, so they want to get a seat ! "

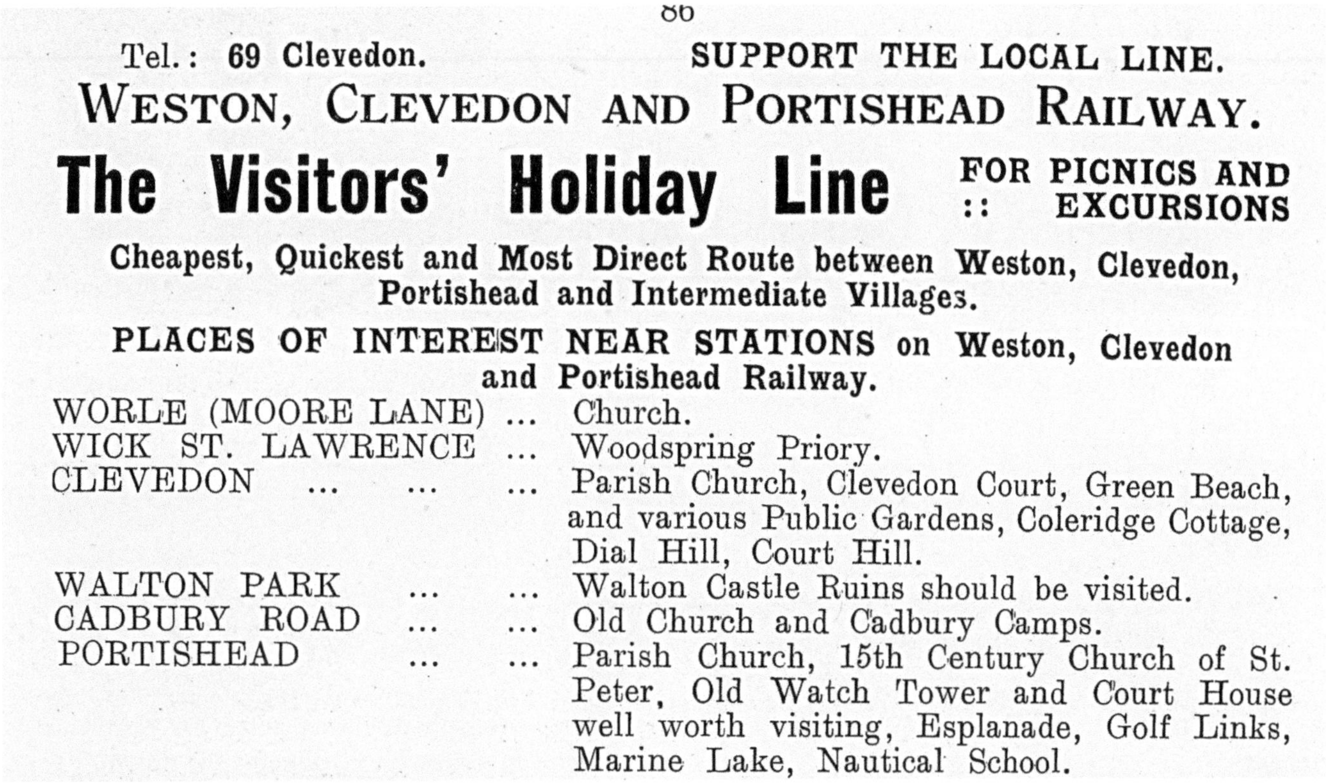

8ö

WESTON, CLEVEDON AND PORTISHEAD RAILWAY.

Tel.: 69 Clevedon.   SUPPORT THE LOCAL LINE.

The Visitors' Holiday Line
FOR PICNICS AND :: EXCURSIONS

Cheapest, Quickest and Most Direct Route between Weston, Clevedon, Portishead and Intermediate Villages.

PLACES OF INTEREST NEAR STATIONS on Weston, Clevedon and Portishead Railway.

WORLE (MOORE LANE) ... Church.
WICK ST. LAWRENCE ... Woodspring Priory.
CLEVEDON ... ... Parish Church, Clevedon Court, Green Beach, and various Public Gardens, Coleridge Cottage, Dial Hill, Court Hill.
WALTON PARK ... ... Walton Castle Ruins should be visited.
CADBURY ROAD ... ... Old Church and Cadbury Camps.
PORTISHEAD ... ... Parish Church, 15th Century Church of St. Peter, Old Watch Tower and Court House well worth visiting, Esplanade, Golf Links, Marine Lake, Nautical School.

Illustration 2.17: An advertisement exhorting the public to support 'the local line', the Weston, Clevedon and Portishead Railway from the *Bristol Channel district guide, c.*1936-1939. (SHC, A/APN/5/32)

the attention of railway managers to the somewhat obvious fact that it will in no case cause them any loss if the tickets in question . . . were made available for the return journey on Saturday night, when a large number of their trains are running absolutely empty. A cheap one day excursion on a Saturday would prove a boon to many travellers.[66]

Sanitation problems

Other problems that the growing seaside towns had to face were those of drainage and the disposal of sewage. In 1849 Thomas Webster Rammell's Report to the General Board of Health on his preliminary enquiry into the sewerage, drainage and supply of water to the people of Burnham was published. At this time, Burnham was advertising itself as a healthy holiday resort with at least one hotel, the Clarence, and many lodging houses where visitors could rent accommodation. However, the lack of anything approaching an integrated drainage and sewerage system caused many visitors to cut short their stay in the town.

Rammell interviewed numerous of the town's inhabitants, asking questions concerning the state of their health and the condition of their houses, and

recording their views on the town's sanitary condition. One of those he interviewed was Robert Wakeham, the landlord of the Clarence, who said

"I have frequently had families in the house who have been prevented staying by the bad smells. Scores and hundreds of people have come to me and said, 'What a dirty place your's is; we've heard of Burnham, but now we see it; at what time does the train go'? The omnibus to the station starts from my house; I never see them after. I have no doubt that hundreds are driven from the place by the bad smells in it".

Wakeham may have been exaggerating somewhat as he also complained that the flooding that the town suffered on a regular basis had cost him over £50 in damage done to his furnishings and the loss of money from visitors who left prematurely but other inhabitants also complained of the lack of drainage in the town. A Mr P.J. Petherick stated that

It does not require a heavy fall of rain to flood Victoria Street, the principal street in the town .. . I have heard visitors say, looking at the water, "This is a watering place indeed!"

A resident doctor who had seen the growth in the amount of visitor accommodation in the town assured Rammell that none of the new lodging

"CLARENCE"
Family and Commercial Hotel,
BURNHAM.

BURNHAM being contiguous to the Bristol Channel, and open to the pure Atlantic breezes, is considered one of the healthiest watering places on the coast.

The above Hotel is situate on the Esplanade, commands extensive land and sea views, and is in the immediate vicinity of the Baths and Medicinal Springs.

houses he had visited had a 'pure' atmosphere and that

> The Royal Parade is very bad; some friends of mine took lodgings in a house adjoining [it], and were obliged to leave them on account of both their children having fever; . . . these houses . . . constitute the best part of Burnham. . . . a very refined lady told me she had been compelled to smoke a cigar during the night, solely for self-preservation from the disgusting smells. I am certain this lady had never smoked before, . . . it was a scented cigar.

If these were the conditions in 'the best part of Burnham', what was it like in the areas where the poorer inhabitants lived? One man who lived with his family in a court with eleven houses in it said that the privy in the middle of the court, which was only three or four steps from his door, was used by all the inhabitants of the eleven houses, a total of 60 people. This privy would be emptied about twice a year but the yard was nearly always wet with the liquid that leaked from it. 'Nasty worm like things with long tails' invaded the house and metamorphosed into flies. His neighbours emptied their chamber pots onto the ash heap which, he said, was between the privy and his house and they threw 'all manner of filth there' as there was nowhere else it could be put. 'Slops' were thrown into the street where they were sometimes six inches deep and had to wait for heavy rain to wash them away. Visitors to the town may never have stayed in properties such as this but the

general atmosphere, particularly in hot weather, must have been noticeable elsewhere in the town.[67]

Following Rammell's report a Board of Health was established for the town and some improvements were made, so much so that ten years later in 1859 the author of a *Guide Book to Burnham* stated with confidence how 'The sanitary condition of Burnham may be said to be now perfect'.[68] This statement as it turned out was slightly premature for as late as 1883 the author of a report to the Local Government Board wrote

> Having regard to the character of the place as a health resort . . . [the visitors should] be assured that in such visits they are not exposing themselves to the risk of contracting preventable disease through the atmosphere of their dwellings being poisoned by sewer air and the water they drink being dangerously contaminated; a guarantee which Burnham at the present time cannot afford them.[69]

Three years later, Rammell conducted a similar enquiry into the drainage and water supply of Clevedon. As far as the town's water supply was concerned, the houses in the upper town relied on deep wells which 'yield a water of hard and often impure quality', and on rain water tanks while the poorer inhabitants in the lower town had shallow wells and the River Yeo which was 'much polluted with the drainage of house refuse'.

Two drains ran into a reservoir in a field owned by Mr Elton of Clevedon Court. When the reservoir was full, it overflowed into a sewer running down to the beach. The mouth of the outfall was above the high water mark and this, according to several of the witnesses at the enquiry 'occasions a considerable stench at times'. Many houses in Upper Clevedon where the visitors stayed, for example those in Wellington Terrace, drained separately and directly into the sea.

> This point is considerably above the level of the sea, and the refuse matter…are brought to the edge of the cliff where they are left to decompose, or find its way down its sides to the beach as best they may. The Hotel drains directly down the face of the sea wall. [This] occasions at times, but especially in the summer season, an intolerable nuisance on the beach.[70]

Privies and cess pits were unable to cope with the amount of waste generated by the towns' permanent populations and their visitors. Following the creation of Local Boards of Health in 1848, Urban Sanitary Districts in 1875 and finally Urban District Councils in 1894 the resorts began to put in proper drainage systems but in many cases the drains merely emptied into the sea off the beaches where the visitors paddled and swam.

In January 1865, entrepreneurs put before the Board of Health in Weston a scheme to turn a problem into a money making resource:

> The sewage disposal question has now assumed an importance which it is impossible to over-estimate, and anyone who will read the evidence given to the Select Committee on Sewage must come to the conclusion that the time is not far distant when the pollution of streams and foreshores will be prohibited by direct legislation.

Their answer to the problem was to lift the town's sewage 'to an elevation which will make any nuisance impossible' and then to use it as fertiliser on the land in the neighbourhood.[71]

Illustration 2.19: An explanation for the smell of the 'ozone' at the seaside (A Charles Keen cartoon from *Mr Punch at the seaside, c.* 1907)

In September of the same year another sewage disposal scheme was put forward by the Lords of the Manors of Norton Beauchamp and Weston-super-Mare. In their letter to the town's council, they said they were considering the reclamation of the Sand Bay foreshore and proposed to pump Weston's sewage into the bay itself. Their engineer was no less than Joseph Bazelgette and the accompanying plan marked the outfall of the sewer pipe 'where, according to the last Admiralty survey, it will always be covered by a fathom of water'.[72]

In 1896, some of Weston's sewage was being discharged into the River Axe so that the current could take it out to sea. William Pople, a fisherman, was employed to empty the Penstock sewage catchment tank. His view was that

> any sewage discharged to the River will not come back as it goes out along Brean to the Channel tide … [This] does not set into Weston so the sewage cannot return … I have never seen sewage in the mud at low tide … With regard to the statement that nuisances have been seen floating amongst the bathers, they do not proceed from the sewers but from the bathers themselves.[73]

Tony Speller, MP for North Devon, said in a debate in the House of Commons in December 1990 that due to the granting of too many planning applications 'far more sewage . . . has to be pumped somewhere. It never occurred to us in years gone by

EVIDENCE OLFACTORY

Angelina (scientific). " Do you smell the iodine from the sea, Edwin? Isn't it refreshing?"
Old Salt (overhearing). "What you smell ain't the sea, miss. It's the town drains as flows out just 'ere !"

that it would be wrong to empty all our debris into streams, rivers and the sea. Now we are paying the penalty'. As mentioned above, it had occurred to some people as early as 1865 but the necessary legislation had not been forthcoming. As recently as May 2011 Surfers Against Sewage set up a live warning system operating at 28 beaches throughout the south of England and Wales, including Blue Anchor, Burnham, Clevedon, Dunster Beach, Minehead and Weston super Mare, to advise surfers and swimmers when raw sewage was present in the water. Ninety five per cent of those they questioned agreed they wished to be warned of this fact.

The pier and entertainment

Early visitors to the sea side had been content with the sea bathing and the surrounding picturesque countryside. They had been happy to make their own entertainment by hiring carriages or horses to take them on excursions to nearby churches and other places of interest. It is true that Mrs Piozzi had complained in 1819 of Weston that when she had 'enquir'd for Books there were but Two in the Town ... a *Bible* and a *Paradise Lost*[74] but this lack had been partly remedied by the provision of a library and a reading room by 1829.

However, it has to be said that most, if not all, of the new day trippers arriving in their thousands from the 1840s onwards were not interested in whether their resort could provide them with reading material. They wanted something more than the sea bathing, which had satisfied earlier visitors, and they did not have the time to take excursions into the surrounding countryside. Rather than make their own entertainment, they wanted it to be provided for them and the resorts did so by licensing the amusements which could soon be found on the newly built piers and elsewhere in the towns.

The seaside pier today is a place of entertainment as it was for much of the nineteenth and twentieth centuries. But its origins lie in commerce and the early Victorian piers were built to enable ships to tie up and discharge their cargoes, whether goods or passengers, at towns which did not have deep water harbours. The 'deposited plan' for Portishead Pier in 1839, for example, marks the height and depth to which the tide rose and fell, showing that it would be possible for paddle steamers to tie up there.[75]

Lack of a pier could deter visitors from landing and thus spending their money in a resort. The Revd Francis Kilvert, while on a visit to Weston in 1872, took his mother on a paddle steamer trip to

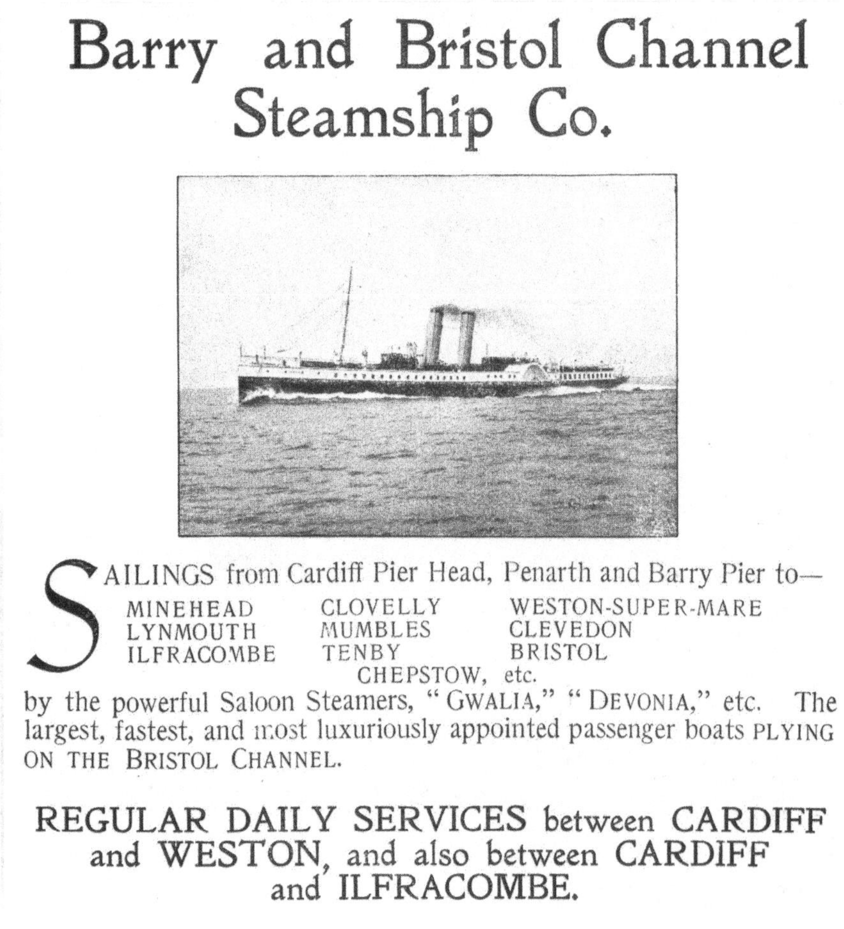

Barry and Bristol Channel Steamship Co.

Illustration 2.20: An advertisement for the Barry and Bristol Channel Steamship Company, *c.*1905. The company offered sailings from Minehead, Weston, Clevedon and Bristol (Adrian Webb)

SAILINGS from Cardiff Pier Head, Penarth and Barry Pier to—

MINEHEAD	CLOVELLY	WESTON-SUPER-MARE
LYNMOUTH	MUMBLES	CLEVEDON
ILFRACOMBE	TENBY	BRISTOL
	CHEPSTOW, etc.	

by the powerful Saloon Steamers, "GWALIA," "DEVONIA," etc. The largest, fastest, and most luxuriously appointed passenger boats PLYING ON THE BRISTOL CHANNEL.

REGULAR DAILY SERVICES between CARDIFF and WESTON, and also between CARDIFF and ILFRACOMBE.

Ilfracombe. He recorded how

> The steamboat was to come round from Clevedon and to be at the Weston Pier at 9.15. She was an hour late in appearing and some time was lost then in lashing her to the pier that the passengers might go on board for there was a good deal of swell . . .

On their arrival at Ilfracombe they found there was no pier where the steamer might tie up and 'the passengers had to be landed in open boats, the ladies being lifted in a scrambling way down off the deck into the boats by the sailors, putting their arms round the sailors' necks'. As this did not appeal to Kilvert's mother, both of them stayed on board.[76]

At this time, Weston itself had had a pier for less than ten years, although the use of steam ships to travel from Bristol to South Wales, passing Weston *en route*, was established by 1826. In that year Mrs Elizabeth Ernst and her family set off from Bristol where they had spent the night at the Gloucester Hotel which she described as 'A large comfortable Inn, which has gradually increased for the accommodation of passengers by the numerous steam packets which start from thence'. All was well until the ship passed Weston when the sea became so rough that Elizabeth, her child and the child's nurse

Illustration 2.21: A view of holiday makers coming ashore from their steamer at a seaside resort without a pier. (A George du Maurier cartoon from *Mr Punch at the seaside, c.*1907).

'could bear it no longer and became very sick . . . As for Ernst' her husband 'he did not suffer at all, but went down and eat a hearty dinner, the fumes of which coming upon deck were dreadful to the poor sick people'.[77]

The town held a public meeting in 1845 at which it was decided a pier was a necessity and the Weston-super-Mare Packet Station, Landing Pier and Ship Company was established as a consequence. Work began but little progress had been made when unusually high tides swept away the stone foundations and the work was abandoned. The idea was commemorated in a poem, the anonymous author of which was perhaps not entirely convinced by the arguments behind the scheme:

> That wonderful Pier!
> 'Twas to bring the Westonians some thousands a year;
> Ships, schooners, and brigs all in multitudes here
> Were to come from Japan and South Wales and Cape Clear,
> And steamers by dozens were soon to appear . . .[78]

The idea was put on hold for nearly 20 years and the foundation stone of Birnbeck Pier was not laid until October 1864. The pier opened on 6 June 1867, proved so popular that in the first three months 120,000 people paid their money to walk on it. The original charge of 1d was quickly raised to 2d as the town needed to recoup the nearly £70,000 that it had cost to build. Kilvert described his family's visit:

> We went to the new pier which connects the mainland with Birnbeck. The 3 children were with us and the sea air seemed to make them wild. They grew so excited, they ran and shouted and screamed and rolled about on the pier, tumbling over and over one another.[79]

This pier provided all the entertainments necessary for a successful visit to the seaside; much to the chagrin of the local shopkeepers and café owners, many visitors never got as far as the town. It had

such dreams of delight . . . that many venture no further; water chutes, switch back railways, try your weight and strength machines, and, above all, a dammed something that may be espied from the shore, like a giant's stride pole with baskets filled with people who paid 1d to be given a good imitation of sea sickness.[80]

It should not be thought that all or even the majority of these pier entertainments were aimed at children. The Cake Walk was mainly for adults and it seems likely the Beckworth Ladies Champion Swimmers were also an adult attraction. Even the swing boats could be patronised by those who would never have considered letting themselves go in such a frivolous way at home.

Birnbeck pier was not the only place entertainment could be found. The road on Knightstone Island leading to the baths was also a popular place for local trades people and entertainers to set up their stalls. In 1891 there was a dispute over the ownership of the road on Knightstone and legal papers survive with the evidence of long term residents as to who could be found on the roadway

Illustration 2.22: Entertainment for adults on Birnbeck pier included the Cake Walk and the Beckwith Champion Lady Swimmers, 1905 (SHC, DD/X/LES/6)

124

BIRNBECK PIER

Weston-Super-Mare.

THE PIER AT WHICH THE STEAMERS CALL. A CONSTANT ROUND OF AMUSEMENTS. LICENSED PAVILION WITH LUNCHEON ROOMS, TEA ROOMS, CLOAK ROOMS, ETC.

SWITCHBACK RAILWAY

WATER CHUTE :: ELECTRIC ORCHESTRA, DANCING, ETC., ETC.

ADMISSION 2d.

☞ During the Summer Months the Birnbeck Pier presents a most animated scene, and hundreds of Excursionists landed here from the Steamers pass the entire day in its vicinity.

Proprietors—WESTON-SUPER-MARE PIER CO.

Illustration 2.23: An advertisement for Birnbeck Pier, 1920 (Adrian Webb)

between 1889 and 1891.

Thomas Davey, junior, who had been in charge of the baths on Knightstone for five years, said 'Scott the magic lantern proprietor paid Mr Griffith', the owner of Knightstone Island at the time

> for permission to exhibit his lantern in the roadway . . . Mr McDonald palmist lecturer also lectured from a stand . . . White the photographer has been there . . . with a wagon on wheels for two years and now a hut or studio . . . Clark the fruiterer would stand on the other side of the road and sell fruit nuts cockles and ginger beer . . . The ice cream man named Coles would stand in front of the photographer . . . Dudd had an Electric Battery fixed on a cart pushed by himself which would stand near the ice cream man and people would patronize him. There was a man with microscopes and he fixed his apparatus against the hoarding for advertising the Baths. A conjuror was also there one season . . . and I have seen a 100 people there at a time.[81]

Phrenology was a popular Victorian subject and Francis Kilvert saw a Mr Hume give a demonstration on the subject in 1872, although he does not appear to have been entirely convinced by the science behind it:

> At 7.30 my Mother and I went to the Assembly rooms to a lecture on craniology and phrenology and mesmerism. A table full of skulls was set out and the lecture was given by a Mr Hume. We had seen it advertised on the pier. He talked a great deal of wild nonsense and examined the heads of two or three of the audience whose moral and mental qualities he praised highly.[82]

A phrenologist was to be found at Knightstone in 1889 and as late as 1935 a Madame Rosetta was still offering her services as a phrenologist to visitors in Burnham whereas Weston had only Madame Ouida, a palmist.

Weston's second pier, the Grand, was opened in 1904. Laurie Lee described it as a 'Magic construction striding the waves, loaded with freaks and fancies, water-chutes and crumpled mirrors' with penny in

Illustration 2.24: Birnbeck pier swing boats attracted holiday makers of all ages, 1905 (SHC, DD/X/LES/6)

the slot machines showing a 'whole series of nightmares', including a drunk's delirium, a haunted grave or a Newgate hanging. He wrote:

> With our mouths hanging open, sucking gory sticks of rock, we groped hungrily from horror to horror. For there were sideshows too, as well as the machines with hair-raising freaks under glass – including a two-headed Indian, a seven-legged sheep, and a girl's eye with a child coiled inside it.[83]

The Grand also had a 2,000 seat theatre which was used as a music hall and for productions of opera, plays and ballet. By 1933, after a fire had destroyed the theatre at the pier's end, a £60,000 new pavilion was built, housing a large undercover funfair rather than a theatre, perhaps an indication of the change in taste of the resort's visitors. After the disastrous fire of 2008, Weston's pier reopened on Saturday 23 October 2010. The pier, which can accommodate 6,700 people, boasts everything from traditional seaside rides, such as dodgems and carousels to state-of-the art rollercoasters. The biggest ride is the 1,000ft Go Kart track split over two levels, which cost £1,000,000 to manufacture, with other attractions including a swinging pendulum ride and two Formula 1 Stimulators costing nearly another million pounds

between them.

In November 1866, at a public meeting in Clevedon, it was decided that the town should have a pier. It was partially constructed from Isambard Kingdom Brunel's second-hand railway lines, presumably to reduce the cost, and was opened on 29 March 1869. The importance given to allowing ships to tie up, regardless of the state of the tide, is shown by the fact that the landing stage at the end of the pier had several levels to allow boats to dock at any time. As with all the other Somerset resorts, there was a charge to walk on the pier and enjoy its amenities. The Council's income from these charges was considerable and they were not willing to forego any of the money raised by them. In May 1896 when a letter from the Secretary of the National Cyclists Union was read at a council meeting, requesting that the pier toll for cyclists be reduced from 4d to 3d, 'the Clerk was directed to reply that the Council could not see their way to reduce the charge'.[84]

As referred to above, Burnham's first pier was built by the Somerset Central Railway in 1858. The

---

Illustration 2.25: A view of the proposed pier at Burnham on Sea. Note the steamers and sailing ships moored alongside and a railway line on the left for ease of transporting cargo, *c.*1858 (SHC)

⚓

town's second pier, built between 1911 and 1914 is claimed to be the shortest in Britain. It also has a claim to fame in that it was the first pier to be built entirely of concrete. However, as it never had a landing stage and was too short for a promenade deck, although it did have a Pavilion, it can hardly have attracted many visitors to Burnham who wouldn't otherwise have gone there.

Minehead had the forerunner of a pier, a quay, as early as the fifteenth century. By the mid sixteenth century it had fallen into disrepair and the townspeople sent a petition to Queen Elizabeth, pointing out the disastrous effect this was having on trade with Ireland and Wales and asking for help to repair it. The Queen does not appear to have been very responsive to their plea as in 1570 George Luttrell was trying to raise money from his neighbours to help with building a new quay.[85] It was another George Luttrell who in 1895 decided that Minehead needed a pier suitable for steamers to tie

up against. The pier was opened in 1901 but before this date visitors to the town would stroll on the quay to admire the view and breathe the healthy sea air. When the pier finally opened it was not universally admired. It was, as one writer stated, 'built in an impossible situation, so that visitors are pleased not to go upon it'.[86]

As well as the entertainments on the piers, all the seaside towns permitted entertainment on the beaches in the summer such as donkey rides, Punch and Judy shows for the children, and Pierrot shows and black face minstrels for the adults. Clevedon refused an applicant who wanted to exhibit a phonograph on the beach in 1896; no reason was given but the council members may have thought it would clash with the Pier Band who were asking to be allowed to hire two extra musicians at this time, which was also refused.[87] In August 1912 Weston permitted the Frank Hucks Waterplane Company Limited to put a hanger on the beach in connection with its flying display and the same month the Anti-Suffrage Campaign, who were using Weston as a base for a fortnight, were allowed to hold two meetings there.[88]

Boat trips were a popular enjoyment and Henry

Illustration 2.26: Burnham's second pier built, between 1911 and 1914, claimed to be the shortest in Great Britain (SHC, A\DGO/1)

Above. Illustration 2.27: Donkey rides on Burnham beach with a carousel and swing boats in the background, *c*.1914 (SHC, A\DGO/1)

Below. Illustration 2.28: Punch and Judy show on Weston beach, 1960s. Professor Staddon had been presenting his show here as early as the 1930s (Sharon Poole)

Peerless on his visit to Weston in 1895 took a trip on the Campbell steamer Waverly to Cardiff, a journey of some 45 minutes. Passenger entertainment was provided on the trip home although Henry's opinion of this was not favourable: 'Music, oh! ye shades of Beethoven and Mozart, what a prostitution of thy sweet art when music is relegated to the tender mercies of a trio of steamboat musicians'. This did not deter him from a trip to Ilfracombe the following day, recounting how on his return the steamer's gangplank had to be laid over another ship to reach the pier at Weston as both steamers were 'crowded from stem to stern, and a good deal of confusion'.[89] The companies that ran the Bristol Channel steamers were only too happy to help advertise the charms of the seaside resorts as much of their trade came to depend on the holiday makers who stayed there. The 39th edition of *The Bristol Channel Travel Guide* which was the official handbook of P. & A. Campbell Limited quoted a Mr G.R. Sims who was staying at Minehead. He said 'You never want to go home again. You want to telegraph to your people to bring the dogs and the birds and the cat, and make Minehead the family address for the remainder of your present time on earth'. Shorter trips around the bays or harbours were also popular, leading to long

Above. Illustration 2.29: Holiday makers at Burnham queuing for a boat trip, 1918 (SHC, DD\S\FRI/2 with acknowledgement to The Francis Frith Collection)

Below. Illustration 2.30: An anonymous cartoon illustrating the possible dangers of a trip in a small boat at the seaside (*Mr Punch afloat, c.*1907)

HOW VERY THOUGHTFUL

Old Lady. "Are you not afraid of getting drown'd when you have the boat so full?"

Boatman. "Oh, dear, no, mum. I always wears a life-belt, so I'm safe enough."

queues for places. These were usually provided by local fishermen or other boat owners. Minehead had at least four pleasure boat proprietors listed in the 1935 Kelly's *Directory* plus the agent for Campbell's.[90]

As well as the bigger companies such as P. & A. Campbell, local boat owners provided excursions to the Bristol Channel islands of Steep Holm and Flat Holm or even across to the ports of South Wales. Paul Hare of Clevedon was one such owner who advertised his 'pleasure yachts' for trips such as this as well as running a 'taxi' service to the pier for passengers arriving or departing by the steamers.[91]

By the middle of the 1930s, all the seaside resort towns had charabanc and coach proprietors, offering day trips out into the surrounding countryside for those staying for a week's holiday. From Minehead, for example, one could take a trip through Porlock and over Exmoor to Lynton and Lynmouth, as well as ones to Allerford, Bossington, Selworthy and Dunster.

Another of the many pleasures of being at the seaside was thinking of one's friends and work colleagues who were unable to be there as well. From roughly the beginning of the twentieth century these unfortunates could be sent a postcard, with a picture of some local beauty spot or interesting building on one side and a brief message on the other to tell them how much one was enjoying the holiday. The cost of sending a card was only ½d until 1918 when it doubled to 1d and the card itself cost 1d. The advent of the cartoon 'saucy' postcard after 1930, many with designs by Donald McGill, brought about a resurgence in popularity and at their height 16 million a year were being bought. Despite problems with censorship in the 1950s, this type of card has never lost its appeal. Other cards were produced to a standard design and the name of a particular resort would be added on the front. Some could have an insert of up to a dozen black and white photographs of local sights such as the Giddy Kipper from Minehead and one from Portishead which read

> You'll find this shrimp I send a treat
> Its not so large but full of meat;
> So raise the flap without a sigh
> There's more inside than meets the eye.

Towards the end of the nineteenth century it began to be realized amongst those responsible for the administration of the seaside resorts that there

Illustration 2.31: Illustrations of a Giddy Kipper postcard from Minehead, *c.*1950 (SHC, A/APN\4\1\3)

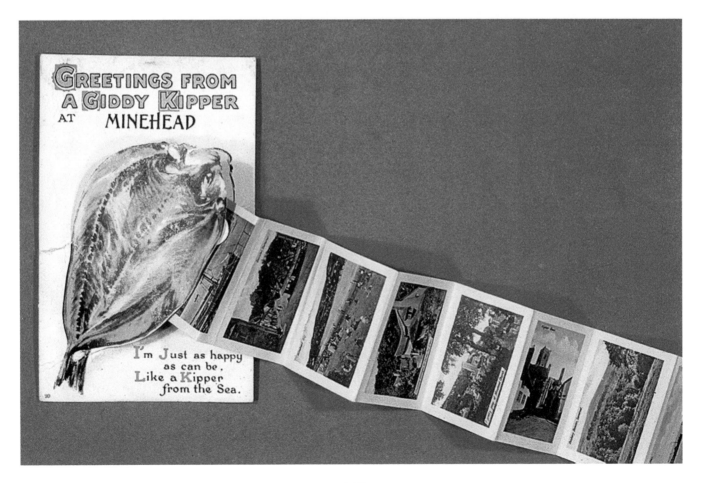

Knightstone Sands, Weston-Super-Mare. No. 19.

Above. Illustration 2.32: A postcard of Knightstone Sands where the writer has used every available space for her message, 1904. The card shows some of the hooded basket chairs which preceded deckchairs (SHC, DD\X\CWL)

Below. Illustration 2.33: Grove Park, Weston, with a leisurely crowd enjoying a musical entertainment, *c*.1914 (David Worthy)

were visitors who did not want non-stop entertainment. They found the beaches and esplanades too crowded and noisy and wanted somewhere quieter to enjoy themselves. In 1886 Weston's Board of Health complained about 'the noise and annoyance on the Foreshore' that had become intolerable 'through the Rabble that frequent there, with their Swing Boats, Shooting Stands and Galleries, Games of 'Aunt Sally', 'Throwing sticks three a penny for Coconuts', Costardmongers, Likeness Takers, Shows of every description, Occupants of tents, etc'.[92] In the 1890s, a Borough guide to Clevedon began to emphasise the peaceful aspects of the town, such as 'The man who seeks repose of mind and freedom from the distracting rush of modern life will not find them among the boisterous merriment and jollity of Weston, . . . but in the midst of the fresh pleasures and beauties of this pretty spot.' For such visitors, the towns provided gardens, perhaps with a boating lake or a bandstand, where people could stroll quietly or sit in the sunshine enjoying a concert. Clevedon's Herbert and Alexandra Gardens were given to the town by Sir A.H. Elton, Bart, in the 1860s. They were described as being 'prettily laid out with well kept flower beds and walks among trees and shrubberies, and are a decided acquisition to the town', being used for flower shows, fetes, band contests and illuminated festivals.[93] The site for Clarence Gardens in Weston was presented to the town in 1883 by Mrs Rebecca Davies, in memory of her husband who had been the first clerk to the Improvement Commissioners. Grove Park was purchased by the Commissioners in 1889 and in 1909 Alexandra Gardens were laid out on the site of the town's original railway station. Blenheim Gardens in Minehead opened in 1925 and Burnham's Marine Lawn Gardens, next to the church, were laid out in 1927. They had 'shelters and seating accommodation, sunken lawns, lily ponds and a pergola' with 'Tudor paths, rockeries and flower beds'.[94]

By the late 1920s and 1930s much of the entertainment on offer at the seaside was organised by commercial companies on behalf of the towns' councils. As an example of this, in 1929 Burnham's Executive Committee produced an annual report showing a net profit of £212 15s 6d against a loss the previous year of £178 12s 11d. This had only been made possible by reducing advertising by 50%, engaging an orchestra for only seven weeks and buying no new deckchairs. By 1934 the Burnham-on-Sea Attractions Limited Company had been formed. The following year it reported that it had entered into a joint scheme with the railway companies for newspaper advertising and as a result had received 1746 requests for the town's official guide. The Playtime Concert Party had been engaged for 12 weeks and the stock of chairs had been increased from 750 to 1400. As a result, and despite the bad weather at Whitsun and cold weather in August, a surplus of £311 had been made and there was hope that this would increase to £435 the following year.[95]

Holiday camps

The twentieth century saw the development of another type of holiday at the seaside, the holiday camp. This provided accommodation, at first in tents, later in chalets, where the holidaymakers could have their meals provided in a dining hall and where some entertainments could be found on site. According to an article in *The Times* in January 1949, in 1939 commercial holiday camps such as Billy Butlin's at Skegness had attracted 30,000 visitors a week. By 1949 the number was 70,000 and up to 7% of annual holidaymakers in Britain went to a camp. The first one in Somerset seems to have been at St Audries Bay which opened in the 1930s. It saw such an increase in the number of its customers immediately after the Second World War that an extension necessitated a completely new sewerage system.[96] By 1951 it boasted a hard tennis court, putting green and bowls pitch for the adults and a sand pit and paddling pool for the children as well as direct access to the beach.[97]

Fred Pontin bought an existing camp at Brean Sands (close to Burnham) and opened it in 1946; the earlier camp on the site had been taken over by the American Army prior to the D-Day landings and many of its existing buildings were damaged at that time. Pontin's brochure of 1948 listed the attractions it provided, including a fancy dress party for children and a gala night for adults, tennis and putting, dancing to a 'first class orchestra' and a beauty queen contest.[98]

Billy Butlin's camp at Minehead opened in 1962 following his success with similar camps in the northeast. Many holiday makers returned there again and again as it provided a safe environment for their children and leisure activities for themselves. Some paid for full board while others chose to cater for themselves while still enjoying the facilities the camp offered. As late as the 1980s, Butlins was publishing its own postcards with views of the amusements laid on in the camps such as the swimming pool, the ballroom and the bars. The importance the company attached to this form of advertising is shown by the fact that it employed German photographers, whose

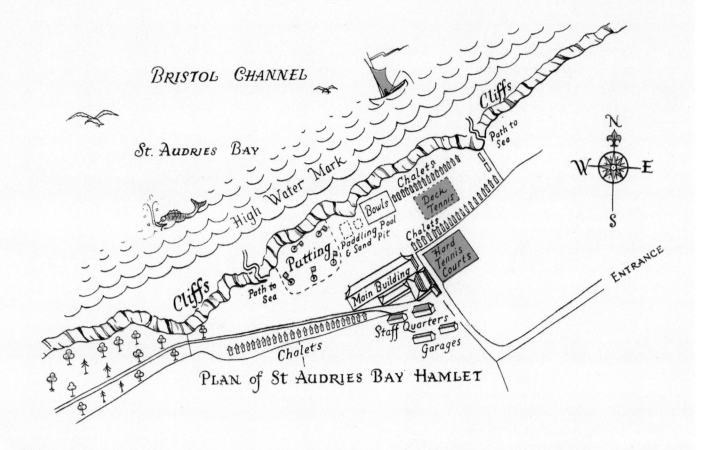

PLAN of ST AUDRIES BAY HAMLET

Above. Illustration 2.34: St Audries Bay holiday camp site, providing putting, tennis, bowls, paddling pool and sandpit for children, 1951 (SHC, A\AIK/1/3)

Illustration 2.35: Above and right come from a Pontin's brochure for Brean Sands Holiday Resort showing an idealised view of ladies sunbathing, the childrens sand pit and the type of chalet available for post-war holidaymakers, 1948 (SHC, A\AIK/1/1)

ATTRACTIONS

Tennis
Putting
Coast Rambles
Motor Excursions
Woodland Picnics
Impromptu Concerts
Fancy Dress Gala Nights
Safe Bathing
Beach Sports
Beauty Queen Contests
Golf at Burnham and Berrow Course

BATHING
TIME

CHILDREN'S FANCY
DRESS GROUP

SUNLIT DINING HALL

Illustration 2.36: A page from a Brean Sands Holiday Camp brochure, listing the entertainments on offer and with a photograph of the dining hall, 1948 (SHC, DD\X\AIK\1\2)

equipment was considered the best available, and the designs were printed in Italy to obtain a deeper colour saturation; nowhere was the water as blue as it was in a Butlins' pool!

A less organised holiday could be had in one of the chalet or caravan sites which began to be developed along the coast before World War II. The first was probably that at Dunster Beach where the first chalet was put up, carefully out of the line of sight of the inhabitants of Dunster Castle, in 1927. Unlike the chalets at holiday camps, these ones could be bought outright and used as a holiday home whenever the owner wished.[99] A camp site, tents rather than chalets, was established at Blue Anchor as early as 1932[100] and, in the summer of 1943, was used by a group of St John's Ambulance Brigade cadets from all over Somerset who stayed there for a week. One of the cadets remembers them being shown to their tents, each sleeping six girls, on arrival and then being allotted their task; the teams in charge of the kitchen, dining tent, latrines and keeping the site tidy were changed every day. The activities included classes in first aid, keep fit on the beach, dancing and crafts, as well as helping out at the

evacuees' nursery at the mill. Any spare time could be spent paddling. There was singing and cups of cocoa around the camp fire at night and on the last evening the girls, and the army cadets whose tents were pitched on another part of the field, were taken in army lorries to a dance in Minehead, returning safely to the camp at midnight. Buckets of cold water provided the washing facilities and on her return home to Burnham the first thing her Mother said to her was that she needed to go and have a bath.[101]

An advertisement in the Clevedon U.D.C. Official Guide of 1970 for Two Acres Holiday Centre at Walton Bay sums up the 'Free-and-Easy 'Do-as you-please'' type of holiday which a chalet, or caravan, provided for those not wishing to be tied to set meal times, or not too keen on the enforced friendliness of a holiday camp. But by the 1980s many of the camps were losing their attractiveness as holiday destinations. This was due partly to the advent of the 'sun, sea and sand' package holiday to Europe, where travel and accommodation were included in a set price. These holidays attracted a younger clientele who were travelling without children. By the 1960s the package holiday was giving most people in Britain their first chance to travel abroad, at first to the beaches of Spain and elsewhere in Europe and by the 1970s to more exotic places such as Morocco and

Illustration 2.37: A family enjoying the sun outside their chalet at Dunster Beach in the 1950s (Hilary Binding)

Illustration 2.38: Blue Anchor camp site in the late 1930s. (Hilary Binding)

Egypt. Fred Pontin organised package holidays to Sardinia in 1963 followed by ones to Torremolinos and Majorca.

The other reason for the decline in the popularity of the holiday camp was perhaps due to the greater expectations people had of their holiday accommodation and surroundings. A writer interviewed several Pentecostalists who were among the 7,136 staying at Minehead in 1985 'in the seedy corner' of the camp reserved for self catering customers. "We have to sleep three in a bed" said one, explaining that the other bed in the chalet was "full of dead fleas". Another complained of having no electricity as the meter in his chalet was broken and

> "What's more, the lavatory don't flush, and we have to empty buckets down. The lady next door's got a mouse – she makes enough fuss about it, you'd think it was a rat".[102]

It was no wonder that the sun and sand and modern hotels of the Spanish Costas and other European resorts proved overwhelmingly attractive to a new, more adventurous, generation of British holiday maker.

Seaside resurgence

It may be now, however, that the wheel has turned

full circle or at least rotated sufficiently for the seaside holiday in Britain to be coming back into favour. That recent phenomenon, the 'staycation', seems to have had an effect on the numbers of visitors taking a holiday of whatever duration at seaside resorts. One national newspaper reported that

> Seaside towns are seeing a dramatic revival in fortunes as rising air fares and the strong euro discourage cash-strapped holidaymakers from going oversees. The trend for 'staycations' has seen the number of visitors to coastal towns increase by 15 per cent in the past two years . . . In April, occupancy rates in seaside hotels rose by almost 10 per cent . . . last month [July] occupancy rates were still almost four per cent higher than last year.[103]

The multi-national companies that now own Butlins, and other holiday camp complexes, realized that they needed to provide more than a chalet and a glamorous grandmother competition to attract customers. As reported in *The Guardian* in 2009

> The Somerset coast is bracing itself for an influx of Gallic mysticism this summer, with news that the French beach soccer team, managed by the

Illustration 2.39: A nostalgic view of the seaside as imagined by the garden designer Sally Leaney, 2011 (Sally Leaney)

enigmatic Eric Cantona, will be visiting Butlins Minehead for an international tournament. The event will add to the resurgent popularity of Butlins as an increasing band of Brits choose to stay at home this summer.[104]

Nostalgia may also be playing a part in this revival of the seaside such as that expressed in an article in another newspaper recently:

> On our seaside holidays, my brother and I ate a diet that consisted almost entirely of sweets, crisps, bright yellow ice cream and fish in batter so amazingly thick, you could have stuck it on your feet and walked across the shingle without it ever disintegrating. And to wash it all down, this heavenly sludge of sugar, fat and food colouring? Pop, of course, by which I mean lemonade, limeade, cherryade and, best of all, Tizer. To this

day, I cannot eat fish and chips without secretly longing for Tizer.[105]

As well as its state of the art pier and ferris wheel on the esplanade, Weston caters for those who remember their bucket and spade holidays by holding a Sand Sculpture Festival every year. Sculptures in 2010 ranged from the 'Rocket' for railway buffs to Shakespeare for the literary minded via the Teletubbies and Wallace and Gromit for younger members of the family.

The final touch of nostalgia is the bathing machine albeit without its wheels, reincarnated as the beach hut where tea can be made and the newspaper can be read, safe in the knowledge that if the rain clouds sweep in, shelter is at hand. One garden designer's vision of the beach hut at the 2011 Taunton Flower Show, 'The Seaside Revisited', was 'designed to evoke childhood memories of long hot summers enjoyed on a west country beach' and was so successful in this that it won a gold prize.[106]

Conclusion

The seaside resorts of Somerset have a long history. Over the course of the last 200 years they have developed from small coastal towns and villages, inhabited mainly by fishermen and agricultural workers, to large urban areas whose permanent populations are among the biggest in the county. These communities increase considerably in size during the holiday season when great numbers of holidaymakers arrive, eager for the entertainments the resorts can offer. Even in these straightened times, the local authorities and private entrepreneurs are willing to invest money in these resorts, knowing that the demand for seaside holidays is still there and increasing. There can be no doubt that at the beginning of the twenty-first century the seaside resort in Somerset is alive and well.

Chapter 2
Notes

1   *Clevedon Borough guide 29* (*c.*1900), 20.

2   W. Hutton, *A description of Blackpool in Lancashire frequented for sea bathing* (1944), 9.

3   T. Hearne (ed), *The itinerary of John Leland the antiquary* vol. 2 (1744), 37-8.

4   J. Wroughton, *Stuart Bath: life in the forgotten city, 1603-1714* (2004), 102-103.

5   SHC, Q\SR\26/53-4.

6   J. Wroughton, *Stuart Bath*, 103.

7   C. Morris (ed), *The illustrated journeys of Celia Fiennes 1682-1712* (1984), 94.

8   British Library, KTOP XII 12i King's floating bath, Weymouth, 1782.

9   SHC, A/AQP/8/46.

10   Anon, *Universal British directory of trade, commerce and manufacture* (1794), 922.

11   SHC, DD\DP/21/2.

12   R. Warner, *A walk through some of the western counties of England* (1800), 82-3.

13   J. Savage, *History of the Hundred of Carhampton in the county of Somerset* (1830), 584.

14   J. Nightingale, *A topographical and historical description of the county of Somerset* (1819), 564.

15   Warner, *A walk*, 79.

16   SHC, A\BTL/2/27.

17   E.E. Baker, *The first guide to Weston super Mare* (1901), 27.

18   Baker, *The first guide*, 13.

19   J. Rutter, *Delineations of north west Somerset* (1829), 47-8.

20   H. and P. Coombs (eds), *Journal of a Somerset rector 1803-1834* (1971), 440-1.

21   J. Rutter, *The Clevedon guide* (1829), 18-19.

22   T.W. Rammell, *Report to the General Board of Health on a preliminary enquiry into the sewerage, drainage, and supply of water, & the sanitary condition of the inhabitants of the parish of Clevedon in the county of Somerset* (1852).

23   SHC, DD\SWD/10/9.

24   J. Salisbury, *A guide or handbook to Burnham and its neighbourhood* (1859), 12.

25   Morris and Co., *Commercial directory and gazetteer of Somersetshire and Bristol* (1872), 225 (advertisement section).

26   T. Smollett, *The expedition of Humphry Clinker* (1771), 145-6.

27   Anonymous, *Mr Punch at the seaside* (n.d.)

28   SHC, DD/S/FRI/8.

29   Rutter, *Delineations*, 48.

30   G. Henning, *An historical account of the medicinal waters or mineral springs of Daviesville, at Burnham . . .* (1836), 20.

31   A. Brown, *New guide to Weston super Mare and the neighbourhood* (1854), 14.

32   W. Plomer (ed.), *Kilvert's diary: selections from the diary of the Rev. Francis Kilvert* vol.2 (1969), 262.

33   SHC, A\AKH/6/3/1 and 2.

34   Information courtesy of Mr Brian Austin.

35   *The West Somerset Free Press*, 10 August 1935.

36   SHC, D\U\M/2/2/6.

37   SHC, DD\X\VZ/5.

38   Rutter, *The Clevedon guide*, 19.

39   SHC, DD\EN/45.

40   SHC, D\U\CL/2/2/1.

41   Henning, *An historical account*, 16-17.

42   J.B. Harley and R.W. Dunning, *Somerset maps. Day and Masters, 1782; Greenwood, 1822* Somerset Record Society 76 (1981).

43   SHC, A\AQP/8/1, 3, 6v, 39, 69.

44   SHC, Q\C\8\6.

45   Henning, *An historical account*, 18.

46   SHC, A\AQP/8/41.

47   J.K. Walton, *The English seaside resort: a social history 1750-1914* (1983), 53-4, 60, 65.

48   Savage, *Carhampton*, 584.

49   H. Binding and D. Stevens, *Minehead: a new history* (1977), 217.

50   Kelly, *Post Office directory of Somerset* (1866), 334-5.

51   Ibid, 309-310.

52   Salisbury, *Burnham*, 65.

53   *Gentleman's Magazine* December 1805, 1098.

54   Baker, *The first guide*, 9-11.

55   Coombs and Coombs, *Journal of a Somerset rector*, 440.

56   Pigot and Co., *National commercial directory 1830* (1830), 733.

57   Hunt and Co., *Directory and topography of Somerset* (1850), 108.

58   SHC, A\APN/5/57.

59   L. Lee, *Cider with Rosie* (1959), 190.

60   SHC, D\B\WSM/2/1/11.

61   C.G. Harper, *The Somerset coast* (1909), 74.

62   E. Fenton (ed.), *A brief jolly change: the diaries of Henry Peerless, 1891-1920* (2003), 20.

63   SHC, D\U\CL/2/2/1.

64   *West Somerset Free Press*, 18 July 1874.

65   *Western Daily Press*, 28 July 1874.

66 *The Times*, 5 June 1907.

67 T.W. Rammell, *Report to the General Board of Health, on a preliminary enquiry into the sewerage, drainage and supply of water . . . of Burnham* (1849), 28-9.

68 Salisbury, *Burnham*, 25.

69 SHC, D\U\B/10.

70 Rammell, *Clevedon.*

71 SHC, DD\X\AUS/127. The 1865 Sewerage Utilisation Act created sewer authorities, and gave town councils and other health authorities powers to dispose of sewerage for agricultural purposes and to take proceedings against persons polluting rivers.

72 SHC, DD\X\AUS/125.

73 SHC, DD\X\AUS/71.

74 Baker, *The first guide*, 27.

75 SHC, Q\RUp/153.

76 Plomer, *Kilvert's diary*, 266.

77 SHC, DD\SWD/10/7.

78 E.E. Baker, *Chronicle of leading events in the history of Weston super Mare during the past fifty years* (1887), 8.

79 Plomer, *Kilvert's diary*, 259.

80 Harper, *Somerset coast*, 75.

81 SHC, DD\VB/4/2/1.

82 Plomer, *Kilvert's diary*, 259.

83 Lee, *Cider with Rosie*, 195.

84 SHC, D\U\CL/2/2/1.

85 SHC, DD/L/P34/2 and 4.

86 Harper, *Somerset coast*, 228.

87 SHC, D\U\CL/2/2/1.

88 SHC, D\B\WSM/2/2/6.

89 Fenton, *A brief jolly change*, 22, 24.

90 Kelly's, *Directory of Somerset 1935* (1935), 624.

91 *New handbook to Clevedon and neighbourhood*, 2nd edition (1868), no page number.

92 J. Walton, *The English seaside resort*, 191-2.

93 *Clevedon the Borough guide* 29 (*c.*1900), 21.

94 *The official guide to holiday resorts in smiling Somerset* (1927), 27.

95 SHC, D\U\B/25/1/1.

96 SHC, D\R\WIL/24/1/160.

97 SHC, A\AIK/1/3.

98 SHC, A\AIK/1/1.

99 B. Concannon, *The history of Dunster beach* (1995), 222-3.

100 SHC, A\APN/4/1/2 Postcard of site postmarked 7 August 1932.

101 Information given by Miss J. Mines of Taunton.

102 R. Kerridge, *Bizarre Britain: a calendar of eccentricity* (1985), 53-4.

103 *The Daily Telegraph*, 27 August 2011.

104 *The Guardian*, 18 May 2009.

105 *The Observer*, 17 July 2011.

106 Sally Leaney, Garden Design, Heale Farm, Corfe, TA3 7BE (sally.leaney@hotmail.com).

Chapter Three

Two Somerset River Ferries

Dr Joseph Bettey and Dr Adrian Webb

Introduction

CROSSING a river by ferry was undoubtedly a cheaper option than constructing a bridge for such a purpose, especially if the river was particularly wide, such as the Avon near its mouth. It was also a much quicker option than having to travel to the nearest bridge, as the poet Samuel Taylor Coleridge advised his friends in 1796 to take the Combwich ferry, rather than travel all the way to Bridgwater.[1] The responsibility for a ferry service fell to the lord of the manor, or more than one if parties on both sides of the crossing held a right to it, whereas bridges were normally paid for from county funds. As Somerset is blessed with numerous rivers so the occurrence of ferries to cross them can be found

from the Middle Ages, some being attached to the rights of owners of manors which benefited from such a facility, others on a less formal basis. One over the Challis Wall rhyne near Pathe (at Othery) was replaced by a temporary bridge in the mid-seventeenth century and later by a more permanent structure,[2] exemplifying the fate of the vast majority of river ferries in Somerset. Of those controlled by the landlord and leased out to a local operator there are many examples.

One early example, operated on the River Axe, is mentioned in 1234 when William Harold paid 8d a year for the ferry and half an acre of land, which in 1515-16 was held by Thomas Hobbs. The ferry was still in use in the 1790s for transporting horses at high tide but was virtually redundant at other times as the river was only two feet deep at low tide.[3] It saw a revival in the early twentieth century with a demand from tourists to visit Brean Down, each paying 6d for the service.[4] Another ferry of great antiquity

Illustration 3.1: Combwich Pill and the ferry slip in 2007 (Adrian Webb)

existed across the River Parrett between Combwich (on the south side) and the White House Inn (on the north side), thought to have been in operation by the mid-thirteenth century. Compared to the ferry over the Axe the ownership of the Combwich ferry was far more complex. It is possible the ferry was valuable enough to have been divided between two parties in 1285 and between four by 1569. One of those quarter shares passed into the hands of the owners of the Anchor Inn (at Combwich) before 1786 and another (possibly a sixth) share existed by 1730 as part of the manor of Otterhampton. One owner left the profits of his share of the ferry to his wife and daughter in 1630, together with possession of a wharf.[5]

The ferry was used to transport cattle, horses and passengers, some of whom in 1404 were impeded by the actions of the Lord of Pawlett, who used stones and timber to block the route between the crossing and the village of Pawlett 'to the damage of the country'.[6] In 1557 it cost a group of officials from the City of Bristol 22d to use the Combwich ferry on the way to Stockland Bristol to undertake manorial duties and musters.[7] The journey across the Parrett was not always easy as Thomas Smyth of Ashton Court, was encouraged by a relation, Elizabeth Gorges, to visit her at Cannington, via the ferry, in July 1637 except 'if it be wyndy wether'.[8] Such advice was a sensible approach to using small boats which could easily be capsized on river crossings. As well as domestic travellers the route between Nether Stowey and Pawlett, crossing the Parrett by ferry, was very important for cattle drovers and dealers.[9] Such a use had existed for some time, as Devon oxen from south and western Somerset were bought in February for fattening on the Somerset levels and also Welsh cattle were bought in

the summer (to follow on) and become fat on the lush pastures of the Somerset lowlands. Cattle landed at Minehead and Watchet would have made their way along the drove road,[10] crossing the ford near Combwich at low tide.

In the later eighteenth century the churchwardens of the parish paid for repairs to a slip, possibly at the end of the causeway where the ferries docked, and the service continued into the late nineteenth century.[11] On the other side of the river the ferry was shared between the owners of Pawlett Gaunt's manor and the Combwich manors in 1589, and a half share of the ferry was let with the inn at the passage in 1810.[12]

At Othery in 1308 there was a ferry across the Parrett, evidently from Burrow to Saltmoor, which was also in use in 1370 and 1515.[13] Although tenants also held some land, one who held Kinglake ferry was responsible for Sowyland clyce, which protected Sowy island, and Kinglake clyce. At neighbouring Aller, from a tenement called the Boathouse (near Bagenham), there was a ferry by 1561 across the rhine dividing Aller from Othery. What is particularly unusual about this was the right (upheld in the mid-seventeenth century at least) to use a temporary bridge every year at harvest time in order to transport hay from Aller moor. In addition to which the ferryman still retained the right at all other times to charge for passages across the rhine.[14] Even though there was a bridge crossing the Parrett at Bridgwater, in 1568 a ferry was used for bringing labourers from Othery to Hamp (near Bridgwater) to work on a substantial engineering project. By going over the water by ferry, rather than from Othery to Bridgwater and then on to Hamp (being 7½ miles) by land, the labourers cut their journey down by two miles.[15] Even in the early decades of the twentieth century a ferry across the Avon at Claverton (just below the weir) required no ferryman to operate it, only the passenger who had to pull themself across by using a rope![16] Such was the diversity and antiquity of some of Somerset's river ferries; the Pill and Rownham operations are examined here in more detail.

PILL FERRY[17]

Ownership

The foundation date for a ferry at Pill, or Crockern Pill (on the south bank of the River Avon) has not, and is unlikely to, come to light. However, the geography at the mouth of the Avon, near

Illustration 3.2: An extract from a chart of 1723 showing The Passage opposite Combwich (SHC, D/RA/9/9).

Avonmouth is such that the Reverend Samuel Seyer, a local antiquary, deduced how important the 'old Gloucester road' (running through Pill to Shirehampton) was to communications between the two counties. He even went as far as to suggest how the ferry 'must have been in common use from the very first habitation of the country; it being the lowest place on the river, where a landing can be made'. His hypothesis hinged upon his observation in the early nineteenth century how it was the only landing place for a mile, thus adding to the importance of the crossing.[18] Evidence for a crossing can be found in the name Passage Leaze is one that was given to the land at Lamplighter's on the Shirehampton side in 'ancient' times.[19]

As for its ownership the ferry was thought to belong to the Abbot of St Augustine,[20] who held it when there was a slip at 'Creocham' (or Crockern) in the reign of Henry II, which came into possession of the Berkeley family.[21] The Berkeleys certainly held some right to the ferry during the reign of Henry VI as Thomas Morgan, passer (or ferryman) brought a petition against the Berkeleys and their servants for using the ferry without paying him any tolls, when Richard Duke of York (d.1460) was lord of the manor of Easton.[22] It is definitely known that the ferry constituted part of the manor of Easton-in-Gordano in the mid-sixteenth century, when it was held by the Morgan family. This can be traced back to the Young family, who held it of Sir William Berkeley by fealty for a quarterly rent of 2d. Some years later Alice Young (born 1477)[23] wife of William Malet of Enmore, the sole daughter and heir of Thomas Young of Easton-in-Gordano, inherited a third of the manor in 1505. This subsequently passed to three Malet brothers, Richard of Ash, Hugh of Enmore and William of Sutton Mallet.[24] Collinson stated how the manor of Easton-in-Gordano was sold by Richard Malet (d.*c*.1548), of Enmore, and Joan his wife, to Richard Morgan esquire in June 1544[25] 'in whose family it remained until the beginning of the present century'.[26] Another record states it was sold in 1547, as appears in the patent roll for that year.[27] The last male Morgan, another Richard, devised the manor to his widow who left it to Thomas Wilkins esquire, her grandson by her former husband, who took the name of Morgan.[28] It is from the time of the Morgan's ownership that a detailed insight of the ferry and its surroundings survives.

Pill was an attractive position for boatmen operating a ferry from at least the middle of the

sixteenth century. Richard White, a 75 year old mariner of Walton, stated the same in 1607 as he knew all of the 'Ryvers Creekes pills and places for the harboringe of Shippinge' within the port of Bristol and the River Avon. It was also possible for small vessels to stay at Crockern Pill without having to take any moorings until the next tide. Although Crockern Pill only had a capacity for six small ships or barks, for the previous 50 years he had known all of the owners, masters of ships, pilots and mariners who had 'free libertie to passe and goe through dyvers lands and pastures adioyninge to the Ryver . . . with men and oxen for the haylinge in and out of shippinge to and from the said Porte of kingrode and hungrode' without having to pay any sum of money for the privilege. This was good for the ferry as there was never going to be the congestion faced at other pills and creeks, as Hung Road was sufficient to hold '. . . and contayne all such shipps Barks and botes as not usually come there'. He also knew of the ferry across the river at Crockern Pill, which he had used to transport himself and his horse at a penny a piece. Although his evidence was corroborated another deponent gave some alternative figure.

John Lullet, a 72 year old husbandman of Easton in Gordano, stated that about 50 years previously he knew that only two, or three, small barks could use Crockern Pill as there were no posts for mooring at that time. His father was ordered by the grandfather of Thomas Morgan to set up two posts for mooring, because before this time vessels 'were usually fastned to the Stakes of the hedges thereunto adioyninge to the spoyle and decay of the same hedges'. These posts laid in the 1550s were 'sett higher in the grownd then the full sea marke', with the new posts recently set up 'above Tenn foote higher in the grownde' than the old posts. He knew that 17 or 18 years ago the Mayor and Commonalty of Bristol had set up two posts, but one which was on the land of Thomas Morgan was removed by Morgan. The corporation had not asked for permission to set up the post on his land and Lullet at that time was the passer, or ferry man, who took the full wrath of Morgan's anger for letting it be set up. Lullet was in a difficult position, as on the one hand he did not want to incur the wrath of the mighty City Council, but on the other he paid Morgan 20s per annum for the office of ferry man, thus finding himself in a no win situation. Nevertheless operating the ferry could not have been easy, as it was known how small ships or barks had been 'overthrowne . . . and certen goods

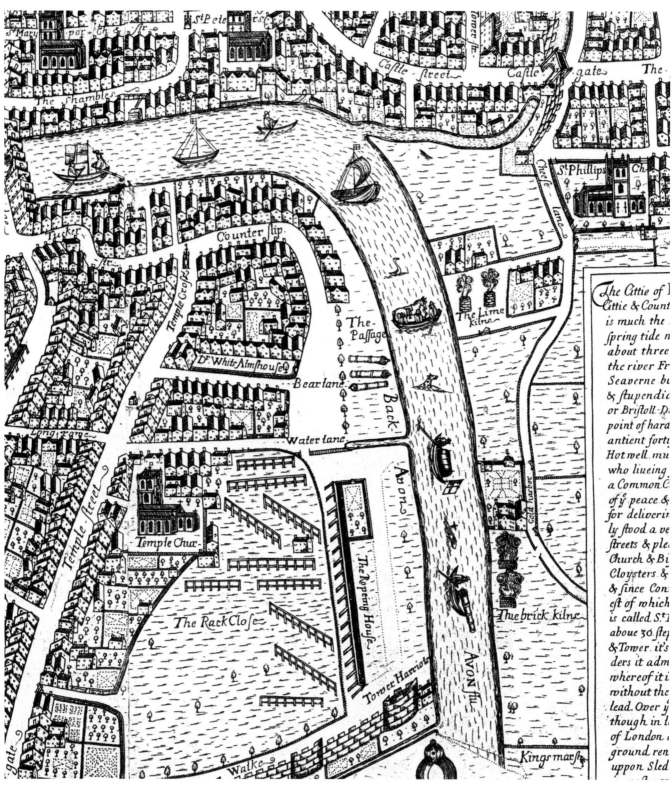

Illustration 3.3: Although crudely drawn this extract from Millerd's map of Bristol of 1673 shows two men and a horse being ferried across the Avon at a place called The Passage (SANHS)

and marchandizes therein being wette spoyled and hurte . . . for want of sufficient moringe posts for their better stayeinge and fasteninge' at Crockern Pill.

The ferry was not an isolated facility at Pill as other facilities in 1607 included two new houses used for victualling maritime visitors, as well as other illegal commodities on offer. Samuel Norton, esquire of Abbots Leigh (aged 60 and upwards) had an intimate knowledge of Crockern Pill and had sat on a commission for surveying and restraint of the transportation of prohibited wares and merchandise within the county of Somerset. He appointed officers to restrain goods within the creek and knew there had been '. . . dyvers prohibited wares conveyed aboorde within the said pill or creeke . . .'. By 1607 Crockern Pill was much more '. . . easie and saffe to lye in then in former tyme yt hath ben and with lesse charge and danger of Anchors Caples and Tacklynge'. The pill was also broader than it had been, which was caused by ships '. . . ridinge lyeinge and moringe . . .' there. Ships lying in the pill also benefited by transporting people across the river, but whether this was from the ferry slip is not clear.[29] Nevertheless the facilities at the ferry on the Somerset side were far better for Morgan establishing the mooring posts, especially as the more ships that moored up so the lord of the manor could earn more revenue from fees, a situation similar to other Somerset ports such as Combwich, Minehead and Bridgwater.

The Morgans courted controversy throughout their ownership of the manor during the seventeenth century. Latimer records a handful of cases in which one of the family had a hand in some matter of controversy concerning navigation and/or the behaviour of the maritime community at Pill. Another Exchequer case, in 1630, revealed how little had changed since the days when Lullett operated the ferry. Ships lying at Pill were still carrying people across the river when they were weather-bound, which provided those mariners with an extra source

of income much to the detriment of the ferryman, Thomas Gethin. Julian Deane widow, aged 60, deposed that she heard her father, former ferryman John Lullett, mention the lord of the manor's great-grandfather sinking posts to improve facilities at Pill. As for Gethin, aged 47 of Crockern Pill, he claimed to be losing £10 per year thanks to mariners ferrying people across the river, something he had witnessed for the previous 12 years he had been passer.[30] Subsequently in 1633 an order by the Court of Exchequer was issued which stipulated, in addition to a heavy fine, several houses interfering with navigation had to be demolished except for one used by the ferry.[31]

It is from the time of the ownership of the manor by Thomas Wilkins Morgan that an indenture between himself, described as 'esquire' of Easton in Gordano, in the one part and John Gilmore, pilot of Easton in Gordano, was drawn up in 1783. Gilmore, who presumably like many of his fellow pilots made

---

Illustration 3.4: An extract from a survey of the River Avon undertaken in the early 1680s, published in 1693. Note how although the ferry is not shown an inlet on the Gloucestershire side shows where King William III landed on 6 September 1690 (Robin and Hillary Bush)

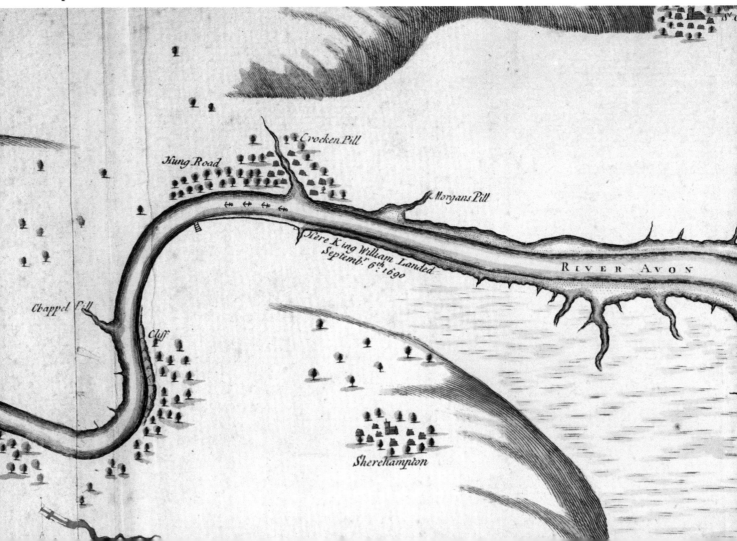

⚓

a good living from the growing shipping trade in the Bristol Channel, paid £280 for the demise of

> all that slip at Passage in the said parish of St Georges Together with the ferry at Passage over and across the River Avon there to the opposite shore in the County of Gloster.

Included in the agreement were two 'passing boats' with their oars and materials, already employed for the use of the ferry (to be returned at the end of the lease), which were in possession of Gamage Henderson, a servant of Morgan. What was also a lucrative part of the deal were all the profits and 'advantages to the Slip Ferry or passage belonging together with free ingress egress regress way and passage to and for the said John Gilmore'. Gilmore took out a 99 year lease on the lives of his children Ann Gilmore aged about 12, John Gilmore aged about 10 and William Gilmore aged about 8, for a yearly rent £1, a 20s heriot as well as suit and service at all yearly courts for the manor of St Georges. What may have not been such a good proposition was the

clause that put Gilmore in the onerous position to have to:

> well and sufficiently repair amend sustain and keep the said slip hereby demised boats and materials . . . with all manner of needful and necessary reparations and amendments whatsoever when where and as often as need shall require

at his own expense.[32] This slip was a not a small run-off from a bank but a substantial stone structure that was an expensive item to repair, requiring masons, labourers and materials that could only be achieved when the tide was right.

The strategic value of the ferry crossing was recorded in September 1768 by Paule St de Beville, a lieutenant colonel of Dragoons. He made numerous

Ilustration 3.5: An intelligence gathering exercise by Paule St de Beville a lieutenant colonel of Dragoons showing the ferry (*Bac*) between St George's and Shirehampton in 1768 (TNA, MF 1/54)

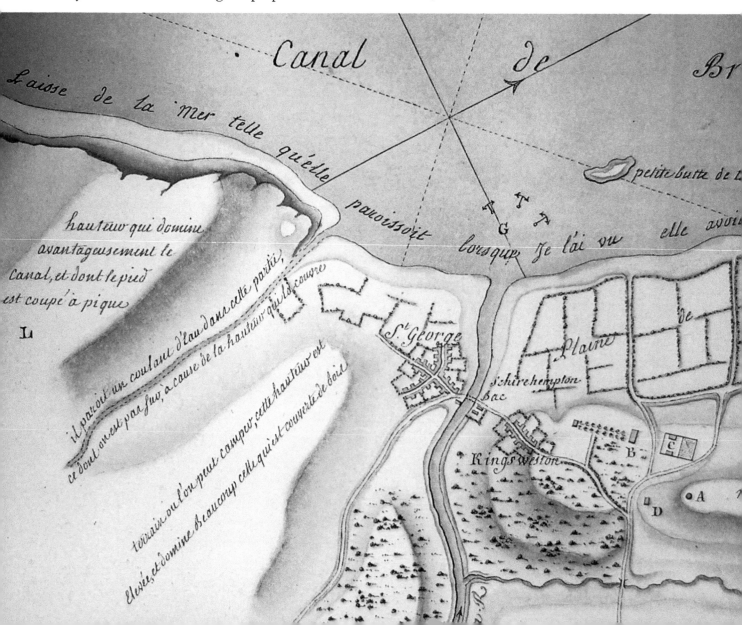

surveys of ports and rivers around the south coast of England, when he included the Rivers Parrett and Avon.[33] These surveys were ordered by the Duc de Choiseul, Minister of War and of the Marine, who, despite having a degree of responsibility for the French policy of providing instruction in hydrographic surveying and navigation,[34] did not instruct Beville to record any hydrography on his surveys of the Parrett and Avon. If he was hoping to use the final product for any type of navigation when it came to an invasion he would have had to overcome some serious inaccuracies in his intelligence gathering. In the Parrett he did not record the two islands by Huntspill, the major shoal in the river or the island adjacent to King Road in the mouth of the Avon. He noted some detail at 'St George', as well as the ferry crossing to Shirehampton and how the area was overlooked by a 'small turret where one keeps a look-out during the war' on the hill above Kingsweston, which he named the Mountain of the Spy.[35]

When the manor of Easton in Gordano came on the market in 1828 a ferry over the Avon was specifically mentioned, along with 'a fishery connected with the manor', a dry dock and dockyard, included in the 1586 acres of land offered.[36] The owners of the manor and the ferry operators, could have made significant amounts of money if those schemes to build a canal at Easton-in-Gordano had become a reality. One such scheme in 1811 proposed building a canal from the River Avon 'at or near Morgan's Pill' to Taunton.[37] This would have brought more vessels and travellers to Pill, potentially increasing the number of passengers using the ferry service. Sadly, what would have been a great feat of civil engineering never materialised, although the development of Portishead and Portbury in the following decades, coupled with the expansion of the railway network, did bring more people to the area. From which it is highly likely that the number of users of the ferry did actually increase in the first half of the nineteeth century.

Lord of the manor of Easton-in-Gordano, the enterprising James Adam Gordon, was responsible for issuing a proposal in October 1840 for the expansion of the maritime facilities at Portbury, a spin-off from which was the development of the infrastructure for transporting goods to and from the area. Improvements were proposed for a road leading directly from Portbury to the ferry at Pill and two more leading from the ferry.[38] Such a venture would have brought added prosperity to the inhabitants at Pill and potentially more business for

the ferry. The ferry was also used to help sell properties that came on to the market in the nineteenth century, such as in 1851 when one enterprising Bristol auctioneer advertised how the farmhouses he was selling, were only a mile distant from the ferry where 'there is easy access'.[39] Similarly, when an inn was sold in June 1886, it was advertised as being immediately opposite the ferry and undoubtedly the first port of call for many travellers.[40]

Presumably Gilmore's investment was not effected when the manor was sold, as on 5 July 1839 the lease appears to still have been active and in the hands of the Gilmore family.[41] In the following year the lease was held by Elizabeth Gilmore, who was the occupier, suggesting that she was running the family business as her husband had passed away.[42] In August 1855 the ferry of Pill was included in the sale of the estates of the late James Adam Gordon esquire, which comprised of over 2,500 acres of land in Clapton, Portbury, Wraxall, Portishead, Tickenham, and Easton-in-Gordano, as well as Dunball (or Dungball) Island at the mouth of the Avon.[43] The ferry was sold as part of a lot of three items. The first was Dunball Island, the second was 'all the manor or reputed manor of Easton-in-Gordano, otherwise St George, with the rights in the Wharf and Commons, and all other the rights, royalties, and appurtenances thereto belonging', and the third was the ferry. Along with the latter was included the passage boats, tolls and privileges 'thereto appertaining', sold with a caveat that the lease of the ferry was determinable on the decease of a life aged 'about 81', at the yearly rent of £1.[44] It is quite possible the life in question was that of John Gilmore as he was ten years old in 1783 when his father took out the lease, making him 81 or 82 in 1855.[45] No burial appears for a John after that date at Easton-in-Gordano, but a James Gilmore, aged 90 was buried on 25 January 1863 in the parish churchyard. So it is possible the lease may have come up for renewal in 1863, although in 1851 and in 1861 Gilmore described himself as a pauper, whose occupation was formerly that of a mariner or waterman,[46] who was described as a pilot in 1799.[47] The estate (comprising of about 450 acres of land) was sold again in June 1879, along with many other things in separate lots, including a boat builder's yard, wharf, riverbank and landing steps.[48]

The ferry was not without problems, one complaint in June 1851 concerned the right of public users to access the upper slip at Pill. The problem arose because the entry to the slip had been enclosed

Illustration 3.6: The slip leading from Lamplighters in 2009 (Adrian Webb)

by the gates of a new Customs house. The upper slip was an alternative departure point and, on that occasion, as the 'rain was pouring in torrents' it was a preferred point of departure. There appears to have been no right to deny access to the slip, but that was not the last time access to one side or other of the ferry route was an issue.[49] In October that very same year there was an issue on the other side of the river, this time concerning posts erected on each side of the ferry slip, as well as a piece of ground 'staked' in front of Lamplighters' Hotel. The problem was caused because the distance between the stakes would only allow one person, or a horse, to travel through it, which had been erected because people had been landing coals illegally; see Illustration 3.7. The stakes were ordered to be put in place by Mr P.W.S. Miles but the objections were on the grounds that the ferry slip had, allegedly, become 'most dangerous to life and property'. There was no doubt that the land was publicly accessible, although at the time the complainant could only recall it being as

such for the previous 40 years. The barrier had also blocked the carriageway and the complainant (styled as 'A Lover of Justice') wanted to know why the Council had allowed such an act?[5]

In the 1850s the service was thought to have been either owned or run by Mr Reed and Mr Russell.[51] Mr Sydney Porter purchased the ferry from the lord of the manor, Mr Richard Bright, in 1880 for £700[52] and in July 1886 the ferry was offered to let through H. Porter, Haywood House, Lodway, Pill[53] for £300 per annum.[54] Shortly afterwards, in 1895, the ferry was once again under the ownership of a lady (Sydney's widow), as it was back in the days of Mrs Ann Morgan. At that time complaints printed in a Bristol newspaper called for the fares for workmen and weekly passengers to be reduced to 6d per week. The matter was brought before the parish council and there were threats of 'an opposition ferry' being set up to compete with the existing one, although how this would have been possible is not clear as the opposition did not have the right to operate such a facility.[55] However, it was not just the fees which were a point of contention, as the frequency at which the ferry operated was also under

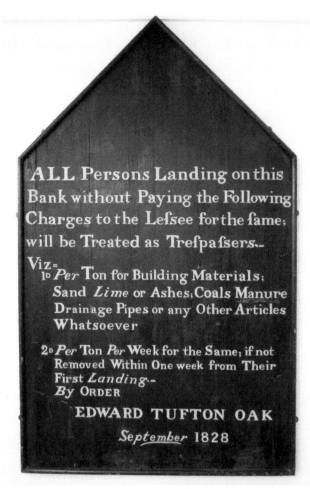

to cross the Avon, being three times the train fare from Bristol to Shirehampton, was questionable, especially when the slips themselves were allegedly in a 'dangerous condition'.[56]

In 1898 Captain Enoch Porter was the lessee who had to pay rates in respect of the ferry to the 'Corporation of Bristol, and to the authorities at Easton-in-Gordano and Shirehampton'. He also had to pave the slip and keep it in good repair, thus as lessee he claimed the right to charge anyone landing on the slip except for pilots, boatmen and others who made a living on the river. When this was brought to court Charles Hunt, a ferryman, stated it was customary to charge people who landed on the slip, although he admitted there were many who did not pay. Joseph Hunt, a boatman of Pill, who was 71, claimed he had seen many people landed at Pill toll free, although he could not comment on similar affairs on the Gloucestershire side as he 'did not like the people who lived there'. It was stated how the right of the river bank was in the public domain and Porter had no right to charge people being landed from boats. Porter's case was not helped as he was unable to produce any deeds to support his claim, and the lease of 1783 did not state such a right, so perhaps Porter realised that was the case and thought it best not to produce them![57]

Porter was known to have lived opposite the ferry and made a good living from it, as he was able

Illustration 3.7: A notice erected at Pill warning of the fines for landing materials illegally, a problem which affected the ferry in 1851 (Helen Todd)

scrutiny in the Press. Calls for the ferry to be kept open from 5a.m. to 12p.m. were made, with comparisons drawn to other ferries and the railway service. Clearly the shilling charged at certain times

Illustration 3.8: A plan of the slipways at Pill and Shirehampton used by the ferry service in 1928 (Bristol Record Office, BristolPlans/arranged/170)

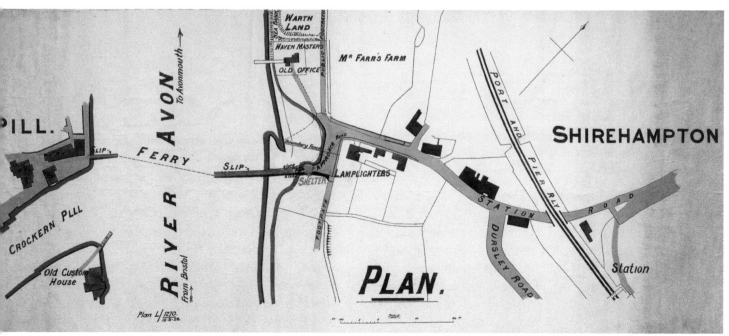

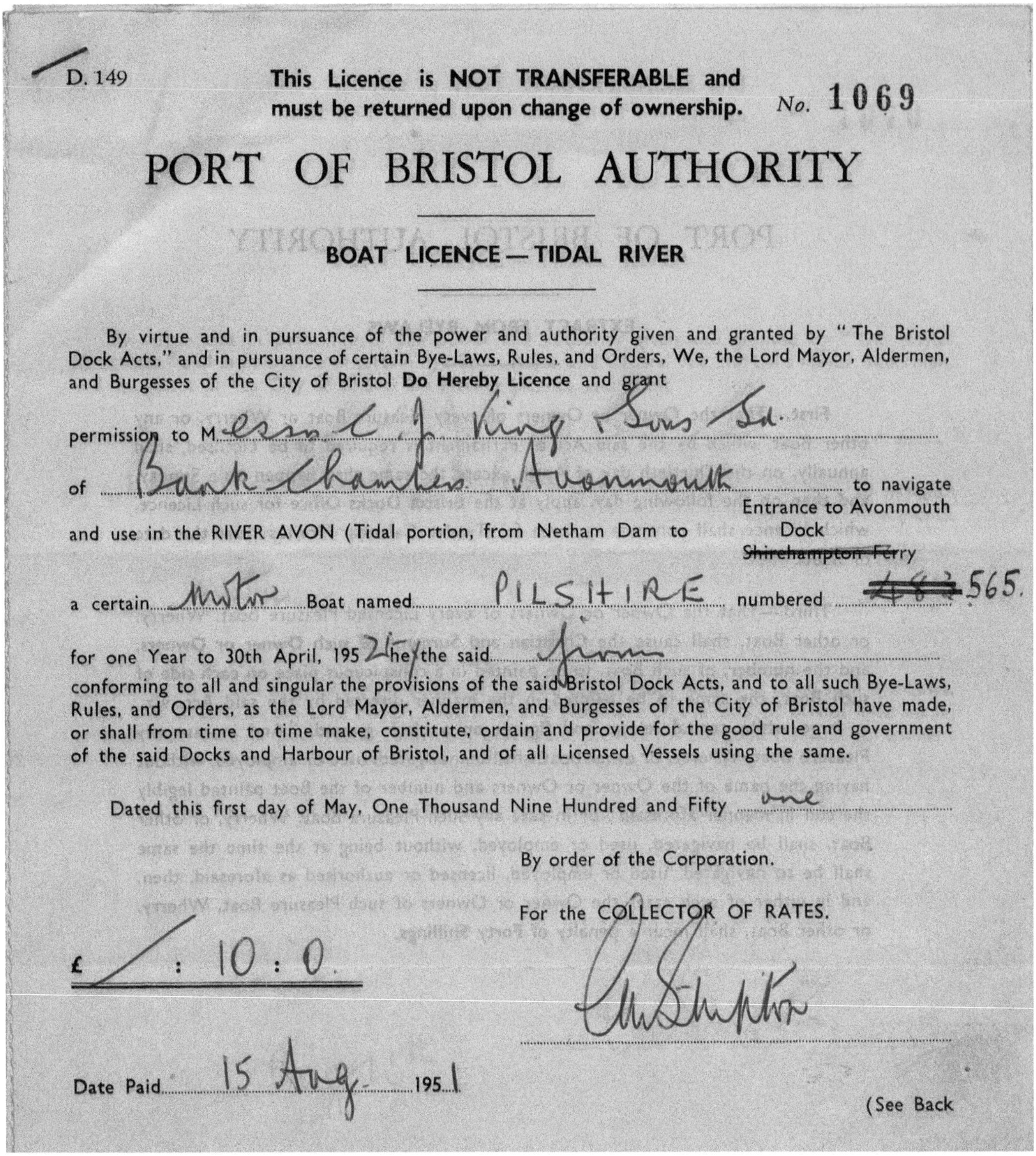

D. 149

This Licence is **NOT TRANSFERABLE** and must be returned upon change of ownership. *No.* **1069**

PORT OF BRISTOL AUTHORITY

BOAT LICENCE — TIDAL RIVER

By virtue and in pursuance of the power and authority given and granted by "The Bristol Dock Acts," and in pursuance of certain Bye-Laws, Rules, and Orders, We, the Lord Mayor, Aldermen, and Burgesses of the City of Bristol **Do Hereby Licence** and grant

permission to M *essrs C. J. King Sons Ltd.*

of *Bank Chambers Avonmouth* .... to navigate

and use in the RIVER AVON (Tidal portion, from Netham Dam to ~~Shirehampton Ferry~~ Entrance to Avonmouth Dock

a certain *Motor* Boat named *PILSHIRE* numbered ~~565~~ *565*.

for one Year to 30th April, 195 2 *the* the said *firm*
conforming to all and singular the provisions of the said Bristol Dock Acts, and to all such Bye-Laws, Rules, and Orders, as the Lord Mayor, Aldermen, and Burgesses of the City of Bristol have made, or shall from time to time make, constitute, ordain and provide for the good rule and government of the said Docks and Harbour of Bristol, and of all Licensed Vessels using the same.

Dated this first day of May, One Thousand Nine Hundred and Fifty *one*

By order of the Corporation.

For the COLLECTOR OF RATES.

£ */* : 10 : 0.

Date Paid *15 Aug* 195 *1*

(See Back

Illustration 3.9: A boat licence issued by the Port of Bristol Authority for the Pilshire in 1951 (BRO)

to send his children to boarding school. When Sidney Porter died, his son John, a superintendent of Bristol Docks, took over and it was his money which paid for the toll house to be built on the Shirehampton side.[58] According to one local historian, Enoch 'weighed 17 stones, had a wonderful strong voice, and was good natured being known to the local children as 'Uncle' Enoch'.[59] The Porter family continued to own the

ferry, witnessing the introduction of motor boats in the mid-1930s, until about 1936 when John Porter was killed in a car fire on the Suspension Bridge.[60]

During World War Two the ferry was run by the Port of Bristol on behalf of the Ministry of Transport.[61] One of the ferries was the M.L. *Pilshire*, owned by Richard John Porter (who died in 1947), Mr Cole-Millard and the Port of Bristol Authority, who passed it over to C.J. King and Son who had it overhauled and surveyed by 11 August 1947. At the same time King and Sons wanted to expand their business by running the *Pilshire* as a passenger ferry between Bristol docks and the mouth of the river, but their application submitted to the Ministry of War Transport was denied; the reasons given were that the river was 'narrow and tortuous', overcrowded with existing traffic and the tides too strong. M.L. *Pilshire* had a capacity to carry 28 persons and other boats owned by King and Son included *Nova* (19 persons), *Nexus* (18 persons) and *Avonshire* (11 persons). Gone were the days when one man operated one craft, as in the financial year of 1948-49 the ferries carried 495,464 passengers!

It was not until 1949 that the ferry boat was returned to the Porter family, when it was run by Mr Millard, son-in-law to the late Mr Porter. Such was the grip the Porters had over the running of the service that Mrs Porter was thought to have watched its every movement. She allegedly recorded the number of passengers (by watching them from the Customs House) by sticking a pin in her pincushion for every person who crossed.[62] Looking at the number of passengers at that time (nearly half a million)[63] she would have needed an awful lot of pins and a very large cushion! King and Sons tried again (in May 1950 by writing to D.W. Gelling Esquire, Senior Engineer Surveyor, Marine Surveyor's Office), due to public pressure, to run river trips using *Pilshire* on such a service rather than as a ferry. They proposed the boat would be manned by two competent men, with only one trip per day in the afternoon during daylight hours and the vessel would leave Shirehampton 30 minutes before high water. Their request to operate between Shirehampton and Hotwells was not approved. They were allowed by the Ministry of Transport in June 1950 to use *Pilshire* to take passengers on a tour of the docks, as long as any children were taken on at the docks and not in the river.

There were more problems with the ferry service, as a letter, of 28 May 1952, from the South Western Regional Board for Industry to King and Son, pointed out numerous allegations against the operation they were running. The complaints included the inconsistent running times of the ferry (causing delays for industrial workers and other passengers), incompetence of the ferry's employees 'involving possible danger to passengers', filthy slipways and a lack of 'uniformity in fares' with 2½d charged for one way and 6d for the other. In reply (of 3 June 1952) to the allegations, King and Son pointed out how the staff were continually being changed (having employed 31 different men between 1947 and 1952) and when there were no ferrymen

available they used trainees. Boats were often delayed due to the tides, but very rarely and, as for the fares, they had been set since 1914 with approval of the Ministry of Transport, so there appears to have been little to worry about. But the Regional Board were not satisfied, as they wrote again in October with another batch of similar complaints and even sent a delegation to try and resolve them, including a former Royal Navy captain.

Tragedy struck at the end of 1952, after King and Sons leased the ferry to Mr Jim Rice, who unfortunately drowned on the very day he took the lease on, but his wife and sons carried on for the seven year term. His death was caused by a heart attack, brought on after he waded into the river to try and rescue a boat which had drifted away. The ferry was then sold to the Hunt Brothers and the Withers who ran it until 1968 when Mr Bob Brown took it over.[64]

Ferrymen and the experience of travelling on the ferry

Outside of the ownership of the ferry some other glimpses of the type of activities connected with its operation can be seen. For example, in 1818 the charge for crossing the river from Pill to Weeks's Hotel was one penny and at that time the local hoteliers prospered from the large number of ships connected with the Avon. This was mainly due to the growing number of packets for Cork and Waterford, but also 'market-boats, sloops, brigs, Indiamen, &c. continually passing to and from Bristol'.[65] It was shortly before this time that Joseph Shepherd, a waterman of Pill, started his career as a ferryman, but disaster struck in 1835 when he accidentally fell overboard into the river and was drowned, despite having over 20 years experience of working the river. The newspaper reported how he fell in at the time of the ebb tide when there was a strong fresh (or current) in the river, at night and, despite seven boats and crews setting off instantly from Pill to try and save him, it was all in vain. His position as ferryman made him a popular figure in the community, one who had worked on the ferry from his teenage years, described as a 'tar for all weathers, cheerful and good natured to every one'. Even more tragic was the fact he left a widow and seven children, but some gentlemen were reported as raising a fund to support them.[66]

Possibly the earliest painting of the ferries is from some time around the early nineteenth century, certainly still well within the Age of Sail. It shows

Illustration 3.10: Pill slipway viewed from Lamplighters, *c.*1830. Is this a ferry boat approaching the shore at Shirehampton, using both man and wind power to speed its course, or, judging by the number of small craft, was it a free-for-all? (Private Collection)

two vessels that could both have been in use as ferry boats, although the two appear to be very different (see Illustration 3.10). The painting shows a small vessel approaching the Gloucestershire side being rowed by two men (sitting down) and a third is adjusting the sail. A fourth man is waiting on the bank with a lasso ready to throw it to the boat in order to secure it safely on its arrival. There are clearly at least two passengers and another four

waiting to be picked up, including a lady carrying a basket on her head.

On the Pill side of the river another small vessel is on the final approach to the slip (see Illustration 3.11). This is a very different vessel to the one approaching Shirehampton. It shows it being operated by a man at each end of the vessel punting their way towards the slip. It has no sails and there is no indication of anyone on the shore waiting to help them tie up, or be held by a rope whilst passengers get in and out of the vessel. It is square-ended and there are two ladies walking towards it carrying goods on top of their heads. There are a lot of people shown behind the two ladies, but whether they were waiting for the ferry is not clear, nevertheless one of

Illustration 3.11: A close-up of the ferry making its way towards the slip on the Pill side, *c.*1830 (Private Collection)

ferry to take the traveller across the water to Pill. It is also quite possible that if the painting was executed in the early 1830s, and it is a ferryman in the foreground, he could well have been Joseph Shepherd who sadly drowned in 1835.[69]

An inhabitant of Shirehampton, Francois Baron (1823-99), recalled being ferried over the Avon 'by "Old Wergen" a bronzed and weather-beaten old sailor', who supplemented his income from the ferry by selling fish. What was particularly memorable to Baron was Old Wergen's medical practice of dipping persons in the river who had been bitten by dogs in attempt to prevent hydrophobia. He recalled how 'sufferers were taken to the middle of the river and then plunged into the water until nearly insensible, and then allowed to recover their breath, when they were again plunged in and after several such submersions were supposed to be safe', although whether they were or not he did not say.[70]

One observer recalled in the 1860s how he observed a ferryboat taking on passengers somewhere along the Avon:

> First, came a lot of market wenches, with their big baskets and Somersetshire hats, looking as though they had dropped out of a last-century engraving; then, a drove of smock-frocked cow-men; then, a young curate and his wife, a soldier on furlough, and two boys home for the holidays.[71]

the two vessels, or possibly both, was operating as a ferry.

Another painting, from around the 1830s or 1840s, possibly shows one of the ferryboats. Francis Greenacre, in his volume *From Bristol to the Sea*, reproduced a painting by Joseph Walter (1783-1856) from a private collection, showing in the foreground a large rowing boat capable of seating around a dozen people. What is more telling is the position of the boat at the foot of the slipway in front of Lamplighters' Hall. In addition to which there is a traveller who is running from the boat towards a steam packet, but a mariner is pointing towards the ferryboat in an effort to persuade the traveller to use the ferry.[67] Although the vessel is unidentified it could well be 'The New and Elegant Steam-Packet' *Eagle*, advertised as stopping at Pill and Lamplighters in 1834; *Eagle* operated from Monday to Saturday under its master, George Walters, tickets for which could be purchased at 60 Broad Quay, Bristol, the Ferry House at Rownham and the 'Hotel' at Portishead.[68] Had the man therefore missed the packet service, or had it not stopped at Lamplighters but at Pill, as one of the ferrymen is pointing to the

From paintings of ferries on the Avon this was not an uncommon appearance. However, travelling on the ferry was not always possible due to adverse weather conditions, such as during a terrific gale in January 1890, which meant passengers could not be landed at Lamplighters. Many areas adjacent to Pill and Shirehampton were also affected by flooding and the ferry could not land on the Gloucestershire side for half-an-hour, as the water level had reached as far up the road as Avonmere House. The water even reached the railway bank but for many living at Pill high tides and floods were commonplace.[72]

It was not just large numbers of passengers who had to be transported across the river. During World War One, horses were kept at Pen Pole Hill for use by the Army but they could only be transported across the river at high tide, due to the steepness of the slipways.[73] Later in the twentieth century a type of corrugated shed was used on top of an oversize ferry boat to transport horses, which was thought to have been in use until the 1940s.[74] The ferryboat was probably a great deal larger than could be seen in the nineteenth-century paintings of it, as the cost of

Illustration 3.12: A view of Pill from Lamplighters Hall showing a ferryboat in the foreground, *c.*1920 (John Rich)

using the ferry in the second half of the sixteenth century was a penny a piece for a man and his horse.[75] Although how many horses at a time could be transported is not known. Four hundred years later (in 1952) the fares varied depending on what time of day a person travelled with 2½d charged up until 8p.m., 3d from 8 until 9, then 4d from 9 until 10 and 6d after that until 10.40p.m. Children up to 14 years were charged at half price and bicycles, perambulators and push chairs (excluding their owners) 3d, but if a passenger with a bicycle wanted a return it was 9d return and tandems 8d single and 1s 2d return.[76]

In February 1952 the ferry was open between 5 a.m. and 10.40 p.m. when the last boat left Pill slip at 10.30 p.m.. Restrictions were also placed on the maximum number of people carried on each journey,

with 30 on a large motorboat, 20 on a small motorboat and 18 in a rowing boat. The ferry operators (C.J. King & Sons Ltd) reserved the right to refuse transport to 'any person, property or animals likely to cause damage, disturbance or discomfort to passengers', with the threat of prosecution if they did. The ferrymen had the authority not to move any boats if they were overloaded, but whether they did or not has not come to light. It is also from this period that some idea of the costs of the whole operation can be found. In 1952 the ferrymen were paid £7 per week, the foreman £8 and the maintenance men £6, overtime averaged at 5s per man. The biggest expenditure for the ferry operators was the wage bill, which rose from £1,616 in 1947-8 to £2,190 in 1951-2, during the same period repairs ranged from £547 to £1,126 per year. There were many other expenses including obtaining river licences, which were 10s for motorboats and 5s for rowing boats. Table 3.1 shows

Table 3.1: Costs, income, expenditure and number of passengers, 1947-1952

Year	1947/48	1948/49	1949/50	1950/51	1951/52
Total expenditure	3257.01.02	3025.06.02	3080.10.10	2879.11.03	4237.19.00
Income	4085.12.08	3691.15.00	3434.08.11	3177.04.09	4181.14.01
Passengers	—	495,464	411,715	379,9757	394,637
Profit	7352.13.10	6744.01.02	6514.19.09	6056.14.00	8419.13.01

Source: BRO, 40095/T/10.

Illustration 3.13: A typical pre-war scene as the ferry pushes off from Shirehampton in the 1930s (John Rich)

the operating costs but does not include the depreciation on the value of the vessel, which at some stage would have become unusable and sold off.[77]

Travel in the ferry was precarious at times, as it was not unknown for it to have been so full that the ferryman could not row it any distance. Just getting on to the boat was difficult enough, as negotiating the narrow plank of wood, which only in later years had a rail, proved precarious for some. That is if they managed to negotiate the slip, which had to be regularly washed down using a five-gallon drum of water, dragged from the Avon and its contents thrown over the slip, time and time again. It was not just Avonmouth that caused people to use the ferry, as the swimming pool and cinema at Shirehampton were a regular draw for those who relied on the ferry to cross over from Somerset in the days before the bridge. People also used it to travel from Pill to catch a train from Shirehampton to Bristol, relied upon the skill of the ferrymen to row against the tide before launching across the river, using the drift of the tide to land precisely on the right spot.[78]

Closure

Many men worked the ferry over the years since the first recorded man, Thomas Morgan, operated it in the early fifteenth century. In more recent times ferrymen included men such as Joseph Dickens in 1851, George Gilmore who lived at Under Banks and James Collins of Pump Square in the 1890s. William Russell of Marine Parade worked it in the 1900s,[79] John Henry Russell was the ferryman in 1911[80] and James Simmons of Under Banks just before World War One.[81] Just before the Second World War an ordinary row boat was known to have been constantly crossing, meaning a lot of hard manual work was involved. When the factories on the Gloucestershire side were finishing for the day, either steam or electric boats were brought into use to cater for the large numbers of passengers making their return journey.[82]

The nature of the work meant men did not serve for a great number of years, such as Amos Buck, ferryman in the 1930s and 1940s,[83] and Tom Paine who was ferryman in January 1958.[84] Some time afterwards Albert Sharp senior took over the business, which was taken over by Albert junior, or 'Uggy', in 1956 until the service folded.[85] The two Albert Sharps were affectionately known as Big Uggy and Little Uggy.

In the 1960s, although the number of users was in decline, access to the ferry slip, despite in previous centuries being part of lease from the lord of the manor, had to be formalised. On 24 January 1962 two justices of the peace, at a court of petty sessions held at Long Ashton, ordered the highway to be stopped up and reserved the right for a public footpath over the land. However, that decision was challenged in certain *ex parte* proceedings in the

Divisional Court of Justice when an order to quash the decision at Long Ashton was made. The Ferry Company claimed the ferry had been in operation since time immemorial across the River Avon between Pill and Shirehampton. It was also claimed, rightly so, how the hobblers and boatmen living at Pill had plied

> their trade in the River Avon . . . since time immemorial exercised customary rights (*inter alia*) for the haulage of boats and the passage of such hobblers and boatmen over and along the said landing slip . . . and hence to the roadway called Marine Parade.

A deed of covenant was subsequently drawn up on 14 April 1966 securing access to the slip.[87] Although access was assured and the County Council ended up with egg on its face, this was not the end of the story.

The construction of the Avonmouth Bridge was the final nail in the coffin for the ferry operators. Subsequently the Pill to Shirehampton ferry closed on 1 November 1974, with Mr Barry Chapman and

Illustration 3.14: The ferrymen seen here in the 1930s used a five-gallon drum to wash down the slip in an effort to keep it clean and safe for passengers. Lads were paid to keep the slip clear of mud.[86] (John Rich)

Illustration 3.15: The entrance to the slip at Pill showing the 'Pill Tidal Gates' with Lamplighters Hall in the background, 2009 (Adrian Webb)

Illustration 3.16: The Avonmouth Bridge, the final nail in the coffin for the ferry, viewed from the bank on the Pill side of the river, 2009 (Adrian Webb)

Mr Albert Sharp junior serving as the last ferrymen,[88] no longer needing the ferry pay box and store house, which became home to the Portishead Cruising Club.[89]

But all was not forgotten, as the experience of the ferry was recorded in 1993:

> climbing the plank, tottering down the steps to sit round the side of the boat, the dockers from Avonmouth, some with bicycles, standing in the centre, the scoop shovels with which the ferryman had to scoop water to scrub the mud off the slipway, the wait when the tide was so low that you see the river bed until the boat could refloat when the tide turned, the swell when Campbell's pleasure boats passed and even perhaps when she stopped to take on passengers from the ferry boat at Pill.[90]

Despite a great deal of local support, it was all too obvious that the ferry was no longer a viable proposition and after centuries of operating between Somerset and Gloucestershire, when millions of passengers crossed the Avon, it was no more. The ferry service was remembered on 30 August 2004 when the route was operated once again. As a fitting tribute, when the last ferryman died (in 2005) a short service was held on a floating pontoon near the site of the ferry, where wreaths were cast on the water and Albert Sharp's ashes consigned to the river by his daughter.[91]

THE ROWNHAM FERRY[92]

For many centuries a valuable link for travellers from Gloucestershire or Bristol going to north Somerset was provided by the Rownham ferry across the river Avon downstream from Bristol. The only alternative route involved crossing Bristol Bridge and proceeding through Bedminster, adding several miles to the journey. Apart from Bristol Bridge there were no bridges across the Avon between Keynsham and the Severn estuary. As a consequence, ferries were an essential feature of economic and social life, and continue to be important in Bristol. Crossing the Avon in a small boat could be hazardous because of the exceptional height of the tides and the fierce currents surging through the narrow channel of the Avon Gorge. The tide could rise by more than 40 feet, and there was a danger of being swept up towards Bristol by the incoming tide or propelled downstream by the retreating flood. Many ships ran aground in making the difficult journey through the winding Gorge, though there are few references to disasters occurring to the ferry.

Throughout the Middle Ages the Rownham ferry was a possession of the Augustinian abbey of Bristol which was founded by Robert Fitzharding in 1140. As well as endowing the abbey with extensive estates along the Severn and elsewhere, Fitzharding had included the grant of Abbots Leigh and the rectories of Portbury, Tickenham and Clevedon, all of which could easily be reached by using the ferry. Fitzharding's grant to the abbey of the rights to the ferry and the income from the tolls which could be raised from travellers, was supplemented by further gifts of land at Rownham to the Augustinian canons. For example, in *c.*1166 Elias of Clifton granted to the abbey a house and land on the Somerset bank of the Avon at Rownham, only reserving to himself and his family the right to cross by the ferry to reach another house which they owned there (*exceptis tamen passagio meo et proprie familie de domo meo apud Reueham*). Later, the name appears as 'Rowenham'. The abbey obtained a further gift of five acres of land at Rownham from Roger of Clifton in *c.*1205, and more land along the river was acquired during the following three centuries.[93] The manor house at Abbots Leigh was used by successive abbots as a country retreat, and many of them spent much time there, crossing from Bristol by the ferry.[94]

Few records of the abbey survive, but late-medieval account rolls show the income from the ferry. In 1491 the right to operate the ferry was let for an annual rent of 12s 0d; by 1511 this had increased to 20s 0d and the lease included 'free passage for the lord abbot and his canons and their servants'.[95] Another late-medieval reference to the ferry comes from the notes on Bristol made by William Worcestre in 1480. He obtained information about distances along the Avon from Bristol to the sea and along the Bristol Channel from 'a certain ferryman, a sailor in charge of the ferry (that is, for going to and fro in a small skiff) across the rivers Avon and Frome, coming from Bristol, at Rownham'. Probably at the same time he crossed the Avon to Long Ashton 'When the tide went out, that is at low-water, I was taken in a little boat along by Rownham village'. This must have involved clambering over the thick mud of the banks on a slippery jetty.[96] There are occasional references in Bristol records to a family known as 'le Passour' who could have derived their unusual name from operating the ferry. A list of those assessed for the tallage or taxation levied by Edward II in 1312 includes Robert le Passour and more significantly Richard le Passour who was assessed for 2s 8d in respect of property he held from the abbot of St

Augustine's abbey. The family continued to be mentioned as resident in Bristol during the later Middle Ages though without specific links to Rownham ferry.[97]

Evidence of the value which the abbey attached to the possession of the ferry is found in the vigorous and successful attack which Abbot William Burton (abbot 1525-1539) mounted against an interloper who attempted to establish a rival enterprise. The culprit was John Kekewich who was lord of the manor of Ashton Theynes on the Somerset bank of the river. Ashton Theynes had belonged to Sir John Inyn (d.1439) of Bishopsworth who was Recorder of Bristol and Chief Baron of the Exchequer. The manor eventually passed to his granddaughter, Alice, who married first Robert Bowring and secondly John Kekewich.[98] He set up a ferry operated by one of his tenants, Thomas Alye. The intrusion led to a protracted suit in the Court of Star Chamber in 1527-8, and the evidence given by more than 20 witnesses provides considerable detail about the ferry. We are not told the rates of the Abbot's ferryman, but Thomas Alye was no doubt

providing a cheaper service, and charged 'of every fote [foot] man a farthing, and for every man and a hors a half-penny for ther passage over the said water'. It is clear from later evidence that horses were regularly carried on the ferry, but the records remain silent on how the animals were persuaded to behave quietly on an open boat. Alye complained that the abbot's men had forcibly taken his boat and rowed it upstream to near the abbey precinct. During the seizure Alye received 'a blowe with a staff and a nother blowe with a fire scrape by reson whereof he was sore sevynyght after'. One witness stated that the ferry was operated by a little boy who on one occasion had asked for his help 'because the water was rough'. John Colman who was Master of St Mark's Hospital known as the Gaunts in Bristol stated that his father, George Colman, had 'occupied

---

Illustration 3.17: An extract from Benjamin Donn's map of the country 11 miles around Bristol, published in 1769. Note how Rownham ferry is marked but no ferry is shown at Pill (United Kingdom Hydrographic Office)

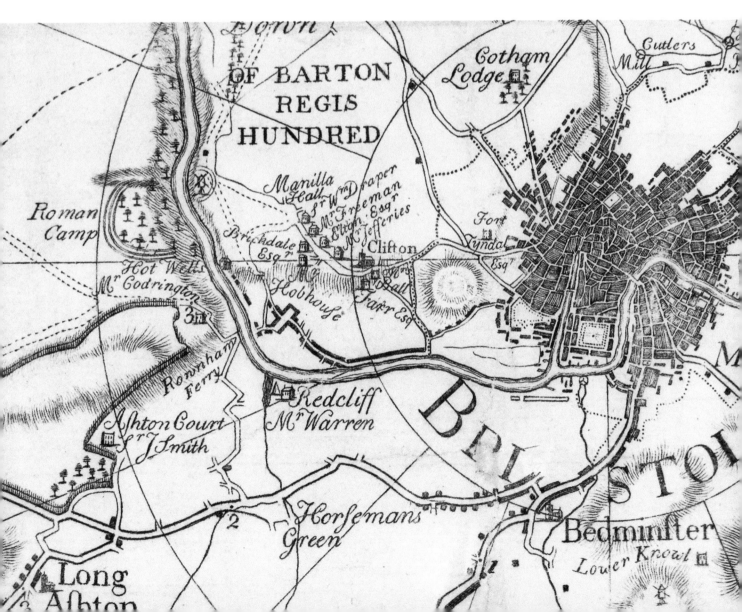

Illustration 3.18: King Edward the Fourth, who crossed the River Avon using the Rownham ferry in 1461 (Society of Antiquaries)

the hole passage with one ferry bote' on behalf of Abbot William Hunt (abbot 1473-1481) from 1475 until the time of Abbot John Newland (abbot 1481-1515) 'and that none other bote was occupied there bye all that time'. Another witness, Richard Bray, of St Stephen, Bristol, recalled that he had helped the ferryman when King Edward the Fourth crossed the Avon by the ferry during his visit to Bristol in 1461. John Squire the incumbent of Clapton-in-Gordano who was 72 years of age drew upon what he had been told 23 years previously by his father who was then aged 90, to state that 'the hole passage called Rownham ferry and five acres of land and all the landing place adjoining' were all part of the endowment of the Augustinian abbey of Bristol. Some witnesses supported John Kekewich, but most confirmed that the sole right to operate a ferry had belonged to the abbey from 'from time out of mind', and supported the abbey's claim. Finally, the abbot himself was able to establish the abbey's rights by producing numerous documents showing gifts to the abbey from its foundation. The earliest document produced by the abbot in support of his claim was the grant to the abbey by Elias of Clifton dated *c.*1166.[9]Following the suppression of the abbey in 1539, the Rownham ferry formed part of the endowment for the Dean and Chapter of Bristol

Cathedral which was established on the site of the abbey in 1542. The first bishop, Paul Bush, must have used the ferry frequently since he spent much time in his manor house of Abbots Leigh and many of his surviving letters are addressed from there. Even after the Cathedral was reluctantly forced by the Privy Council to surrender ownership of Abbots Leigh in favour of Sir George Norton, the Dean and Chapter retained their right to the Rownham ferry.[100] For accounting purposes the cathedral administrators regarded the ferry as an outlying part of their manor of Blackswarth or Blacksworth on the eastern side of Bristol, and it is seldom possible to distinguish the rent of the ferry from other payments received from the manor. A survey of Chapter estates by Dean Edward Chetwynd in 1619 shows that the ferry, together with a house and three acres of land, were let to Dame Jackson for 13s 4d per annum, and that she had sub-let it for 24s 0d.[101] She might have sub-

Illustration 3.19: A section of the fine map of Clifton made for the Society of Merchant Venturers by Jacob de Wilstar in 1746. The inn and other properties on the Clifton side of the river are listed in the accompanying schedule as belonging to the Dean & Chapter of Bristol Cathedral. (Copyright Merchant Venturers' Archive in the Bristol Record Office).

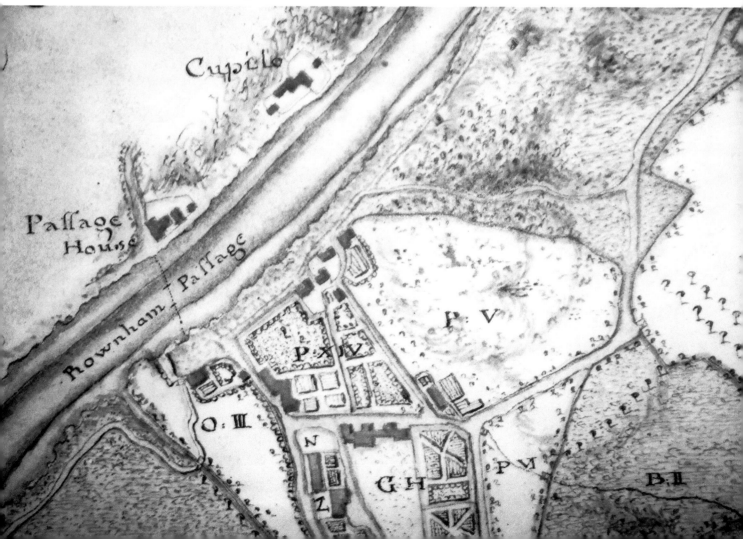

Illustration 3.20: Lithograph by T. Bedford *c*.1830 showing the Rownham ferry and the paddle steamer Beaufort. The paddle steamer may have been added for effect since there is no record of such a vessel at the time. (Copyright Bristol Museums, Galleries and Archives).

let the ferry to another party, or employed a ferryman, as in 1630 John Gaynard of Clifton was ferryman.[102]

For the convenience of passengers waiting for the ferry, inns were established on both sides of the river. The intrepid traveller on horseback, Celia Fiennes, visited Bristol in 1698. She was impressed by the numerous ferries across the Avon and wrote:

> They have little boates which are called Wherryes such as we use on the Thames, soe they use them here to convey persons from place to place.

After exploring the city she crossed by Rownham ferry to visit the Smyth family of Ashton Court.

> Here I ferry'd over the Avon that comes up to the town with a great tyde in two parts; about 6 mile off it joyns the Severn. . . . Then I went to Aston [*i.e.* Ashton Court] a mile from the water side thro' a fine park.[103]

The importance of the ferry is evident from the fact that both the crossing and the roads leading to it are clearly marked on early maps. They appear on Saxton's map of Gloucestershire of 1577, on Donn's map of 11 miles around Bristol of 1769 and on Isaac Taylor's large scale map of Gloucestershire published in 1777. The ferry features in a survey of the manor of Clifton of 1625 and is shown in Jacob de Wilstar's beautifully-drawn map of Clifton which was made for the Society of Merchant Venturers in 1746. Wilstar's map shows a Passage House on the Somerset side and Rownham Inn (later known as Rownham Tavern) with a garden and two acres of pasture on the Bristol side.[104]

Surviving eighteenth and nineteenth century leases granted by the Dean and Chapter of Bristol of their manor of Blacksworth and of the right to operate the ferry show its profitability. Several of the leases for three lives were granted to successive members of the Elton family, and later to Eltons and Tyndalls. The annual rent for the whole manor remained fixed at the modest sum of £6 15s 0d, but the ferry was sub-let for much larger sums. In 1716 it was sub-let to Thomas Day, a butcher from Clifton, and in 1733 sub-let to his widow, Joan Day. In 1748 she sub-let it to William Bucher or Busher of Clifton for £100 per annum. The lease included Rownham Inn and also

All the benefit, profit and advantage of the Passage over the River Avon there called Rownham Passage with free liberty of keeping boats for passing and repassing the said river on both sides thereof for the carrying over and landing of Passengers, Horses and Cattle at the Slips there with free use of the said Slips and premises aforesaid. And also to prevent and hinder all persons whatsoever from keeping of any Boat or Boats for passing and repassing Passengers, Horses and Cattle over the said river . . . and any part of the river thereabouts between the said City of Bristol and the Hotwell House.[105]

Some of these leases survive in the extensive collection of legal documents and estate records of Robert Codrington, an attorney who lived at Rownham in the parish of Long Ashton. When he died in 1764 his records passed to his brother-in-law, Oliver Calley of Wroughton, Wiltshire, and are now part of the Calley family archive in the Wiltshire Record Office.[106] Codrington's papers include an inventory of Passage House Inn dated 1745. This lists a parlour, fore-room, middle-room, back-room, kitchen, pantry, five chambers, a brewhouse and a cellar. There were several beds, cooking and brewing equipment, plates, cutlery, malt, hops, hogsheads of beer, bottles of wine and rum. Evidently the house provided ample facilities for the entertainment of passengers waiting for a suitable state of the tide for the operation of the ferry.[107] The final surviving lease of Blacksworth manor and the ferry was granted by the Dean and Chapter to Arthur John Knapp and Joseph Bissell in 1856. It was still for three lives at the same annual rental of £6 15s 0d. This lease is particularly interesting since instead of naming the three lives as the holders of the lease or members of their family as was generally done, the lives named were of young members of the Royal Family, the Prince of Wales aged 16, Prince Alfred aged 12 and Prince Arthur aged 6. No doubt because of their superior lifestyle they were expected to live longer.[108] In fact, the lease only lasted ten years since, as will be shown later, the building of the Suspension Bridge altered the whole running of the ferry.

The rapid growth in popularity of the Hotwell Spa during the eighteenth century attracted crowds of people from all over the country and from the West Indies, as is witnessed by the numerous monuments in Bristol churches to the memory of those who failed to benefit from the therapeutic water and are buried there. The heights of Clifton and the scenery of the Avon Gorge likewise attracted an increasing number of tourists, especially during the summer months, and many of these visitors crossed the Avon by the Rownham ferry. A Bristol guidebook of 1793 noted that 'Many ladies and gentlemen cross the river at Rownham Ferry and walk to the sweet and wholesome village of Ashton to eat strawberries and raspberries with cream'. The fare for foot passengers was one half penny.[109] Others crossed to admire the grandeur of the Avon Gorge and the beauty of Leigh Woods. The Avon Gorge was famous for the splendour of its scenery, the excellence of the riding to be enjoyed on Clifton Downs and for the woodland walks. Visitors were drawn by the awe-inspiring rocks, the ever-changing river, the remarkable geology and the range of botanical specimens to be found. Many contemporary writers enthused about the dramatic scenery and spectacular views, including the novelists Tobias Smollett, Maria Edgeworth and Fanny Burney and the poets Alexander Pope, Robert Southey and George Crabbe, although the Cornishman, Humphry Davy, was surely exaggerating when he wrote 'it almost rivals Penzance and the beauties of Mount's Bay'.[110]

As the visitors to the Hotwell Spa brought increased business to the ferry, so the development of industries on the Somerset side of the river led to more passengers using the crossing. During the late seventeenth century there are references to stone quarries and to a lime kiln being established at Rownham by Sir Hugh Smyth. The stone was pennant sandstone which could be split into slabs and large quantities were sent to Bristol from a wharf by the ferry landing stage. It was used for paving, flagstones and as roofing tiles. In 1684 a reverbatory lead-smelting furnace was built downstream from the ferry. It was known as a Cupola since this was the name commonly given to such furnaces in Bristol. During the eighteenth century large-scale clay extraction and brick-making was undertaken upstream from the ferry. The bricks were used to build the large cones used by the Bristol glass industry which became such a distinctive feature of the city. Potters used the clay to make the large pots in which the molten glass was collected.[111]

An unusual event in 1857 brought an unexpected rush of passengers for the ferry. A murder had been committed in Leigh Woods and the horrific details of the case roused great interest in Bristol. On the Sunday following the discovery of the body more than 14,000 crossed the river to view the site where the corpse was found, and later returned to Bristol. With a fare of ½d for each crossing this could have brought the ferryman an unexpected return of nearly

£60 for the day.[112] A consequence of the influx of wealthy visitors to the Spa and to Clifton was to provide another source of information concerning the Rownham ferry. Many artists came to produce views of the dramatic landscape which they could sell to tourists, and their work frequently shows the ferry. Well-known artists who depicted the ferry in their paintings of the Avon Gorge included Francis Danby, Samuel Jackson and Rolinda Sharples. One of Danby's paintings shows a coach and horses being conveyed, and Rolinda Sharples includes the over-crowded ferry with a horse among the passengers. Likewise, a watercolour of *c.*1836 by Samuel Jackson shows the ferry about to leave from near the Hotwells with several people and a horse crowded into the small open boat. The tide was not full, and passengers had evidently had to cross an expanse of mud to reach the ferry. In the river a steam tug is shown towing a sailing vessel upstream to the port of Bristol. The two towers or abutments which were to support the Clifton Suspension Bridge are shown already in position, although the Bridge was not to be completed for another 18 years.[113] Many other views of the Rownham ferry in operation can be found in the numerous early photographs of the Bristol docks, the Avon Gorge, Hotwells House and the Rownham Tea Gardens. For example, a photograph of 1867 taken from the Somerset side of the river shows the small, open rowing-boat which still operated as the ferry with the clearly marked Rownham Tavern on the Bristol side. Although planks are laid across the thick mud of the banks, access to the ferry must have been difficult for passengers, except at high tide. A photograph of *c.*1870 taken at low water shows Brunel's Entrance Lock to the Floating Harbour and the ferry which at low tide consisted merely of a bridge of planks laid across three boats.[114]

In view of the exceptional tides and current of the Avon, it is remarkable that so few references to

Illustration 3.21: Hotwells and Rownham ferry by William Williams, 1784 just a few years after a servant was drowned whilst using the ferry (copyright Bristol Museums, Galleries & Archives, reference BMG J26)

Illustration 3.22: Rownham ferry by John Field *c.*1800-1820 (copyright Bristol Museums, Galleries & Archives, reference BMG K6260)

disasters have been found. A solitary example from the early seventeenth century shows the danger which could be encountered even at low tide. John Snygge, eldest son of the prominent Bristol lawyer, George Snygge, had dined with Sir Hugh Smyth at Ashton Court at Christmas 1610, and returning to Bristol on horseback decided to avoid the ferry and ride across the shallow river at low tide. This was not a wise plan since the horse was unable to cope with the muddy bottom of the river. The rider was thrown off and subsequently drowned.[115] It could be that less eminent victims of the vagaries of the river are concealed within the coroners' records. An eighteenth century disaster is recorded in a London newspaper of 1780:

> a gentleman's servant was crossing by the ferry at Rownham on horseback, his horse took fright and leaped overboard, and notwithstanding all the assistance given, he was drowned; the horse swam to shore.[116]

The likelihood that other tragedies were not uncommon is evident from the fact that it was recorded as creditable that during the period 1867 to 1926, when the ferry crossing had been moved upstream following the completion of the Suspension Bridge, and when the number of passengers was much reduced, only two fatalities were recorded.

Local sources reveal numerous complaints during the nineteenth century concerning the conduct of the ferrymen, extortionate charges and the dangers involved in making the crossing. In 1799 the Merchant Venturers complained about the charges levied by the ferryman and ordered their clerk to make the crossing and report on the prices. No action seems to have resulted from this.[117] Further complaints about charges on the ferry were made by the Merchant Venturers in 1836. On this occasion they addressed their concerns to Bristol Corporation

ROWNHAM - FERRY TO BE LET.

To be LET by TENDER, for a Term of Seven Years, from the 25th March, 1847, ROWNHAM-FERRY, with the Ferry-boats and Tackle belonging thereto; and the well-accustomed INN or TAVERN, called *Rownham Tavern*, for many years past in the occupation of the late Mr. David Llewellin.

The Lessors do not bind themselves to accept the highest tender, and no tender will be received after the 11th of February next.

For the Conditions of the Lease, &c., apply, post-paid, to Messrs. CROSSMAN & LLOYD, Solicitors, Thornbury.

Illustration 3.23 An advertisement from *The Bristol Mercury* of 23 January 1847 offering a seven-year lease of the ferry.

who in turn wrote to George Rogers the long-serving clerk to the Dean and Chapter of Bristol cathedral. After some months delay the Chapter Clerk replied setting out the times of operation and the charges authorized for the ferry. The regular hours of crossing were:

25 March to 29 September	6.00am – 9.00pm
29 September to 25 March	7.00am – 8.00pm

The charges were:

For 1 person ½d
For a horse 1d

The complaints arose because outside the established hours of operation the charge was left to the discretion of the ferryman.[118]

Further complaints continued to appear in the local press, largely from people who felt that they had been overcharged for being taken across the river outside the regular times. Others complained about the state of the boat or the difficulty of negotiating the muddy slipways.[119] Bristol Corporation considered these and other complaints on several occasions, but felt unable to act as the ferry was the property of the Dean and Chapter. One councillor, Dr Thomas Green, was particularly concerned about the subject and frequently raised it in council. In 1847 he 'called the attention of the house to the mismanagement of the ferry at Rownham which possessed the unenviable reputation of being the most ill-conducted ferry in the kingdom'.[120]

The advent of steam power brought additional hazards for passengers on the ferry, since the increased speed of ships passing up and down the river meant that small boats could easily be swamped in their wake. An example was brought before the Bristol magistrates in 1860 by the Revd J. Birtill of Leominster who was on the ferry with his wife and five children, together with a dozen other passengers,

Illustration 3.24: Isambard Kingdom Brunel whose suspension bridge brought on the demise of the Rownham ferry (Ian Coleby Collection)

when the steamer *Ely* went down the river at great speed. The ferry was dashed about in all directions and he considered it a marvel that the passengers escaped with their lives. Apart from complaining to the owners, the Steam Navigation Company, the magistrates did not think they had any jurisdiction unless someone had been killed. The ferry operator did however offer to pay the legal expenses of a young woman whose clothes had been ruined by the spray from the dirty water of the river.[121]

The construction of the Suspension Bridge was eventually to bring an end to the long history of the Rownham ferry, but its demise was protracted. Work began on the Bridge in 1831, but shortage of funds, problems with the contractors and the difficulties of the undertaking meant that the Bridge was not opened until 1864. The building of the bridge was fiercely resisted by the Dean and Chapter and by the lease holder. This is evident from Brunel's concern in 1849 when he wrote to the Secretary of the Bridge Trustees expressing confidence that the construction could soon be completed, except for the problem of the rights to the ferry:

> what is to be done with the Ferry? If you can devise and procure relief from this I think I will manage the Bridge. What can be done – Is it hopeless?

Later in the year Brunel wrote again,

> I think I can manage all except the Ferry. If you will get that burden or bug-bear (for it is more

alarming than it ought to be) removed, I think I can see my way set to work . . . .[122]

Brunel's problem was eventually to be resolved by a handsome payment of compensation to the Dean and Chapter. In 1866 the rights to the ferry were sold to Bristol Corporation by the Ecclesiastical Commissioners on behalf of the Cathedral Chapter for £10,000.[123] Changes to the landing arrangements were made necessary by the construction of the Bristol and Portishead Railway along the Somerset side of the river. The Act of Parliament for the Railway received the Royal Assent in June 1863. The railway line resulted in the final demolition of the Cupola which had survived as a 'Chocolate House' providing a resort for visitors from the Hotwell Spa.

The ferry continued to operate having been moved a short distance upstream away from the Bridge. The slipway which led down to the ferry can still be seen at low water, just downstream from the lock by which ships entered the Cumberland Basin. During its final years the ferry was run by members of the Wort family. George Wort and his son, John Wort, were the ferrymen from 1867 until 1926, and a brother-in-law, W.C. Woodward, was in charge until the final closure in 1932. [124] The decline in passengers in the final years is evident from a letter addressed to the Corporation in 1866 by George Wort the ferryman and keeper of the inn which was now known as Rownham Tavern. He stated that during the previous six months 149,508 passengers had used the ferry, representing a considerable decline. This he attributed to the opening of the Bridge and the

Illustration 3.25: Photograph of the ferry, *c.*1860, before the position was moved to accommodate the new lock entrance (copyright Bristol Museums, Galleries & Archives, reference BMG J5124)

closure of the popular Tea Gardens on the Somerset side of the Avon. It is a remarkable tribute to the usefulness of the ferry and the link which it had provided to and from north Somerset, that even though the Hotwell Spa no longer attracted crowds of visitors and the Bridge had created an alternative route, almost 300,000 passengers a year were still being carried[125] Further problems were created for the Rownham ferry by the major alterations made to the river to provide easier access for ships coming up to Bristol. The re-alignment of Brunel's Entrance Lock to the Cumberland Basin in 1873 interfered with the Bristol departure point of the ferry and made it necessary to move the ferry crossing upstream some 200 yards.[126] It continued to carry passengers across the Avon for another 60 years, but finally ceased to operate on 31 December 1932, thus bringing to an end more than eight centuries of work in conveying travellers and tourists across the Avon.

Conclusion

It is highly likely that the from late medieval times the ferry needed to transport livestock and humans across the River Avon was a substantial vessel. This must have changed very little until the introduction of steam power in the 1820s. Evidence for this can be seen in the pictorial collections of the Bristol Museums, Galleries and Archive, such as the 1784 painting in illustration 3.21. How this size of vessel varied between Pill and Rownham is not known. However, travellers using the latter crossing point appear to have been more prolific, suggesting that a larger vessel may have been needed at Rownham to cope with demand. This theory has some credibility when illustration 3.11 is taken into consideration, which shows only smaller craft in operation at Pill in the first half of the nineteenth century.

Both ferries were most likely in existence before being first documented. Despite the Reformation Rownham remained in ecclesiastical ownership and both proved to be viable propositions. However, Rownham was much more lucrative than Pill, as can be seen through the terms of their leases, with Pill being offered, in 1783, on a 99 year lease; both were offered on a seven year lease during the nineteenth century. This state of affairs continued until the introduction of new technology. For Rownham its days were numbered thanks to Brunel's genius, but for Pill it was the motorcar and the Avonmouth Bridge that finally caused its demise. Their fate, like many small ferry services across the country, was sealed. Fortunately a few of the smaller services still survive to this day in the South West, in places like

Teignmouth, Devon, and the chain ferry across the River Tamar at Torpoint, and King Harry near Falmouth, but alas not in Somerset.

Acknowledgements

The authors gratefully acknowledge the assistance received from Dr Jenny Gaschke of Bristol Art Gallery and Andy King of Bristol Museum at M Shed in selecting illustrations, Francis Greenacre for information on the history of the Avon Gorge, and the staff of the Record Offices in Bristol, Taunton and Chippenham for their help with the archives.

Chapter Three

Notes

1   M. Langley and E. Small, *Estuary and river ferries of South West England* (1984), 36.

2   M.C. Siraut, 'Othery' in R.W. Dunning, *A history of the county of Somerset volume VIII The Poldens and the Levels* (2004), 136.

3   R.J.E. Bush, *Somerset stories* (1990), 16.

4   P. & A. Campbell Ltd, *The Bristol Channel district guide* (1921), 148

5   R.W. Dunning and M.C. Siraut, 'Cannington' in R.W. Dunning (ed.), *A history of the county of Somerset volume VI Andersfield, Cannington, and North Petherton hundreds (Bridgwater and neighbouring parishes)* (1992), 75.

6   C. Ross (ed.), *Cartulary of St Mark's Hospital, Bristol*, BRS vol. 21 (1959), 133. I am grateful to Philip Ashford for this and the following four references.

7   D. Livock (ed.), *City chamberlain's accounts in the sixteenth and seventeenth centuries*, BRS vol. 24 (1966), 69.

8   J. Bettey (ed.), *Calendar of the correspondence of the Smyth family of Ashton court 1548-1642*, BRS vol. 35 (1982), 131-2.

9   J. Savage, *History of the hundred of Carhampton* (1830), 381.

10 J. Billingsley, *General view of the agriculture in the county of Somerset* (1794), 103-4.

11 Dunning and Siraut, 'Cannington', 75.

12 R.W. Dunning and M.C. Siraut, 'Pawlett' in R.W. Dunning (ed.), *A history of the county of Somerset volume VI Andersfield, Cannington, and North Petherton hundreds (Bridgwater and neighbouring parishes)* (1992), 268.

13 Siraut, 'Othery', 136.

14 R.J.E. Bush, 'Aller' in R.W. Dunning (ed.), *A history of the county of Somerset volume III* (1974), 61.

15 BRO, F/Au/1/9.

16 *Somerset County Herald*, 19 March 1938.

17 The research for this section and the introduction was undertaken by Dr Adrian Webb.

18 Revd S. Seyer, *Memoirs historical and topographical of Bristol and its neighbourhood, from the earliest period down to the present time* vol. 1 (1821), 71.

19 E. Thomas, *Shirehampton* (1983), 78.

20 *The Bristol Mercury and Daily Post*, 1 October 1898.

21 W. Barrett, *The history and antiquities of the city of Bristol* (1789), 90.

22 E. Wigan, *A tale of Gordano* (1950), 54-5.
23 Sir J. Maclean, 'Notes on the Family of Yonge, or Young, of Bristol, and on the Red Lodge' in *Transactions of the Bristol and Gloucestershire Archaeological Society for 1890-91* (1891), 231-3, 242-5.
24 *Somerset & Dorset Notes & Queries* 20 CLXXV (December 1932), 265.
25 *Calendar of State Papers Foreign and Domestic, Henry VIII* 19:1, 507.
26 Revd J. Collinson, *History and antiquities of the county of Somerset* . . . III (1791), 149-50.
27 *Somerset & Dorset Notes & Queries* 20 CLXXV (December 1932), 265.
28 Collinson, *Somerset* . . . III, 149-50.
29 TNA, E 134/5Jas1/Mich2. White's information was corroborated by Richard Richardes, aged 80, of Weston in Gordano, mariner.
30 TNA, E 134/5CHAS1/MICH38. John Gethin who was killed on his boat in the King Road, in the Bristol Channel, during an affray with Bristol merchants in 1587. In 1608 13 sailors, five of them surnamed Gethin, were mustered from Hewelsfield parish (C.R.J. Currie, N.M. Herbert (Editors), A.P. Baggs, A.R.J. Jurica, 'Hewelsfield and Brockweir', *A History of the County of Gloucester: Volume 5: Bledisloe Hundred, St. Briavels Hundred, The Forest of Dean* (1996), 150-159).
31 J. Latimer, *Annals of Bristol in the seventeenth century* (1900), 111, 124, 141, 237.
32 SHC, DD/PN5.
33 TNA, MF 1/54.
34 A.J. Turner, 'Advancing navigation in eighteenth-century France: teaching and instrument-making in the port of Rochefort' in *The Mariner's Mirror* 91:4 (2005), 535.
35 TNA, MF 1/54.
36 *The Derby Mercury*, 2 April 1828.
37 *An Act for making a navigable canal from the River Avon, at or near Morgan's Pill, in the parish of Easton-in-Gordano, otherwise St George's, in the county of Somerset, to or near the River Tone, in the parish of St James in Taunton, in the said county, and a certain navigable cut therein described* (1811).
38 *The Bristol Mercury*, 31 October 1840.
39 *The Bristol Mercury*, 20 December 1851.
40 *The Bristol Mercury and Daily Post*, 12 June 1886.
41 SHC, DD/PN5.
42 Plan for dockising the Crockerne Pill in the county of Somerset - November 1840 schedule for the parish of St. George otherwise known as Easton in Gordano (http://www.origins.plus.com/pillnewdock.htm, accessed 15 April 2012; I am grateful to Phillip Ashford for this reference).
43 *The Bristol Mercury*, 7 July 1855; *The Law Times*, 21 July 1855, 192.
44 *Somersetshire. Particulars of the manors and estates, of the late James Adam Gordon, esq., deceased, intended to be sold by auction, by Messrs Fargus, at the White Lion Inn, Broad-street, Bristol, on Thursday, the 9th day of August, 1855, and on Thursday, the 16th day of August, 1855, at one o'clock in the afternoon* (1855), 35. I am grateful to Ann Nix for acquiring a copy of this catalogue for the library of the Somerset Archaeological and Natural History Society.
45 SHC, DD/PN5.
46 Easton-in-Gordano census for 1851 and 1861.
47 1799 Voluntary Contribution published electronically by the Bristol Historical Database Project (http://www.uwe.ac.uk/hlss/history/staff_pwardley_bhd p.shtml).
48 *The Bristol Mercury and Daily Post*, 7 June 1879.
49 *The Bristol Mercury*, 14 June 1851.
50 *The Bristol Mercury*, 25 October 1851.
51 Ex inf Mr Albert Sharp, Pill hobbler, related to M.R. Bunce in 1993 (typescript held at Pill Library).
52 E. Thomas, *Shirehampton* (1983), 78.
53 *The Bristol Mercury and Daily Post*, 27 July 1886
54 Thomas, *Shirehampton*, 78.
55 *The Bristol Mercury and Daily Post*, 20 June 1895.
56 *The Bristol Mercury and Daily Post*, 21 June 1895.
57 *The Bristol Mercury and Daily Post*, 1 October 1898.
58 *South Avon Mercury*, 1 November 1974.
59 Thomas, *Shirehampton*, 78.
60 Ex inf Mr Albert Sharp, Pill hobbler, related to M.R. Bunce in 1993 (typescript held at Pill Library).
61 Ibid.
62 Ibid.
63 BRO, 40095/ T/10.
64 Ex inf Mr Albert Sharp, Pill hobbler, related to M.R. Bunce in 1993 (typescript held at Pill Library).
65 P. Egan, *Walks through Bath, describing every thing worthy of interest connected with the public buildings, the rooms, crescents, theatre, concerts, baths, its literature, &c including Walcot and Widcombe, and the surrounding vicinity; with sketches of Prior-Park-House, the rocks of Wick, Corsham-House, and its fine collection of paintings: also an excursion to Clifton and Bristol Hot-wells, with a visit to Lord de Clifford's house, and some remarks upon its pictures: the whole forming a complete guide to the visitors of the above city* (1819), 253.
66 *The Bristol Mercury*, 28 February 1835.
67 F. Greenacre, *From Bristol to the sea. Artists, the Avon Gorge and Bristol Harbour* (2005), 117.
68 *The Bristol Mercury*, 11 October 1834.
69 *The Bristol Mercury*, 28 February 1835.
70 E. Thomas, *The continuing story of Shirehampton* (2002), 90-1. I am grateful to Dr Bettey for finding this reference.
71 J. Estagel, 'Sor Eustachio. A tale of three Christmases' in *Bentley's Miscellany* lxii (1867), 648.
72 *The Bristol Mercury and Daily Post*, 24 January 1890.
73 The horse boat was kept on the Shirehampton side, until 1954 when Mr Sharp 'burnt it down' (ex inf Mr Albert Sharp, Pill hobbler, related to M.R. Bunce in 1993 (typescript held at Pill Library)).
74 Ex inf Mr John Rich, Pill, 2009.
75 TNA, E 134/5Jas1/Mich2.
76 BRO, 40095/ T/10.
77 BRO, 40095/ T/10.
78 Ex inf Mr John Rich, Pill, 2009.
79 I am grateful to Mary Mason for supplying me with these references from the parish registers.
80 J. Jeremiah, *the Bristol Avon: a pictorial history* (2005).
81 I am grateful to Mary Mason for supplying me with these references from the parish registers.
82 *Somerset County Herald*, 19 March 1938

83   Ex inf Mr Albert Sharp, Pill hobbler, related to M.R. Bunce in 1993 (typescript held at Pill Library).

84   SHC, A/BEA 1/4.

85   *Bristol Evening Post*, 10 July 2002. Mr Sharp passed away in 2005 (*Mercury*, 10 November 2005).

86   Langley and Small, *Estuary and river ferries*, 20.

87   SHC, A/AJV1.

88   *South Avon Mercury*, 31 May 1974.

89   J. Rich, *Pill and district past and present* (1991), 21.

90   Ex inf Mr Albert Sharp, Pill hobbler, related to M.R. Bunce in 1993 (typescript held at Pill Library).

91   *The Bristol Mercury*, 10 November 2005.

92   The research for this section was undertaken by Dr Joseph Bettey.

93   D. Walker (ed.), *The cartulary of St Augustine's Abbey, Bristol,* Bristol & Gloucestershire Archaeological Society Record Series 10 (1998), 598, Add. Doc. 24.

94   J. Bettey, *St Augustine's Abbey, Bristol,* Bristol Historical Association (1996), 20.

95   A. Sabin (ed.), *Two compotus rolls of St Augustine's Abbey, Bristol,* Bristol Record Society (BRS) 9 (1938), 184, 262, 284-5.

96   F. Neale (ed.), *William Worcestre: the topography of Medieval Bristol,* BRS 51 (2000), 437.

97   E.A. Fuller, 'Tallage of 6 Edward II (1312) and the Bristol Rebellion', *Bristol and Gloucestershire Archaeological Society Transactions* 19 (1893-5), 232-7; Bristol Record Office (BRO), P/AS/D/CS N4; P/AS/D/CS B2. I am indebted to Dr Adrian Webb for these references.

98   Collinson, *Somerset . . .* II (1791), 288, 296.

99   Walker, *Cartulary,* 598; G. Bradford (ed.), *Star Chamber proceedings,* Somerset Record Society 27 (1911), 94-108.

100 Bettey (ed.), *Records of Bristol Cathedral,* BRS 59 (2007), 21-5.

101 A. Sabin (ed.), *Some manorial accounts of St Augustine's Abbey, Bristol,* BRS 22 (1960), 155-7, 159.

102 TNA, E 134/5ChasI/Mich38.

103 C. Morris (ed.), *The journeys of Celia Fiennes* (1947), 238-40.

104 BRO, SMV 6/5/4/3

105 Wiltshire Archive Service (WAS), 1178/611/3.

106 For fuller details of Robert Codrington's collection of documents *see* J. Bettey, 'Records of two 18th century attorneys in North Somerset' in *Somerset & Dorset Notes & Queries,* XXXV (September 2005), 452-6.

107 WAS, 1178/653, 654, 680.

108 BRO, DC/E/11/1 Leases of Blacksworth manor, 1856.

109 W. Matthews, *Guide to Bristol* (1793), 37.

110 J. Bettey, *Bristol observed* (1986), 82.

111 WAS, 1178/616, 651, 654, 678; L.J.U. Way, 'Leigh Woods' in *Bristol & Gloucestershire Archaeological Society Transactions,* 36 (1913), 71, 75-7, 97.

112 *John Bull & Britannia* 17 October 1857.

113 Further details including copies of the work of Samuel Jackson and numerous other artists who produced works on the Avon Gorge can be found in F. Greenacre and S. Stoddard, *The Bristol landscape* (1986); and in F. Greenacre, *From Bristol to the sea* (2005).

114 Many early photographs were published in a remarkable series of books by Reece Winstone. See for example R. Winstone, *Bristol's earliest photographs* (1970), *Bristol's suburbs long ago* (1985), *Bristol as it was 1874-1866* (1996).

115 H.E. Roslyn, *The history of the antient Society of St Stephen's ringers* (1928). I am grateful to Francis Greenacre for this reference.

116 *Gazetteer and New Daily Advertiser,* 22 July 1780.

117 BRO, SMV2/1/1/13 Merchant Venturers' Hall book f.104, 1 August 1799.

118 *The Bristol Mercury* 20 February 1836; 6 August 1836. George Rogers succeeded his father as Chapter Clerk in 1791. He retained the post until 1838.

119 *The Bristol Mercury* 6 February 1847; 23 July 1853; 6 August 1853; 5 August 1854.

120 BRO, M/BCC/CCP/1/6 Bristol Corporation Minutes 6 February 1847. Dr Thomas Green (1803-78) was a wealthy surgeon living in Queen's Square. He served as Councillor from 1842 to 1853 and was an Alderman 1853-77.

121 *The Bristol Mercury* 14 July 1860. I am grateful to Dr Adrian Webb for the references from the Bristol newspapers.

122 R.A. Buchanan, 'Brunel in Bristol' in P. McGrath and J. Cannon (eds), *Essays in Bristol and Gloucestershire History* (1976), 227-8.

123 John Latimer, *Annals of Bristol in the nineteenth century* (1897), 418.

124 Langley and Small, *Estuary and river ferries,* 22.

125 D. Large (ed.), *The port of Bristol 1848-84,* Bristol Record Society, 36 (1984), 70.

126 BRO, DC/E/40/68/4 Bristol Dock Improvements 1864-5. See also R.A. Buchanan & N. Cossons, *The Industrial Archaeology of the Bristol Region* (1969), 42-3, 236.

Chapter Four

Thomas Surbey's 1701 Survey of Minehead Harbour

Paul Hughes

Introduction

EXMOOR RUNS down to the sea on the Somerset coast at Minehead, where the high moor's rock outcrops into the turbulent waters of the Bristol Channel. That turbulence comes from the moon endowing those waters with severe tidal characteristics. Whether flooding east or ebbing west, all the tidal streams here run with great strength. During spring (or big) tides the elevation of the water surface has a substantial, vertical range of ten metres. The beach here lies rather level. Between extreme tidal elevations of high water and low water, the water's edge flexes across the beach some four hundred metres. Consequently, the harbour dries out to well beyond its perimeter, even at low neap (or small) tides. The harbour's firm, shingle and sand beach is ideal for well-found boats to sit out the period across low water. As the neap tidal range exceeds four metres, the natural beach in the Minehead vicinity only needed protection from large swells to provide a commodious harbour with a near enduring facility.

Port appearances vary from light open fabrications where waves pass freely through pilings, to heavy closed concretions that prevent waves passing through their solidity. Both port types (in itself a word going back to Old English) attracted several different Middle English words; wharf appeared by 1067, harbour by 1150, quay 1306, staith 1338, jetty 1412, pier 1453, mole 1545, and landing 1609. Various Minehead port facilities take up that profusion of different names. Early Minehead documents talk of a jetty, then later a quay. Thomas Surbey (1676-1703) refers to that construction and his own projection as a pier, but with the spelling peer. From 1901 to 1940 a pier did exist at Minehead, therefore illustration 4.1 sets out the actual positions of the first facility, the present quay and the demolished pier. To add to the complex lexicon, the current sailing directions describe the present solid construction as a breakwater.[1] As this breakwater runs out from Quay Street, for clarity, I favour calling that structure which forms the port facility a quay.

In 1701, Minehead's two MPs elicited expert opinion on the improvement of their local harbour. That opinion, expressed in a set of plans and associative commentary, has so far attracted little attention.[2] This article examines that document more thoroughly, placing it within a context of both the locality, contemporary art work, and other hydrographic cartography. Appendix 4.1 is a transcription of the manuscript.

Old harbour works

The early history of Minehead's port facilities is overshadowed by an early eighteenth-century document giving a one sided version of events.[3] A recent archaeological report provides some evidence for the chronology of events in the port's construction,[4] with other published interpretive histories offering only limited success in bringing a more fulsome account to light.[5] However, made up of ordinary domestic goods, the record of the port's extensive trade is not the direct concern of this article. What is, is the development of Minehead's harbour infrastructure and the inhibiting influences involved. The development had two parts. First the developers needed investment with which to build a harbour; they also continually needed to raise revenue to maintain the harbour against substantial wear and tear. Secondly, the developers' efforts interfered with nature and caused siltation inside the harbour, foreshortening the harbour's available depth and requiring further expense.

Illustration 4.1: A plan of Minehead port

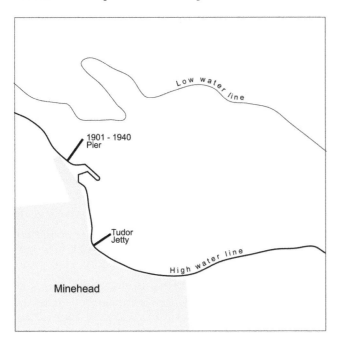

The area's initial port facility lay closer to Dunster than Minehead, but when the Luttrell family, of Dunster Castle, became lords of the manor, they began to make a record of port constructions in the bay sitting before Minehead. In the main, the Luttrells financed the port, to bring in coal for domestic fuel, and limestone with which to make both fertiliser for their estate and mortar for building works.[6] However, lying between high and low water, the facility was not private but a common quay. This meant that while all had a right to use it, its upkeep was to be borne by all. At times merchants and ship owners endowed the port.[7]

The townsfolk combined with Lady Margaret Luttrell (d.1438) in 1421 to construct a new wooden jetty.[8] As this ran to decay, between 1485 and 1509 Sir Hugh Luttrell (d.1521) erected another small jetty.[9] No remains of those structures now exist, though Surbey gives an indication of their positions. However, these were sufficient to buttress a port which provided revenue to the king and therefore needed customs regulation.[10] Together they allowed ships of between 60 and 100 tons to trade from the port as far as France and Ireland.[11] In the sixteenth century, the port possessed 12 ships, 20 barques, and 29 shipowners.[12]

With the Luttrells also exercising authority through their office of Vice-Admiral the public's interest in the town sought their own influence as port burgesses. Beyond the financial, the port needed physical control and with more trade came the need for greater maintenance. Together this resulted in a grant of Burgesses and the office of Harbour Master in 1558-9.[13] Twenty years later Thomas Luttrell considered the jetty useless and, rather than burden the townsfolk, he drew in considerable funding to keep it in repair.[14] Some other new quay may have been functional two years before the alleged tsunami of 1607.[15] Unfortunately, none of these structures was sufficiently durable 'against the violence of the sea and tempest whereunto it lay open'.[16] From 1609 onwards, with the burgesses in default of the conditions of their grant, George Luttrell (1560-1629) set himself to build a quay stretching out toward permanent water (that is, beyond the low water mark), investing more than £5,000.[17] However, he wanted to spend more than the allowed revenues would supply. The result of this was an application from the Luttrells for a new Act of Parliament in 1700.[18]

Although compared to Bristol, Minehead was always small, there were reasons why such a port should command parliamentary time. The Luttrells, the main local landowners, held powerful positions in London. With water by far the most efficient way to transport goods, the Minehead port facility was more important to West Somerset and North Devon than Bristol could be. The Bristol approaches are open to the full blast of the prevailing south-westerly onslaught, from which the bay at Minehead, or an improved harbour, was able to offer refuge. Often, pilots of ships in the Bristol trade would board and land through Minehead.[19] Therefore Minehead was useful to Bristol; but of equal importance was the government's rising need of new ports for defence against the ever encroaching French.

Thomas Surbey as civil engineer

Until the eighteenth century, the local port fabricators at Minehead never did succeed in building a harbour of sufficient robustness to ordinarily withstand the sea. The quay's seaward reinforcements had begun disintegrating in 1696, if not earlier. Nevertheless, at the start of the eighteenth century, the dawn of the canal age, Britain was in the throes of new architectural practices. Having gained legislation allowing proper financial support, in the summer of 1701 the Luttrells decided to resort to the coming new profession of civil engineer with which to advise them how to improve the port. Beyond the desired harbour extension, there were two things further to consider, how to strengthen the whole harbour so that it could withstand the sea's ravages, and how to curtail the siltation.

Although the heir, Tregonwell Luttrell, was by then aged eighteen, his stepfather, Sir Jacob Banks MP (1662-1724) in London, and his uncle, Colonel Alexander Luttrell (d. 1714) in Somerset, had long had the conduct of his business, and which they continued to do so in this harbour affair. Edmund Dummer MP (1651-1713), secretary of the navy, was also a renowned civil engineer and shared with Banks a mutual parliamentary and naval interest; they had at least two links in common. Therefore Dummer sent his capable friend, Thomas Surbey, to assess Minehead's needs.[20]

Very little is known of Surbey's background. He appears to have been the son of William, a nailer, and Mary, of Nether Gornal, Staffordshire who took him to All Saints, Sedgley, for christening on St. George's day 1676.[21] He is next recorded on 1 May 1699, taking a stagecoach from London to fulfil an engagement with York Corporation.[22] Journeying through Huntingdon and Stamford, he made sketches of locks on the Great Ouse and River Welland. His main achievement was a survey of the estuary from York to Hull. After also undertaking a minor survey of the Studley Royal estate at Ripon for John Aislablie MP (1670-1742), he eventually returned to London by horseback during the latter part of May and early June. From Nottingham he detoured to Derby then on to Warwick; then in Coventry and then Oxford he made further architectural sketches. In addition to remarks on dredging the Thames, his journal includes plans of locks on the River Wey leading up toward Guildford. The recording of his demise bears more certainty than that of his genesis. In Oxford, he met friends from Plymouth, and that was home to the half-brother who outlived him.[23] His account of travel from London to York, what he did while in Yorkshire, and then back to London extends to thirty-three folios and a large folded chart.[24] Surbey's notes and meandering through England in 1699, also show him sighting Sir Christopher Wren's provincial architectural interests of Newby Hall, the Sheldonian Theatre, Queens College Library, Tom Tower of Christ Church, modifications at Salisbury cathedral, St. Mary's Church at Warwick, Nottingham Castle, and the Royal Exchange.

The Yorkshire and Somerset documents are the only two presently known that exhibit Surbey's work. The document at the Somerset Heritage Centre holds the separate productions of two people in one binding.[25] Surbey's pair of plans now form the front and end pieces to Dummer's eight folios of writing that sit in between. Dummer added to the complexity, for his text contains two of his own letters to Banks, within one of which he inserted the text of Surbey's letter to Dummer. The folios conclude with Surbey's estimates, compiled after his return to London. In the interim years, the document resided in Dunster Castle until passing to the Somerset County Record Office in 1958. Prebendary Hancock made a black and white reproduction of Surbey's general quay plan, representing it as a map of the town of Minehead, but did not comment on the folios of text.[26] Binding and Stevens with their own reproduction of Surbey's general plan considered his manuscript work as 'rather crude'.[27] In my opinion, for accuracy and clarity, Surbey's work is of cutting edge quality for its time. For completeness, illustration 4.14 reproduces that same general plan of the quay in colour. For the first time the full text of the written part of the document is transcribed in appendix 4.1 and Surbey's particular

quay plan is reproduced in illustration 4.15.

In addition to the document now in Somerset, Dummer kept a copy himself.[28] I have located neither that copy nor any personal archive of Dummer manuscripts. However, the National Archives and the British Library do hold collections of his Admiralty and private business correspondence, journals, drawings and cartography. That pair of draughts, or plans, by Surbey of Minehead is the singular survival of several that Dummer eventually forwarded to Sir Jacob Banks.

The Minehead survey

In the early summer of 1701 Banks asked Dummer to provide technical advice about Minehead harbour. On 7 July, Dummer gave Surbey twelve written questions that he should find answers to while in Minehead. Surbey wasted little time, for taking only one day to prepare for his journey, he set out from London on 9 July. He waited upon Colonel Luttrell at Ven (near Taunton) on the 12th, and arrived in Minehead later that day. Travelling by horseback, he was able to take the direct route of some one hundred and sixty seven miles. Although he omits mention of what he did on the Sabbath, for the accounts he regarded it as a working day. Then on Monday, with his usual energy, Surbey viewed both the quay and Greenaleigh Point, from which the quay's constructors quarried its building stone, thereby providing his fifth answer. That quarry sits 'within two mile' north-west along the coast from the harbour, where Exmoor itself tumbles into the sea. There the beach builds up a loose mass of the Hangman Sandstone Formation, of purple, grey and green sandstone and reddish-brown mudstone.

Surbey immediately sought the advice of those with relevant knowledge and experience, particularly the ship masters who used the harbour, and the harbour's 'gentlemen trustees', successors to the former burgesses. The advice of the shore officials and of those who navigated the harbour stood in conflict, and so he asked Luttrell to come and meet with them. By then Luttrell had fallen ill and could not come, explicitly leaving the final say to Surbey. Surbey twice lamented upon Luttrell not coming to meet and discuss the issues with the involved parties within the port. Not to be put off, during his seven and a half days in Minehead, Surbey took sufficient measurements to prepare one draught of the quay's general disposition, and another draught to show particulars of both the pier as it then existed and his design for its extension. With the moon full on

Thursday night, his week's stay enabled him to witness both spring and neap tides.[29] Taking measures at the end of the quay, he found springs rose twenty-eight feet (8.53 metres), and neaps twenty-two feet (7.50 metres) at the most, but the harbour dried out on every tide, fulfilling his first answer. He proposed additional seaward strengthening and extending the quay south-eastwards. To alleviate the wind causing a potential whirlpool, he proposed inserting timber stops both within and to the south-east of the harbour.

Surbey left Minehead half way through Sunday the 20th. Taking half a day more on the return journey; perhaps he met adverse weather or had become more prudent, having lamed a horse two summers before. Back in London he discussed the survey over two and a half days with Dummer. In the interim Surbey increased the number of his draughts to six, finalising fair copies of them for Dummer on Monday 28 July. Dummer had directed Surbey to hand his findings personally to Batson, the proprietor of the coffee house near the Royal Exchange.[30] The medical profession dominated this meeting place, but Dummer and others in the maritime trade also used it.[31]

Surbey then went on to other things. Unfortunately so did Dummer, for he forgot about the Minehead survey, not even beginning to compile his report to Banks until 9 August. Banks seems to have found out something was remiss; he either learned of Dummer's preoccupations, or of Surbey's engagement elsewhere, or even that Surbey's deliberations were laying ready in-wait at Batson's coffee house. Whatever, not hearing from Dummer or Surbey, Banks wrote to Dummer on the 12th wanting to know the result of Surbey's survey. Dummer's statement that Surbey returned on the 29th stands at odds with Surbey's accounting. It took Dummer a further six days before he could muster an apology and give Banks the drawings, estimates and Surbey's considerations. Dummer went to the extent of transcribing Surbey's words, yet it is clear that the draughts are from Surbey's hand. Dummer offered to provide further harbour consultancy but he expected Banks to contract his own builders.

Surbey's plans

Surbey does not say what instruments he used for his survey, or whether he used any existing maps or plans. Dummer's 'delineator' of a contemporary survey drew decorative cartouche supporters girding themselves with a surveying chain.[32] With a length of

twenty-two yards, chains need two people to operate them, therefore long measures in the written estimates suggest that Surbey did indeed have someone helping him. He used dividers, and for a surveyor, a compass and a spirit level were ordinary items. As for earlier maps, Minehead was a place of sufficient note in 1575 for Saxton to insert it on his map of England. Each of the county maps of Somerset by Speed (1611) and Blaeu (1648) then rise in decorative quality, showing ships in the channel and a title cartouche with supporters. While this decorative tradition flourished, those atlases' purpose was to map the land, and their scale gave little opportunity for local detail beyond stylised town representations, or insets of cities.

Yet the coast in Minehead's environs does enjoy an early map of a somewhat larger scale than those of the county. Although entitled *The Somersett coast upon Severn* this view, of about 1544, is of military defences rather than an hydrographic map or civil engineering plan. However, this is more of a view as seen from seaward, which means it is oriented with south at the top of the paper. Like the county maps, it includes several ships along the main channel, and three ships anchored in Minehead's offing. Although it includes four groynes west of Minehead, the map's main purpose is to show features such as gun emplacements. It interestingly exhibits a perspective view, with ships reduced in size as they recede in their distance from the observer.[33]

The portrayal of Minehead quay on the Bristol Channel chart, which Captain Greenvile Collins (*c*.1644-1694) published in 1693, is probably the earliest depiction of it to have survived. Admittedly small scale, Surbey also had this as an indicator. Collins even lamented on the chart's quality, blaming the engraver who had lost the original Severn draught and forcing substitution of another.[34] That chart, particularly in the Minehead area, gives a poor rendition of the foreshore.

Surbey's large-scale 'general' plan sets a north point over the sea, giving an approximately north-west-by-north up orientation in a landscape layout; see illustration 4.14.[35] This orientation comes from that found in the larger scale 'particular' plan (see illustration 4.15). Measuring 20.8 inches wide by 15.8 inches high (0.528m x 0.401m), the scale is approximately 4.6 inches to half a mile. Without a graticule, this is a simple plan of the area. His one mile distance between church and quay, contrasting with the actuality of three-quarters of a mile, may well reflect the large difference in elevation between

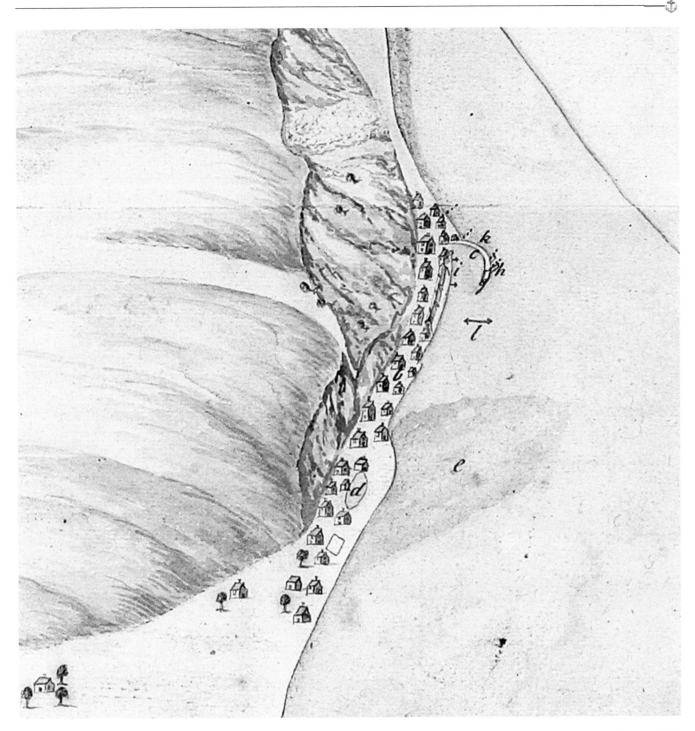

the quay down on the beach and the church up on the hill.

Given in illustration 4.14, the plan locates the quay's general surroundings: low-water mark, high-water mark, Bratton stream, twenty-nine houses in High Town, thirty houses in Quay Town, four isolated houses in between, North Hill, and Warren Point. High Town's widely spread houses surrounded with trees contrasts sharply with the closely spaced twin row of houses in Quay Town (detailed in illustration 4.2). Illustration 4.3 shows his portrayal of St Michael's church with a double roof, in contrast to its present-day triple roof. As they were not

Illustration 4.2: The houses of Quay Town, 1701 (SHC, DD/L/1/58/15)

important to his objective, he omitted roads, paths, gardens and fields, and showed North Hill as bare as it was in the nineteenth century.

Both plans give the appearance of once-rich illumination, for traces of colour are visible, but the colours are now very faded indeed. On the general plan and perhaps the brightest, he sets the north point in yellow, blue and red. He marks the uplands with a grey wash and brown accents, the foreshore with a brown/yellow or pale pink wash, and tree-tops

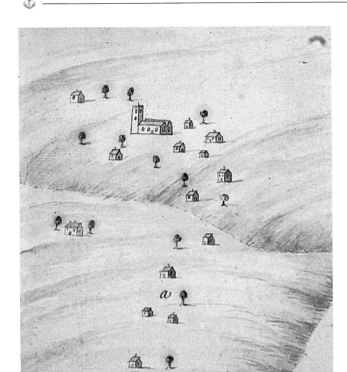

Illustration 4.3: Twin roofed St. Michael's church, 1701 (SHC, DD/L/1/58/15)

the page, corresponds directly to the elevation view across the top of the page. Uppermost of all are three cross-sectional views of the quay. Measuring 21 inches by 15.6 inches (0.533m x 0.396m), this plan at a scale of about 4.4 inches to 200 feet needs no graticule for such a small area.

On the particular plan of the quay, in illustration 4.15, he drew a long lane, describing it as the town's only street. On the lane's seaward side, in way of the harbour, he shows a sea wall, explicitly stating it is to protect the houses against the sea; see illustration 4.4. He indicated the passage to the Customs House, and immediately north-west of the harbour inserted a shipwright's yard. In the elevation, he sketched a double-storey house either side of Quay Street, and further low buildings which were standing in the way of the present The Old Ship Aground pub and St Peter's church; see illustrations 4.5 and 4.6. The plan and cross sections show the vertical batter on either side of the quay, a stepped parapet consisting of a six feet high embrasured outer wall and a step taking up half the width of the working apron; see illustration 4.7. The inner quay wall contains four stair flights connecting the apron and strand; see illustration 4.8. He showed the then existing backwork of stone projecting seaward from the quay's outer wall, as seen in illustration 4.9; Surbey designed this in order to catch the long shore drift, which he described throughout his report as sullage, being the subject of Dummer's seventh question.

He drew four posts used for mooring ships at the bottom of the page, inexplicably separated from the quay. By drawing the long shore drift that had recently accreted under the mole-end he lost a little clarity; this is because he put his design for the quay extension on top of the drift sketch. With one exception, he drew his intended remedies to the harbour's problems in red following Dummer's style. As the harbour was exposed, in windy conditions when a swell got up and the tide was in, ships in the harbour would plunge about badly and occasionally sink one another. Surbey proposed solving this in two ways: first by providing more protection with a 100 feet quay extension, and secondly by erecting two short timber stops from the seawall out into the harbour to inhibit whirlpool development. To prevent or reduce sullage under prevailing conditions, he proposed inserting four timber groynes into the existing long-shore drift, and adding one new backwork. To inhibit problems from a south-east wind, to which the harbour would remain exposed, he proposed a timber and stone stop combination, colouring the stone part of this yellow on his plan.

green. He left the east side of buildings uncoloured, darkened the north side, and indicated blue slate roofs. He highlighted and underscored with red. While he effected land elevation by intensity of colour and a broken surface, the degree of fading undergone since 1701 rather affects his representation.

The general plan answers the second question, showing where the harbour lies in respect to the lee offered by the land, the depth of shelter to be had within Minehead bay, and the proximity of the quay to the low-water mark or permanent water. With the same north-west-by-west up orientation but in a portrait layout, the quay's even larger scale particular plan puts Quay Street along the length of the page, with the quay's bulk jutting out from the street essentially at a right angle. This plan, in the centre of

Illustration 4.4: The modern sea wall – protecting property, 2011 (Author)

Illustration 4.5: The modern quay elevation, 2011 (Author)

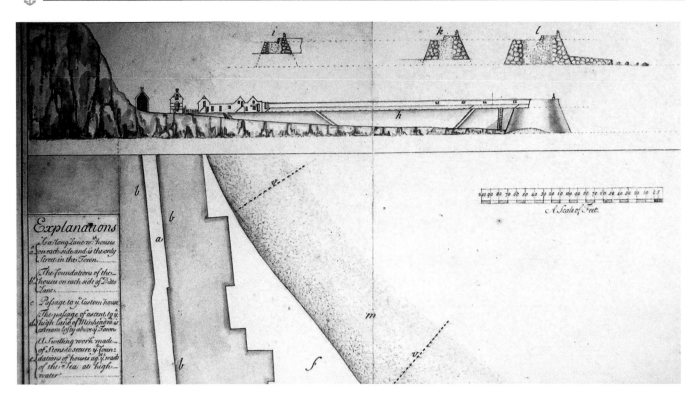

Illustration 4.6: Surbey's quay elevation, 1701 (SHC, DD/L/1/58/15)

These answered Dummer's third and fourth questions.

The plan, elevation and cross-sections answer the sixth question. Surbey specifically asked the client to refer to the draughts for further queries. The remaining questions concerned the adequate foundations, and freedom from the need to neither pile nor erect cofferdams. Despite Surbey charging Banks for six pairs of draughts, with Dummer retaining one for himself, Banks can only have received five pairs. Presumably Surbey kept his originals. In the main, the survey provided two results. One was the estimations of labour and material costs for Banks and Luttrell to consider, in extension of his eleventh answer; including silt removal, he estimated the total cost at less than £4,000. Figures of material scantlings, or dimensions, backed up the conclusive twelfth. The other result was the several working copies of the particular plan, elevations and cross-sections containing Surbey's new design for the use of the final undertakers.[36]

The harbour after Surbey

Surbey gave detailed building figures for Minehead in the same way as he had done in Yorkshire, two years previously. At about 18d per day, masons got the same in Minehead as carpenters got in Derby. In contrast, his own consultancy fee of £1 a day was one and a half times that which Collins charged the king for similar work.[37] The £2 he paid as coach fare to York compares neatly with these approximate eight days horse hire of 27d per day. These transport costs and expert fee compare similarly to modern prices, that is, if one considers rail fares but not car hire plus fuel. Omitted, but possibly hidden within Surbey's claim, is Dummer's take or cut for his own efforts and advice. However, the £1 Surbey charged for each pair of draughts was low compared to that of about 13s 4d which Collins invoiced for his works.

With plans to hand, construction work did not begin immediately. It took until 1704 for the Luttrells to contract Daniel Dennell, as their otherwise unknown construction engineer who closely followed his advice. However, within seven years the construction timber had perished, forcing the Luttrells to once again combine with the townsfolk to secure further parliamentary backing to raise tolls for more construction. This time, beginning in 1712, they encased the quay with stone, using lime mortar. With occasional set backs from the ever-destructive weather, construction persisted into 1716, when they finally succeeded with a much more durable edifice than anything that had existed before.

Through Parliamentary publicity the quay grew to a large size in the public's imagination, leading the astronomer, Edmund Halley (1656-1742), to portray it as monstrously large in 1702; in fact, several miles long and a mile wide (see illustration 4.9).[38] After the harbour works inspired by Surbey's designs were finally complete, and while passing through

Illustration 4.7: The stepped apron, 2011 (Author)

Illustration 4.8: Quay and batter and steps, 2011 (Author)

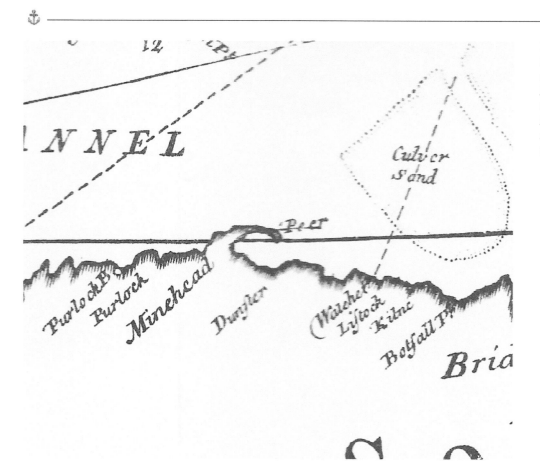

Illustration 4.9: Edmund Halley, *A new and correct large draught of the Channell between England and France with the coast of Ireland St. Georges & Bristoll Channell and several of the most noteable harbours at large* (London, 1710)

Minehead some time before 1724, Daniel Defoe (1660-1731) wrote:

> Minehead, the best port, and safest harbour, in all these counties, at least, on this side: No ship is so big, but it may come in, and no weather so bad, but the ships are safe when they are in; and they told me, that in the great storm anno 1703, when in all the harbours and rivers in the county, the ships were blown on shore, wreck'd, and lost, they suffered little or no damage in this harbour.[39]

A minor artist, George Wood, painted *The prospect of Dunster Castle* in the early eighteenth century. In 1735 he painted another local prospect, as in illustration 4.10; this is of Minehead town, its harbour and the estuary. A number of aspects combine to allow our designation of Wood's talent as naive. He exaggerated the vertical components of the church tower, North Hill, distant Welsh hills, and the quay's skirt wall. His bird's-eye view, achieved by a mid-canvas horizon, should have diminished that component. Nevertheless the view exposes the harbour well, but gives it a large footprint compared to that of the town. He caught a reflection of the

leaden, overcast brown skyscape in the river's smooth water surface; and surrounded that reflection with a milky calmness. In contrast, a westerly wind which filled the sails and stretched out the flags borne by half a dozen ships in the estuarial offing, these should have disturbed that calm surface. However, that wind gave the ships steerage way; but it was the dominant power of the flood-tide which drove them eastward, upriver. In this painting, Wood captured a view shortly after the Minehead interests had completed the work under Surbey's design; it was at a moment in the tidal cycle with the water risen enough to partly fill the harbour. He portrayed over thirty people on the foreshore, all standing and apparently gazing out into the estuary – probably at the nearer of the ships under sail, towing its boat, wearing a large red ensign and a long pennant at the topmast. Dark brown dots along the quay's apron could represent other, more distant people, or, more likely, cargo goods. Moored inside the harbour sit another half dozen ships, but of a smaller size. Altogether, Wood demonstrates the maritime prosperity of Minehead's harbour rather well, and clearly shows the long-shore drift, or sullage, problem accumulating outside the quay wall.

Storms continued to do damage, but the construction after Surbey had a more durable nature

The prospect of Minehead-Key, from Conagree, near Dunster, exactly Delineated by Geo: Wood 1735.

1 Conygar   3 part of Middle Town   5 The Key   8 The Beech   10 to Porroc-Point
2 The Church   4 The Lower Town   6 Blenheme   9 The Marshes   11 Wales

Illustration 4.10: George Wood's painting of The prospect of Minehead-Key, 1735 (National Trust)

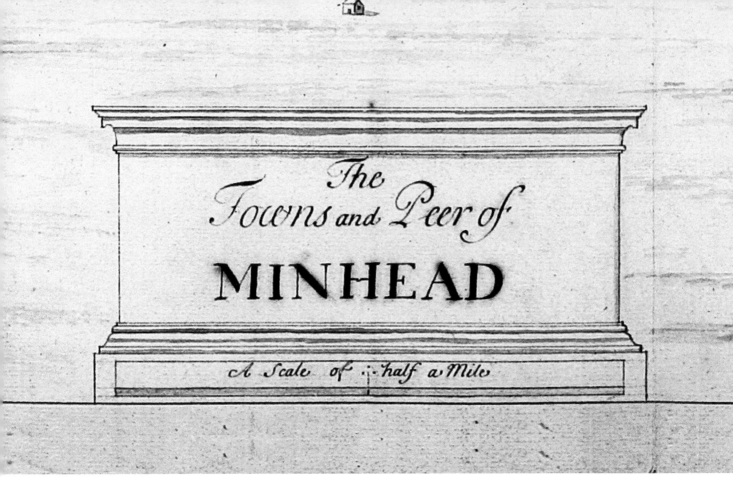

Illustration 4.11: The rococo cartouche detail from the general plan, 1701 (SHC, DD/L/1/58/15)

than anything achieved before.[40] Inevitably, the quay needed to be maintained through to the end of the eighteenth century, with another Act in 1823.[41] By which time civil engineers had re-discovered cement and concrete. Ultimately they had advice from that most eminent of all early civil engineers, Sir Thomas Telford (1757-1834), but it was not until 1895 that the final act concerned with the pier's construction appeared.[42] Modern concrete, matching that of the whole promenade fabricated in the first years of the twenty-first century, now encases the uppermost seaward part of the quay. Some control of the harbour began to pass from the residual trustees to Municipal Authorities in 1894, yet it was not until 1952 that the Luttrells finally surrendered their interests.[43] Whilst the office of Harbour Master continues into the present, West Somerset District Council now hold the more modern and over-arching office of Statutory Harbour Authority.[44]

Surbey's cartography

Whilst in Yorkshire, Surbey wrote three letters to Edmund Dummer. The terseness of those references did not then allow much appreciation of that correspondence's significance. In contrast, Dummer's own words in the Minehead document now show

their collegiality to have been greater than that of mere correspondents. Dummer, the elder by twenty five years, was a very well connected man with wide experience who delegated work to Surbey. While a young man in Portsmouth, Dummer accelerated his own learning in draughtsmanship as assistant Surveyor of the Navy under Sir John Tippetts (d.1692). Dummer advanced to draw many Mediterranean views and plans of the Thames, Portsmouth, Plymouth, Livorno and Genoa showing a very high degree of skill.[45] With their association that began no later than July 1698 and possibly the year earlier, Surbey, in turn, came to gain from Dummer's expertise. If Surbey is less flamboyantly baroque than Dummer, perhaps this shows best in Surbey's 1701 Minehead cartouche where he anticipates the sober rococo style by half a century.

After Collins's survey of the 1680's, the Navy established a practice of employing the assistance of Trinity House of Deptford Strond in survey work.[46] The 1698 survey of the English south coast has so far formed the primary evidence for consideration of Dummer as a cartographer.[47] However, he was more the directing progenitor in London than the actual surveyor on the coast. In fact the resulting atlas is very likely to have been the actual product of Surbey's hand.

Unlike Collins, neither the Luttrells, Dummer nor Surbey indicated any intention of publishing the

Minehead survey. When Murdoch Mackenzie (1712-1797) did rise to publishing a new general coastal chart of Somersetshire, in 1771, it merely brought the exaggerations of Collins, Halley and Wood into order.[48] In fact, beyond the Ordnance Survey's shoreside work, Surbey's plans reigned supreme for over a century. Not until 1831 was Lieutenant Denham's chart of Minehead anchorage published, replete with at least some of Surbey's building suggestions.[49]

Conclusion

Surbey's autographed reports demonstrate that he and Dummer worked together from at least the summer of 1699 through to the ensuing two summers. Whether or not that association extended to a period any earlier is not of main importance. Primarily this article sets out the place of Surbey's Minehead plans within their cartographic context, and their relevance to the harbour of today.

As Adrian Webb demonstrated, it was normal to improve a chart.[50] Whilst John Seller copied or improved Dutch charts, Collins on the other hand wittingly undertook a new survey. But the old ways persisted and the south coast surveyors used Collins's charts whenever they could. However, in 1698 Dummer and Wilshaw demonstrated original work by adding soundings. Perhaps having learned from that, that aspect is one of the inputs which Surbey so brilliantly achieved in Yorkshire. Yet with his

Minehead work Surbey rose to an even higher degree of surveying and cartography, by emulating Collins and making his own large scale draught of a place. At Minehead he achieved not a mere improvement of someone else's work, but an original and highly detailed survey.

All these surveyors and cartographers worked within a map making cusp as the process began to morph from an art to a science. Exactly within the period of Surbey's work, Halley was reviving the earlier interest in triangulation from a maritime perspective at the Royal Society, and John Adair was undertaking its practice in Scotland. Some time after, Mackenzie came to publish triangulated charts, and it was he who invented the station pointer. Also within this cusp, cartographic publications stood somewhat nondescript and utilitarian. Still a new technology at the turn of that century, printing was then limited to monochrome production. When the booksellers illuminated maps with colour they found an additional market. In his Minehead draughts, Surbey achieved that decorative facet rather well for his client, and augmented it with an informing narrative. He found it expedient to copy several draughts out in full colour by hand, rather than resort to the then still underdeveloped technological revolution of printing. For the engineering consultant, drawing designs to explain needs, theirs was a time of much change for the techniques involved.

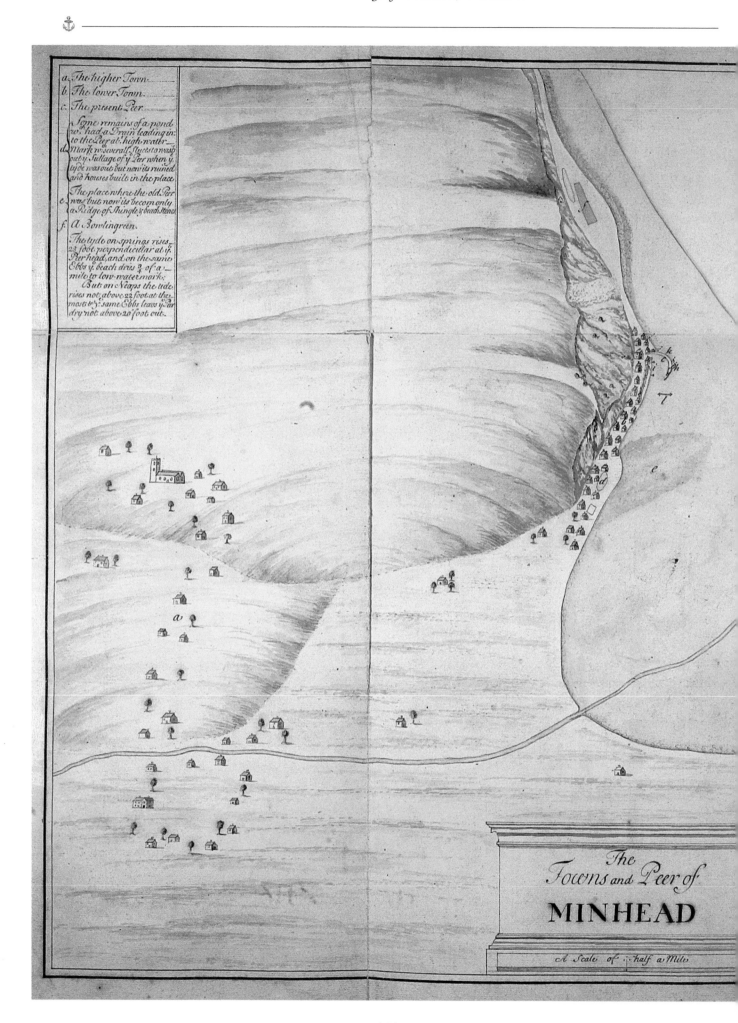

a. The higher Town.
b. The lower Town.
c. The present Peer.

d. Some remains of a pond
w.ᶜʰ had a Drain leading into the Peer at ye high-water-
Mark w.ᵗʰ severall sluces to wash
out ye Sullage of ye Peer when ye
tyde was out but now its ruind
and houses built in the place.

e. The place where the old Peer
was but now its becom only
a Ridge of Shingle & beach Stones.

f. A Bowlingreen.

The tyde on springs rises
23 foot perpendicular at ye
Peer head, and on the same
Ebbs ye beach dries ⅜ of a
mile to low-watermark;

But on Neaps the tide
rises not above 22 foot at the
most & ye same Ebbs leaves ye air
dry not above 20 foot out.

The
Towns and Peer of
MINHEAD

A Scale of ½ half a Mile

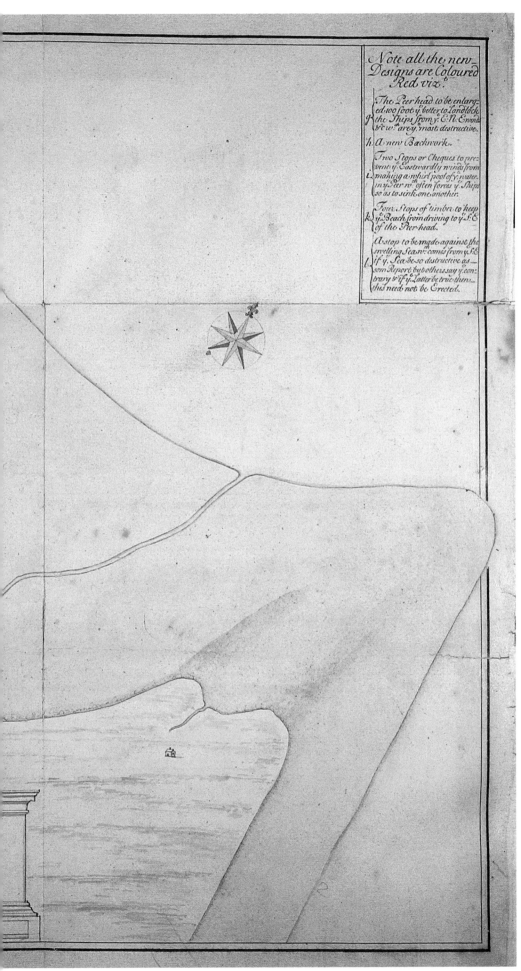

Illustration 4.12: Surbey's general map, 1701 (SHC, DD/L/1/58/15)

Appendix 4.1

A transcription of Somerset Record Office, DD/L/1/58/15

This document contains:

front piece	Surbey's general quay plan
f1r	title page: survey and description
f2r	beginning of letter from Dummer to Banks 9th August
f2v-f4v	the questions Dummer set Surbey, 7th July
f2v-f4v	the answers Surbey gave Dummer, 28th July
f5r+v	conclusion of first letter from Dummer to Banks
f5v	Surbey's charge account for Banks
f6r	title page: dimensions, scantlings and estimate
f6v-8r	the dimensions, scantlings and estimate
f8r-8v	second letter from Dummer to Banks, 18th August
end piece	Surbey's particular quay plan

[*Writing on map*]

	The Towns and Peer of MINHEAD
	A Scale of half a Mile
a.	The higher Town
b.	The lower Town
c.	The present Peer
d.	Some remains of a pond w$^{ch.}$ had a Drain leading in to the Peer ab$^{t.}$ high water Mark w$^{th:}$ severall Sluces to wash out y^e Sullage of y^e Peer when y^e tyde was out but now its ruined and houses built in the place
e.	The place where the old Peer was but now its becom only a Ridge of Shingle & beach stones
f.	A Bowlingreen.
	The tyde on springs rises 28 foot perpendicular at y$^{e.}$ Peer head, and on the same Ebbs ye beach dries ¾ of a mile to low-water mark: But on Neaps the tide rises not above 22 foot at the most & y^e same Ebbs leavs y^e Peer dry not above 20 foot out
	Note all the new Designs are Coloured Red vizt.
g.	The Peer head to be enlarged 100 foot y$^{e.}$ better to Landlock the Ships from y^e E:N:E: winds &c w$^{ch:}$ are y^e most destructive.
h.	A new Backwork.
i.	Two Stops or Cheques to prevent y^e Easwardly winds from making a whirl pool of y^e water in y^e Peer w$^{ch:}$ often forces y^e Ships so as to sink one another.
k.	Four Stops of timber to keep y^e Beach from driving to y^e S:E: of y^e Peer-head.
l.	A stop to be made against the swelling Sea w$^{ch:}$ comes from y^e S:E if y^e Sea be so destructive as som Report but others say y^e contrary & if y^e Latter be true then this need not be Erected.

Opposite. Illustration 4.13: The title page from Surbey's report of 1701 (SHC, DD/L/1/58/15)

A

Survey & Description

of the

Defects of y^e Peer

at

Minehead

with

An Esteemate of ye Charge

to

Repair ye Same

1701

[*f1r*]

A Survey & Description
of the
Defects of ye. Peer
at
Minehead
with
An Esteemate of ye Charge
to Repair ye Same
1701

[*f1v*]
[*blank*]

[*f2r*]

London the 9th of August 1701

Sir

According to your desire I dispatched to Minehead Mr Thomas Surbey to inspect the Deficiencys of that Peer, and to observe the scituation, and manner of it's annoyance together with the Remedys, and the Charge it will require, to render it safe and usefull, he went from me the 9th of July and returned the 29th following he was instructed as well as I could from the generall Idea I have of Such things, without seeing my self this matter in particular, on which he hathe made very naturall observations, and hath returned a very clear and Judicious Answer to the Same, In the following Account, and that you and the other Gentlemen concern'd may be Master of the Method I have taken therein, in Order to the giving you and them the best view of the nature of this Affair, I have thought fit to transcribe my Letter to him, and his Answers to each Article set one against the other for your better discerning, how to apply your own Judgment to the understanding thereof, with which he hath made two drawings one generall the other more particular describing the Conditions andCircumstances of the Peer only, and I conclude with my own opinion upon the whole, for as full an information as I can at present give on this Subject, the Letter follows

[*f2v*]

Questions made by Mr Dummer about the Condition of the Peer at Minehead.

London y^e. 7th of July 1701

Mr Surbey
Sr Jacob Banks desireing my opinion and Assistance touching the removeall of the Sullege within the Peer at Minehead, and what may be done for prevention of the Same for the future, I desire you will go thither with what speed you can and take a view of the Condition therefore with it's Scituation and Circumstance in respect to the Querys following. (Viz^t).

Answered by Thomas Surbey
S^r In Obedience to yours of the 7th, Instant I departed London the 9th and arived at Minehead the 12th. (having first waited upon Coll. Lutterell at Ven' near Taunton) on Monday the 14th. I went to view the Peer and the rocks from whence came the materialls with which it is built, and remaining all the week, I advised with the Masters of Ships and others the most Antient and best Acquainted with this place, but finding their reports very opposite with relation to the impedimen^{ts} of the Peer, I wrote Coll. Lutterell (p[er] his own Order) acquainting him with what I had done and desired he would meet with some of the Trustees to hear the opinions of the aforesaid Masters and others together but the Messenger brought Answer that he was ill and not well able to come but would Leave it to me, and having Considered their Argume^{nts} humbly offer the following Account in Answer to the instructions you gave me.

[*Tables to follow*]

[*f3r*]

	Questioned &c		Answered &c
1st	What is the rise of tides on Springs how far the strand is dry at low water at the same time without the utmost extent of the Peer.	1st	The rise of tides on Springs at the Peer head are 28 foot and the Strand (or beach) is near ¾ of a mile dry on the same Ebbs which may be about 8 foot Perpendicular below the Surface of the ground at the Peer head but on neaps not above 2 and the rise not above 22 foot.
2dly	In what manner the land bendeth and windeth with respect to the Headlands or bays towards Bristoll & towards yᵉ South.	2dly	I have taken a draught of the place to which I refer for the bearing of the Headlands.
3dly	Observe from the Highest land about the Peer how the Stream or Current runs on the flood and Ebb, how the Eddys set alternatively and how near or far from the Shore.	3dly	The Tyde from the Ocean that takes mails at Pembrook sets over to Comberton which is to the Westward of Minehead and then away to the Holms so that the Current on floods or Ebbs never comes near Minehead by a mile except from the Northerly winds it may sometimes be forced in but there is generally an Eddy tide both wayes Nevertheless there runs a great grown sea when the wind is at S.W. though at the same time it blows right of Shore which is prodigious high land therefore it cannot make any raging Sea here as some of the Masters conceive but it's the troubled water which comes from the Ocean that makes these grown seas which are generally very great so as to roul the beach to the Eastward and if the wind shift to the West and North the beach still rouls toward the Harbours mouth and when it get's into the Lee of the Peer head it Lodges untill the wind veers to the Eastward of the North and then it rouls into the Peer and Choakes up the Entrance as may more plainly appear from the Draughts.
[*f3v*] 4thly	How the most constant wind blow in the year with respect to the Peer either obliquily by the Shore or more directly upon the head what the Antient men say touching the first building of this head and what observation they have made touching it's present defect and where ever the like have happened and what they think is the reason of the present mischief and how they would go a bout to reform it.	4thly	The most constant winds are here as at other places of England generally to the Southward of the west but these do them no harm save moving the beach as aforesaid but the wind that is chiefly destructive to them comes from the NE. to the E.N.E. which blows almost full into the Harbour and comeing obliquily against the townside forces all the water into the Peer to a turnado or rather a Whirlpoole, whereby the Ships often Sink one another to the number of 6 or 7 at a time and as to the Antient mens report of this defect they say it was not altogether so bad formerly untill a Ledge of rocks were taken away from about the place where the moring post now stands and where expended about the back work which was almost entirely ruined about for or five years since.
5thly	What are materialls and manner of the work of the Peer and whence they were brought for makeing the same.	5thly	The materials are Ruf Stone of all Magnitude from about 25 or 30 tuns downward and are to be got on the Shore within two miles of the place.
6thly	What dimension the Peer is now of with a generall plat of its's scituation together with its adjacent Shores to the next head Lands either way with proper prophiles of the said peer.	6thly	The peers breadths and highths being so various I refer to the draught also to that and the second paragraph for the bearing of the head lands and to the dimensions &c for the new work which I have designed
[*f4r*] 7thly	What means or force must be used to remove the present matter which annoys the Peer.	7thly	The Sullage now in the Peer must be carried by Carts about 30 or 40 Rods into yᵉ wash of the Sea and then it will work of

8^{thly}	What is the Soil the peer stands upon and what is it's foundation.	8^{thly}	The peer stands upon firm hard Red Earth mix'th with Stones but the Shingle is about 7 foot deep which must be dug out for the foundation.
9^{thly}	Whether Pileing is consistant with it for makeing breakwaters or a receptacle for the annoying Sullage.	9^{thly}	Pileing or rather post set into the ground must be to check the rouling of the Beach and I humbly conceive their proper places will be as per the draught.
10^{thly}	Or if Chest work be more proper ask the price of mens Labour and Charge of materialls of timber Stone Iron and all other necessary kinds.	10^{thly}	Chest work will be a needless Charge seeing the tyde leaves the Peer dry, Masons have 18 or 20^d per day, and Labourers 14^d, but as to task work finding materialls they account for building houses with ruf Stone 2^s per rope which is their way of measuring and a rope is 20 foot long and one foot high in any kind of wall not above two foot thick, measuring over all doors and Windows but they say to work such work as is the parrowpit wall on the peer which is three foot thick at bottom and 2 foot aloft by 6 foot high both faces and filling being wrought with good lyme and Sand is worth 5^s:6 or 6^s per rope but for the ruf work of the peer there is no body can give any esteemate per foot yard rod or otherwise as for timber the best may be delivered for about 35^s per tun and Ironwork is about the same as at London.
[f4v] 11^{thly}	Describe your own thoughts and make a generall Esteemate as to manner and Charge and in what time the present defects may be removed and prevented	11^{thly}	I have described all that I conceive proper for Cure of the present defects and considered the Charge may amount to near 4000 Pounds but the latter is very uncertain seeing none of the Natives could give me any better Acco^t. then in the last foregoing paragraph but as to time I humbly conceive it may be performed in two years if diligently followed.
12^{thly}	When you are on the place and see more of the natuire of it than my Suggestions arise to, towards the Coming at a true Judgment of the manner of the defects and it's amendment let me know the difference, or omission in these Instructions. I am yor Affectionate friend and Servt. EDummer To Mr Thomas Surbey	12^{thly}	As to coming at a true Judgment of the defects one ought to be there all seasons of the year for from the reports of the seamen and others I found the defects as numerous and different as were the numbers of men I conversed with which made me humbly desire Coll. Lutterell and the other Gentlemen Trustees to meet on the place and hear all that could be said by the Masters of Ships and others altogether, whereby one might better Judge of the real defects by the most solid arguments, but the Coll. being indisposed I could have no such hearing nevertheless I hope have discovered all the materiall Impediments and most effectuall wayes to remove the same all which I humbly Submit to your Judicious Correction and remain Sr Your Hon^{rs}. most London ye 28th.July.1701. humble obed^t. serv^t. Thomas Surbey
			To Edmund Dummer Esqr.

Duely weighing the foregoing Questions and Answers together with the observations which obviously arise from the same it is evident that the Sullage do annoy only the point of the peer, which makes it certain that there is a Constant Counter force of Sea that rouls upon the Shore from the N.W. without the Peer and from the S.E. within the Peer at the same time and meets at the head where it's coagitation dissolves the impetus from either side and admits rest to the Soyl that constantly mixes with the troubled Sea and produces the annoyances complain'd of, so that when it is once Lodged neither the impetus, from the one hand or from the other how great so ever it is able to remove it either way, saving that one sees sometimes that the impetus of the Sea within is too weak for that without wh^ch removes the Sullage from the head to the Letter P. for by means of the projection of the whole body of this peer from the Land the Course of the waves being by it broken let the wind blow so strong as it will the motion of the Sea begotten thereby (That passing by the outside of the Peer, will be contrary to that within the peer for all such kind of Winds that in respect to the generall Scituation of the peer it self tend to produce this defect It seems to me therefore reasonable for makeing a Solid Cure for this evill to take nature for a Guide which makes a provision of it self, for the lengthening of this peer and shews it to be too short, But least that should not be an Entire remedy provision must be made to give interruption to the rouling Ballast both wayes by proper break waters for whatsoever lessens the impetus moderates the means of this annoyance therefore, O.R. which shews the additional Length of the Peer stained red, and the breakwaters and Stops marked with the Letters, U.N & S. ought also to be done to the North West and in my opinion the other works [f5v] stained yellow or that stained red marked W.T. on the South East should also be built and these will equally break the impetus of the waves each way and produce less violence therein or turn the Course of all the Sullage or so lodge it that little there of shall be any more brought to the head it now rest's at, this to me appears the sum totall of the defect together with it's amendment which in the performance if the best Husbandry be used the Charge will be the Less Mr Surbey who has enquired into the materialls and Labour, as men there understand it, is of opinion it will cost near 4000 Pound all which with the drawings thereof I submit to your Consideration and that of your friends and remain

S^r your most humble servan
E Dummer

I have herewith inclosed Mr Surbeys Charges and have kept one set of draughts for my further use in Case you shall have any occasion of my judgment hereafter

The Honble. Sr Jacob Banks Kn^t. is to Tho. Surbey D^r.				
for Surveying Minehead Peer &c Viz^t from July ye 9th to the 26th Inclusive 1701	£	s	d	
To 4 days rideing from London to Minehead & 7.½ days spent there, drawing two draughts of the place and peer and considering the impediments, and designing some new works to be erected for the better securing the Ships in the peer and 4½ days returning to London again, in all 16 working days at 20^s per day	16	00	00	
To a horse for D^o. Journey	01	16	00	
To expence for Subsisting horse and self upon this Journey	04	08	00	½
To drawing the 6 Coppys of the draughts I made at Minehead at 20^s each, Including Coulouring &c	06	00	00	
To a report made to Mr Dummer in Answer to the instructions he gave me and attending him about the same above 2½ days	02	10	00	
Totall	30	10	00	½
To Sr Jacob Banks Kn^t				

[f6r]

Dimencons Scantlings
and
An Esteemate of
the
New works Designed
to
Repair yᵉ Defects
of
Minehead Peer
1701

[f6v + f7r title]

Dimencons Scantlings and an Esteemate for Inlargeing the Peer at Minehead one Hundred foot with Severall Backworks according to the Draught herewith Delivered vizt.

[f6v]

Dimencons and Scantlings &c						
				feet	feet	feet
Diging or Scavell work	Outside	Length Breadth Depth	165 22 7	25410		36802
	Inside	Length Breadth Depth	92 16 3	4416		
	Backwork	Length Breadth Depth	218 8 4	6976		
				36802		
Walling	The out side and end	Length height to the upper Alter and 7 foot in ground Thickness {alow} 20} {aloft} 6}	160 41 mean 13	85280		144218 all dry
	The Inside	Length height to yᵉ 1ˡˡ. Alter } and 4 foot in ground }] Thickness {alow 14} {aloft 4}	90 32 mean 9	25920		
	After wall	Length height Thickness	140 5 3	2100 21918 9000		
	Shingle filling	Length Breadth height	84 50 26	144218 109200 x 2500 111450		111450 all dry
	Parrowpit	Length Height Thick in the mean	160 6 2½	48 Rope to be wrought with good lyme and Sand		
	Backwork	Length height in the mean Thickness	281 13 6	21918	v	
	Shingle filling	Length Breadth Height	75 30 10	2250	v	
	Great Stones for to Cover the Shingle filling	Length Breadth Thickness	75 30 4	9000	v	

[f7r] An Esteemate			£	s	d
Scavell work &c	To scavell work or diging work for all the foresaid foundations	1363 yds at 12 d per yard	68	03	00
	To a Draine to Carry of the tyde and keeping Cleer the same till the foundation is laid		25	00	00
	To fetching and setting the blockstone for the outside or face walling according to the foresaid dimentions	144218 foot at 4d per f^t.	2403	12	02
	To filling the Inside with Shingle according to the Dimentions aforesaid	111450 at ½d per foot	232	04	00
	To the parrowpit wall containing 48 Rope at 6s per rope		14	08	00
			2743	07	02

[f7v]

Dimentions and Scantlings &c				
			foot	feet
Bond timbers or Taylings	18 bond timbers	Length .... 40 Size ..... 10 by 10 inches	495	
	18 Crosses for D°.	Length .... 9 Size ..... 10 by 10 inches	112	607
	To lay 3 beds of d°. Bond timbers and Crossings to contain 6 of each in a bed at proper Heights to keep the peer from Spreading		607	
Cabshaw &c	Cabshaw	Length............................. 150 Size ..... 12 by 10 Inches	125	
	15 Landtys	Lengths from 15 to 18 foot Size........ 8 by 9 Inches	128	421
	15 Crosses	Length .... 4 foot size 7 by 8 Inches	24	
	6 fenders	Length .... 36 foot Size .... 12 by 12	144 421	
To timber stops or backwork	for 4 times 35 post for} No{Length from 15 to 20 foot backworks vizt. } 140{Size or Diameter from 8 to 14 Inch			
	To ruf cleft wood or timber about 1600 foot of rayl to be fastened to Do. Post to prevent the Shingle from rouling past each of the 4 Stops			
Whirle stops	To 2 other stops of Stone or timber by the town Side to prevent the water from Whirling round the peer with the E.N.E. wind &c			

[*f8r*]

An Esteemate		£	s	d
	Brought Over	2743	07	02
To bond timbers and taylings &c	607 feet at 18d per ft. wrought	45	11	06
Cabshaw fenders and Landtys &c	421 Dᵒ. at 20d per Dᵒ.	35	01	08
To the 4 rows of Post &c for Backworks	at £30 each	120	00	00
To 2 whirle Chequs at	£25 each	50	00	00
50 Cask containing at Least 1 butt each	at £20 apeice	50	00	00
To two boats and oars &c		50	00	00
To Chains and fids &c		60	00	00
To Carting the Shingle out of the peer		50	00	00
To 2 Sheads for houseing the Cask and othe things in the two bays where the Stone must be got		25	00	00
To repairs of boats and Cask and other unforeseen Incidents		300	00	00
		3529	00	04

London 18ᵗʰ August 1701

Dear Sʳ

    I must put my hand on my mouth and Submit to your Censure, for being the Cause of delaying the Survey of Minehead from you,

I gave directions to Mr Surbey to leave it for me at Batsons Coffee house as soon as the whole was written fair and digested to the figure you now have it in, and he left it in Batsons hand accordingly, But he neither minded to give it me nor I remembred the directions I had given, by reason of my own business, there it hath lay'n 'ere since Monday last for which I am extreamely sorry [*f8v*] How ever you have it Compleat and well Considered, with all the stepps of Circumstance in defect, Dimension of the work propounded to be done and the Charge thereof, that is required, and an indifferent workman will discern from thence the whole manner of it, to do either the whole, or part according as you and the other Gentlemen shall think fit,

For my own Judgment, I have Considered of the whole as necessary to make the peer entirely safe and usefull, But perhaps some may judge the expence too great, and if less of the work propounded be done, it may be sufficient for your purpose as to the abating of the Sullage from the Head of the Peer and be Content to be Secured from that annoyance only wherein I shall acquiesce to your pleasure who must cut your Coat as you have Cloth and still retain my opinion that the whole designed will more absolutely Compleat it's generall benefit, For whether you perform the whole or that part only, namely the Lengthening the peer, and those other works on the back thereof intended to interrup the Course of the Sullage there, I am perswaded the defects in generall are so caused as set forth in the Answers to the Querys, and the remedys thereof must conform to the manner described in the said Survey, who ever shall undertake the same it will not consist with my Affaires to meddle with it, But I can to serve you direct any body you shall employ, and visit the same once or twice a year for your Satisfaction, and Mr Surbey haveing other business cannot at present be depended on

But be that as it will in case you have plenty of mony and come to a resolution upon this subject what next to do (the ground work being thus laid and described with great accuracy and pains) I will give you the best assistance I can further when you need it,

In the mean time I advise that you take fitting time to Consider before you begin it, for to enter upon works of this nature before the whole scheme for the performance thereof be established will not be so well for these sort of expences, or any mistake are very Chargeable with which (earnestly asking your pardon for this delay) I take leave to offer thus much in further Answer to yours of the 12ᵗʰ Instant and remain

    D Sʳ your most humble servt.
        E Dummer

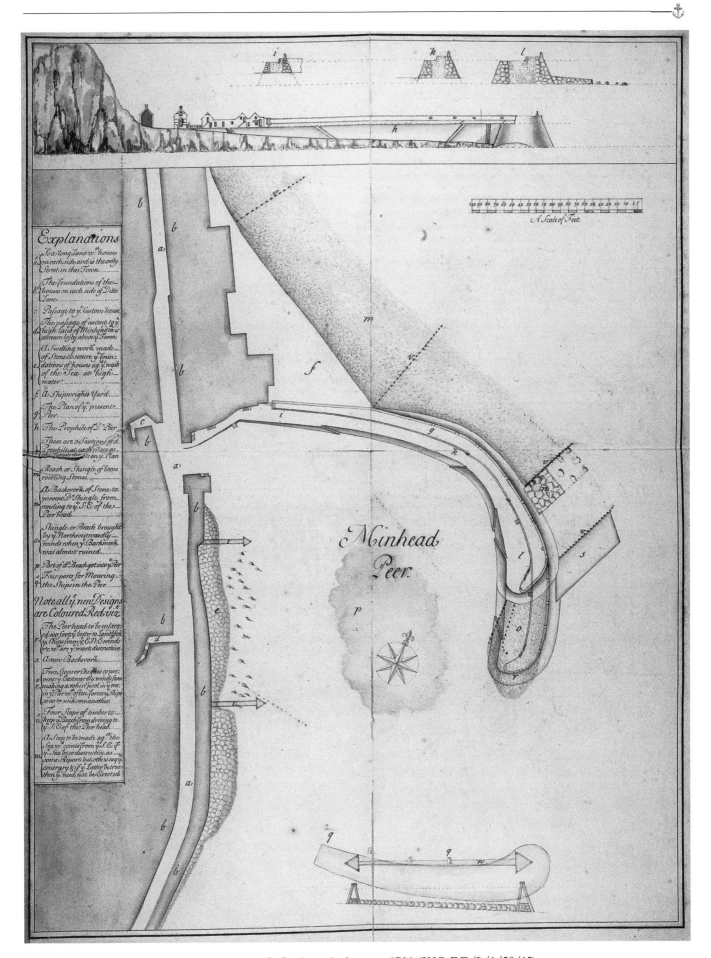

Illustration 4.14: Surbey's particular map, 1701 (SHC, DD/L/1/58/15)

[*Writing on map*]

A Scale of Feet	
Minhead Peer.	
a's	Is a long lane wth houses on each side and is the only street in the town.
b's	The foundacions of the houses on each side of Ditto Lane.
c	Passage to ye Custom house.
d	The passage of ascent to ye high land of Minehead wch. is extreme lofty above ye Town.
e	A Swelling work made of Stone to secure ye foundations of houses agst. ye wash of the Sea at high water.
f	A Shipwrights yard.
g	The Plan of ye present Peer.
h	The Prophile of D^o Peer.
ikl	These are 3 Sections of d^o. Prophile of each place as the letters denote on ye Plan.
m	Beach or Shingle of loose rowling Stones.
n	A Backwork of Stone to prevent D^o Shingle from rowling to ye S:E: of the Peer head.
o	Shingle or Beach brought by ye Northwestwardly winds when ye Backwork was almost ruined.
p	Part of d^o. Beach got into ye Peer
q's	Four posts for Mooring the Ships in the Peer.
Note all ye new Designs are Coloured Red vizt.	
r	The Peer head to be enlarged 100 foot ye better to Landlock ye Ships from ye E:N:E winds &c wch. are ye most destructive.
s	A new Backwork.
t's	Two Stops or Cheques to prevent ye Eastwardly winds from making a whirlpool in ye way in ye Peer wch. often forces ye Ships so as to sink one another.
u's	Four Stops of timber to keep ye Beach from driving to ye S.E. of the Peer head.
w	A Stop to be made agst. the Sea wch. comes from ye S.E. if ye Sea be so destructive as some Report but others say ye contrary & if ye Latter be true then ye need not be Erected.

Notes

1 United Kingdom Hydrographic Office (UKHO), *West coasts of England and Wales pilot* 17th edition (2008), 124.

2 SHC, DD/L/1/58/15.

3 SHC, DD/L/1/58/16 was published in F. Hancock, *Minehead in the county of Somerset* (1903), 286-99.

4 Somerset Historic Environment Record, R. McDonnell, *Minehead sea defence scheme* (2001), 2 volumes unpublished.

5 J. Collinson, *History and antiquities of the county of Somerset* (Bath, 1791), ii, 26-33; Hancock, *Minehead*, 230-325; H. Binding and D. Stevens, *Minehead a new history* (1977), 49-72; L. Lamplugh, *Minehead and Dunster* (1987).

6 M. Stammers, *The industrial archaeology of docks & harbours* (2007), 25; Oxford, Bodleian Library, Rawlinson A.187 f.196-9 Minehead port accounts, 1651.

7 Lamplugh, *Minehead*, 29; Lamplugh, *Minehead*, 8.

8 Hancock, *Minehead*, 37, quotes the term 'juttee'.

9 Hancock, *Minehead*, 288.

10 Lamplugh, *Minehead*, 29.

11 Hancock, *Minehead*, 233.

12 Binding and Stevens, *Minehead*, 60, quoting from SHC, DD/L/1/55/1.

13 The National Archives (TNA), L.T.R. Originalia Roll, 1 Eliz., Part 3, Roll 112; this is given in Collinson, Somerset, Appendix E, 430-8, Minehead charter in Latin.

14 Binding and Stevens, *Minehead*, 54, quoting from SHC, DD/L/P 29/34.

15 Binding and Stevens, *Minehead*, 54, quoting from the Minehead parish register.

16 Binding and Stevens, *Minehead*, 58, quoting Luttrell's 1609 petition.

17 Journal of House of Commons, 28 March 1610; Collinson, *Somerset*, ii, 27.

18 House of Lords, *An act for the recovering, securing and keeping in repair the harbour of Minehead, for the benefit and support of the navigation and trade of this kingdom*, Public Act, 12 & 13 William III, c.9. This record is dated 1700.

19 G. Collins, *Great Britain's coasting pilot* (London, 1693), 11; Collins also stated this for Barnstaple.

20 For a biography of Dummer see the *Oxford Dictionary of National Biography* or E Cruickshanks *et al*, *The House of Commons 1690-1715* (2002), volume iii, 931-3.

21 Dudley Archive Office, Sedgley parish registers, 1558-1684.

22 York City Archives, accession 65.

23 TNA, PROB 6/78 f.234v (page 147).

24 I gave some exposition of the chart and journal in 'Thomas Surbey's 1699 Survey of the Rivers Ouse and Humber', *Yorkshire Archaeological Journal*, 66 (1994), 149-90; P. Hughes, 'Some civil engineering notes from 1699, *The Local Historian*, 26:2 (May 1996), 102-114; P. Hughes, 'Thomas Surbey's dredger' in *The Pilot* 233 (April 1993), 4; P. Hughes, 'Drawing the paddles', *Waterways World* April 1997, 83.

25 SHC, DD/L 1/58/15.

26 Hancock, *Minehead*, 288.

27 Binding and Stevens, *Minehead*, 63.

28 SHC, DD/L 1/58/15 f.5v.

29 *London Post with Intelligence Foreign and Domestick* 5th April 1700, 1.

30 SHC, DD/L 1/58/15 f.8r.

31 *Daily Courant* 9 June 1720, 1.

32 This: *A survey of the ports on the south west coast of England from Dover to the Lands-end*, exists in manuscript form, of which twelve copies can be found, but it can also be readily seen as http://www.geog.port.ac.uk/webmap/dummer

33 British Library, Cotton Augustus I.vol.1.f8; part reproduced in *MHS1*, 1.

34 See the plate of '[The Severn or Channell of Bristoll]' in Collins, *Coasting pilot*. For the comment concerning the loss of Collins's own chart see page 12 in part one of his *Coasting pilot*.

35 Surbey differentiates the two drawings as one general and the other particular.

36 SHC, DD/L 1/58/15.

37 SHC, DD/L 1/58/15 f.8r; National Maritime Museum, ADM/A/1805.

38 E. Halley, *A new and correct chart of the channel between England & France* (1702).

39 D. Defoe, *A tour through England and Wales* (1948), i, 267.

40 Gloucester Record Office, D1799/C192: includes reference to storm damage at Porlock and Minehead quays, 16 March 1770.

41 *Whitehall Evening Post* 7th March 1799, 1; 4 Geo IV c.xiii *An Act for more effectually improving and keeping in repair the pier and harbour of Minehead in the county of Somerset*, recited 12&13 W.3 c9, 10 Ann c.24, 11 G.2 c8, & 10 G.3 c26.

42 Hancock, *Minehead* (Appendix K, 447). Hancock actually wrote *Sir John Telford*; a John Telford figures in three pieces of the Thomas Telford correspondence but he was neither celebrated nor a knight. 58 & 59 Victoria c.lxix *An Act to confirm certain provisional orders made by the Board of Trade under the general pier and harbour act 1861 relating to Minehead Morecambe and Woody Bay* (1895).

43 15&16 Geo.6 & 1 Eliz.2 c.xxix *Pier and harbour order (Minehead) confirmation act* (1952).

44 G. Farr, *Somerset harbours* (1954), 147–9. The pier was finished in 1714.

45 British Library, King's MS 40 + 43 and Lansdowne 847. For expositions of Dummer's work see: C. Fox, 'The Ingenious Mr Dummer: rationalizing the Royal Navy in late seventeenth-century England', *eBLJ*, 2007, article 10; & Lucia Nuti, 'To make the whole progress a lineall visible Demonstration: The journal of Edmund Dummer', *Word & Image*, xv (1999), 299-302; M. Duffy, 'Edmund Dummer's "Account of the General Progress and advancement of his Majesty's new dock and yard at Plymouth"', December 1694', *The Naval miscellany volume VI*, Navy Records Society (NRS) 146 (2003), 93-147.

46 C. Sergison, *The Sergison papers*, NRS 89 (1950), 106.

47 G.P.B. Naish, 'Hydrographic surveys by officers of the navy under the later Stuarts', *Journal of the Institute of Navigation*, ix(1) (1956), 47-55.

48 Reproduced on page 102 in volume one of this series.

49 Lieut. H.M. Denham, *Anchorages on the south shore of the Bristol Channel, i.e. Linmouth, Minehead, Porlock, and Watchet* (1831).

50 http://www.geog.port.ac.uk/webmap/dummer/ therein he gives a lucid explanatory exposition.

51 Combe Martin, Devon.

Chapter Five

Sea Fishing in Somerset: Past, Present and Future

Commodore Bill Kelly

Introduction

AS A MECHANICAL engineering apprentice, nearly 50 years ago, I worked on commissioning the first power station at Hinkley Point on the Somerset coast. I spent many sunny afternoons sitting on the grassy cliff tops overlooking Bridgwater Bay and the remains of Lilstock harbour, knowing that there were fish running past the seawater intake caisson attached to the power station. I had seen them in the screens of the water intake. Now returned to Somerset with a more mature interest in fishing I have

Illustration 5.1: Hinkley Point Water Intake Caisson in Bridgwater Bay, 2009 (© Copyright Ken Grainger) (Licensed for reuse under this Creative Commons licence)

revisited some of my fisherman's marks. I wonder about both the history of fishing in the sea off the Somerset coast and what fishing might be like in 50 years time. I plan to use an ecosystem approach to explore the complex development of sea fishing in Somerset's coastal waters from the Middle Ages to today and, from this, to suggest prospects for the future. Viewed from the parallel perspectives of social need, technological opportunity, and statutory regulation, the progressive regimes of fishing activity will emerge as wholes that are greater than the sum of their parts. The systemic extrapolation of this model should offer a possible prognosis for sea fishing in Somerset in 2060.

An ecosystem approach

It is useful to explore possible relationships between human and fish activity by considering Somerset's coastal margins as an ecological system. Ecology can be defined (1) as the study of the complex relations of animals and plants to their organic and inorganic environments.[1] A systems approach is a way of making sense of fishing as one of these complex relations by considering the emergent property of a simple set of notions and then aggregating these properties such that the whole is greater than the sum of its parts.[2] The notions that I plan to explore are economic demand, technological opportunity, and statutory regulation.

A thousand years of supply and demand for sea fishing in Somerset

The consumption of fish was an important part of life in the early medieval period, and their catching, preparation, storage, and cooking played an equally significant role in everyday life. This is not surprising as in 730 A.D., according to *Regia Anglorum*, Bishop Winfrid of Colchester apparently:

> … found so much misery from hunger, he taught the people to get food by fishing. For, although there was plenty of fish in the seas and rivers, the people had no idea about fishing, and caught only eels. So the Bishop's men got together eel nets from all side, and threw them into the sea. By God's help they caught three hundred fish, of all different kinds.[3]

The Christian Church, growing in power and influence, did much to encourage the consumption of fish, both freshwater and sea varieties, during lent and on non-meat days.

Under the control of the Bishop of Wessex by the middle of the tenth century, Taunton was a principal market town with easy access to the market and mint on the coast at Watchet and the other inland markets and mints at Langport, Ilchester, and Crewkerne. Towards the end of the eleventh century when Saxon Britain united under the house of Wessex, Somersetshire emerged from the kingdoms of Wessex and Dumnonia with western coastal hundreds, administrative areas linked to one hundred households, based on Cannington, Willington, and Carhampton. A string of coastal forts and lookout posts originally established by Alfred the Great had contributed greatly to repelling Viking invaders from the Somersetshire coast. These fortifications were connected by a military road or herepath, so that troops could track and oppose amphibious assaults by Viking raiders.

The Somerset Herepath[4] started from a ford on the River Parrett at Combwich, past Cannington hill fort to Over Stowey, over the Quantocks at Triscombe and up onto to Exmoor with clear views of the approaches to likely landing places where the

Somerset rivers met the Bristol Channel. These were, in the main, the established communes of coastal folk in Combwich, Lilstock, Watchet, Minehead, and Porlock. Watchet was an important coastal town with a Saxon market, first noted in about 900 A.D., and a mint for local coinage,[5] some of which was later discovered in Scandinavia. A Viking raid on the town in 918 A.D. recorded in the Anglo Saxon Chronicle as:

> Nevertheless, they eluded them at night, by stealing up twice; at one time to the east of Watchet. There was a great slaughter each time; so that few of them came away, except those only who swam out to the ships. Then sat they outward on an island, called the Flat-holms; till they were very short of meat, and many men died of hunger, because they could not reach any

Illustration 5.2: A map of Somerset's burghs and mints (T.J. Hunt and R.R. Sellman, *Aspects of Somerset History*)

meat.[6]

Sea fishermen also sailed from Porlock where, later, a market was established, and the Vikings, thought by some to have based themselves on Flatholm, frequently plundered Porlock Bay. The Vikings were also a trading people and their first currency in Britain was probably fish, as was the case in Norway and in Iceland up to the close of the last century. Sild, hring, or herring, is still a term in use to mean money, and the scad or scat (the horse mackerel often corrupted to scot), a fish of the same genus, had the same meaning in North Britain. There are suggestions of fish-money in the expression 'scot-free'. Earl Harold, son of the Danish Earl Godwin of Wessex and soon to become King Harold of England, landed at Porlock when he returned from exile in Ireland to challenge the authority of King Edward, as also recorded in the Anglo Saxon Chronicle for 1052 A.D.:

> Then was Harold come out from Ireland with nine ships; and then landed at Porlock, and there much people was gathered against him; but he failed not to procure himself provisions.[7]

The sea and river fish of the coastal margins of Somersetshire would appear to have been more than sufficient to satisfy the needs of local coastal communities, such as Porlock and Watchet, their religious masters, and for tribute for the Earl of Wessex. There is little evidence of the extent of sea fishing or populations, but it is thought that whereas the human population of Somerset was sparse by modern measures, at about 50,000, the fish population was near abundant. One Medieval source gives an account of a conversation between a master and one of his serfs in 1000 A.D. as:

> Master: Where do you sell your fish?
> Fisherman: In the town.
> Master: Who buys them?
> Fisherman: The citizens. I cannot catch as much as I can sell.
> Master: What fish do you take?
> Fisherman: Herring, salmon, porpoises, sturgeon, oysters, crabs, mussels, periwinkles, cockles, plaice, sole, lobsters, and the like.[8]

The uncertainty of the early months of the reign of King Harold encouraged, firstly, Harald Hardrada, King of Norway, and then Duke William of Normandy to invade England, the failure of the former and success of the latter in 1066 led to a fundamental restructuring of English social life under King William the Conqueror. The Normans

---

Illustration 5.3: Fishing from boats in 1555 (http://www.york.ac.uk/res/unnatural-history-of-the-sea/images/content/gallery/gbap3large.jpg)

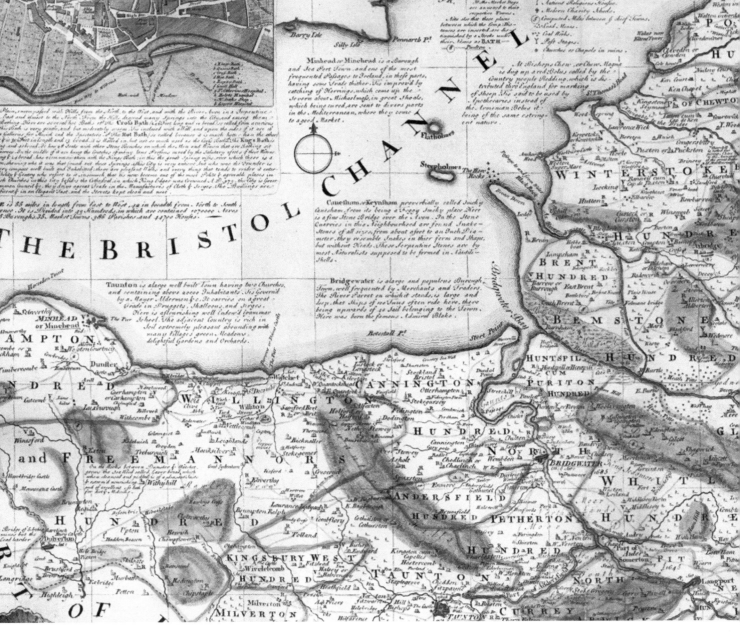

Illustration 5.4: An extract from Bowen's map of Somerset, showing the Hundred of Cannington (SANHS)

introduced a form of feudalism with authority based on ownership of land. The King, anticipating his frequent absences in France as a French duke and his need to subjugate his rebellious Anglo Saxon subjects, granted feuds or fiefs to his loyal barons in return for feudal services thereby transferring land guardianship to his supporters from the earls who sided with Harold. The larger, at-risk fiefdoms, such as along the coast of Somerset, were granted to the more loyal barons. A dispersed social structure based on burghs, markets, and mints was replaced by manors with resident vassals of the King, who owned all the land of England, at the centre of his granted fiefs. The Normans, descended from Vikings themselves, were a resolute sea fishing and sea trading race as well as being devoutly Christian. The influx of Norman culture encouraged people to migrate to towns, in which specialist trades and markets grew up, and led to growth of church building. The population of

Somersetshire increased, and social life tended to centralise in larger towns.

Manors along the coastal hundreds of Somerset, where the King did not directly hold them, were honoured to members of his family and the faithful Norman nobles who accompanied William the Conqueror to Hastings. William de Mohun held most of the land to the west of the Quantocks, where he built his castle and administrative town and market at Dunster, William de Falaise held Stogursey, and Roger de Courseulles held Cannington as lords and tenants-in-chief. In the coastal margins, sub-tenant holdings flourished around the streams and estuaries such as the Rivers Hawkcombe, Avill, Washford, Doniford Brook, Holford, and the Aller.

The lord of the manor usually retained some land as demesne that he required his serfs to cultivate and rented the remainder to sub-tenants in return for their feudal services. Fish in the rivers and in coastal waters belonged to the Lord of the manor, and he had first call on any that were caught particularly those that had a medicinal and scarcity value such as lamprey and sturgeon respectively. The former was reported to have contributed to the death of Henry the First in 1135, and the latter was so favoured as to be protected by an Act of Edward the Second. A thriving market in dried cod, a commodity in which the Danes had traded for many hundreds of years, would have existed, and the market at Watchet might well have supplied Earls Godwin and Harold of Wessex. The new Norman masters would also have had a taste for Danish dried cod.

Fish made a crucial contribution to diet, not only because of Lent and non-meat days. In eight century Wessex, river fish predominated, but, by the eleventh century, sea fish, above all herring, were commonly eaten, and the herring consumed in towns were probably produced by an organised fishing and processing industry. There is evidence that medieval fish-tanks excavated in Taunton contained fish bones, predominantly sea species that include hake, conger eel, herring, and plaice.[9] The medieval market had developed to include more sea fish species because of demand and choice. Recent research suggests that long-distance fish trade had begun by late Saxon times, and, at the end of the first millennium A.D., consumption of marine fish such as cod in parts of Northern and Western Europe went up sharply. It was not clear how much this was local fishing, and how much the result of organised long-distance trade. According to researchers, the distinction is important because 'the emergence of commercial fishing represents a watershed in the intensity of human use of the sea' and represents a fish event horizon.[10]

Dunster market was in existence by 1222 when plans for a new market at Watchet were suppressed to protect it. In 1253, Reynold de Mohun secured a charter for a Monday market and granted freedom from toll to fishermen and corn-mongers and on transactions of 12d or less.[11] In the medieval Dunster market town, the large castle household encouraged traders to bring food produce and fine cloth and supplied the market with by-products from its slaughterhouse and kitchen fat. Ports at Dunster and Watchet, and later Minehead, encouraged a market in fish, cloth, and products coming from or attractive to traders from Wales and Ireland. It is likely that the fortunes of the extensive coastal fishing industry and of local cloth making were inter-related in the market, and its employees would have created a demand for food.

Life in fourteenth century Somerset was significantly affected by what was later called 'the Hundred Years War' with France, the Black Death and by the end of the North Atlantic Medieval Warm

Period and the beginning of its Little Ice Age. By the early stages of the 100 Years War, the English crown lost control of Normandy but retained power in the Southern district of Gascony[12] with which there was a lucrative maritime trade with the coastal ports of Somerset in salt, wine and wool. Military encounters between French and English ships in the South West Approaches might have restricted international trade in salted herrings and other fish taken from the more Northern waters around the British Isles. It has been suggested that sea temperatures fell by nearly 1 degree Celsius between the high of the Warm Period and the low of the Little Ice Age[13] and, though the effect of water temperature on fish populations is complex, it is likely that herring, mackerel and cod became more abundant in the Bristol Channel.

At the same time, the population of Somerset reduced by as much as 50 per cent because of the impact of the Great Pestilence or Black Death. The plague is thought to have been imported to England from Gascony in 1348, through the port of Weymouth, and then spread north throughout

Illustration 5.5: The west door of St Georges Priory Church, Dunster, 2011 (Bill Kelly)

Somerset to Bristol and Gloucester by overland or coastal trade before affecting the whole of England. After 1350 there was a dietary shift towards meat and away from fish, perhaps especially away from the unpalatable dried, salted and smoked herring, for there are signs of more variety and greater discrimination in fish consumption. Fresh and salted fish were an important commodity in Dunster market and for the castle. Thirteen dozen fish from Dunster were shipped to Poole in the early fifteenth century probably for onward shipment to Sir Hugh Luttrell, the then owner of the Dunster estate, who often requested local fish to be sent to him in Harfleur. A shipment in 1419 included a pipe of salmon, a pipe of scallops, 220 hake, four casks of herring, eight saltfish and 13½ dozen ling and mullet.[14] The Luttrells strongly asserted their right to fish caught around the

Illustration 5.6: Plaque in Weymouth recording the Black Death, 2002 (Mark A Wilson)

coast, and, in 1484, Avill manor had a new fish weir next the sea, and the new port in Minehead had developed with their investment in new jetties.

The early Minehead harbour area lay on a creek some way south of the present quay, at the then mouth of the Bratton Stream. Though this was adequate for small fishing boats and coasters, it was from the beginning difficult to maintain a sufficient depth of water for the ocean going vessels on which Minehead's international trade depended. There are references to problems with silting as early as the fourteenth century, and to the construction of jetties in the fifteenth century, with a proportion of the manor's harbour tolls being left with the townsfolk for their upkeep.[15] Minehead succeeded in retaining its deep-water facilities into the sixteenth century though, at the accession of Elizabeth the First, the condition of the port was becoming critical for successful mercantile and fishing trade. The port of Bridgwater, in use from about 1200, was by this time an important trading port; however, Somerset's sea

fishing fleet remained concentrated in the Minehead area. It is likely that this fleet would be aware of new fishing grounds discovered by John, and later Sebastian, Cabot during their voyages off the East coast of the New World over the continental shelf of Newfoundland. They sailed out of Bristol in the *Matthew* sponsored by Bristol merchants, with a warrant from Henry the Seventh to claim new territories and resources, but English fishing boats did not immediately exploit the abundant stocks of fish in the New World.

Whilst there is evidence that fishing boats from Minehead sailed to the Newfoundland fishing grounds at the end of the seventeenth century,[16] it is highly likely that Minehead's fishing boats were not equipped to fish effectively for cod off the Newfoundland coast as they probably were fitted with drift nets for herring fishing in shallow seas. Herring and sprat were the abundant Clupeidae or pelagic fish that inhabited the more northern waters of the Celtic Sea and Irish Sea whereas pilchard, sardine and anchovies were common in more southerly waters of the south coast of Devon. Local climatic conditions and environmental effects would cause large blooms of plankton to drift in the open sea currents into the Bristol Channel, and the huge schools of Herring-like fish followed them to feed. It was also known that herring press inshore to breed in the shallow waters of bays and estuaries. West Somerset fishers would have adopted the practice of drifting gill-net fishing during late summer in shallow water of the Bristol Channel for herring.

Fishermen from Porlock, Watchet and Minehead may well have been driven close to bankruptcy, when in 1630 two merchants, Yeomans from Bristol and Jacob Andrews of Bridgwater, cornered the salt market and raised prices by 300 per cent. The following year, in 1631, John Waydon and John Preist, partners of Watchet and Julia Stone, Richard Miles and Joane Miles were all charged with stockpiling salt at the Quarter Sessions.[17] Two notable Minehead fishermen, Gregory Tylye and John Williams who died in 1675 and 1680 respectively, owned salt upon their deaths. Tylye's boats, half owned by him, were the *Thompsin* and the *Seaflower,* and it is quite likely that he benefitted from the notable shoals that came up the Bristol Channel in November 1668. When the shoals were about 12 miles off Minehead harbour, many boats set sail to take advantage of glut. Nine years later in November 1677 huge shoals of herring, 'the like not known' were reported off Porlock, and so great was the plenty that fishing boats from the Lyme Regis area sailed into the Bristol Channel to

Sea Fish

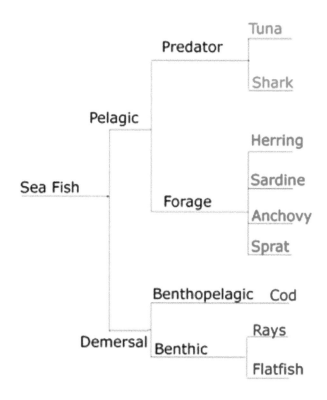

Above. Illustration 5.7: Pelagic and Demersal Sea Fish, 2011 (Bill Kelly)

take advantage of the catch.[18]

Clearly the West Somerset ports were a hive of activity in the winter. Fresh herring were being landed, salted, cured, packed and dispatched onto small coasters for the trip to Bristol or being loaded onto larger vessels for overseas markets. A voyage of the *Betty* to the Caribbean, probably around 1670, was connected to the business of Hoare and Company of Bridgwater. The master of the *Betty* was Robert Dashwood and the full manifest was 307 barrels of white herring, 50 barrels of red herring, three hogsheads of peas and one barrel of powder. In a letter, the company agent is requested to send the ship on to another West Indian island if no market for the herring could be found in Barbados.[19]

It seems that not all herring from this period were caught in drift nets. A survey of Watchet from September 1719 shows that herring were caught from the shore. What is also significant is that there were eighty people involved in catching herring which was probably about eight or ten times as many as at Porlock and possibly even more than were fishing at Minehead. The breadth of the foreshore at low tide was clearly a significant factor in limiting the number of operatives, that area being narrower at Porlock than along the beaches east of Minehead. Current

Below. Illustration 5.8: Drift Net fishing, 2007 (José Ramón García Ares)

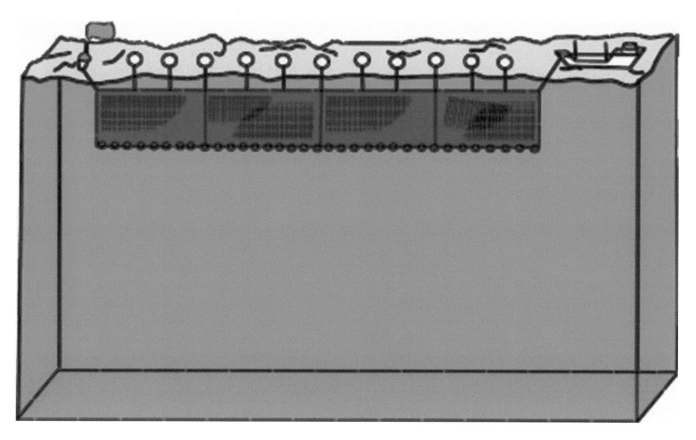

maps show that at low tide the beaches within two kilometres of Porlock harbour are up to a maximum of 200m wide, whilst in the same vicinity of Watchet harbour they are 500m wide and at Minehead reach 1,000m in width to the east of the harbour since the beach shelves gently there.[20] Stake nets were in use north along the Somerset coast as far as Sand Point, the home of Woodspring Priory established by William de Courtenay in 1210.

Evidence of the decline of herring fishing in both Minehead and Watchet was collected by Edmund Rack during his travels throughout Somerset between 1781 and 1787. Rack remarked that in Minehead

> in the early 1700s upwards of 40 vessels were employed to Ireland. Many other vessels were employed in the West India, Virginia, and Straits trade, and 4000 barrels of herrings were then caught, cured and shipped here annually for the Mediterranean. But all this is now nearly at an end. The trade is lost, the herrings have left the coast and there are at present only 5 or 6 vessels belonging to this port.[21]

In Watchet he recorded

> here there was a very large fishery but the herrings having left the Channel, that is much declind of late years. The fish mostly caught here now are shrimps, prawns, crabs, plaice, flounders, whiting, salmon peal and some cod. There are also porpusses, dogfish and sharks occasionally on the coast. There being only 7 vessels now belonging to the port, 2 of which are Bristol traders, the rest colliers bringing coal from Wales.[22]

Shoaling herring during the autumn periods of the early nineteenth century were few and far between off the West Somerset coast. Huers, from their high ground perches such as Hurlestone Point above Porlock and Blue Anchor Bays, had been accustomed to spotting the feeding or spawning schools of fish by observing either their natural predators circling around and above the school or, at night, the effervescence of the plankton on which they were feeding but they had little to report to the boatmen of Porlock and the net men of Minehead in 1800. The concern of West Porlock fishermen over the lack of herring and other fish was recorded by visitors to the village in 1813[23] but despite the decline, the fishermen hung on, perhaps with increasing difficulty. Minehead had probably had more than enough locally caught herring in the past but perhaps to underline the extent

of the decline a small tonnage of herring was brought into Minehead from St Ives. In 1830 Porlock had many fishing boats, but, with the exception of the herring season when many people were involved in its fishery,[24] few were in continuous employment throughout the year. The failing economics of Porlock's herring fishery was probably one of the reasons why in late 1832 or early 1833 there was huge agitation in Porlock when it was alleged that the non-resident rector was about to introduce tithes on the herring catch. The remaining 27 stake and net fishermen at Watchet in 1847 were considerably fewer than those recorded operating there in a similar manner at the beginning of the eighteenth century.[25]

Whilst the population of sea fish visiting the Bristol Channel was decreasing, the population of the people of Somerset was flourishing, nearly doubling between 1800 and 1850 from 260,000 to 400,000. The spread of Brunel's railway from Bristol to Taunton with a branch line to Watchet and Minehead encouraged folk to move to the towns of Somerset which were growing as industrial rather than agricultural centres. The West Somerset Railway Co, formed under Sir Peregrine Fuller Palmer Acland's chairmanship, encouraged the transition of the coastal towns from fishing and cloth-making to seaside tourism. The local demand for sea fish was satisfied by timely shipments from the South Devon coast fisheries and North Sea fisheries, and Somerset's fishing industries continued to decline as its traditional markets for sea fish were supplied by rail. Somerset's population doubled again between 1850 and 2000.[26] The shoals of herring did not return to the Bristol Channel, and by the middle of the nineteenth century many thousands of tonnes of fish were moved about the British Isles by rail. Refrigerated rail and road transport of fresh and frozen fish from the East and South coast developed to satisfied local demand for sea fish in Somerset and the boatmen of the coastal resorts turned their hands to tourism and sport sea fishing.

The impact of twentieth century nuclear technology on the fisheries of the Somerset coast should not be ignored in that the Severn Estuary with its strong tidal currents and characteristic salinity and sedimentary patterns made it a most suitable site for the location of nuclear power stations from Berkeley in Gloucestershire to Hinkley Point on the West Somerset coast. The 1950s' regime of planning regulations reflected the wisdom of the day that the Bay was an almost barren habitat for pelagic and demersal sea fish. We now have an enormous amount of intelligence about the fish assemblages in

Illustration 5.9: Sir Peregrine Fuller Palmer Acland Bt. (Image is courtesy of Lady Gass)

Bridgwater Bay and the variation of salinity and temperature profiles in the Bristol Channel during the latter half of the twentieth century. The cooling water discharge in the Bristol Channel from Hinkley Point is a plume of sea water 10 degrees Celsius above sea temperature and it diffuses rapidly into the Severn tidal flows with insignificant heating effect. Research since the installation of the power stations shows that fish assemblages in Bridgwater Bay had stabilised,[27] but the Stert Flat fisheries were already in steep decline and the West Somerset commercial fishing fleet laid up.

It was reported by the Director of Fisheries Research of MAFF in 1994 that:

Two small part-time boats work out of Minehead setting pots and taking out angling parties. On Stert Flats, to the east of Hinkley Point, 2 fishermen maintain ranks of about 100 fixed stowe or stake nets. These are intended to catch shrimps, but also catch a small quantity of other species such as mullet, rays and sole. From July to October one, occasionally both, of the stakenetsmen also erect a hang net which is a 800 m long curtain of netting around 3 m high that traps a variety of fish on the falling tide.[28]

It was noted in the same report that there were many more boats operating out of the South Wales ports, some of which were catching a few herring in the colder winter months.

Sea fishing technology and science

Sea fishing has, since pre-Saxon times, been an activity either pursued from the foreshore or at sea from boats.[29] There is little, surviving evidence of line fishing, whether it was from shore or boats, off the Somersetshire coast, but examples of medieval fish hooks were discovered on other parts of the English coast.[30] Like that of fishing line, there is also no evidence of fishing nets used from boats off the

Illustration 5.10: Stert Point, 2008 (Roger Cornfoot)

boats.[29] There is little, surviving evidence of line fishing, whether it was from shore or boats, off the Somersetshire coast, but examples of medieval fish hooks were discovered on other parts of the English coast.[30] Like that of fishing line, there is also no evidence of fishing nets used from boats off the Somersetshire coast during Saxon times as they would likely be made from dried nettles or stripped bark of willows common in the area. They would not have been preserved. Lave nets would have been used both from boats in shallow water or from the shore so that the fisherman could raise the net, held on the sea floor, when a fish was felt to be caught in the net.

Early foreshore fishermen, particularly from sandy beaches along the Bristol Channel that experience high tidal ranges, developed the technology of tidal v-shaped fish weirs that constrain the ebb of contained tidal waters through a mesh net or basket at the apex. Fish weirs were established on Dunster foreshore by the twelfth century when William de Mohun gave a fishery to the Prior of Dunster. By 1266, there were four on the manor, and there were five weirs on the beach at Minehead in 1299[31] that may have used willow bark nets or baskets to collect fish. Work on weirs was part of the labour service owed by tenants.

Fishing was recorded in the thirteenth and

fourteenth centuries, and fish weirs or fishing stakes at sea and nethangs, stakes at high water, were let in the late fifteenth century for 7s 6d. Assuming a later rate of letting of 3d each, there may have been 30 weirs. In 1469, a man was accused of selling a sturgeon caught in his weir instead of taking it to the lord of the manor according to ancient custom. One tenant took three named fishing stakes in 1521 and another took a weir in about 1570 for 11 good dishes of fish and the chief fish, presumably sturgeon.

Surviving weirs usually comprise a V-shaped bank composed of large boulders in the intertidal mud.[32] The weir arms are over 100 foot long and, at the apex, a sluice allows water out but traps fish on the outgoing tide. Some have posts to support netting or wattles. The stakes or nethangs took the form of a crescent or triangle of wooden stakes driven into the foreshore about 4 or 5 feet apart. Rows of stakes or 'hangs' were up to 500 ft long and nets hung on them caught fish as the tide receded. At least ten survive alongside Dunster beach and some remained in use in the early twentieth century.

By 1795, the right of fishery on Dunster and Minehead stands was let with the warren. 50 years later, the warrener was a fishmonger and laver dealer and in 1871 employed a fisherman and woman who both resided at Warren House to mend nets. In the

Lave Net

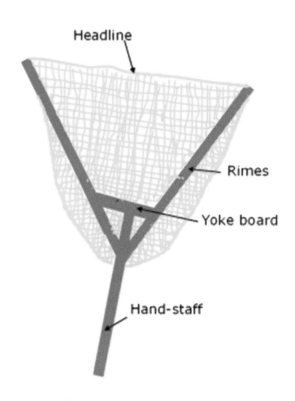

Headline

Rimes

Yoke board

Hand-staff

(Above) Illustration 5.11: Lave net, 2011 (Bill Kelly)

to be worth £10,000 a season and a ton a day went to Taunton market where poor families preserved them for later use. Some herring were also caught in stake nets in the autumn and winter at the same period.

Farther north-east along the estuary into Bridgwater Bay and beyond, the intertidal area was, and still is, fine, sedimentary mud and unsuitable for weir structures so net-hangs were driven into the intertidal mud to support nets. The nets were either conical form or gill nets, and the fish they caught were retrieved by mud-horse fishermen. The mud-horse is a sledge with a large surface area in contact with the unstable, intertidal mud such that the surface pressure could support the weight of a fisherman and his catch.[33] The fisherman pushes the mud-horse across the mud surface to his nets at speed to prevent his feet sinking into the mud, collects fish from gill nets and shrimps from more closely woven nets. It is dangerous work as the mud is never in a stable state, it returns to a fluid suspension as the tide rises, and the intertidal areas become an integral part of the Bridgwater bay-Newport Deep sediment gyre in the Severn Estuary.

There is evidence that the size of boats sailing around the coast of Northern Europe increased three-fold from about 18 tonnes to 55 tonnes[34] at about the same time as a significant increase in consumption of marine fish around 1000 A.D.. This represented an increase of over 40% in boat length for similar boats probably resulting from needs of increased fishing rather than improvements in technology. Nevertheless, longer hull length allowed larger sail area and greater towing power, leading to the emergence of bottom trawling alongside drift netting.

(Below) Illustration 5.12: Fish weir off the West Somerset coast, 1970s (Somerset County Council HER image 1783)

Illustration 5.13: A mud horse, c.1970. When an image of a mud horse was published in 1965, the accompanying text read: 'Mudhorses, for the unitiated, are devices made toboggan fashion but having a simple super-structure or framework like a light, or small kitchen table turned upside down. Mudhorses are pushed across the soft, deep mud. Their chief use is on the homeward journey, when they are laden (on the rails of the upside down table legs, so to speak) with sacks of shrimps, baskets, and seives. But mudhorses are also useful in that they take much of the weight of the pushing fisherman . . .'. (Bill Kelly, 2011)

The origin of trawling, described as the dragging of nets across the seabed, can be quite precisely dated because of a complaint made to Edward III in 1376 requesting that he ban a new and destructive type of fishing gear. The commons petition to the King complained that:

> where in creeks and havens of the sea there used to be plenteous fishing, to the profit of the Kingdom, certain fishermen for several years past have subtily contrived an instrument by which fishermen take such quantity of small fish that they do not know what to do with them; and that they feed and fat their pigs with them, to the great damage of the commons of the realm and the destruction of the fisheries, and they pray for a remedy.[35]

The report of the commission appointed to look into the complaint stated that the net was six metres long and three metres wide. At the ends of a 3 metre wooden beam were two iron frames formed like a rake, and the top of the net was attached to the beam, while the bottom had a rope weighted with lead and many great stones. The lower part of the net ran along the seabed, scaring fish into the bag, held open by the beam above. The commissioners could not see their way to an outright ban of what would be easily recognizable today as the beam trawl, but they determined that it should be used only in deep water and not in the waters of coastal estuaries and bays. The invention of the beam trawl in the fourteenth century marks the first of two fishing revolutions. The second would happen in the late nineteenth century with the addition of steam power to trawling vessels that allowed them to operate with larger nets in deeper water irrespective of wind and currents. The fishing boats operating out of the West Somerset ports were mainly drift and seine net fitted, and there is no evidence to suggest that any boats operating out of Minehead were trawling. They may have sailed to the Newfoundland Banks at the end of the seventeenth century but in all probabilities they were driftnet and long-line fitted.

The enlightenment of the nineteenth century introduced new science and technology to fishing and brought about a major change in the culture and fortunes of the West Somerset fisheries. The poor state of the Minehead and Porlock harbours and the decline of the Bristol Channel fisheries did not support the conversion of their fishing boats to steam power and what small boats remained on the West Somerset coast were net or long-line fitted. In the mid nineteenth century there was widespread unrest in the net and long-line fishing communities as a result of the increase in trawling with steam boats. Steam power for both boat propulsion and winches enhanced the capability of boats to cover more and varied ground at greater speeds. By 1863 this unrest was acknowledged by the Government, and a Royal Commission was established. Thomas Henry Huxley, a fellow of the Royal Society and friend of Charles Darwin, was one of the commissioners, and the Commission shared his view that, contrary to common perceived experience of fishermen, the use of the beam trawl has no significant impact on fish populations.

About the same time marine biologists were conducting studies of the Celtic and Irish Seas to establish the populations and breeding distributions of sea fish. As a result of these advances in marine science and discussions at an International Fisheries Exhibition in London in 1883, a new Royal Commission was established in 1883. However, Huxley continued to hold to the view that '. . . nothing we do seriously affects the number of fish . . . And that any attempt to regulate these fisheries [including herrings] seems consequently from the nature of the case to be useless.[36]

Never-the-less this Commission concluded that the inshore fisheries, including the Bristol Channel, should be regulated under a single management structure. The success of marine science in acknowledging public perceptions of overfishing was such a strong lobby in Government that funds were made available to establish the Marine Biological Association of the United Kingdom in Plymouth in 1884 with Huxley as its first President and Ray Lankester as Secretary. Four years later their work reinforced the recommendations of the Royal Commission, and coastal Sea Fisheries Committees were put in place. The emerging understanding of fish behaviour during the twentieth century coincided with the accurate mapping of tidal and residual coastal currents, the engineering of underwater echo sounders, and development of precise global positioning systems. The combination of these initiatives resulted in both better charting of the coast, seabed structure and water column behaviour and improved understanding of fish habitats.

Before the middle of the twentieth century fishing nets and lines were made from biodegradable woven or braided hemp or sisal fibres that restricted size and weight of the gear that could be handled by small boats. Small boats favoured long-line fishing where a length of line, which maybe kilometres long, would be laid out in mid-water for pelagic fish and just off the sea bed for demersal fish, with individual hooks

attached to snoods. In 1938 du Pont invented nylon. It was used as a very stiff line for nets and long-lines but was replaced in 1958 by a much softer, more flexible monofilament which permitted smaller meshes for nets. Nets constructed from these new, monofilament fibres were light enough to be handled by small, internal-combustion powered boats that could also handle modern long-lines up to 50 kilometres in length. In recent times monofilament nylon has been replaced by new polymer materials with good resistance to water absorption and light degradation. The ease of handling polymer nets allowed single boats to employ large ring nets or purse-seine nets covering the pelagic fish water column of an area the size of a cricket pitch.

The pre-twentieth century technology of fish finding relied upon visual evidence of feeding or spawning shoals of fish by observing either their natural predators circling around and above the shoal or, at night, the effervescence of the plankton on which they were feeding. These observers would have a good idea where and when the shoals might appear, and the location of the fish would have been marked by celestial or terrestrial bearings from a celestial or

Illustration 5.14: Thomas Henry Huxley, 1888/91 (W. & D. Downey)

terrestrial fixed mark. By the middle of the twentieth century, pelagic fish shoals could be found in the open seas using echo finders, but coastal spotting would still be by human eye. The gravel and sandy bottoms off the West Somerset coast favoured by herring for spawning would be well marked on charts and easily found with global positioning system devices if fish succeeded in reaching the Bristol Channel having evaded the nets of the steam-driven, offshore fishing boats. Demersal fish, on the other hand, would inhabit charted ground and would be found with precise navigation systems. Sports fishing boats operated along the Somerset coast would have sophisticated echo sounding gear and global positioning systems capable of marking sea bed structures to within a few metres.

Statutory regulation of sea fishing

Medieval rights for fresh-water fisheries are held in the 'common of fishery', a manorial sharing arrangement similar to those for the common fields. Salt-water private rights, mostly for tidal stretches of rivers or for shellfish, were abolished in the Magna Carta, to be succeeded by the English 'public right of fishing' from intertidal ground in tidal waters.

In 1376 Edward the Third received a commons petition requesting that he ban the use of trawl nets. No law was enacted as a result, but commissioners determined that beam trawls should be used only in deep waters and not in waters of coastal estuaries and bays. Echoes of this original complaint continued as trawling was systematically restricted from coastal waters of England, France and Holland who for many years controlled sea fishing through the Hanseatic League. Even in the late Tudor period there was an understanding that trawling was a destructive form of fishing, but it was not perceived to be so ecologically disastrous as to prevent its continued use on commercial grounds.

The Tudor Navy ships' companies in Henry the Eighth's days were recruited from the fishing smacks, but the Reformation itself had destroyed much of the fishing trade. In Tudor times, Minehead possessed more ships and sailors suitable for the Navy than any other Bristol Channel port, and indeed a sketch of coastal defence measures at the time shows several large vessels anchored in the bay.[37] In 1563, William Cecil, advisor to Queen Elizabeth the First, argued for Parliament to pass an act, later to become known as 'Cecil's Feast', making it unlawful for anyone to eat meat during Lent. The punishment would be either three months in jail or a fine of 3 pounds. In a

handwritten codicil, Cecil attempted to calm those of a more Puritan persuasion, who hated such Catholic traditions of fish days, by explaining that this act was for economic reasons only. A bill also made Wednesday, Friday and Saturday fish days. At the same time, an act to encourage English merchant fishing fleet was passed.[38] Although the act did not specifically remove the liability of imported fish to poundage, in practise this seems to have happened as imports of Irish fish disappeared and others have suggested that the ends for the two acts together were to maintain the supply of competent English seamen for the Tudor Navy.

The Fisheries Act of 1705 further attempted to encourage British sea fishers:

Our Sovereign Lady and the Estates of Parliament taking to consideration the great and many advantages that may arise to this Nation by encouraging the Salmond White and Herring fishings they being not only a natural and certain fund to advance the trade and increase the wealth thereof but also a true and ready way to breed seamen and set many poor and idle people to work And albeit there be several good acts already made to encourage and carry on that trade yet they are either in dissuetude defective or do not answer the present circumstances.[39]

The War of the Spanish Succession was placing increasing demands on manning for the Royal Navy

Illustration 5.15: King Edward the Third's effigy in Westminster Abbey

as new naval bases were acquired through the Treaty of Utrecht to support the expanding British Empire.

The introduction to the White Herring Fisheries Act in 1771 continued the process whereby fishing around the coast of the British Isles was encouraged, stating that:

> Whereas the carrying on and improvement of the British White Herring Fisheries are of great importance to these kingdoms, by increasing the trade and navigation thereof, and being a nursery for seamen, and otherwise a means of employing and providing for great numbers of industrious poor, provided that reasonable encouragement be given to such persons as are willing to carry on the said fisheries.[40]

During the eighteenth and nineteenth century Government provided bounties to British fishermen allowing them to profit from large fish populations around its shores. Promoting the British fishing industry and improving the harbours they use helped to maintain a nursery of seamen for the Navy as well as feeding a growing population during the early days of empire and industrialisation.

The Royal Commission of 1863, established to investigate the complaints of coastal net and long-line fishermen to trawling, gave rise to the Sea Fishing Act of 1865. This Act permitted fishermen to ply their trade whenever, wherever and however they pleased and put into law Thomas Huxley's contention that the regulation of sea fishing was futile. However, after another Royal Commission in 1883 and the establishment of the Marine Biological Association in Plymouth in 1884, the Sea Fisheries Regulation Act was placed on the statute book in 1888. This Act gave rise to Sea Fisheries Committees which were administered by the then new County Councils. Twelve Committees were formed for the English and Welsh coastal regions with significant sea fisheries, the Devon Sea Fisheries Committee and the South Wales Sea Fisheries Committee covered the Bristol Channel as far east as the Devon/Somerset border and Nash Point, south of Bridgend, on the Welsh coast respectively. Somerset County Council administered its Bristol Channel coastal fishery. After many small changes to the Sea Fisheries Act were consolidated in the 1966 Act and in the Sea Fish (Conservation) Act 1967, which regulated sizes of both fishing gear and landed fish, the Somerset coastal waters were managed by the Somerset Rivers Authority then by the Environment Agency. The main tasks of the Committees and other agencies were to keep trawlers

capable of working offshore out of the inshore areas where they had been destroying spawn and nursery fish and to rebuild fish stocks in these areas.

The collapse of the herring fisheries, eventually acknowledged in the 1970s, resulted in closure of these fisheries for a few years into the 1980s. The accession of the United Kingdom to the European Community in 1973 and its introduction of the Common Fisheries Policy in 1983 significantly empowered member governments to create sustainable fisheries in their inshore waters, initially out to 3 miles but then extended to 6 miles in 1997. The Environment Act 1995 had profound implications for inshore fisheries as it empowered fishery ministers, sea fishing committees and the Environment Agency, to regulate for the protection of marine environment.

A millennium of development of Somerset's sea fishing ecosystem

The so-called sea fish event horizon of eleventh century North-Western Europe was noted as the emergence of commercial fishing in human use of the sea, though the question as to whether this use was for long-distance trade or local fishing remains unanswered. The Norman settlers in the British Isles brought with them the Norse traditions of sea trade and fishing, and the people of the Somerset coastal communities were known to be fishing from the shore and in small boats. The extent of fishing was unregulated except by the local market community and the lord of the manor, and the Norse technology of the day used natural fibre nets, fish weirs and small estuary boats suitable for river navigation. The equilibrium of the ecosystem was one of sea fish abundance.

Sea fishing during the late Medieval period might be characterised by thriving markets in Somerset coast ports with reduced population of people because of plague and reduced maritime trade during a period of European war during a period of cooling sea water resulting from the onset of a little ice age. Slightly larger and longer boats, developed with improving wood technology, that were capable of laying beam trawl nets but these were not permitted in coastal waters by the Crown commissioners of the fifteenth century. It is highly likely that this was a period of continuing sea fish abundance, particularly herring-like fish and their accompanying food shoals and predators, in the Bristol Channel, and the beach and small boat fishermen of the Somerset coastal communities will have taken full advantage of it

Illustration 5.16 A rare image of fishing using nets in boats off the Somerset coast during the 1680s (SHC, DD/L1/10/35A)

during the winter seasons to supply their own needs and those of their markets. The equilibrium of the Bristol Channel ecosystem was likely to have been largely sustained as a system with sea fish abundance whilst human population recovered.

The sea fishing grounds off the Newfoundland coast presented an all-season opportunity, and the British commercial exploitation of them at the end of the seventeenth century included larger boats from Minehead. Though the effects of the Little Ice Age bottomed out around the middle of the eighteenth century, the winter assemblage of herring in the Bristol Channel began gradually to diminish possibly perhaps because of overfishing by fishermen from Somerset and their county neighbours. To meet the burgeoning needs of the Royal Navy for experienced seamen the Government provided financial

incentives for coastal communities to develop fishing skills and facilities for herring in particular. Nevertheless, these encouragements were insufficient to keep the harbours of Minehead, Watchet and Porlock well maintained, and they had fallen into decline by early in the nineteenth century. Edmund Rack evidenced this decline in about 1787. The ecosystem was exhibiting signs of stress, and equilibrium was shifting towards a much reduced pelagic sea fish population and its accompanying plankton food species and fishy predators in the Bristol Channel.

Within a hundred years the Bristol Channel experienced the early effects of the post Little Ice Age warming and the visiting shoals had all but disappeared whilst population of Somerset had doubled with the coming of the railways. The technology of the industrial revolution, particularly the advances in steam engine design, that could be transferred to the engines and winches of fishing boats, and the development of marine science created a public debate out of which emerged the first real regulation of inshore sea fisheries. The Royal Navy also underwent a revolution in its manning in that the need for engineering skills was added to those of seamanship, and whilst fishing and fishermen were encouraged nationally, it was the deep water fishing ports of the British Isles that prospered rather than the smaller coastal harbours of Somerset. As fishermen, mostly outside the Somerset coastal regions resorted to steam power to plunder their offshore fisheries, technology had a significant influence on the Bristol Channel ecosystem. The ecosystem became unsustainable from a reducing sea fish population perspective.

A further decline of fish assemblages in the Bristol Channel continued throughout the twentieth century at the same time as an increase in Somerset's population, but perhaps more significantly the open ocean temperature increased by nearly 1 degree Celsius compared with the low of the Little Ice Age. The salinity and water temperature in the Bristol Channel, whose major influence is the fresh water run-off from the River Severn and its tributaries, remained more or less constant during the preceding 100 years. The herring that had disappeared from the Bristol Channel also began to disappear from its littoral seas and, with the food shortages during the world wars of the first half of the century, the lack of regulation of Britain's inshore fisheries under the 1888 Act resulted in overfishing in the Celtic Sea. The offshore fisheries continued to be unregulated until the second half of the century when the Common Fisheries Policy of the European Union, informed by politically active marine scientists, regulated the catch through total allowable catch regimes for each species of sea fish. Protection of fish stocks became the driving force for the regeneration of European offshore and inshore fisheries, and in particular the Bristol Channel, as sustainable ecosystems. Commercial herring fishing was temporarily banned and even the catch of leisure and sport fishermen of the Somerset coastal harbours who catered for holiday visitors was regulated.

Sea fishing in 2060 Somerset; the next 60 years of supply and demand

It is assumed that the sea temperature will not fall in another period of cooling. The causes of the Little

Ice Age and the sharp increase in temperature at the end of the twentieth century are both unproven though it is highly likely that a mixture of volcanic and solar activity, ocean current variations, and human activity contributed to both, and it is very probable that the trend will continue. Future sea temperatures in the Bristol Channel are not likely to support the presence of plankton in quantities necessary to attract the large shoals of herring and their predators seen in the eighteenth century.

Although the UK market for sea fish remains generally strong, that for herring collapsed at the end of the twentieth century because of the offshore fishing ban in the North Sea and Scottish fisheries. Small quantities of herring were imported from North America to satisfy the British market.

Another assumption is that the population of Somerset, both permanent and seasonal, is likely to grow at such a rate as to nearly double by the end of the next 50 years.[41] Sea fish are also likely to remain an important diet for Somerset people both for their traditional appeal and their source of nutritional oils. The demand for sea fish in Somerset should easily be sourced through the fisheries industries on the south and east English and Scottish coasts, though there will always be a more exclusive market for locally drift net and line-caught herring-like and white fish from the Bristol Channel

The fish assemblage of the Bristol Channel is likely to remain mainly bottom-feeding rays, eels and white fish. However, at the end of 2011, an inshore fisherman from Minehead reported the return of the autumn run of herring with up to 5,000 fish in his nets. The fisherman with 50 years experience said "I have never seen anything like this, and I don't think anyone else around here has, either".[42] This report is corroborated by the International Council for the Exploration of the Sea, an independent community of marine researchers set up to coordinate and promote marine research on oceanography, the marine environment, the marine ecosystem, and on living marine resources in the North Atlantic. It published advice in June 2012 suggesting that the stock of herring in Celtic Sea had attained its largest level since 1960 and that fishermen had reported increasing quantities of herring.[43]

Two major national power generation projects may, if commissioned, have a significant influence on the Bristol Channel ecosystem. The more likely project is the building of new pressurized-water-reactor nuclear power stations at Berkeley on the Severn Estuary and Hinkley Point on the West

Somerset coast of the Bristol Channel. Both of these projects, carbon-free and historically safe in their operation, are replacements for existing installations that are being decommissioned. They should have no more influence on the characteristics of the Bristol Channel over the next 50 years than the existing power stations had during the past 50 years.

The less likely and more ecosystem invasive project is the installation of a tidal barrier across the lower Severn Estuary between Brean Down in Somerset and Lavernock Point in South Wales. This installation, if commissioned as presently proposed to

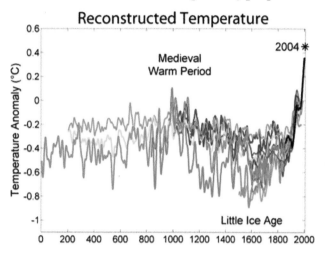

Figure 5.1: Northern Hemisphere temperature reconstruction; the red shows proxy data, and the black shows instruments, 2005. (Robert A. Rohde / Global Warming Art)

generate an average of 8640 MW from the twice daily tides of the Bristol Channel, will have significant impacts on temperature and salinity distributions and sediment transport within the Bristol Channel off the Somerset coast. These inshore fisheries are likely experience a significant change in fish assemblage by species and quantity.

Sport and recreational sea fishing from the Somerset shore and boats will continue to be an important leisure activity and for some, like the 'grow your own' allotment hobby, may become a 'catch your own' movement. Sea fishing in Somerset has a significant input to local economies and supports many businesses from bed and breakfasts to suppliers of tackle and boats. In ways similar to the commercial inshore fisheries, it is likely that data will be collected on the extent of sport and recreational fishing as it expands off the Somerset coast.

Sea fishing technology and science

It is likely that improvements in science and technology of fishing vehicles and their gear employing electric power and composite materials will not affect the inshore fisherman's capability to catch different species of sea fish and greater numbers of them. Technology will permit the more accurate and timely monitoring of both fishing boat activities and fish assemblages and movements. Inshore fishing technology appropriate for the Somerset coast of the Bristol Channel is unlikely to advance beyond the existing drift nets and long-lines used at present unless the abundance of herring seen in the eighteenth century returns.

Fish finding technology has improved with the deployment of LIDAR (Light Detection and Ranging) systems that have the capability of penetrating water to depths of tens of metres and are therefore suitable for detecting shoals of fish in littoral seas. These improved data acquisition techniques, which also include more sensitive sonar devices as well as implanted electronic fish tags, are all directed towards improving the accuracy of data used by marine scientists to evaluate levels of fish stocks by species. The Common Fisheries Policy of the European Union sets for its member nations fish catch quotas by species based on the total allowable catch for the stock level of a species,[44] and the data to establish these allowable catches is provided by the International Council for the Exploration of the Sea.

It is significant that data collection has vastly improved since the end of the twentieth century such that the research conducted by members of the International Council for the Exploration of the Sea is grounded in extensive data of fish population and catch by species. The Council provides fisheries advice that is consistent with the broad international policy norms of maximum sustainable yield (MSY), the precautionary approach, and the ecosystem approach.[45] Most of the stocks on which the Council advises are managed using stock-specific total allowable catches (TACs). Fishing affects fish stocks through the fishing mortality rate (F) applied to the stocks. Yield or production (Y) of a fish stock can be highly variable but, on average, it is related to stock size (SSB), which in turn depends on mortality rate (F). That is, for each F, there is a long-term yield Y and an average stock size B. The relationship between F, Y, and B is called the production function. The peak of the production function is MSY, the fishing mortality generating this peak is F_{MSY}, and the average stock size is B_{MSY}.

Figure 5.2 (over) gives a hypothetical yield or production and spawning-stock biomass versus fishing mortality, and Figure 5.3 (over) shows Surplus

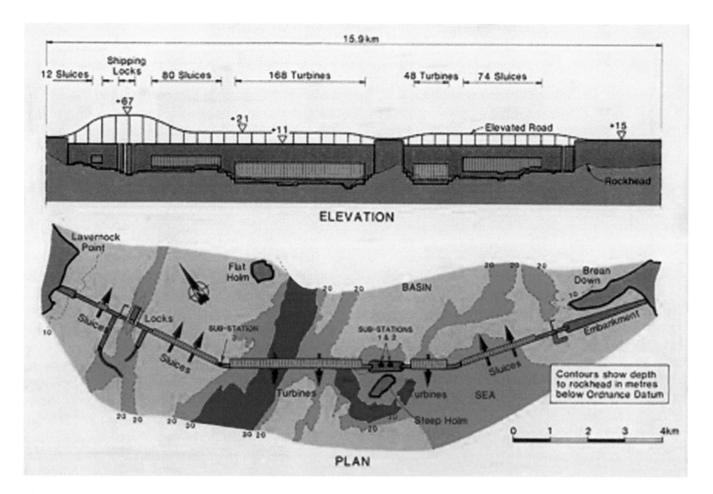

ELEVATION

PLAN

Illustration 5.17: Plan showing the proposed location of the Severn Barrage, 2006 (David Kerr)

Production versus Spawning-stock Biomass. Surplus production is the catch that can be harvested without changing the stock size.

Control of the local surplus production of a fish species using the local total allowable catch is a maturing regulator that should if implemented in the near future facilitate the herring and white fish stock recovery in the Bristol Channel. However, implementation will need to be accompanied by an enhanced system of monitoring commercial fishing. Fishing boat monitoring has traditionally been carried out using sea surface and aerial patrol, on-board observers, fishing boat logs and dockside recording. Modern communications technology permits the on-board installation of boat identification electronic-chips that uniquely identify the boat whilst communicating its activities through satellite systems and global positioning systems. This suggests a wholly new meaning for 'fish and chips.'

Statutory regulation of sea fishing

Following the UK Government's 'Review of Marine Fisheries and Environmental Enforcement',[46] the Marine and Coastal Access Act was passed in 2009. New measures for the management of marine special areas of conservation and marine conservation zones were introduced, including the creation of the Marine

Management Organisation responsible for all marine planning, regulation and licensing. For inshore regions, such as the Bristol Channel, the Sea Fisheries Committees created by the 1888 Act and administering County Councils were considered to have inadequate powers to manage this new protection and conservation role and they have been abolished and replaced by Inshore Fisheries and Conservation Authorities. The Devon and Severn Inshore Fisheries and Conservation Authority oversees the Somerset Coast of the Bristol Channel district and is accountable for managing the exploitation of sea fisheries resources in the area and managing any marine conservation zones that are established in the area. This sets aside the confusion that existed at the end of the twenty-first century as to the extent of responsibility for inshore fisheries between the old Sea Fisheries Committees and the Environment Agency, the latter of which was responsible for the Somerset coast of the Bristol Channel. The Devon and Severn Authority has as its mission statement 'to lead, champion and manage a sustainable marine environment and inshore fisheries, by successfully securing the right balance between social, environmental and economic benefits to ensure healthy seas, sustainable fisheries and a viable industry'.[47]

The Devon and Severn Authority consists of a mix of elected councillors from each local authority that borders and defrays the expenses of the

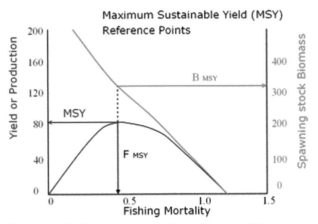

Figure 5.2: Yield or production and spawning-stock biomass versus fishing mortality, 2011 (Bill Kelly)

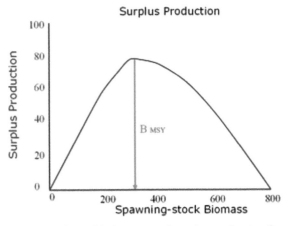

Figure 5.3: A graphical account of surplus production for a range of spawning stock biomasses, 2011 (Bill Kelly)

Authority; representatives from the Marine Management Organisation, Natural England and the Environment Agency; and others appointed by the Marine Management Organisation to present the interests of sea fishing communities. Councillors from Somerset County Council and North Somerset Council attend the Devon and Severn Authority meetings to represent historic Somerset's marine interests. The Authority's area includes Natural England's Severn Estuary Special Area of Conservation and Sites of Special Scientific Interest of Bridgwater Bay and the coast between Lilstock and Blue Anchor where fishing activity is regulated. Even bait collection is subject to fisheries legislation as a sea fisheries resource, and management measures may be necessary to monitor and effectively manage bait collection from the intertidal zone at sustainable levels taking account of both environmental impacts and local economic factors.

Research into sea angling is a priority activity under Devon and Severn Authority Action Plan, and a full

audit of this sector is being undertaken in order to make decisions over possible future development for the sea angling sector in the whole district, in particular in the Bristol Channel and Severn Estuary area.[48] The Authority also intends that its Recreational Sea Angling Project will highlight areas of bait collection. Enforcement officers have continued to support Natural England in the development of the netting licences for Bridgwater Bay.

The Marine Management Organisation operates a satellite-based vessel monitoring system from its fisheries monitoring centre in Newcastle to support its monitoring, control and surveillance operations. The system is used to track the positions of fishing vessels. The Organisation investigates and takes appropriate enforcement action when breaches of the regulations are identified, assisted by the Royal Navy's Fisheries Patrol Squadron. This enforcement work is crucial to ensuring high compliance with fisheries regulations so that fish stocks are exploited in a sustainable way to assist the long-term economic survival of the fishing industry and to protect a valuable natural food resource.

The future of inshore fishing, both from boats and from the shore, off the Somerset coast is now the responsibility of a national Marine Management Organisation and a local Fisheries and Conservation Authority with the combined aim of creating sustainable fisheries. It is likely that the Common Fisheries Policy of the European Union will be reviewed and updated in the near future because it has not delivered its key objective of an economically viable fishing industry which minimises impacts on marine ecosystems. The health of fish stocks and profitability of fishing businesses have deteriorated, while centralised bureaucracy has proliferated. The UK is calling for radical reform leading to a simplified, regionalised Common Fisheries Policy with incentives for fishermen to operate sustainably and profitably. These measures and work on developing UK marine planning, regulating and licensing policy will help make UK fisheries economically sustainable and provide greater benefits to coastal communities through tourism and enhanced local sales of fish. The Department for Environment, Food, Rural Affairs published 'Fisheries 2027', a long term vision for sustainable fisheries and direction for everyone with an interest in marine fisheries. Its overall priority is:

> to get the best possible long-term economic benefits for society through effective management and moderate levels of exploitation, within the two

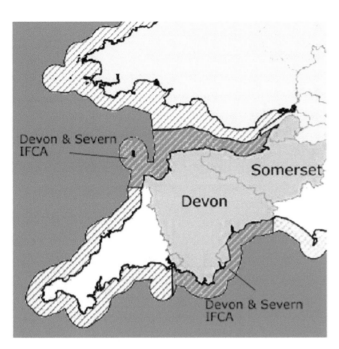

Illustration 5.18: Devon and Severn Inshore Fisheries and Conservation Area, 2011 (Bill Kelly)

Illustration 5.19: Royal Navy Fisheries Patrol vessel, HMS *Severn*, 2006 (Torsten Bätge)

following constraints:

Fishing is managed according to an ecosystem-based approach, including use of the precautionary approach to make sure that we maintain healthy ecosystems and protect rare, vulnerable or valued species and habitats. This means more environmental protection than before, especially in the context of climate change and the need to increase the resilience of the marine environment.

Access to fisheries continues to be available to small-scale fishing vessels, even if in some cases that is not the most economically efficient way of harvesting the resource. This is because the wider economic, social and environmental benefits of small-scale fishing can outweigh the comparative inefficiency in harvesting the resource and make a significant economic and social contribution to the lives of individuals and coastal communities, for example, by providing jobs, attracting tourists, providing high-quality fresh fish and maintaining the character and cultural identity of small ports throughout England.[49]

There are no current proposals for Maritime Conservation Zones off the Somerset coast that might further constrain Somerset's inshore

fishermen.[50]

An ecosystems approach to sea fishing in 2060

According to a marine ecology researcher at the University of Liverpool, Chris Frid, the causes of recent, unprecedented declines in fish populations might be attributed to marine pollution and climate change by the fishing industry. Chris Frid counters that overfishing has also altered the way the ecosystem works, pointing out that

> Everybody would like to see the rebuilding of fish stocks and this can only be achieved if we understand all of the influences, human and natural, on fish dynamics . . . fish communities can be altered in a number of ways, for example they can decrease if particular-sized individuals of a species are targeted, as this affects predator and prey dynamics. Fishing, however, is not the sole cause of changes to marine life-pollution is another example . . . No one factor operates in isolation and components of the ecosystem respond differently to each individual factor.[51]

The traditional approach to fisheries science and management has been to focus on a single species. This can be contrasted with the ecosystem-based approach that considers the condition of the ecosystem and the activities of all species operating within it. In 2007, a group of scientists offered the following rules for ecosystem-based fisheries:

> Keep a perspective that is holistic, risk-averse, and adaptive.
> Question key assumptions, no matter how basic.
> Maintain old-growth age structure in fish populations.
> Characterize and maintain the natural spatial structure of fish stocks.
> Characterize and maintain viable fish habitats.
> Characterize and maintain ecosystem resilience.
> Identify and maintain critical food web connections.
> Account for ecosystem change through time.
> Account for evolutionary change caused by fishing.
> Implement an approach that is integrated, interdisciplinary[52]

The Centre for the Environment, Fisheries, Aquaculture Science, an executive agency of the UK Department of Environment, Food, and Rural Affairs formed in 1997 from the former Directorate of Fisheries Research, collects offshore and inshore data to support the development of sustainable fisheries management. Their work includes a project to develop and pilot an 'Ecosystem Approach to Fisheries in the southwest of the UK':[49] Specifically, it will support managers and stakeholders by:
- the development, testing and reporting of indicators to assess the status of the ecosystem and the impacts of fishing
- the development of decision tables to see the effects of different management options and to choose among them.

Indicators are being developed and piloted for the fishing impacts most likely to compromise UK policy commitments. In practice, this means indicators for vulnerable species (with an emphasis on skates and rays), vulnerable habitats, the fish community and associated ecosystem.[53]

The project is seeking to establish the links between these indicators of ecological state and indicators of fishing pressure, as measured for the main fisheries in the southwest and taking account of environmental variation and change. From knowledge of the links, the project will seek to determine the management actions needed to achieve the desired values of indicators and hence the desired state of vulnerable species, vulnerable habitats, and the fish community. This information will be used to develop decision tables that allow managers and stakeholders to see the consequences of different management options for the fishery, target species, and other parts of the ecosystem.

The Marine Conservation Society and other organizations offer advice to members of the public who eat sea fish with an eye to sustainability. According to the marine conservation biologist Callum Roberts, four criteria apply when choosing seafood.

> Is the species in trouble in the wild where the animals were caught?
> Does fishing for the species damage ocean habitats?
> Is there a large amount of other species taken with the target species?
> Does the fishery have a problem with discards—generally, undersized animals caught and thrown away because their market value is low?

The Devon and Severn Inshore Fisheries Conservation area is made up of a complex mix of sub-areas which present very different issues for its single management to consider. Differences in vessel ownership, size, gear, crew and location all influence

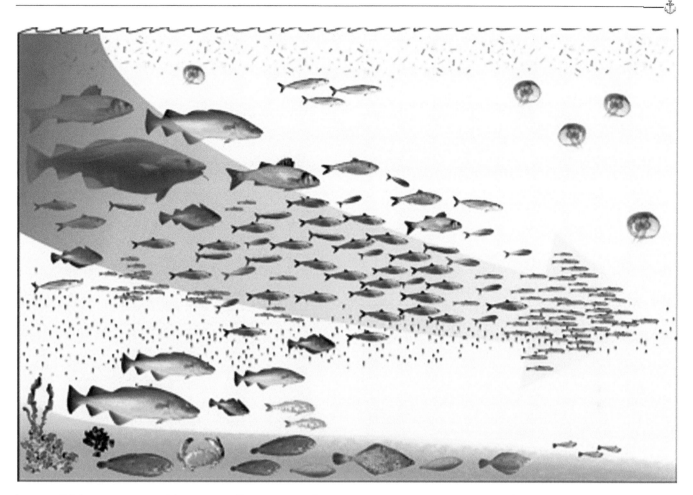

Illustration 5.20: The Pelagic/Demersal food web 2009 (© Hans Hillewaert / CC-BY-SA-3.0)

how fishing communities contribute to the Authority's policy and practise formulation. Risk and profitability of fishing activity in the Bristol Channel will affect the issues raised by Somerset's fisher folk, and county-wide socio-economic issues will be presented by the Somerset and North Somerset Council representatives. The Marine Management Organisation and the Devon and Severn Inshore Fisheries Conservation Authority will need to balance these views and priorities in the diverse Devon and Severn inshore areas.

So will these new management arrangements for Somerset's fisheries balance the expectations and needs of the communities that work or take their leisure fishing the Bristol Channel with the aspirations of the lobby groups concerned with conserving its marine environment? The Devon and Severn Inshore Fisheries and Conservation Authority has the power to distinguish between the needs of one type of fishing in one area and another type in another area whilst developing marine conservation in the light of designated marine conservation zones. The Authority will have to decide where and what kind of fishing can continue and will have to move away from the default notion that all fishing is bad in all places at all times.

Taken together, fisheries economics, marine

science and legislation may well create by 2060 a view of the Bristol Channel and Severn Estuary as an ecosystem in which its unique marine food web connections are better understood. The marine planning, regulation and licensing actions of the Marine Management Organisation and Devon and Severn Fisheries Conservation Authority may have produced a sustainable fishery that is risk-managed, resilient to shock and adaptive to climate change whilst providing environmental and economic benefits to the coastal communities of Somerset. There is no doubt that Somerset's fisher folk have played a significant role in shaping the ecosystem that is the Bristol Channel over the past thousand years and their engagement in measures to secure a sustainable marine environment for the future will be essential.

Chapter Five
Notes

[1]   M. Common & S. Stagl, *Ecological economics* (2005), 1.

[2]   P. Checkland, *Systems thinking, systems practice* (1981), 92-8.

[3]   D. Green, *Fishing in early Medieval times* (2003), http://www.regia.org/fishing.htm#3 (accessed February

2013).

4   C. Gathercole, *Somerset extensive urban survey – Nether Stowey archaeological assessment* (2003), 3.

5   C. Gathercole, *Watchet*, Somerset Urban Archaeological Surveys (2003), 3.

6   *Anglo Saxon chronicle*, part II http://omacl.org/Anglo/ (accessed February 2013).

7   *Anglo Saxon chronicle*, part V http://omacl.org/Anglo/ (accessed February 2013).

8   T. Wright, *Medieval sourcebook: the dialogue between master & disciple: on labourers, c. 1000* (1998).

9   M. Aston and E. Dennison, 'Fishponds in Somerset' in *Medieval fish, fisheries and fishponds in England*, BAR British Series 182 (1988), 395.

10 J.H. Barrett, A.M. Locker and C.M. Roberts, 'The Origins of intensive marine fishing in Medieval Europe: the English evidence' in *Proceedings of the Royal Society* (2004), 2420.

11 M. Siraut, 'Dunster economic history' in *Victoria County History of Somerset*, forthcoming.

12 M. Keen, *The Hundred Years War*, http://www.bbc.co.uk/ history/british/middle_ages/hundred_years_war_01.shtml (accessed February 2013).

13 National Oceanic and Atmospheric Administration National Climatic Data Center, *Paleoclimatic Data for the Last 2000 Years*, http://www.ncdc.noaa.gov/paleo/globalwarming/index.ht ml (accessed February 2013).

14 M. Siraut, 'Dunster economic history' in *Victoria County History of Somerset*, forthcoming.

15 C. Gathercole, *Somerset extensive urban survey - Minehead archaeological assessment* (2003), 5.

16 Ibid, 5.

17 Rev. E.H. Bates Harbin, *Quarter Sessions records for the county of Somerset 1625-1639*, SRS 24 (1908), 24.

18 P. Ashford, 'The rise and fall of the Bristol Channel herring fishery with especial reference to Porlock Somerset, 1530-1830' in *The Mariner's Mirror* 92:1 (2006), 23-30. I am grateful to Philip Ashford for these references.

19 TNA, C 104/12 Part 1, folio 158r. I am grateful to Philip Ashford for this reference.

20 Ashford, 'The rise and fall', 23-30.

21 M. Mcdermot and S. Berry (eds), *Edmund Rack's survey of Somerset* (2001), 83.

22 Ibid, 83.

23 R. Ayton, *Voyage le long de la cote de la partie meridionale du Pays de Galles en 1813*, in *Nouvelles annals des voyages de la geographie et de l'histoire ou recueil* (1824), 65-74. I am grateful to Philip Ashford for this reference.

24 J. Savage, *History of the Hundred of Carhampton in the county of Somerset* (1830), 143.

25 W.H. Norman, *Tales of Watchet harbour* (1988), 120. I am grateful to Philip Ashford for this reference.

26 http://en.wikipedia.org/wiki/Somerset (accessed February 2013).

27 P.A. Henderson, R.M.H. Seaby and R. Somes, *Fish and Crustacean captures at Hinkley Point B Nuclear Power Station: report for the year April 2006 to March 2007* (2007), 7.

28 M.J. Gray, *The coastal fisheries of England and Wales in 1994*, Fisheries Research Technical Report No. 100 (1995), 63.

29 J.M. Gilman, 'An ancient industry', in *Somerset Countryman* 20:1

30 J.M. Steane and M. Foreman, 'The archaeology of Medieval fishing tackle, in *Waterfront Archaeology: Proceedings of the third international conference on waterfront archaeology held at Bristol, 23-26 September 1988* (1991), 88-91.

31 M. Langtham, 'Ancient monuments at sea; the fish weirs of Minehead' in *Country Life* (17 Nov 1983), 1458-60.

32 M. Aston and E. Dennison, *Fishponds in Somerset*, Medieval fish, fisheries and fishponds in England, BAR British Series 182 (1988), 401.

33 M.C. Brown, *Mud horse fishing in Bridgwater Bay,* unpublished note provided by Dr A. Webb.

34 C. Roberts, *The unnatural history of the sea* (2007), 20.

35 Roberts, *The unnatural history*, 131.

36 P. Winterbottom, 'Management of English and Welsh inshore waters and the Marine Bill, 2008' in *The Journal of Water Law* (2008), 145.

37 D. Taylor, 'Somerset's sixteenth century maritime trade' in *The maritime history of Somerset I* (2010), 1.

38 Ibid, 11.

39 *The Fisheries Act* (1705).

40 *White Herring Fisheries Act* (1771).

41 *Population projections for Somerset*, Somerset Intelligence Network, www.sine.org.uk (accessed February 2013).

42 *Western Daily Press*, 2 December 2011.

43 International Council for the Exploration of the Sea, 'Ices Assessed Stocks - Summary Of New Advice Published In June 2012' in *International Council for the Exploration of the Sea (ICES) advice in June 2012* (2012), 19.

44 International Council for the Exploration of the Sea, *EC request on evaluation of a modified harvest control rule for managing the stock of western Horse Mackerel (Divisions IIa, IVa, Vb, VIa, VIIa–c,e–k, and VIIIa–e)* (2012).

45 International Council for the Exploration of the Sea, *Report of the ICES Advisory Committee, 2011*, ICES Advice; Book 1 (2011), 2-6.

46 Department for Environment, Food and Rural Affairs (DEFRA), *A marine bill* (London, 2006).

47 T. Noble, *The work of the Devon and Severn Inshore Fisheries & Conservation Authority in the Severn*, see slide 4 http://www. severnestuary.net/sep/forum/SEF2012/SEF2012 DSI TN. pdf (accessed February 2013).

48 Ibid, slide 5.

49 DEFRA, *Fisheries 2027 – a long-term vision for sustainable fisheries* (2011), 6.

50 T. Hooper, *Finding Sanctuary final recommendations summary Summer 2011* (2011), 16, http://webarchive.nationalarchives. gov.uk/20120502152638/http://www.finding-sanctuary.org /resources/download/1201.pdf,(accessed February 2013).

51 C. Frid, 'Marine ecologists to help rebuild decreasing fish stocks' in *Science Daily* (Rockville, 2006), http://www.sciencedaily.com/releases/2006/02/060216233 254.htm (accessed February 2013).

52 R.C. Francis, M.A. Hixon, M.E. Clarke, S.A. Murawski, and S. Ralston, 'Ten commandments for ecosystem-based fisheries scientists' in *Fisheries* 32:5 (Seattle, 2007), 217.

53 Centre for Environment, Fisheries & Aquaculture Science (CEFAS), http://www.cefas.defra.gov.uk/our-science/ ecosystems-and-biodiversity/ecosystem-approach-to-

Glossary

Anabaptist. A Christian Protestant sect with its roots in sixteenth century Switzerland and Germany. Believers considered that infant baptism was not scriptural, so, as adults they were re-baptised as believers. Each congregation was autonomous.

Boarding and landing. Undertaken out at sea these opposite processes involve much jeopardy to usually, a pilot's life. A pilot boards a ship from a launch; a pilot lands onto a launch from a ship.

Brigantine. A small ship with two masts, the foremost one being square-rigged. The rearmost mast had sails similarly shaped to a yacht.

Draught. The old name for a chart used for navigation.

Drover. A person who walked cattle or sheep to and from market, mainly in the pre-industrial era since there was no efficient means of land transport for large numbers of animals. Drovers would have accompanied cattle and sheep in transit over water.

Embrasure. An opening or indentation, as in a battlement.

Epuipages. A carriage with horses and attendants.

Hydrographic. All things relevant to mapping and recording the navigable waters of the world and adjacent land.

Fishing mortality rate (F). Fishing catch (including discards) divided by mean spawning fish stock size.

Indentured servant. A servant indebted to a sea captain for their free passage across the Atlantic Ocean. The debt was redeemed by landowners buying the indenture from the captain in the New World which paid the debt but meant that the servant was bound for a certain number of years to work for the landowner.

Long-shore drift. The transportation of sediments (clay, silt, sand and shingle) along a coast at an angle to the shoreline.

Maximum sustainable yield (MSY). Maximum catch that maintains yield or production rate at maximum growth rate for that biomass.

Neap tides. Derived from the Anglo-Saxon word nepflods. These are medium tides, opposite to spring tides.

Privateer. A privately owned ship whose owners and masters had been commissioned by their home government to embark on acts of war against enemy shipping. Essentially a warship, but not owned by the government's navy.

Recusant. A person who refused to attend public worship in the Anglican church on grounds of faith, usually a Catholic.

Road. An area of relatively sheltered shallow coastal water where ships could safely come to anchor.

Serge. A woollen fabric made especially in the Taunton area of Somerset during the seventeenth century.

Skiff. A very small sailing vessel with one triangular sail attached to the mast.

Sloop. A one masted trading vessel with triangular sails to the fore and aft of the mast.

Spawning stock biomass (B). Size of the spawning fish stock.

Spring tides. The tides range at its maximum height.

Square-rigged. This means that the ship is propelled with the wind by the primary sails which are carried on horizontal spars that are perpendicular to the masts. Thus many sails were of a square rather than a triangular shape.

Stop. This is an obsolete word for an obstruction (timber or stone) inserted in order to hinder water whirling within an open harbour, or to reduce the effect of swell entering.

Sullage. The deposition of mud and silt by water.

Surplus yield or production. Catch that can be taken without reducing the size of the biomass.

Triangulation. A method of surveying in which an area is divided into triangles, the baseline is measured and the angles measured and the lengths of the other sides calculated trigonometrically.

Vagrants. Poor and homeless people who moved from place to place in search of work or succour. Clearly, many would have needed to steal in order to survive.

Weigh anchor. To haul up an anchor or anchors so a sailing vessel could get under way.

Wherry. A clinker built rowing boat. By act of parliament in 1555, a Thames wherry was 22 and a half feet long and 4 and a half feet wide and could be rowed by one or two men.

Yield or production of a spawning fish stock (Y). Measure of a fish stock to replace itself.

Woodforde, James, 53
Woodlief, John, Captain, 5
Woodward, W.C., 149
Worcester, William, 140
Wordsworth, William, 85, 87
Wort, George, 149, John, 149
Worth, James, 19
Wren, Christopher, Sir, 155
Yeates, family, 56
York, Richard of, 3rd Duke of, 125
Young, Alice, 125, Thomas, 125

Index of Place Names